Greece
a country study

Federal Research Division
Library of Congress
Edited by
Glenn E. Curtis
Research Completed
December 1994

On the cover: The Parthenon built on the Acropolis in Athens as a temple to the goddess Athena

Fourth Edition, First Printing, 1995.

Library of Congress Cataloging-in-Publication Data

Greece: a country study / Federal Research Division, Library of Congress ; edited by Glenn E. Curtis.—4th ed.
     p. cm. — (Area handbook series, ISSN 1057–5294) (DA Pam ; 550–87)
     "Supersedes the 1986 edition of Greece: A Country Study, edited by Rinn S. Shin."—T.p. verso.
     "Research completed December 1994."
     Includes bibliographical references (pp. 341–362) and index.
     ISBN 0–8444-0856–5 (hc : alk. paper)
     1. Greece. I. Curtis, Glenn E. (Glenn Eldon), 1946– .
II. Library of Congress. Federal Research Division. III. Series. IV. Series: DA Pam ; 550–87
DF717.G78 1995   95–32388
949.5–dc20   CIP

Headquarters, Department of the Army
DA Pam 550–87

For sale by the Superintendent of Documents, U.S. Government Printing Office
Washington, D.C. 20402

Foreword

This volume is one in a continuing series of books prepared by the Federal Research Division of the Library of Congress under the Country Studies/Area Handbook Program sponsored by the Department of the Army. The last two pages of this book list the other published studies.

Most books in the series deal with a particular foreign country, describing and analyzing its political, economic, social, and national security systems and institutions, and examining the interrelationships of those systems and the ways they are shaped by cultural factors. Each study is written by a multidisciplinary team of social scientists. The authors seek to provide a basic understanding of the observed society, striving for a dynamic rather than a static portrayal. Particular attention is devoted to the people who make up the society, their origins, dominant beliefs and values, their common interests and the issues on which they are divided, the nature and extent of their involvement with national institutions, and their attitudes toward each other and toward their social system and political order.

The books represent the analysis of the authors and should not be construed as an expression of an official United States government position, policy, or decision. The authors have sought to adhere to accepted standards of scholarly objectivity. Corrections, additions, and suggestions for changes from readers will be welcomed for use in future editions.

Louis R. Mortimer
Chief
Federal Research Division
Library of Congress
Washington, DC 20540–5220

Acknowledgments

The authors are indebted to numerous individuals and organizations who provided materials, time, advice, and expertise on Greek affairs for this volume.

Thanks go to Ralph K. Benesch, who oversees the Country Studies/Area Handbook Program for the Department of the Army. Former United States Ambassador to Greece Monteagle Stearns and Carol Migdalovitz of the Congressional Research Service, Library of Congress, provided initial recommendations of chapter authors. Invaluable assistance to the research process was supplied by Elizabeth Prodromou of the Princeton University Institute of International Studies; Brigitte Regnier of the Organisation for Economic Co-operation and Development; John Topping of the Library of Congress; Dr. Yannis Skalkidis of the Hellenic Committee for the HOPE Program; and Dr. George Psacharopoulos of the World Bank.

The Press and Information Office of the Embassy of Greece in Washington, the Bernice Huffman Collection of the Library of Congress, and Sam and Sarah Stulberg contributed numerous timely photographs.

The authors appreciate the advice and guidance of Sandra W. Meditz, Federal Research Division coordinator of the handbook series. Special thanks go to Marilyn L. Majeska, who managed the editing and production process, assisted by Andrea T. Merrill; to Wayne Horne, who designed the book cover and the title page illustrations for the five chapters; to David P. Cabitto, who provided graphics support and, together with the firm of Maryland Mapping and Graphics, prepared maps; and to Tom Hall, who compiled geographic data.

The contributions of the following individuals are gratefully acknowledged as well: Catherine Schwartzstein, who edited the chapters and performed the final prepublication editorial review; Barbara Edgerton and Izella Watson, who did the word processing; Sandi Schroeder of Schroeder Indexing Services, who compiled the index; and Janie L. Gilchrist, David P. Cabitto, and Stephen C. Cranton, who prepared the camera-ready copy.

Contents

List of figures

Preface

This volume replaces *Greece: A Country Study,* originally published in 1969 and revised in 1977 and 1985. In the years after completion of the 1985 edition, significant political and international events have altered Greece's position, and some changes have also occurred in Greek society and the economy. Among the most important intervening events have been the end of the Cold War, eruption of several national conflicts in the Balkans, and Greece's increased political and economic integration into the structure of the European Union (EU).

The purpose of this study is to present an objective and concise account of the dominant social, economic, political, and national security concerns of contemporary Greece. Sources of information include scholarly journals and monographs, official reports of governmental and international organizations, foreign and domestic newspapers and periodicals, and interviews with individuals who have special knowledge of Greek affairs. Brief comments on some of the more useful, readily accessible sources appear at the end of each chapter. Full references to these and other sources used by the authors are listed in the Bibliography.

The contemporary place-names used in this study are generally those approved by the United States Board on Geographic Names, as set forth in the official gazetteer published in 1960. Many place-names in Greece, however, have standardized international forms (for example, the conventional form Corfu is used rather than the Greek form Kerkira, and Athens is used rather than Athinai). Where appropriate, when the conventional form is used, the vernacular is provided in parentheses. Administrative units, shown in figure 1, are uniformly given in the vernacular. Contemporaneous personal names are universally given in their Greek form (for example, Konstantinos Karamanlis rather than Constantine Karamanlis); historical figures such as Aristotle and Alexander the Great, however, are given in their standardized forms. Table A provides the full Greek and English names for organizations whose acronyms recur in the text. Table B is a chronology of the most significant events of Greek history. The dictionary used was *Webster's Tenth Collegiate Dictionary.*

Measurements are given in the metric system; a conversion table is provided to assist those who are unfamiliar with metric terms (see table 1, Appendix). The Appendix also provides other tabular material on social, economic, government, and military matters.

The body of the text reflects information available as of December 1994. Certain other portions of the text, however, have been updated. The Introduction discusses significant events and trends that have occurred since the completion of research; the Country Profile and the Chronology include updated information as available; and the Bibliography lists recently published sources thought to be particularly helpful to the reader.

Table A: Organizations and Political Parties and Their Acronyms

Acronym	Greek Term	English Translation
Organizations		
ADEDI	Anotati Dioikousa Epitropi Dimosion Ipallilon	Supreme Civil Servants' Administrative Committee
DEI	Dimosia Epicheirisi Ilektrismou	Public Power Corporation
EAM	Ethnikon Apeleftherotikon Metopon	National Liberation Front
EDES	Ethnikos Dimokratikos Ellinikos Stratos	National Republican Greek League
ELAS	Ethnikos Laikos Apeleftherotikos Stratos	National People's Liberation Army
EOKA	Ethniki Organosis Kyprion Agoniston	National Organization of Cypriot Fighters
GSEE	Geniki Synomospondia Ergaton Ellados	General Confederation of Greek Workers
IKA	Idryma Kinonikon Asfaliseon	Social Insurance Administration
OGA	Organismos Georgikon Asfaliseon	Agricultural Insurance Organization
OSE	Organismos Sidirodromon Ellados	Greek Railroads Organization
OTE	Organismos Tilepikoinonion Ellados	Greek Telecommunications Organization
PEEA	Politiki Epitropi Ethnikis Apeleftheroseos	Political Committee of National Liberation
SEV	Sindesmos Ellinikon Viomikhanion	Association of Greek Industrialists
TEVE	Tameio Emporikon Viomihanikon Epihiriseon	Tradesmen's and Craftsmen's Fund for the Self-Employed
Political parties		
EK	Enosis Kentrou	Center Union
ERE	Ethniki Rizopastiki Enosis	National Radical Union
KKE	Kommunistikon Komma Ellados	Communist Party of Greece
ND	Nea Demokratia	New Democracy
PA	Politiki Anixi	Political Spring
PASOK	Panhellinion Socialistiko Kinima	Panhellenic Socialist Movement
SYN	Synaspismos	Coalition

Table B: Chronology of Important Events

Period	Description
2600 B.C.	Early Minoan civilization produces cultural artifacts, beginning 1400 years of Minoan culture on Crete, including introduction of alphabet.
1400s–1300s B.C.	Mycenaean civilization reaches peak on Greek mainland.
1050–800 B.C.	Dark Age of Greece; earlier cultural gains lost in period of stagnation and decline.
Ninth Century B.C.	Homer writes *Odyssey* and *Iliad*, greatest epic poems of Greek classical literature.
Eighth Century B.C.	Athens, Sparta, and other city-states emerge and develop trade relations.
750–500 B.C.	Era of colonial expansion and cultural diffusion into Italy, eastern Mediterranean Sea, and Black Sea.
490 B.C.	Greeks defeat Persians at Marathon, ending First Persian War.
481–479 B.C.	After Persian occupation, Greek victories at Salamis (naval) and Plataia (land) end Persian threat permanently and cut cultural ties with Near East.
450s B.C.	Rule of Pericles begins golden age of Athens, including masterpieces of sculpture, architecture, dramaturgy, and philosophy.
421 B.C.	First phase of Peloponnesian War (Athens against Sparta) ends inconclusively after ten years of fighting.
404 B.C.	Second phase of Peloponnesian War concludes with Sparta's defeat of Athenian navy, ending Athenian golden age.
Fourth Century B.C.	City-states decline; Macedonian Empire rises.
336 B.C.	Alexander the Great takes throne of Macedonian Empire after assassination of Philip II.
323 B.C.	Alexander dies after establishing largest empire in history, reaching North Africa and Afghanistan.
ca. 300 B.C.	Fragmented Hellenistic kingdoms begin struggle for power.
280 B.C.	Pyrrhus of Epirus begins long series of battles between Greeks and Romans, including Greek participation in Punic Wars on side of Carthage.
86 B.C.	Athens conquered by Rome.
31 B.C.	Mark Antony's defeat at Battle of Actium brings final integration of Greece into Roman Empire.
31 B.C.–A.D. 180	Pax Romana, peaceful period of cultural flowering and rise of Greeks into empire's ruling elite.
313	In Edict of Milan, Emperor Constantine establishes Roman Empire's toleration of Christianity
364	Roman Empire officially split into Latin Roman (western) and Greek Byzantine (eastern) empires.
Fifth century	Greek Orthodox Christianity rises as official religion of Byzantine Empire, which dominates former Roman Empire after fall of Rome; schism with Roman Catholic Church deepens until final break in 1054.
567–867	Byzantine Empire declines and shrinks as Slavic and Islamic groups expand from West and East.
867	Macedonian Dynasty begins expansion, cultural and economic growth, and consolidation of Byzantine control in Balkans.
1071	Decline of Byzantine Empire accelerates with Seljuk Turk capture of Emperor Romanus IV.
1204	Fourth Crusade sacks Constantinople; Greece divided into small units by Western occupiers.

Table B: Chronology of Important Events

Period	Description
1261–1453	Palaeologus Dynasty solidifies Byzantine Empire, withstands increasing pressure from Ottoman Turks.
1453	Ottoman Turks capture Constantinople, ending Byzantine Empire; most of Greece in Ottoman hands.
1453–1821	Greece, except for Ionian Islands, remains part of Ottoman Empire.
1821–32	Under intellectual influence of the Enlightenment and with intervention by France and Britain, Greek War of Independence liberates part of modern Greece.
1828	Ioannis Kapodistrias becomes first president of fledgling Greek state.
1832	Treaty of Constantinople places Greece under British, French, and Russian protection, defines its boundaries, and names Otto of Wittgenstein ruler.
1844	First constitution establishes democratic parliamentary government system, reducing Otto's power.
1854	Britain and France prevent Greece from taking Ottoman territory in Thrace and Epirus, humiliating Otto.
1862	After series of coups, Otto forced to abdicate.
1864	New constitution establishes powerful parliament; Prince William of Denmark named king as George I.
1866	First revolt on Crete against Ottoman rule.
1875	George accepts principle of parliamentary majority party forming government, ending fractious minority administrations.
1875	Kharilaos Trikoupis becomes prime minister, beginning quarter-century of government domination by him and ideological opposite Theodoros Deliyannis.
1881	After Great Power pressure at 1878 Congress of Berlin, Ottoman Empire cedes Thessaly and part of Epirus to Greece.
1886	Britain and France blockade Greece after Deliyannis mobilizes troops to profit from Serbian-Bulgarian conflict.
1897	Financial collapse ends with national bankruptcy.
1908	Young Turks overthrow government in Constantinople, beginning reform of Turkish politics and society.
1909	Military coup at Goudi overthrows Greek government; Eleutherios Venizelos chosen to head new government.
1912–13	Balkan Wars add southern Epirus, Macedonia, some Aegean Islands, and Crete to Greek territory.
1915	Venizelos resigns over King Constantine's failure to support Allies in World War I, beginning constitutional crisis termed the National Schism.
1917	Constantine passes crown to his son Alexander; Greek forces join Allies for remainder of war.
1920	Treaty of Sèvres establishes Greek enclave around Smyrna in Asia Minor.
1922	After disastrous military defeat in Asia Minor, Smyrna is sacked and Greek forces withdraw.
1923	Treat of Lausanne cedes all territory in Asia Minor to Turkey; huge influx of Greek refugees in exchange of ethnic minorities between Greece and Turkey.
1928	Chaotic period of government coups ends; second Venizelos golden age begins.
1930	World financial crisis initiates new political and economic unrest in Greece.
1932	Venizelos resigns; National Schism reemerges.
1936–41	Dictatorial regime of General Ioannis Metaxas.

Table B: Chronology of Important Events

Period	Description
1941	Nazi forces invade Greece; start of four years of destructive occupation; National Liberation Front founded as resistance movement.
1943	Resistance splits; communist-dominated EAM faction, major element of resistance activity, forms resistence government in Greece.
1944	Athens liberated; Greece assigned to British sphere by agreement with Soviet Union; communist insurgency leads to fall of Papandreou government.
1945	Varkiza Agreement ends insurgency; White Terror persecution of leftist resistance forces.
1946–49	Civil War between communist Democratic Army of Greece and government.
1947	Massive United States aid starts with Truman Doctrine.
1949	Marshall Plan aids reconstruction period of Greek economy and society following World War II and Civil War.
1950	Martial law lifted; first civilian elections held; two decades of economic growth begin.
1955	Konstantinos Karamanlis named prime minister, beginning eight-year regime; violent terrorist campaign of National Organization of Cypriot Fighters (EOKA) begins against British occupation of Cyprus and for union with Greece.
1963	Karamanlis's resignation begins period of instability and increased leftist influence.
1967	Military junta takes power, begins seven-year regime and period of international isolation; King Constantine goes into exile.
1973	University student uprisings and radicalization of junta increase social resistance to regime.
1974	Turkey invades Cyprus in response to coup attempt against Cypriot President Makarios; military regime replaced by new Karamanlis civilian government; voters abolish monarchy; democratic institutions restored.
1975	New constitution establishes republican government; Communist Party of Greece legalized; Turkish Federated State of Cyprus declared.
1981	Panhellenic Socialist Movement (PASOK) ends postwar conservative control of government, begins eight-year rule with broad reform program under Andreas Papandreou; Greece gains full membership in European Community (EC).
1986	Constitutional amendments curtail presidential power.
1987	Incident in Aegean Sea brings Greece and Turkey to brink of armed conflict.
1989	Two elections yield stalemated coalition governments after scandals undermine PASOK support.
1990 April	Konstantinos Mitsotakis's New Democracy (ND) party wins half of Assembly seats and forms new government.
1991 September	Declaration of sovereignty by Yugoslav Republic of Macedonia arouses nationalist outcry in Greece against possibility of EC recognition of country under name Macedonia; Greek campaign against recognition begins.
December	Soviet Union dissolves, beginning revision of Greece's national security position and military doctrine.
1992 August	Privatization of mass transit brings general strike against Mitsotakis government economic policies.
1993 March	EC adopts five-year economic reform program for Greece.
June	Political Spring party formed, based on nationalist hard-line Macedonia policy and drawing support from ND.

Table B: Chronology of Important Events

Period	Description
October	After austerity program and scandals weaken ND, Papandreou again is elected prime minister.
November	Maastrict Treaty goes into effect, creating new levels of cooperation in the European Community and redisignating that organization as the European Union (EU).
1994 February	Greece imposes unilateral trade embargo on Former Yugoslav Republic of Macedonia; EU declares embargo violates international law.
April	Assembly revokes citizenship of exiled King Constantine; border incident brings Albanian crackdown on Albanian Greek minority.
1994 June	End of Greece's six-month presidency of EU; Greece expels thousands of illegal Albanian immigrants.
1994 Fall	Diplomatic dispute with Turkey aroused by Greek claims to territorial waters in Aegean; armed conflict narrowly avoided.
1995 March	Assembly elects Konstantinos Stefanopoulos president as compromise candidate, averting parliamentary stalemate and early elections.
1995 June	Assembly ratifies United Nations Convention on the Law of the Sea, bringing new Turkish threats of war if the treaty terms implemented in Aegean Sea.

Country Profile

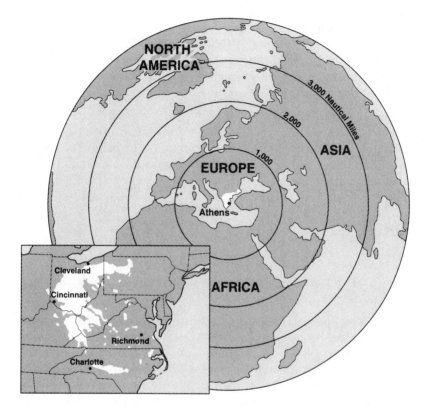

Country

Formal Name: Hellenic Republic.

Short Form: Greece.

Term for Citizens: Greek(s).

Capital: Athens.

Geography

Size: 131,957 square kilometers.

Topography: About 80 percent of territory mountainous. Nine geographically and historically defined regions (six mainland, three insular). Most extensive lowlands are plains of Thessaly in northeast. Highly irregular coastline marked by many bays, coves, and inlets. No point on mainland peninsula more than 100 kilometers from sea. Coastline total length 15,000 kilometers. About 20 percent of land area composed of over 2,000 islands, ranging from small rock formations to Crete, fifth largest island in Mediterranean Sea.

Climate: Predominantly hot, dry summers and cold, damp winters, with some variation at higher elevations and inland. Northern mountains have cold continental winters and more precipitation. Coastal regions and islands parched by dry summer winds. Rainfall greatest along west coast, least on east coast and on Aegean islands.

Society

Population: According to 1991 official census, 10,264,156, of which 51 percent female; predicted to remain stable through the year 2010.

Ethnic Groups and Languages: About 98 percent of population ethnic Greeks; largest minority groups Albanians, Armenians, Bulgarians, Macedonian Slavs, Pomaks, Turks, and Vlachs. Influx of Albanian refugees in 1990s a source of tension. Modern Greek spoken on mainland and most islands; existing regional dialects do not impede communication.

Religion: Officially established church Orthodox Church of Greece, to which 97 percent of population belongs. Small numbers of Roman Catholics, Muslims, various Protestant groups, and Jews.

Education: About 93 percent of population over age fifteen literate. Nine years of education free and compulsory; next three optional years, also free, divided into college preparatory and technical programs. Fewer than 10 percent of students in private schools. State-controlled university system highly competitive; postsecondary technical and vocational schools also available.

Health: Health care reorganized in 1980s into state-run National Health Service, to which private facilities added after 1990. Distribution of facilities and medical personnel uneven, concentrated in Athens and Thessaloniki; shortages of nurses and specialized personnel everywhere. Health insurance dominated by state organizations with varying coverage programs.

Economy

Salient Features: Very slow growth in early 1990s, hindered by expanding debt in public sector, except for specific branches. In early 1990s, heavily regulated sectors (transportation, telecommunications, utilities) liberalized to streamline and expand market economy and resource allocation, with large-scale support from European Union (EU) funds. Government control of prices and wages ended early 1990s. Flourishing underground economy based in small enterprises and service sector.

Energy: Consumption increased by 42 percent 1982–92, generation by 48 percent 1980–90. Main electricity sources coal-burning (66 percent) and liquid-fuel-burning (23 percent) thermoelectric stations and hydroelectric stations (10 percent). Role of coal expanding. Nearly all electricity from government-owned plants.

Mining: Small percentage of economy but based on significant mineral wealth, especially lignite, bauxite, ferronickel ores, magnesite, sulfur ores, ferrochrome ores, kaolin, asbestos, and marble. Crude oil, rapidly depleted, extracted only in north Aegean Sea.

Manufacturing: In 1991 contributed almost 18 percent of gross domestic product and employed 19 percent of labor force. Principal products textiles, clothing and footwear, processing of food, beverages, and tobacco, chemical products, construction materials, transportation equipment, and metals (iron, steel, and aluminum). Predominance of small enterprises prevents economies of scale and limits research and development. Some industries showed substantial growth in early 1990s.

Agriculture: Labor force and share of national productivity declining through 1980s and early 1990s. About 3.7 million hectares used for crops and pasturage, 59 percent in plains. Landholdings small and labor-to-land ratio high compared with West European standards. Livestock production 30 percent of agricultural total. Major crops tobacco, cotton, sugar beets, grains, vegetables, fruits, olives, and grapes. Main agricultural exports grains, fruits, vegetables, and tobacco products.

Services: Tourism major source of foreign currency, growing annually with strong government subsidy. Banking and finance diversified widely in early 1990s, providing vital credit and investment support for national economy. Shipping services also major foreign-exchange earner.

Foreign Trade: In 1990s increasingly focused on EU, where trade barriers lowest. Main partners Germany, Italy, France, and Britain. Exports 50 percent manufactured products, 30 percent agricultural, and fuels and ores 18 percent. Imports 40 percent manufactured goods, 25 percent raw materials and fuels, 21 percent equipment, and 14 percent foods. Annual oil import from Organization of the Petroleum Exporting Countries (OPEC) averages US$1.5 billion to US$2 billion in 1990s. Extensive investment in manufacturing in Albania, Bulgaria, and Romania.

Currency: Drachma; exchange rate in May 1995 US$1 equaled approximately Dr230.

Fiscal Year: Calendar year.

Transportation and Telecommunications

Ports and Shipping: Main ports Heraklion (Crete), Igoumenitsa, Kavala, Patras, Piraeus (serving Athens), Thessaloniki, and Volos; 116 smaller ports also handle passengers or freight. Merchant fleet, 1,407 vessels in 1994, drastic reduction from 1980s size because of expanded overland transport and international shipping slump. No navigable rivers; six-kilometer Corinth Canal connects Ionian Sea with Aegean Sea, cutting 325 kilometers from voyage between seas.

Roads: Automobile travel expanded rapidly in 1980s and early 1990s. Road congestion a serious problem in Athens and Thessaloniki. In 1990 some 38,312 kilometers of roads in service, of which 21,000 kilometers paved and 116 kilometers express roads. Road network to be expanded significantly in late 1990s with EU aid.

Railroads: Standard-gauge routes totaled 1,565 kilometers in 1994, of total 2,503 kilometers in network run by state Greek

Railroads Organization. Railroad construction generally ignored in favor of road and air transportation until 1980s, when modernization and extension programs began, especially on Athens-Thessaloniki line. In 1992 some 214 diesel locomotives in service. Athens-Piraeus electrified urban line of twenty-six kilometers upgraded in early 1990s.

Civil Aviation: State-owned Olympia Airways monopolizes air travel, operating American-made jets to most points in Europe and the Middle East and selected destinations in the Far East, Africa, and the United States. Nine international and twenty-eight domestic airports in operation; new airport planned at Spata to serve Athens region.

Pipelines: None in operation in 1995; in late 1990s, EU will finance 520 kilometer natural gas pipeline from Bulgaria to supply Thessaloniki and Athens and upgrade industrial development in northeastern Greece.

Telecommunications: Development of modern communications lines has been slow. In 1992, 5.3 million telephones in service. Government monopoly of broadcasting ended 1987, bringing significant diversity in radio and television programming.

Government and Politics

Government: Form prescribed in 1975 constitution and 1986 amendments on executive power. Divided into executive, legislative, and judicial branches. Main executive body is Cabinet, chosen by prime minister; cabinet reflects policy of Assembly, which can dismiss it with no-confidence vote. President has limited, mostly ceremonial powers. Legislature is unicameral Assembly of 300 members serving four-year terms; Cabinet has strong role in introducing legislation. Judiciary is independent, divided into criminal, civil, and administrative courts; judges appointed by presidential decree on advice of Judicial Council.

Politics: Dominated by two parties, Panhellenic Socialist Movement (Panhellinion Socialistiko Kinima—PASOK) and New Democracy (Nea Demokratia—ND), since 1981, with some smaller parties exerting influence. Strong role of personal connections and personalities rather than institutions in everyday relations, with movement toward emphasis on mass appeal and issues in mid-1990s. PASOK government under

Andreas Papandreou elected 1993.

Administrative Divisions: Fifty-one provinces are basic element of subnational government. Local governments are 359 municipalities (over 10,000 population) and 5,600 communes (5,000 to 10,000 population). Monastic center of Mt. Athos has status as autonomous region outside regular structure.

Foreign Relations: Defined by membership in EU and North Atlantic Treaty Organization (NATO), providing strong link to Western Europe. End of Cold War reduced strategic role in NATO, leaving traditional enmity of Turkey and unresolved occupation of Cyprus as key issues. Heavy postwar reliance on United States lessened in early 1990s, more diversified position sought. Conflict in former Yugoslavia and in Albania major regional concerns, affecting trade and immigration policy; Macedonian independence provokes strong nationalist feeling.

National Security

Armed Forces: Hellenic Armed Forces divided into army, air force, and navy, with reserve components. Ground forces (Hellenic Army) include 113,000 active personnel, of whom 100,000 conscripts, with 350,000 reserves; Hellenic Air Force 26,800 personnel, of whom 14,400 conscripts; Hellenic Navy 19,500 personnel, of whom 7,900 conscripts. Terms of active-duty service range from eighteen to twenty-three months.

Major Military Units: Army in one field army divided into four corps plus Higher Military Command of the Interior and the Islands, headquartered in Athens. First and second corps defend northern border, third and fourth corps defend Turkish border and islands. Organization includes nine infantry divisions plus specialized units. Three air force commands, one based in Larisa, two in Athens. Tactical Air Command is main combat command. Eight major air force installations. Three navy commands: fleet (operational), Naval Training Command, and Naval Logistics Command.

Military Budget: Highest percentage of defense expenditure among NATO countries, about 5.5 percent of gross national product in early 1990s. Equipment purchase and modernization targeted to specialized needs dictated by doctrine and defense posture.

Internal Security Forces: Police, reorganized in 1984 into single national paramilitary unit of 26,500 called Hellenic Police (Elliniki Astinomia—EL.AS). Special security forces include special tasks and missions units for riot control, Special Forces Squad for special threats, and Counterterrorism Squad, expanded in mid-1990s. Ministry of Public Order directs security forces. Customs Police, Hellenic Police, and Okana (state drug agency) are major narcotics agencies.

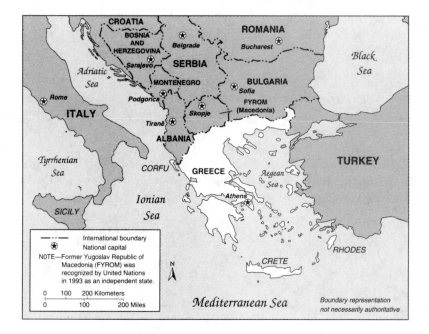

Figure 2. Geographic Setting, 1994

Introduction

FOR GREECE, THE TWENTIETH CENTURY has been a period full of violence and uncertainty. The last years of the century, however, have brought the potential for political stability in a slowly maturing democratic system, and for economic prosperity as a part of a European continent undergoing unprecedented unification. Democracy, the theoretical basis of governance since the foundation of the modern Greek state in 1832, has had its longest and most consistent application in the era that began with the toppling of the military junta in 1974. Economic growth, which virtually stopped in the 1980s, showed signs of revival in the early 1990s, aided by substantial infrastructural aid programs and strict economic guidelines from Greece's partner nations in the European Union (EU—see Glossary). On the negative side, Greece's traditionally difficult relations with neighbor Turkey remained extremely tense as a series of territorial issues were still unresolved in the mid-1990s. And the violently unstable regions of the former Yugoslavia, just to Greece's north, renewed the threat that the wider Balkan turmoil of earlier decades might begin a new chapter.

Rooted in the Minoan and Mycenaean civilizations of the third millennium B.C., the cultural heritage of Greece has evolved without interruption despite four centuries of Ottoman rule (fifteenth through nineteenth centuries) over the entire Greek peninsula. In the eighth century B.C., Greeks began establishing colonies throughout the Mediterranean and Black sea regions, spreading a cultural influence that remains in modern times. Following the development of the Greek polis as the dominant political entity on the Greek peninsula, for several decades in the fifth century B.C. Athens was the center of unparalleled political and cultural accomplishment. Among the contributions to modern civilization that emerged from Greece in that period are the art forms of a group of great sculptors and dramatists, the philosophical approaches of three great thinkers, and the governmental innovations of the great Athenian leader Pericles. After the fall of the Athenian Empire around 400 B.C., Alexander the Great extended his short-lived empire deep into Central Asia. Between his death in 323 B.C. and the Ottoman occupation in the 1450s, Greece was a culturally influential part, first of the Roman Empire, then of the Byzantine Empire.

The Greek War of Independence (1821–32) resulted from a convergence of internal and international circumstances that simultaneously revived the Greek national consciousness and weakened the hold of the Ottoman Empire. The modern Greek state emerged from its struggle for liberation under close control of the European Great Powers and with quite vivid irredentist longings. In the nineteenth century, the West placed men from noble families of two countries, first Bavaria and then Denmark, on the new throne of Greece. For more than a century after independence, nationalist expansionism and extreme political factionalism hindered smooth development and brought frequent intervention by Britain and France. Progressive regimes such as those of Prime Minister Eleutherios Venizelos, in the first decades of the twentieth century, were interspersed with heavy international debt, military juntas, struggles between the monarch and elected government officials, and chaotic changes of government. Although the size of the Greek state increased in several stages in the nineteenth and early twentieth centuries, Greek irredentism suffered a serious blow in 1922 when Turkish forces drove the Greeks out of the Smyrna enclave that had been established along the west coast of Asia Minor, causing a huge refugee movement that changed Greece's demography.

Greece was directly involved in the two world wars, suffering devastating damage from the Nazi occupation of 1941–44. The political schism that had begun in the early 1900s between royalists and republicans then fueled a disastrous civil war immediately following World War II.

Greece emerged from the calamitous 1940s shattered economically, socially, and politically. Recovery was remarkably fast in the economic sphere and to some degree in society, but for another thirty years the left side of the political spectrum was suppressed in the wake of Civil War anticommunism, enabling conservative factions to dominate. The final stage of that domination, the totalitarian military regime of 1967–74, gave way to a broad spectrum of political activity and parliamentary representation that has prospered since 1974.

In the postwar period, Greece's foreign relations have been determined by the need for economic and military security, provided first by Britain, then by the United States and the European Community (EC—see Glossary). In that period, two aspects of international geopolitics dominated Greece's foreign policy: the Cold War between the Soviet Union and its allies and the West and the latest stages of Greece's long-term struggle with Turkey over control of the two countries' overlapping territorial claims in the Aegean Sea. The Cold War ended with the collapse of the Soviet Union and its alliances in 1991, but the tensions with Turkey, represented most concretely in the dispute between Greece and Turkey over the status of the island of Cyprus, continued unabated into the mid-1990s. Turkey took control of part of the island in 1974 in response to a Greek nationalist coup attempt. The autonomous state declared at that time in northeast Cyprus on behalf of the Turkish minority remained a major irritant to relations into the mid-1990s. In several instances in the 1980s and the 1990s, the two nations narrowly averted war over the status of territory or resources in the Aegean Sea. The presence of vocal nationalist factions in Greece and Turkey pushed the respective governments away from positions of conciliation on the issues of the Aegean and Cyprus, despite substantial sentiment for harmonious relations between the two members of the North Atlantic Treaty Organization (NATO—see Glossary).

After Greece achieved full EC membership in 1981, economic and political ties with more prosperous European nations grew steadily and greatly benefited Greece. However, in 1991 the emergence of new independent states from the collapsed Republic of Yugoslavia on Greece's northern border caused strains in this relationship. In opposition to EC policies, Greece defended the aggressive actions of traditional ally and trading partner Serbia toward Bosnia and Herzegovina, and in the same period Greece waged a vigorous campaign against recognition of Slavic Macedonia, another fragment of former Yugoslavia that declared independence in 1991.

Greek society is characterized by substantial ethnic and cultural homogeneity. An estimated 98 percent of citizens are of Greek descent, with small minorities of Albanians, Armenians, southern Slavs, Turks, and Vlachs. In the 1990s, the foremost minority problem has been the influx of illegal Albanian immigrants from across the northwestern border.

Migration within the borders of Greece has assumed definite patterns. Although the net shift of Greek citizens from rural to urban areas began with the first wave of industrialization before 1900, the economic growth of the post-World War II period was accompanied by a more intense urbanization that moved more than 2 million residents out of rural areas in the postwar decades.

Greece's religious homogeneity matches its ethnic makeup and reflects tradition born in the later years (fourth century A.D.) of the Eastern Roman Empire. The Orthodox Church of Greece, the established state religion, is the professed faith of 97 percent of Greek citizens. In recent decades, the church, which maintains substantial influence outside the strictly theological realm, has defended its doctrine in disputes with secular groups over social issues such as the legalization of abortion and civil marriages. Freedom of religion is a constitutional guarantee, although proselytization by some groups has been restricted.

Both the education and the health care of Greek citizens are overwhelmingly dominated by state agencies. Greek society affords great respect to education because of Greece's venerable classical heritage and because Greeks traditionally have seen education as the key to social advancement. The centralized education system, the lower levels of which underwent major reform in the 1970s, oversees most of Greece's postsecondary institutions. The shortage of university positions has put great pressure on secondary students and created a "brain drain" by forcing many to attend universities abroad.

Health care in Greece also has undergone substantial reform in the last two decades, although uneven distribution of health resources such as doctors, nurses, and clinics is still considered a major problem. The National Health Service, established in 1983 to centralize health care, has exerted varied degrees of control according to the political complexion of the government in power. This variation changes the ratio of public and private health care; since 1990, however, private medical practices and private hospitals have increased.

The economic progress of modern Greece has been very uneven, with few periods of sustained growth. Despite periodic modernization programs that began in the late nineteenth century, until the middle of the following century Greece remained predominantly an agricultural nation. Then, following the destruction of much of its infrastructure in World War II and the Civil War of 1946–49, the Greek economy grew, with substantial Western aid, at a phenomenal rate in the 1950s and the 1960s. An important aspect of this growth was the development of the industrial sector into a significant part of the national economy, which was bolstered by a number of large investment projects backed by West European nations. The most important elements of this growth were the shipping, chemical, pharmaceuticals, metallurgy, and electrical machinery industries. By the early 1970s, however, a major economic crisis developed. Caused by the inept economic policies of the military regime, an international fuel crisis, and excessive borrowing in the public sector, the crisis brought production growth to a standstill in many parts of the economy for the next fifteen years. Budget deficits and inflation climbed in the 1980s, bringing a series of stabilization policies that included tax reform and privatization of state enterprises.

Among the continuing structural problems of the Greek economy are the substantial size of the underground economy, the predominance of small enterprises, the need for more efficient taxation procedures, the failure of privatization programs, and excessive spending by the public sector. However, in the early 1990s closer integration of national economies in Europe and stringent EU requirements for continued participation in union aid programs spurred reforms and streamlining by Greek economic policy makers. By 1994 inflation had dropped significantly, and growth occurred in several long-stagnant manufacturing industries, spurring the hope that private investment might stimulate another period of growth.

In the postwar period, Greece's traditional trade partners were consistently European (the top three were Germany, Italy, and France), with the United States the most important partner outside the EC. In the early 1990s, major gains were made in trade with nations of Eastern Europe and the former Soviet Union. Nevertheless, the most important aspect of Greece's foreign trade policy was increased integration into the EU system, a process that had entailed liberalization of trade policy in the late 1980s and meeting stringent standards for deficits, production growth, inflation, and unemployment by 1998 under the EU Convergence Plan.

Beginning with the military regime of General Ioannis Metaxas (1936–41), the left wing of Greek politics was forcibly excluded from participation in government—a policy bred in the National Schism between royalists and republicans and reinforced after World War II by the bitterness of the Civil War fighting between communist guerrillas and the national government. Although the exclusion ended technically with legalization of the Communist Party of Greece in 1974, the Greek left took control of the government for the first time in 1981

with the triumph of Andreas Papandreou's Panhellenic Socialist Movement (Panhellinion Socialistiko Kinima—PASOK). In
the fourteen years that followed, PASOK and the main conservative party, New Democracy (Nea Demokratia—ND), gained
alternating majorities in the unicameral legislative Assembly.
Although the two parties started the 1980s with drastically
opposed positions on issues of national security and domestic
economics, by the early 1990s both positions had moved
toward the center in many respects. This centrist drift was especially true of PASOK, which during the 1980s dropped much of
its socialist program as well as its opposition to Greek participation in NATO. In this period, political campaigns were waged
more on accusations of corruption and malfeasance than on
divergent policy approaches. Under these conditions, experts
pointed to the disenchantment of the Greek electorate as a
major cause of the two changes in majority control between
1989 and 1993 and the inability of either party to form a government after the 1989 elections.

Meanwhile, even lacking significant policy differences, the
two major parties maintained a hold on power that made emergence of significant new political groups increasingly difficult.
The strongest new party to emerge in the early 1990s, Political
Spring, was dedicated to the single issue of preventing world
recognition of independent Macedonia. At the same time, the
next-largest party, the Communist Party of Greece, lost significant support. Both PASOK and the ND expected a new generation of leaders to emerge in the mid-1990s once long-time
stalwarts Papandreou and Konstantinos Karamanlis retired.

Even in the more liberal political climate that has prevailed
since 1974, the free exchange of political ideas has been hampered by a long tradition of individual patron-client relationships that take the place of the Western-style interaction of
coherent interest groups. For example, labor unions are not
permanently active in pursuing their members' goals, and environmental groups have exercised rather inconclusive influence
over government policy toward consumption of natural
resources and pollution.

The focus of Greek foreign policy changed somewhat in the
early 1990s with the curtailment of Greece's strategic responsibilities in NATO, although the resentment of the 1980s toward
perceived Western domination had dissipated in most political
circles. Despite Greece's enthusiastic support of EU unification
goals, however, its policy toward the fragmented states of the

former Yugoslavia caused friction with other member states. The main sources of friction were Greece's lobbying to prevent recognition of an independent state of Macedonia and Greece's refusal to honor the UN embargo on its erstwhile ally and major trading partner Serbia, in response to Serbian actions in Bosnia and Herzegovina. Both positions had substantial support in the Greek electorate and influential parts of the Greek media. As a result, in 1993 and 1994 Greece struggled to avoid isolation within the European body.

Another major source of regional friction, the refugee movement from Albania into northern Greece, raised tensions with that neighbor and temporarily halted the large-scale aid initiative that Greece had begun after the fall of Albania's last communist regime. By the end of 1994, however, Greece had made gestures of reconciliation that improved relations, and the border situation was under negotiation.

In 1947 the United States initiated a large aid program to prevent communist guerrillas from defeating Greek government forces in the Civil War. With that program, the United States replaced Britain as Greece's most important source of material aid and national security protection—a relationship that was to last until the end of the Cold War in the early 1990s. Greece joined NATO in 1952 as an extension of the anticommunism policy established as a result of the Civil War. Beginning in the mid-1970s, Greece's most immediate national security problems have been associated with a variety of conflicts with Turkey. The major components of that clash have been the Turkish occupation of part of the island of Cyprus; conflicts over sea and air jurisdiction in the Aegean Sea; and the existence of a substantial Muslim population in Greece's easternmost province, which borders on Turkey. Since Turkey's invasion of Cyprus in 1974, a number of international forums and individual arbiters have failed to resolve the fundamental conflict of national security positions between the two neighbors.

Greece's designated Cold War role in NATO was the support and basing of United States and West European forces in the eastern Mediterranean, considered a crucial location in the event of a land attack in Europe by Warsaw Pact (see Glossary) forces. After 1991, Greek national security policy concentrated more heavily on defense against a possible Turkish attack in the Aegean Sea or in Cyprus. In that period, Greek military policy has been to seek diversification of its foreign support and supplies; accordingly, the United States presence has waned although bilateral defense agreements remain in place. In the early 1990s, military doctrine turned fully toward smaller units with enhanced mobility and firepower and modernization of specific types of equipment seen as most supportive of that approach.

A number of economic indicators provided a generally positive outlook for Greece in 1995. The strong likelihood that the PASOK government would not have to face an election for the next two years improved the prospects of reducing the budget deficit and the inflation that for many years had combined to impede economic growth. In mid-1995, experts predicted that the annual inflation rate would be slightly below 10 percent at the end of 1995 and 8.5 percent in 1996. Given increased public investment (including the start of construction on the Spata international airport), Greece's gross domestic product (GDP—see Glossary) could rise by 2 percent in 1996. (Between 1992 and 1994, average annual GDP growth was 0.4 percent.)

The public-sector deficit was generally identified as Greece's most pressing economic problem at the beginning of 1995. The 1994 national budget projected a deficit of Dr2.4 trillion (for value of the drachma—see Glossary), a figure that was exceeded in that year by about Dr360 billion. Despite the overshot on Greece's borrowing requirement, the final figure was well within EU requirements for that stage. The 1995 budget, which includes government borrowing equal to 10.7 percent of GDP, also met the targets of the EU's Greek Convergence Program. Experts did not expect Greece to exceed its 1995 public borrowing estimate, but they believed that budgeted expenditures for 1995, based on anticipated revenue increases of 26.9 percent from newly stringent tax enforcement policies, were unrealistically high. The budget also relies on a very low 1995 interest payment rate on the public debt, 3.6 percent. Overall, government debt was expected to rise from its 1994 level of 116.9 percent of GDP to 117.4 percent of GDP in 1995.

The government's inability to collect taxes from the many self-employed Greek citizens has been a major cause of Greece's high public debt. In 1994 more than 70 percent of personal income tax came from salaried individuals whose incomes were easily documented. A series of measures devised by the Ministry of Finance to curtail rampant tax evasion by companies and individuals encountered obstacles early in 1995. After a court ruled the ministry's suspension of trade privileges an unconstitutional punishment for corporate tax evasion, the process of naming violators slowed noticeably, although the ministry's close monitoring of transaction documents continued in the first half of 1995.

Plans were announced for a special tax police force with the power to arrest offenders, expediting the lengthy court procedures that had hindered enforcement in the past. At the same time, new excise taxes went into effect on tobacco products and gambling establishments. To improve collection of taxes on self-employed citizens, a new law bases assessments on presumed rather than reported earnings. In early 1995, farmers, merchants, and other self-employed Greeks demonstrated and struck against the new system, and the powerful General Confederation of Greek Merchants claimed that it would cripple Greece's retail market. Despite resistance, revenue collection rose substantially in the first half of 1995.

Privatization remained a key economic issue in the first half of 1995. After 1993 PASOK policies, which had alienated the business community in the 1980s by favoring nationalization, shifted to a more pragmatic stance toward privatization and gained support from the Association of Greek Industrialists and other business groups. Experts cited opposition from labor organizations and the ND's failure to support PASOK privatization programs as the causes of Greece's generally slow progress in this area; little privatization of any kind was achieved in the first half of 1995.

The privatization of state enterprises, a program that received a serious blow in November 1994 with the suspension of sales of shares in the state-owned Greek Telecommunications Organization (Organismos Tilepikoinonion Ellados—OTE), was scheduled to continue in 1995. Plans called for shares in OTE and the Public Petroleum Corporation to become available on the Athens Stock Exchange sometime in 1995. However, poor performance and high levels of indebtedness by OTE were expected to decrease the value of its shares. The emergence of private competition was expected to challenge OTE and another government monopoly, the Public Power Corporation (Dimosia Epicheirisi Ilektrismou—DEI). Plans called for two privately owned wind-energy plants to be built on Crete in 1995, providing the first major test of private power production in Greece by more than doubling Greece's installed capacity of wind energy.

Several EU assistance programs targeting Greece offered an average of US$10 billion per year from 1995 through 1999. Disagreements between Greek authorities and the European Commission (see Glossary) about supervisory control of EU public works projects prevented utilization of much of the money allocated for the first half of 1995, however. Most of the large projects for which such assistance had been designed (most notably in the so-called Second Delors Package) never got underway; the main exception was the new Spata international airport near Athens, which was scheduled to begin construction in the fall of 1995 after an agreement was signed with the German Hochtief corporation in July. That deal creates a private-public joint venture that will manage the airport for its first thirty years.

In June 1995, the Ministry of National Economy reported increased private investment in Greek industry. With the aid of substantial government subsidies, investment rates for 1995 were considerably above those for 1994. Concentrated on machinery and commercial building, the investment trend was expected to continue into 1996. Experts warned, however that investment must focus more strongly on infrastructure and retraining of the labor force to achieve long-term growth.

In mid-1995 the Ministry of Labor reported declining investment and rising unemployment in some sectors of the economy, mostly traditional industries that were unable to apply new technology, and find new markets as other industries were restructuring. The most notable losses occurred in the garment and textile industries. The latter industry, which accounts for 40 percent of Greece's industrial exports and 25 percent of its overall industrial product, has declined because of outmoded equipment and competition from imported materials. Meanwhile, expansion continued into the mid-1990s in the food and beverage industries, mining, services, trade, transportation, and banking.

The tourism industry, whose growth in the early 1990s had been an important part of the national economy, suffered setbacks in the summer of 1995. In July an announcement by the United States Department of State of an indefinite terrorist threat against American tourists in Greece, together with similar warnings in the German media, seriously reduced the normally substantial summer tourist income from those countries. Such publicity exacerbated Greece's reputation as a haven for terrorists, which had worsened with a series of assassinations and bombings in 1994. Long-standing friction with United States antiterrorist intelligence agencies resulted in dismissal of the chief of the national police's Antiterrorist Service in early 1995.

As 1995 began, a number of political issues and questions were on the agenda for Greek policy makers. A key question, the prospect of parliamentary elections being forced by a stalemate over the choice of a new president, was avoided when Andreas Papandreou withdrew from presidential consideration in November 1994 and compromise candidate Konstantinos Stefanopoulos was elected and inaugurated in March 1995. That outcome, which avoided a fifth national election in a period of six years, was a great relief to all parties and to the Greek public as well.

The compromise ensured that the present government would remain in power until the next scheduled parliamentary elections in October 1997. Such stability would greatly improve Greece's chances of meeting the long-term requirements of the EU's Convergence Program, which provides the guidelines for full participation and benefits in that organization. Experts believed that PASOK would now feel free to take some of the unpopular steps (such as reductions in public-sector spending) needed to gain control of the economy.

At the beginning of 1995, both parties proposed a number of constitutional amendments. Among the fifty-two changes to be discussed were proposals to prescribe specifically the separation of church and state; strengthen privacy rights by prohibiting storage of data on an individual; and formally abolish the death penalty (which has not been applied since 1972). Also on the table were proposals to reinforce the constitutional status of the Assembly and the political parties; specifically state Greece's commitment to the EU and to European unity in general; strengthen the independence of the judiciary and establish a Supreme Judicial Council; and reform conditions of employment in the public sector. ND leaders added a proposal upgrading the president's power to convene meetings and to issue proclamations (the last constitutional amendments in 1986 had weakened presidential powers substantially) and a proposal for reform of election campaign financing. PASOK declared all amendments except for the presidential powers provision open for negotiation.

By the end of 1994, both major political parties were seriously divided into two or more factions, threatening the ability of each to make headway with the electorate between 1995 and the next elections. Experts viewed the conflicts as a healthy sign of democratic change as a new generation debated the proper direction for the future. The public also was uncertain about its political direction: in a national poll in mid-1995, the ND and PASOK, still the two leading parties, each received only 25 percent support, with 30 percent of respondents declaring themselves undecided.

In 1995 the parties faced the imminent retirement of three long-time leaders belonging to the pre-World War II generation—Papandreou, who had led PASOK for the entire twenty-one years of its existence, President Konstantinos Karamanlis, an ND leader active in Greek governance since 1951, and former prime minister Konstantinos Mitsotakis, also of the ND.

The compromise selection of Konstantinos Stefanopoulos—former leader of the now-defunct Democratic Renewal Party and at age sixty-nine also a veteran politician—as president in March 1995 was a pragmatic move by both sides and a great relief to observers who feared a bloody and indecisive battle over the successor to Karamanlis. In the event, Stefanopoulos received 181 votes, eleven more than the required number, on the third and decisive ballot in the Assembly, and PASOK party discipline enforced the party's official support for a one-time political rival. Also vital to this result was the support of the nationalist Political Spring party, which held eleven seats in the Assembly.

Throughout the first half of 1995, Papandreou vowed to remain as prime minister—although he was physically able to work only briefly each day, and his young wife received substantial criticism from within PASOK and in the media for her increasingly visible role in everyday policy making. Papandreou's professed aim was to bind together PASOK's two increasingly opposed factions, which were labeled the loyalists and the reformists. The reformist faction of PASOK, favoring closer ties with the EU and openly calling for Papandreou to step down, was led by a group of ambitious younger politicians including Minister of Industry, Energy, and Technology Konstantinos Simitis, former EU Commissioner Vasso Papandreou (no relation to the prime minister), and former Deputy Minister of Foreign Affairs Theodoros Pangalos. As Papandreou continued to hold power in mid-1995 without naming a successor, several candidates jockeyed for position, and Pangalos emerged as the most outspoken critic of Papandreou. Among

Papandreou loyalists, the most likely candidates to succeed the prime minister were Minister of Foreign Affairs Karolos Papoulias and Assembly Speaker Apostolos Kaklamanis.

The ND, meanwhile, faced a rebellion against party leader Miltiades Evert, who was portrayed by a dissident faction as out of touch with the party's political base and accountable for the ND's perceived loss of influence. The leaders of this movement were the former minister of industry, energy, and technology, Andreas Andrianopoulos, and a group of little-known younger politicians. Evert was able to consolidate his position in the first half of 1995 because of his party's generally favorable results in the local and regional elections of late 1994 and because of his victories in various skirmishes with the internal opposition. Former Prime Minister Konstantinos Mitsotakis, who had criticized some Evert policies and to whom many dissidents had looked as a possible replacement for Evert, remained uncommitted in the first half of 1995. Experts believed that wiretapping and bribery charges, which had stood against Mitsotakis until Papandreou dropped them in January 1995, would prevent Mitsotakis from mounting a challenge to Evert.

At the beginning of 1995, Greece's four main foreign policy problems were its tense relations with neighboring Albania and Turkey, continuing conflict in the states of the former Yugoslavia, and Greece's unresolved objections concerning the name and certain policies of the Macedonian state to the north (recognized internationally since 1993 under the cumbersome name Former Yugoslav Republic of Macedonia—FYROM). Thus Greece continued to find itself in a dangerous national security position between a powerful and influential historical enemy, Turkey, and a chronically unstable region, the Slavic Balkans, at a time when the United States military presence in Greece had been greatly reduced.

Relations with Albania improved early in 1995 with the release of four Greeks jailed in Albania under sedition charges in 1994. In March a meeting between Papandreou and Albanian Prime Minister Sali Berisha yielded a mutual commitment to sign a treaty of friendship before the end of 1995. Such a treaty would provide human rights guarantees for the Greek minority in Albania, improve the status of illegal Albanian refugees in Greece, resolve border issues, and address issues of banking and economic cooperation. Relations improved further when Greece arrested members of the Greek extremist

Northern Epirus Liberation Front, who planned an attack on an Albanian border post.

On the issue of Macedonia—or Skopje in the official Greek terminology that uses the capital city as the country name—Greek officials continued to complain that the government of President Kiro Gligorov remains adamantly opposed to constructive dialogue. However, the elimination of spring elections from the political scene improved the prospects that Greece could make concessions on the Macedonia issue. In the first half of 1995, negotiations by the United Nations (UN) and other intermediaries failed. The use of the term Macedonia in the name of the new nation that emerged from Yugoslavia to Greece's north is objectionable to Greece because that name (and the sunburst design that FYROM included in its national flag) is associated with the Greek empire of Alexander the Great and the present-day northern province of Greece. In conjunction with reckless nationalist rhetoric in FYROM, the name usage has conjured fears of irredentist expansionism into Greek territory. Although compromise was reached on secondary issues, the name question did not yield to any compromise suggested in the first half of 1995. In September talks were set to resume at the foreign ministry level, under United States and UN sponsorship, in New York. This new stage provided hope that the long impasse would finally end, stabilizing one portion of the Balkan region.

Meanwhile, Greece's unilateral embargo of non-humanitarian goods crossing into FYROM, imposed in 1994 in response to that nation's use of the name Macedonia, yielded negative results for Greece as well as for FYROM. The European Commission brought suit against Greece in the European Court of Justice for unjustified restraint of European trade, world opinion was decidedly against the Greek move, and Greek businesses complained of lost revenue and markets. As the court prepared a verdict in mid-1995, Greek diplomats had ample incentive to find a compromise that would avoid two potential sources of embarrassment: an international verdict against a key foreign policy of the Papandreou government and the admission that Greek diplomacy could not resolve a major foreign policy question independently without Western assistance.

Although preliminary indications were that the court would declare the issue outside its jurisdiction, in May Greek and FYROM diplomats proposed an interim "small package" of mutual concessions, including changes in FYROM's flag and in the description of the country in the FYROM constitution and a lifting of the Greek embargo. Amid criticism that such a package would be an admission of failure for Greece, this strategy was abandoned. The Greek blockade of FYROM thus continued through the first half of 1995, as France, Germany, and other EU member countries intensified their objections and UN-sponsored negotiations made no progress. The blockade's severe impact on FYROM's national economy exacerbated ethnic tensions in that country, where hostility between the growing Albanian minority and the Slavic majority threatened to further destabilize Greece's northern border.

A second embargo issue, the international blockade on trade with Serbia imposed by the UN in 1992, also hurt the Greek economy by eliminating an important trading partner except for illegal shipments. Besides commercial ties, Greeks also carried into the 1990s their historical loyalty to Serbia on cultural and religious grounds. In a 1995 poll, over 60 percent of Greeks named Serbia the foreign country for which they had the highest regard. After years of vocal opposition to the UN policy and violation of the embargo at various levels, in May 1995 Greece joined five other regional trading partners of Serbia to lodge an official protest and demand compensation from the UN.

The diplomatic stalemate and Serbian advances in Bosnia and Herzegovina, which in 1995 continued to threaten the Balkans with a wider war, offered Greece an opportunity to repair its international diplomatic image and hasten the end of the UN embargo by acting as a neutral negotiator—provided that the Western powers found some diplomatic value in Greece's close ties with Serbs in Belgrade and in Bosnia. In June 1995, the Greek Ministry of Foreign Affairs was very active in negotiating the release of UN hostages taken by Bosnian Serb forces in Bosnia. At the same time, the official Greek position was that the UN peacekeeping force should remain in Bosnia and Herzegovina, but that any NATO rapid-reaction force, under consideration as a potentially anti-Serbian military unit of the Western powers, must remain under the peacekeeping mandate of the UN. At the same time, the Greek government reiterated that its NATO forces would aid in a withdrawal of UN forces from Bosnia but would not participate in a NATO attack on Serbian positions in Bosnia.

Experts expected that the summer of 1995 would be significant in Greek-Turkish relations because of recent expansion of

Turkey's navy, the conflict within NATO over location of the organization's Aegean headquarters at the Greek city of Larisa, the prospect of Cyprus's achieving membership in the EU, and increased tension over control of the continental shelf in the Aegean.

Greek-Turkish reciprocal funding vetoes in NATO continued to hinder the financial and strategic planning of that organization, as they had in the early 1990s. Fearing loss of leverage over negotiations on Aegean Sea issues, Turkey vetoed funding for the Larisa base of NATO ground forces, part of a NATO package proposal that also included Multinational Division Headquarters and Air Subheadquarters in Greece. Greece responded with a veto of funding for the Izmir NATO base in western Turkey. In June the United States intensified its pressure on Turkey and revised the proposal on Land Forces headquarters, the most urgent of the issues, to better accommodate the Turkish position.

In June the issue of Aegean control heated up when Greece ratified the United Nations Convention on the Law of the Sea, which establishes a twelve-mile continental shelf—giving Greece the legal right to extend its current six-mile limit and in effect nullifying Turkish claims to territorial waters in the Aegean Sea between the Turkish mainland and the Greek islands adjacent to the coast. Having lost this stage of its longstanding battle for control of the Aegean, Turkey, besides Israel and Venezuela the only country not to sign the treaty, threatened war if Greece applied the treaty in this way. An exchange of harsh language and accusations continued through the summer. The Turkish government repeated its claim that Greece was harboring, training, and exporting some of the Kurdish terrorists whose bombs and violent attacks have destabilized Turkey—a claim that Greece denied categorically.

In March 1995, the EU made a commitment to begin discussion of proposed membership for Cyprus and Malta (strongly urged by Greece) to begin within six months of the end of the EU's Intergovernmental Conference in 1996. The commitment also provided Cyprus the same political links with the EU as other prospective members such as the Czech Republic, Hungary, Poland, and Slovakia. Although Greeks hailed the commitment as a step toward the withering of the Turkish enclave in Cyprus, and only Turkey recognized the enclave as a separate nation, the EU's handling of that de facto division was left to membership discussions.

After the EU made its Cyprus commitment, Greece withdrew its veto of a proposed customs union between the EU and Turkey, which Turkey had eagerly sought to improve commercial ties in Europe and which was scheduled to go into effect in 1996. Greece's approval carried with it the requirement that a review be made after one year of implementation to determine the union's effect on the Greek textile industry. In any event, Turkey's prospective new position was jeopardized in 1995 by the European Parliament's disapproval of human rights practices in Turkey.

In the first half of 1995, nationalist rhetoric in Greece continued to describe Turkish plots to stir irredentism in the Turkish minority in western Thrace as a base for a Turkish invasion and capture of that Greek province. That strategy was seen as one of three elements of Turkey's offensive position toward Greece, the other two being Cyprus and the Aegean Islands. In May the Turkish navy's acquisition of nine new naval vessels—whose identity was a matter of dispute—brought accusations that Turkey planned to attack the Greek Aegean Islands and Cyprus and become a naval superpower in the Mediterranean. Although overall Turkish military superiority is assumed in all Greek national security doctrine—since 1970 the Turkish army has been the largest NATO force in Europe, and since the mid-1970s its military expenditures have been the highest percentage of gross national product (GNP—see Glossary) aside from Greece's—nationalist factions in Greece used this assertion to urge additional weapons development programs for the Hellenic Navy, which now is building a full-sized navy yard in Cyprus.

In mid-1995, the Greek government, assured that it would remain in power until 1997, announced a set of guidelines as initial bargaining positions on major European issues at the EU Intergovernmental Conference in 1996. Together with overall strong support of social, financial, and political cohesion in Europe, the statement supported EU membership for Cyprus and Malta; dismissed the concept of categorizing EU member nations according to varying speeds of development (a proposed standard of measurement by which Greece would be in the third and most disadvantaged group of nations); and insisted that the EU must achieve unanimous positions on foreign policy issues that are vital to the national interests of member nations.

In 1995 the government moved toward reform in its national defense establishment. In 1990 and 1993, the incoming Mitsotakis and Papandreou administrations had recalled retired generals with connections to the party in power to assume high staff positions, causing resentment and resignations among senior officers who lost promotion opportunities. New legislation would appoint chiefs of the general staff and service chiefs to fixed terms, and it would strengthen the Assembly's oversight of the Ministry of Defense. Through its Foreign Affairs and Defense Committee, the Assembly would have to be consulted in long-term defense and spending policy as well as changes in the command structure.

Domestic security organizations also were involved in controversies in the first half of 1995. In March the minister of justice, Georgios Kouvelakis, resigned in a dispute over alleged corruption in the administration of the national prison system. Kouvelakis, whose investigations had led to charges against an influential senior official, claimed in his resignation statement that his activities had been obstructed by the undersecretary to the prime minister. Also in March, the police beating of pensioners demonstrating for improved benefits brought the resignation of high police officials in Attica Province. Later that month, the minister of public order, Stelios Papathemelis, resigned rather than ordering police to break up a blockade by farmers striking against the new tax policy.

Thus the road to much-needed economic and political reform, as well as the road to improved national security, proved rather uneven in 1995. Nevertheless, major events proved that Greece was still on the road and moving in the right general direction, despite obstacles in its internal politics and in its traditional foreign policy positions.

August 31, 1995   Glenn E. Curtis

Chapter 1. Historical Setting

THE BURDEN OF HISTORY lies heavily on Greece. In the early 1990s, as new subway tunnels were being excavated under Athens, Greece's museums were being filled to overflowing with the material remains of the past: remnants of houses from the Turkokratia (the era of Ottoman rule); coins and shops from the period of the Byzantine Empire; pottery remains from the Greek workshops that flourished during the Roman Empire; and graves, shrines, and houses from the classical period when Athens stood at the head of its own empire. The glories of ancient Greece and the splendor of the Christian Byzantine Empire give the modern Greeks a proud and rich heritage. The resilience and durability of Greek culture and traditions through times of turmoil provide a strong sense of cultural destiny. These elements also pose a considerable challenge to Greeks of the present: to live up to the legacies of the past. Much of the history of the modern state of Greece has witnessed a playing out of these contradictory forces.

An important theme in Greek history is the multiple identities of its civilization. Greece is both a Mediterranean country and a Balkan country. And, throughout its history, Greece has been a part of both the Near East and Western Europe. During the Bronze Age and again at the time of the Greek Renaissance of the eighth century B.C., Greece and the Near East were closely connected. The empire of Alexander the Great of Macedonia brought under Greek dominion a vast expanse of territory from the Balkans to the Indus. The Byzantine Empire, with its heart in Constantinople, bridged the continents of Europe and Asia. Greece's history is also closely intertwined with that of Europe and has been since Greek colonists settled the shores of Italy and Spain and Greek traders brought their wares to Celtic France in the seventh century B.C.

A second theme is the influence of the Greek diaspora. From the sixth century B.C., when Greeks settled over an expanse from the Caucasus to Gibraltar, until the dispersal of hundreds of thousands of Greeks to Australia and Canada during the 1950s and 1960s, Greeks have been on the move. The experience of the diaspora has been and continues to be a defining element in the development of Greece and Greek society.

The third major theme is the role of foreign dependence. Until 1832, the Greek nation had never existed as a single state. In antiquity, hundreds of states were inhabited by Greeks, so the Greek national identity transcended any one state. For much of their history, Greeks have been part of large, multiethnic states. Whether under the suzerainty of the emperors of Rome or the dominion of the Ottoman Empire (see Glossary), much of Greek history can only be understood in the context of foreign rule. In more recent times, the fortunes of Greece have been linked in integral ways to the struggles of the Great Powers in the nineteenth century and the polarizing diplomacy of the late twentieth-century Cold War. The history of Greece and the Greek people, then, is bound up with forces and developments on a scale larger than just southeastern Europe. To understand the history of Greece, one has to examine this complex interplay between indigenous development and foreign influences.

Earliest History

Migrations from the east brought the foundations of new civilizations to the Greek mainland, the island of Crete, and the Cyclades Islands east of the Peloponnesian Peninsula (more commonly known as the Peloponnesus; Greek form Peloponnisos). The Minoan civilization (in Crete) and the Mycenaean civilization (on the mainland) developed distinctive social structures that are documented in archaeological records. The dominant Mycenaean civilization then declined for a 250-year period known as the Dark Age of Greece.

The Stone Age

The earliest stages of settlement and social evolution occurred in Greece between 10,000 and 3000 B.C., building the foundation for major advances to begin shortly thereafter. Current evidence suggests that Greece was settled by people from the Near East, primarily Anatolia. But some historians argue that groups from Central Europe also moved into the area. Extensive archaeological remains of a number of farming villages of the Neolithic Era (the last period of the Stone Age, approximately 10,000 to 3000 B.C.) have been discovered in the plains of Thessaly in present-day east-central Greece (see fig. 7). Larger villages built between 3500 and 3000 B.C. show that in that period society was becoming more complex, and that an elite group was forming. Shortly thereafter, craft specialists began to appear, and the form of social organization shifted from tribalism to chiefdoms. Population increased in this period at a slow rate.

Meanwhile, the island of Crete (Kriti) was first inhabited around 6300 B.C. by people from Anatolia. These early groups brought with them a wide range of domesticated plants and animals. They settled at Knossos, which remained the only settlement on the island for centuries. Only in the final phase of the late Stone Age, did the civilization on Crete begin to advance, and only then did real farming villages appear in other parts of the island. The social structure remained tribal, but it set the stage for change.

The Origins of Civilization: 3200–1050 B.C.

The second millennium B.C. saw the evolution of two powerful Greek civilizations, the Minoan in Crete and the Mycenaean on the mainland. During the early Bronze Age (3000–2200 B.C.), major changes occurred in both Crete and mainland Greece. In both cases, there is evidence of rapid population growth associated with the establishment of trade connections across the Aegean Sea to Anatolia and the Near East. The Cyclades (Kiklades), islands between Crete and the mainland, were settled at this time and seem to have flourished as stepping stones between Europe and Asia. Both the Cyclades and the mainland developed complex societies featuring skilled craftsmen and political elites.

The Minoans

The civilization that developed in Crete is called Minoan after the mythical King Minos. The Minoan culture began producing sculpture and pottery in approximately 2600 B.C., inaugurating what was known as the prepalatial (early Minoan) period. Then about 2000 B.C., the Minoans began constructing the palaces that became their trademark. The palace-building protopalatial (middle Minoan) period, which lasted until about 1450 B.C., included flourishing economic, political, and social organization and active trade in the eastern Mediterranean, as well as the first appearance of writing in the Greek world. In the latter part of this period, Minoan traders ventured as far west as Spain. The large, ornate palaces had a distinctive design, were built at population centers and were the scene of elaborate religious ceremonies. The destruction of

5

many of the society's palaces by a severe earthquake began the postpalatial (late Minoan) period. In that period, the rival Mycenaean civilization took control of Crete's Mediterranean commerce, and by 1200 B.C. development of the Minoan culture had ceased.

The Mycenaeans

The civilization that took root on the mainland is called Mycenaean after the first major archaeological site where this culture was identified. The Mycenaeans, an Indo-European group, were the first speakers of the Greek language. They may have entered Greece at the end of the early Bronze Age, in the middle Bronze Age, or in the Neolithic period. The excavation of exceptionally wealthy graves, and the size and spacing of palace foundations, indicates that the Mycenaeans formed an elite and a chieftan-level society (one organized around the judicial and executive authority of a single figure, with varying degrees of power) by the late Bronze Age (ca. 1600 B.C.). Mycenaean palatial society was at its zenith in the thirteenth and fourteenth centuries B.C. At some point in the middle of the fourteenth century, Mycenaeans, whose society stressed military excellence, conquered Knossos and the rest of Crete (see fig. 3).

The Mycenaeans employed a form of syllabic writing known as Linear B, which, unlike the Linear A developed by the Minoans, used the Greek language. It appears that the Mycenaeans used writing not to keep historical records but strictly as a device to register the flow of goods and produce into the palaces from a complex, highly centralized economy featuring regional networks of collection and distribution. Besides being at the center of such networks, palaces also controlled craft production and were the seat of political power.

Each palace on the mainland seems to have been an autonomous political entity, but the lack of historical records precludes knowledge about the interaction of the palatial centers. These small-scale polities stand in marked contrast to the huge contemporaneous states of the Near East. Archaeological findings in Egypt and the countries bordering the eastern Mediterranean Sea show that the Mycenaeans reached those points. Nevertheless, the Mycenaeans seemingly were able to avoid entanglement in the conflicts of the superpowers of the eastern Mediterranean, such as the Hittites and the Egyptians. They were content to be lords of the Aegean for a time.

Between 1250 and 1150 B.C., a combination of peasant rebellions and internal warfare destroyed all the Mycenaean palace citadels. Some were reoccupied but on a much smaller scale, others disappeared forever. The precise circumstances of these events are unknown, but historians speculate that the top-heavy system, whose elite based their power solely on military might, contained the seeds of its own destruction.

The Dark Age, 1050–800 B.C.

During the late Bronze Age (1550–1200 B.C.), a confluence of events caused mainly by local factors brought about the downfall of all the major cultures of the Near East. Undoubtedly the earlier incidents of decay influenced the collapse that came later to some extent, but other factors were usually the primary causes. As it affected Greece, this phenomenon is commonly called the Dark Age; it extended approximately from 1050 to 800 B.C.

The art of writing was largely lost after the fall of the Mycenaean palaces, so the only documentary source for this time is the work of the poet Homer, who wrote in the ninth century B.C. The period generally was one of stagnation and cultural decline. The disruption that followed the collapse of the Mycenaean palaces was great. Groups of people migrated to different areas, and the population declined, probably reaching its nadir in the tenth century B.C.

Archaeological records indicate that in the Dark Age most people lived in small communities in remote areas supported by subsistence farming. Organizationally Greece was a chiefdom society. Most trade and contacts with cultures in the Near East and elsewhere lapsed.

The Era of the Polis

As early as 900 B.C., Greece again expanded contacts with civilizations to the east, and Greek civilization became more complex. The rise of empires, most notably the Athenian Empire, brought a more sophisticated economy, trade, colonization, and war.

The Renaissance of the Eighth Century B.C.

Developments in the eighth century B.C. enabled states to reemerge. The ports of Argos and Corinth, on the eastern shore of the Peloponnesus, grew very fast, trade with the Near

Figure 3. Centers of Mycenaean Civilization, ca. 1400 B.C.

East began to flourish, and increased domestic production enabled a new, wealthy elite to rise. Commercial activity centered on the acquisition of metals from the Near East for the manufacture of luxury goods. In this process, the Greeks came in contact with and adopted the alphabet of the Phoenicians, as well as other innovations that accelerated change in Greek civilization.

Colonies in the Mediterranean

Between 750 and 500 B.C., the Greeks founded colonies in many parts of the Mediterranean Basin and the Black Sea, beginning to exert their cultural influence, which remains in these regions to the present day. Around 730 B.C., permanent Greek colonies were established, based on the metals trade at

Ischia and Pithecusai on the coast of Italy. Shortly thereafter, Corinth sent out agricultural settlers to Corfu (Kerkira) off the coast of northwest Greece and to Syracuse on Sicily. These settlements set the trend for the earliest colonization movement to the west. Southern Italy and Sicily became known as Magna Graecia (Great Greece) because of the extent and density of colonization that followed the initial ventures.

More than 150 colonies were established in Italy, along the coast of northern Greece, in the Bosporus, and on the Black Sea coast. The chief incentive for colonization was the need for additional land for agriculture and living space to accommodate population growth; colonies established by other civilizations, such as Miletus in Asia Minor, also challenged the Greeks to expand.

The Rise of Athens and Sparta

The concept of the polis (city-state) began to evolve with the development of aristocratic clans to replace chiefdoms. Clan rivalries yielded single powerful figures who were termed tyrants because they achieved domination in outright power struggles within the aristocratic group and among clan centers. Because they often were marginal clan members, the success of the tyrants created a new criterion for power: ability rather than birth. This change was a crucial element in the development of the polis, which came to be a politically unified community covering an average of 200 square kilometers and based on a small urban center. When the tyrants were overthrown after one to three generations, the institutionalized structure they created remained and became an important legacy to the modern world.

In the eighth century and early seventh century B.C., Sparta began to develop as a militant polis with a rigid social structure and a government that included an assembly representing all citizens. Meanwhile, Athens became the largest polis, combining several regions of the peninsula of Attica. Under the leadership of the aristocrat Solon, Athens developed a social system in which power was based on wealth rather than aristocratic birth. Citizens of various wealth categories were allotted different positions of power. Thus, in different ways Sparta and Athens built states that included wider sectors of society in their political activity than had any previous society, and the basis of democracy was laid.

The Persian Wars

The consolidation of the Persian Empire under Cyrus the Great in the sixth century B.C. posed a major threat to the fledgling states of Greece. The resolution of the clash between East and West was to shape the entire future of the region. For the Greeks, it was a question of survival; for the Persians, on the other hand, occupation of Greece was simply part of their imperial plan. Nonetheless, the Persian Wars are significant because they resulted in a separation between Greece and the Near East after centuries of fruitful interaction.

The First Persian War in 490 B.C. was a brief affair. Intending to punish Athens for its participation in a raid in Asia Minor, Persia sent a small force by Persian standards, about 20,000 infantry and 800 cavalry. The Greeks met this force with 10,000 troops at the plain of Marathon on the west coast of Attica. The combination of Greek tactics, the superiority of their armor, and the new phalanx formation proved decisive in the battle; the Persians were routed.

The Second Persian War of 481-479 B.C. was a very different proposition. Persia's king, Xerxes, planned to lead a huge expedition to conquer all the Greek states. The Greeks formed the Hellenic League, which included Sparta and its allied states. Other Greek states went over to the Persian side.

In 480 B.C., Xerxes invaded Greece with a huge fleet and an army of over 100,000 men. After overcoming fierce Spartan resistance at Thermopilai, the Persians occupied central Greece and the Greeks retreated south to the Peloponnesus. All of Attica was captured and Athens sacked. On the seas, however, the Greeks completely destroyed the Persian fleet in the Bay of Salamis. Xerxes retreated hastily to Asia, then suffered a great land defeat the next year at the Battle of Plataia, in which the superiority of Greek armor and tactics was the deciding factor. Persian expansionism never threatened Greece again.

The most important result of the Persian Wars was a barrier between Greece and the Near East that ruptured a vibrant cultural zone including Phoenicia, Lydia, Egypt, and other cultures of the Near East. The barrier would not be broken until the middle of the next century, and the concept of a divided Asia and Europe became permanent.

The Athenian Empire

Once the Persian menace had been removed, petty squabbling began amongst the members of the Hellenic League.

Theater at Epidaurus, known for its unusually fine acoustics, built
fourth century B.C.
Courtesy Peter J. Kassander

Sparta, feeling that its job was completed, left the association, and Athens assumed domination of the league. Under the leadership of Themistocles and Kimon, Athens reformed the alliance into a new body called the Delian League. By using monetary contributions from other member states to build its own military forces, Athens essentially transformed the Hellenic League into its own empire.

In the 450s B.C., Pericles (ca. 495–429 B.C.), known as the greatest statesman of ancient Greece, laid the foundation of imperial rule. Athens set the level of tribute for the member states, which were now subject to its dictates, and it dealt harshly with failures to pay. Athens also began regulating the internal policy of the other states and occasionally garrisoning soldiers there. At its height in the 440s B.C., the Athenian Empire was composed of 172 tribute-paying states. Athens now controlled the Aegean.

The enormous wealth entering Athens from subject states financed the flourishing of democratic institutions, literature, art, and architecture that came to be known as the golden age of Athens. Pericles built great architectural monuments, including the Parthenon, to employ workers and symbolize the majesty of Athens. The four greatest Greek playwrights—Aeschylus, Aristophanes, Euripides, and Sophocles—wrote during the golden age.

In society and government, lower-class Athenians were able to improve their social position by obtaining land in the subject states. Pericles gave more governing power to bodies that represented the citizenship as a whole, known as the demos. For the first time, men were paid to participate in government organizations and sit on juries. Many states outside the empire felt quite threatened by the growth of Athens, creating a volatile situation in the mid-fifth century B.C.

The Peloponnesian War

Hostility toward Athens brought about the longest war of antiquity, the Peloponnesian War (also called the Great Peloponnesian War to distinguish it from an earlier conflict in the Peloponnesus between 460 and 445 B.C.). In 431 B.C., Athens faced a loose alliance headed by Sparta (see fig. 4). The first phase of the war (431–421 B.C.) pitted the most powerful fleet in the Mediterranean (Athens) against one of the strongest armies ever assembled in the ancient world. In this phase, Athens abandoned the countryside of Attica to the invading Spartans, who reinvaded Attica every year, attempting to force the surrender of the population within the city walls. After neither strategy gained a decisive advantage, a peace was signed in 421 B.C.

The second phase began in 414 B.C., when Sparta repulsed an Athenian invasion of Sicily. With aid from Persia, Sparta built a large navy that finally destroyed the Athenian navy in 404 B.C. at Aigispotamoi. Thus ended the Athenian Empire and the golden age.

The Polis in Decline, 400–335 B.C.

Following the collapse of Athens, Sparta controlled an empire that encompassed much of present-day Greece. Sparta's tenure as head of the empire was shortened, however, by a combination of poor leadership, wars with Persia and with Sparta's former allies, and social weakness at home. Sparta suffered a drastic shortage of manpower, and society neared revolution because of the huge amounts of wealth falling into the hands of a few. Thebes, Thessaly, and a resurgent Athens were able to carve out small domains for themselves because of Spartan ineptitude. In the next fifty years, however, Sparta's rivals

obtained only temporary advantages over other ambitious states. Thebes, for example, crushed the Spartan army at the Battle of Leuctra in 371 B.C., dominated the peninsula for ten years, then declined rapidly.

In the fourth century B.C., many Greek states suffered bloody class struggles over money and land. During this conflict, the kings of Persia contributed large amounts of money to whichever side would provide the best advantage to Persian interests.

Hellenistic Greece

Weakness in the established states promoted the rise of a new power, Macedonia, under the inspired military leadership of Alexander the Great. Alexander left no legacy of stable governance, however, and the Macedonian Empire that he created fragmented shortly after his death into a shifting collection of minor states.

Philip II of Macedonia

On the fringes of the Greek world, Macedonia's people spoke a form of Greek, but the country had different customs and social organization. Macedonia had not followed its southern neighbors in the evolution of the polis, but had retained a chiefdom form of society in which local headmen still wielded considerable power. In a period of twenty-five years, however, Macedonia became the largest empire yet in antiquity, solely as a result of the genius of Philip II and his son, Alexander. A man of exceptional energy, diplomatic skill, and ruthlessness, Philip totally reformed the Macedonian army when he came to power in 359 B.C. Wielding this new weapon, he conquered all the peoples of the southern Balkans, culminating in the defeat of Athens and Thebes in 338. As he was planning to invade Asia, Philip was assassinated in 336. The task of expanding the empire eastward was left to his son.

The Fire from Heaven: Alexander the Great

At the death of his father, the twenty-year-old Alexander became king. A natural warrior, he also received a formal education under the philosopher Aristotle. Alexander lived only thirteen years after his accession to the throne, but in that time he created the largest empire ever seen, and he had perhaps a greater impact on Western civilization than any other man of the ancient world. As with many great men, his life is shrouded in myth and legend.

In 334 B.C., after securing his base in Greece, Alexander invaded Asia Minor with 30,000 troops, quickly capturing the Turkish coastline to deprive the Persian fleet of its ports. Using brilliant tactics, he then defeated a much larger Persian army under Darius in a series of battles in northern Syria. Alexander then captured Egypt and Mesopotamia, defeating 100,000 Persians in a climactic battle at Guagamela in 331 B.C. Before dying of a malarial fever at age thirty-three, Alexander conquered Afghanistan and parts of India as well.

Alexander used both military and administrative skills to build his empire. He was able to integrate the various peoples he had conquered into a unified empire by devising appropriate forms of administration in each region. In Egypt he became the pharaoh. In Mesopotamia he became the great king. In Persia, however, he kept the indigenous administrative system intact under joint Persian and Macedonian rule. He founded hundreds of new settlements, encouraging his men to marry local women. And he manipulated the local religions to legitimize his own rule. In creating his empire, Alexander changed the face of the world.

The Hellenistic Monarchies

Alexander's death resulted in a twenty-year power struggle that divided his empire into several parts, including mainland Greece and Macedonia, Syria and Mesopotamia, and Egypt. By 280 B.C., new Hellenistic monarchies, whose leaders ruled by force and lacked Alexander's organizational ability, were fighting each other and suffering internal struggles as well.

In this period, parts of Greece were able to achieve some degree of autonomy within confederacies or leagues, most of which were governed by oligarchies. As the leagues became dominant, smaller political units, such as Athens, lost most of their political power. In this process, states of larger size and greater complexity replaced the polis.

The Hellenistic kingdoms mingled elements of Greek culture with Near Eastern cultures. Some of the kings founded colonies to establish garrisons in foreign territory, and in such places intermarriage between Greeks and non-Greeks became common. The Greek language spread and was used as the lingua franca for culture, commerce, and administration throughout the Near East. Greek art forms also became prevalent in

The temple of Apollo at Corinth, ca. sixth century B.C.
Courtesy Jean R. Tartter

the region. The old rigid form of social organization characteristic of the polis was discarded. Greek towns were now a part of
a larger entity, based not on kinship or residence but on power
and control. A new power elite arose, made wealthy by the conquests of vast new territories and the payment of tribute. At the
same time, peasants suffered greatly from higher levies to support the upper class. The weakness of the agricultural producers, combined with constant warfare among kingdoms, made
the Greeks vulnerable to a new Mediterranean power, Rome.

Greece in the Roman Empire

Over a period of about 250 years, Greek territory gradually
was incorporated into the Roman Empire. The Greek and
Roman worlds each changed significantly because of the interaction that resulted.

The Conquest of Greece

As the constant military conflicts of the Hellenistic kingdoms raised revenue needs, the tax burden on both rural and

17

urban populations rose. Meanwhile, the Persians, Parthians, and Bactrians threatened from the east; and Roman expansionism in southern Italy and the western Mediterranean set the stage for repeated clashes between Rome and various Hellenistic rulers. The vibrancy, resilience, and resourcefulness of the Roman Republic finally proved to be too much for the fragile kingdoms of the East.

In the fourth and third centuries B.C., military conquests in central Italy brought Rome into direct competition with the city colonies of Magna Graecia in southern Italy, especially Tarentum (Taranto) and Syracuse. In 280 B.C., Pyrrhus, king of Epirus, began a long period of confrontation between the Greeks and the Romans when he fought a series of battles against the Romans in southern Italy. In this period, however, Rome's major adversary in the Mediterranean was the powerful empire of Carthage, just across the Mediterranean in modern Tunisia, with which Rome fought the Punic Wars over a period of forty-five years. Greek forces also became involved in the campaigns of the Punic Wars, setting the stage for future conflicts with Rome.

The most important episode occurred during the Second Punic War (218–207 B.C.). Campaigning in Italy, the Carthaginian leader Hannibal allied with Philip V of Macedonia, then the most powerful ruler in the Balkans, to protect supply lines from North Africa. Rome responded by supporting Philip's many enemies in the Balkans as they fought the First Macedonian War (215–213 B.C.), which expanded Roman interests into the Balkans. In the Second Macedonian War (200–197 B.C.), Rome's first major military expedition into the Greek world met with brilliant success. Philip lost all his territory outside Macedonia, and the victorious commander Flamininus established a Roman protectorate over the "liberated" Greek city-states. The fortunes of Greece and Rome were henceforth intertwined for about the next 500 years.

The final incorporation of Greece and the Greek East into the Roman Empire came in 31 B.C. after the Battle of Actium, on the western shore of Greece. There, rule of the Roman Empire was settled when the Roman emperor Octavian defeated the navy of Mark Antony. Because Antony had based his land forces in Greece, the victory of Octavian made the Greek world an integral and permanent part of the Roman Empire. The yoke of empire on Greece was relatively light, however, and many Greek cities approved the new order. Rome demanded only two things from its Greek holdings—security and revenue.

Creation of the Graeco-Roman World

The period from 31 B.C. until the death of Marcus Aurelius in A.D. 180 is often referred to as the era of the Pax Romana, or Roman Peace—a phenomenon that actually occurred only in the central areas of the empire, including Greece and the Greek East. The peace and security of the first two centuries A.D. promoted a cultural flowering and economic growth in the Greek world, as well as integration of Greeks into the ruling elite of the empire.

Peninsular Greece was divided into two provinces: Achaia, incorporating central and southern Greece, and Macedonia, which included Thessaly, Epirus, and Macedonia proper. Because these provinces were not required to support Roman occupation forces, their fiscal burdens were relatively modest. Greek cities became the financial, economic, and administrative core of the eastern reaches of the empire. The first result of this role was economic growth and prosperity—Greek cities such as Athens, Corinth, Alexandria, Miletus, Thessaloniki, and Smyrna flourished as both producers and commercial centers. From this settled prosperity, an urban Greek elite arose.

Decentralized Roman provincial administration created spaces for local men to rise in power and status, and, beginning with the reign of Emperor Vespasian (A.D. 69–78), significant numbers of Greeks even entered the Roman Senate. At the same time, life in Greek cities incorporated Roman features, and new generations of "Romanized" Greek citizens appeared. An example of such new Greek citizens was Herodes Atticus, a fabulously wealthy financier and landowner from Athens, who rose to be consul of Rome in A.D. 143, and whose bequests still adorn his home city.

On the other hand, several Roman emperors such as Hadrian and Marcus Aurelius actively embraced Greek culture and traditions, encouraging the hellenization of Roman culture. Together, Latin and Greek became the dominant languages of the empire. Literature, art, oratory, rhetoric, education, and architecture all drew on Hellenic roots from the age of the Greek polis. During the Pax Romana, Greece and Greek culture were a vital part of the Roman Empire.

Constantine and the Rise of Christianity

By the second century A.D., Christianity and Hellenism had come into close contact in the eastern Mediterranean. In the early fourth century, the policies of Emperor Constantine the Great institutionalized the connection and lent a lasting Greek influence to the church that emerged.

Although Christianity was initially practiced within Semitic populations of the Roman Empire, by the first century A.D. Greeks also had learned of the teachings of Christ. In that period, the epistles of Paul to the Ephesians and the Corinthians and his preachings to the Athenians were all aimed at a Greek audience. Other early Christian theological writers such as Clement of Alexandria and Origen attempted to fuse Christian belief with Greek philosophy, establishing the Greek world as the home of gentile Christianity.

A combination of internal turmoil and the threat of invasion by various nomadic tribes to the north and east led to a crisis in the third century. The Germanic Heruli sacked Athens in A.D. 267. The Goths, the Alemanni, the Franks, and the Vandals all made significant incursions into the empire. In the east, the Sassanians revived the moribund Persian Empire and defeated Roman armies several times during the third century.

The chaos of the third century raised deep social and economic problems throughout the empire. Taxes increased to expand the army, driving the peasantry further into poverty. The economy nearly collapsed as the coinage was devalued to provide the vast amounts of metal needed to pay the army. Inflation was rampant. Manpower was scarce because of huge military losses, plagues, and the weakened condition of the peasantry. Such traumas set the Latin West and the Greek East onto separate historical trajectories. The urban centers of the East, built upon the structure of the old Greek polis, endured the crises much better than the other areas of the empire.

The reigns of Diocletian and Constantine mark a critical turning point in the fortunes of the empire. Constantine became emperor of Rome in A.D. 305. He built on the foundations laid by his predecessor, Diocletian, and consolidated the empire after a chaotic third century in which the average reign of a Roman emperor was less than five years. The reforms that Diocletian and Constantine introduced brought temporary stability. Diocletian responded to geographic fragmentation by dividing the empire into two major parts to be ruled by separate emperors. Constantine's Edict of Milan, issued in 313, established the empire's toleration of Christianity; his personal conversion continued over a number of years.

In 330 Constantine advanced the separation of the eastern and western empires by establishing his capital at Byzantium and renaming it Constantinople. In 364 the empire was officially split. The western empire was to be ruled from Rome, the eastern from Constantinople. For those in the eastern territory that had been dominated by the tradition of the polis, the transition from a Latin Roman empire to a Greek Byzantine empire was an easy one. Constantinople inherited the cultural wealth of the Greek city-state as a solid foundation and a symbol of civilization in its empire.

The Byzantine Empire

The Byzantine Empire was established with the foundation of Constantinople, but the final separation of the eastern and western empires was not complete until the late fifth century. With its political structure anchored in Greek tradition and a new religion stimulated by Greek philosophy, the Byzantine Empire survived a millennium of triumphs and declines until Constantinople fell to the Ottoman Turks in 1453 (see fig. 5).

Separation from Rome

Two crises between A.D. 330 and 518 helped shape the Greek part of the empire. The first was the invasion by barbarian Huns, Visigoths, and Ostrogoths in the fifth century. Constantinople averted the fate of Rome, which fell to similar onslaughts, by a combination of skillful bribery and a strong army. Thus, as the West was carved into minor kingdoms, the East remained largely intact, and the balance of power in the former Roman Empire moved conclusively to the East.

The second major crisis was religious in nature. In the East, great heresies such as Arianism, Nestorianism, and Monophysitism drew on the rich Greek metaphysical tradition and clashed with the emerging Roman Catholic Church in the fourth and fifth centuries. Among the challengers was an eastern branch of the church with Greek as its language, closely bound to the political world of Constantinople. The Greek Orthodox Christian empire established at this time would bridge Asia and Europe for centuries.

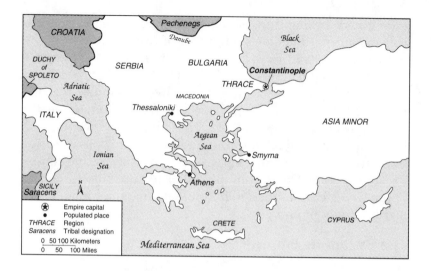

Figure 5. The Byzantine Empire, Early Eleventh Century

Justinian and the Empire of the East

Justinian (r. A.D. 527–65) laid the foundation on which the Byzantine Empire would rest for nearly a century. An ambitious and dynamic leader, he greatly expanded the empire's territory by conquering the southern Levant, northern Africa, and Italy, in an effort to recreate the domain of the old Roman Empire. Justinian's administrative reforms created a centralized bureaucracy, a new fiscal system, and a provincial administration. The codes of Roman law were revised and unified in the Justinianic Code, which remains to this day a cornerstone of European jurisprudence. These reforms greatly advanced the unification of the diverse peoples of the empire in a Hellenic context. In the end, Justinian's institutional reforms proved far more lasting than his military conquests.

The Decline of the Empire, 565–867

Justinian's wars brought the empire to the verge of bankruptcy and left it in a vulnerable military position. Threats from both East and West plunged the empire into a spiral of decline that lasted for nearly 300 years. The first menace from the East came from the Persian Sassanid Empire. Sassanid forces took Palestine, Syria, and Egypt, and even threatened

Constantinople at one point. A more serious threat soon developed with the advent of Islamic expansionism. Exploding out of the Arabian Peninsula, Muslim forces swept northward and westward, taking Egypt, Syria, Iraq, Iran, and Afghanistan. Portions of Asia Minor were wrested from the Byzantine Empire, and twice between A.D. 668 and 725 Constantinople was nearly overrun by Muslim forces.

The other major threat to the empire came from the West. During the late sixth and seventh centuries, Slavic peoples began to invade the Balkan Peninsula. Major cities such as Athens, Thebes, and Thessaloniki were safe behind defensible walls. Much of the indigenous population of the Balkans, Greeks included, fled, especially to Calabria at the southern tip of Italy, or relocated their settlements to higher, more secure regions of the Balkans. Under these conditions, urban centers no longer were the basis of Byzantine society in the Balkans.

But the Slavic arrivals were unable to preserve their own distinct cultural identities; very soon their hellenization process began. Greek remained the mother tongue of the region, and Christianity remained the dominant faith. Although the Slavic invasions and Islamic conquests of the seventh and eighth centuries shrank the Byzantine state, it survived as a recognizable entity grounded more firmly than ever in the Balkans and Asia Minor.

Revival and Collapse, 867–1453

When a new dynasty, which came to be called Macedonian, took the throne of the Byzantine Empire in 867, its forces began to roll back the tide of Islamic expansion. Antioch, Syria, Georgia, and Armenia were reconquered. The Byzantine fleet regained Crete and drove Muslim pirates from the Aegean Sea, reopening it to commercial traffic. Consolidation of the Balkans was completed with the defeat of the Bulgarian Empire by Basil II in 1018.

Orthodox missionaries, including Cyril and Methodius, led the proselytization of Bulgaria, Serbia, and eventually Russia. The military conquests of the Macedonian Dynasty initiated a period of economic growth and prosperity and a cultural renaissance. Agriculture flourished as conditions stabilized, and, as emperors increasingly used land grants to reward military service, the area under cultivation expanded. The prosperity of improved agricultural conditions and the export of woven silk and other craft articles allowed the population to grow. Expanding commercial opportunities increased the influence of the nearby Italian maritime republics of Venice, Genoa, and Amalfi, which eventually gained control of the Mediterranean trade routes into Greece.

The prosperity of the Macedonian Dynasty was followed by a period of decline. In the late eleventh century, a Norman army, allied with the pope and commanded by Robert Guiscard, ravaged parts of Greece, including Thebes and Corinth. Civil war among rival military factions impaired the empire's ability to respond to such incursions. In a disastrous loss at Manzikert (in present-day eastern Turkey) in 1071, Seljuk Turks from Central Asia captured Romanus IV, one of the first rulers after the end of the Macedonian Dynasty. Through the next century, the empire became more and more a European domain. The worst humiliation came in 1204, when marauders of the Fourth Crusade plundered Constantinople, carrying off many of its greatest treasures.

Greece was carved up into tiny kingdoms and principalities ruled by Western princes. Venice gained control of substantial parts of Greece, some of which were not relinquished until 1797. Architectural remains from the Venetian period are still visible in the Greek countryside and ports.

Only the actions of the Palaeologus Dynasty (1261–1453) prevented the empire from falling. The Palaeologi recaptured Constantinople and most of the southern Balkans, but the end of the empire was not long delayed. A new force, the Ottoman Turks, arose from the east in the wake of the Mongol invasion led by Genghis Khan in 1221. Late in the fourteenth century, Asia Minor and the Balkans fell to the Ottoman Turks, but Constantinople still held out. Finally the forces of Mehmet the Conqueror took the capital city after a lengthy siege. Constantinople would again be the center of a Mediterranean empire stretching from Vienna to the Caspian Sea and from the Persian Gulf to the Strait of Gibraltar—but now it would be as a Muslim city in the empire of the Ottomans. The great Greek Byzantine Empire had come to an end.

The Ottoman Era

When Constantinople fell in 1453, the Ottoman conquest of the Orthodox Balkans was assured. By that time, most of peninsular Greece was already in Ottoman hands. The other remaining bastions of Hellenism held out for a short time longer. The kingdom of Trabzon (Trebizond), at the southeast corner of the Black Sea, fell in 1461. During the sixteenth century, the Ottomans took Rhodes (Rodos) and Chios (Khios) in the Dodecanese Islands (Dodekanisos), Naxos in the Cyclades, and Cyprus. In 1669 the island of Crete capitulated after a lengthy siege. Only the Ionian Islands west of the Greek Peninsula remained outside the Ottoman sultan's grip; instead, they were part of Venice's expanding empire. The Greek world would remain an integral part of the Ottoman Empire until 1821, when one small portion broke away and formed an independent state. But a significant part of the Greek population would remain Ottoman until 1922.

The Nature of Ottoman Rule

The Ottoman state was a theocracy, based on strict notions of hierarchy and order, with the sultan exercising absolute, divine-right power at its pinnacle. The system first divided subject peoples into the domain of the faithful, the Muslims, and the domain of war, the non-Muslims. An individual's obligations and rights were determined by position in one of these groups. Conversion by foreign subjects to Islam was possible, but the Ottomans did not demand it. Instead, further religion-based classifications were used to rule the subject population.

The non-Muslim community was divided into *millets* (see Glossary), administrative units organized on the basis of religious affiliation rather than ethnic origin. Accordingly, the four non-Muslim *millets* were Armenian, Catholic, Jewish, and Orthodox; the last was the largest and most influential. The *millets* enjoyed a fair amount of autonomy. At the head of each was a religious leader responsible for the welfare of the *millet* and for its obedience to the sultan. The head of the Orthodox *millet* was the ecumenical patriarch of Constantinople. The patriarch's position as *ethnarch,* or leader of the nation, also gave him substantial secular powers. This combination meant that the institution of the Orthodox Church played a vital role in the development of Greek society during the Ottoman era.

In practice, the extent of the empire made control dependent on a complex, decentralized administrative hierarchy. Living on their estates, designated local military leaders, the *sipahi,* assumed many of the responsibilities of local rule. Over time, the estates became hereditary and stopped serving their intended function. In Greek territory, this policy left massive landholdings controlled by the Ottoman Turks and worked by dependent Greek peasants.

As the *sipahi* system broke down, a form of provincial administration took its place. The empire was divided into regions that were governed by pashas, who in turn subdivided their realms into smaller units overseen by beys. The Orthodox *millet* included two types of local government. Ottoman officials and religious judges adjudicated civil and criminal cases involving Muslims and Orthodox citizens. Orthodox priests and Christian primates collected taxes, settled disputes, and effectively governed at the local level. At times the two systems competed, and at times they operated in coordination; the result was complexity, abuse, and cynicism. In this atmosphere, people sought security in direct patronage relationships with individuals in power. The Ottoman system discriminated against the non-Muslim population by imposing special levies of money and labor, and various restrictions were placed on personal freedom. In court, testimony of a Muslim would always be accepted over that of a non-Muslim. Marriages between Muslims and non-Muslims were illegal. Most hated of all was the forced conscription of male children for service in military or civil service. The burden on the subject population became even heavier and more capricious when the empire began suffering military defeats by Russia in the eighteenth century.

Some parts of Greece were able to escape the direct effects of Ottoman rule. The remote mountains of central Greece, for example, were called the Agrapha, the "unwritten", because the empire had no census or tax records for the region. Other areas were granted special status because they filled particular needs of the empire. Beginning in the late seventeenth century, the Phanariotes, a group of Greek merchant families in Constantinople, gained bureaucratic power by serving the sultan as diplomats and interpreters. In the eighteenth century, the Phanariotes were appointed *hospodars*, or princes, of the Romanian provinces Moldavia and Wallachia.

The official role given the Orthodox Church in the *millet* system made its situation in Greek society paradoxical. On the one hand, it helped to keep the Greek language alive and used its traditional educational role to pass on the Greek cultural heritage and foster a sense of cultural identity. On the other hand, the Ottoman authorities expected the church to maintain order. The church became a very conservative institution that protected its role by isolating Greeks from the great intellectual currents of the West, first the Reformation and later the

Remains of a Turkish mosque, Metsovon, Epirus
Courtesy Sam and Sarah Stulberg

Enlightenment. Secular influences first touched Greek society not in Greece but in the communities of the diaspora.

As the feudal system crumbled, control over such a vast domain became increasingly problematic. Because a standing army would have been prohibitively expensive, non-Muslims were assigned as *armatoliks*, or armed guards, of specified areas and paid from local taxes. This system was abused flagrantly by independent groups of armed men, some with official sanction and some without, who roamed the countryside and abused the peasant population. Myths have turned the bandits into proto-revolutionaries, but to contemporaries in Greece and elsewhere, they were a force to be feared.

The Greek Diaspora

During the years of Ottoman domination, Greek speakers resettled over a wide area inside and outside the empire.

27

Greeks moved in large numbers to Romania, along the coast of the Black Sea, and into all the major cities of the empire and became merchants and artisans. Over 80,000 Greek families, for example, moved into the territories of the Habsburg Empire. Thousands more settled in the cities of the Russian Empire. Commercial dealings between the Ottoman Empire and the outside world were increasingly monopolized by Greeks. Important merchant colonies were founded in Trieste, Venice, Livorno, Naples, and Marseilles. Amsterdam, Antwerp, London, Liverpool, and Paris also received sizeable Greek populations.

The diaspora communities played a vital role in the development of Greek culture during the Ottoman occupation. Greek enclaves in foreign cultures reinforced national identity while exposing their inhabitants to new intellectual currents, including the ideology of revolution. Many diaspora Greeks became wealthy, then helped to support communities in Greece by founding schools and other public institutions.

Out of the Ottoman Empire

After gaining independence from the Ottoman Empire early in the nineteenth century, Greece became a monarchy ruled by representatives of European royal houses. Domestic politics and relations with neighbor states began a pattern of persistent turmoil.

The Conditions for Revolution

The modern state of Greece came into existence as a result of a protracted, bloody war against the Ottoman Empire between the years 1821 and 1832. The significance of the Greek War of Independence transcends the bounds of Greece and its history. It was the first major war of liberation after the American Revolution; it was the first successful war for independence from the Ottoman Empire; it was the first explicitly nationalist revolution; and it provided a model for later nationalist struggles.

The Greek War of Independence was the result of several factors. The ideology of a specifically Greek national consciousness, which had earlier roots, developed at an accelerated pace in the late eighteenth century and early nineteenth century. The uprising of 1821 followed other Greek efforts to confront Ottoman rule directly. The most important of these events was the Orlov Rebellion of 1778–79. Inspired by the belief that Russia's war with the Turks signaled that country's readiness to liberate all the Christians in the Ottoman Empire, a short-lived uprising took place in the Peloponnesus beginning in February 1778. Under the ostensible leadership of the Russian Orlov brothers, the venture quickly failed because of poor organization and the lack of a coherent ideology, rapidly degenerating into looting and pillaging by both sides, but it set a precedent for violent resistance to Ottoman rule. The Orlov Rebellion also prompted oppressive measures by the Sublime Porte (the Ottoman government) that increased resentment against the empire.

The intellectual basis of nationalism came from the affluent and prominent diaspora Greeks of the eighteenth century. The two most prominent leaders of this group were Adamantios Korais and Rigas Velestinlis. Korais, primarily an educator, advocated the education of Greeks about their ancient heritage as the path toward emancipation. He played no active role in founding the modern Greek state. The fiery revolutionary Velestinlis wrote a blueprint for a new Greek state that would arise from the ashes of revolution against the empire. He was executed by the Turks in 1798.

In 1821 Greece met three major requirements for a successful revolution: material conditions among the populace were adverse enough to stimulate mass support for action; an ideological framework gave direction to the movement; and an organizational structure was present to coordinate the movement. Greek intellectuals had provided the language and ideas necessary for a nationalist struggle. And episodes such as the Orlov Rebellion provided a collective memory of violent resistance that made action feasible. During the 1810s, the other two conditions developed, then all three converged in the early 1820s.

The economy of the Ottoman Empire was seriously damaged by the general depression of commerce that followed the defeat of Napoleon Bonaparte in 1815. Near-famine conditions prevailed in most of the Balkan Peninsula, but the problem was not addressed at any level of Ottoman government, and resentment grew among the rural populace. The Greek movement also developed organizational leadership during the 1810s. The Filiki Etaireia, or Society of Friends, founded in Odessa in 1814, was the most important of many clandestine revolutionary groups that arose. Unlike other such groups, it was able to

29

attract a substantial membership while remaining undetected by Ottoman authorities. The organization brought together men from many levels of society to provide an organizational base for the dissemination of revolutionary ideas and for coordinated action. By 1820, then, only a spark was required to set the revolution ablaze.

The War of Independence

Despite decades of intellectual and logistical preparation, in actuality the Greek struggle for independence demonstrated little unity among supporting elements. Only the intervention of European powers protecting their own geopolitical interests ensured the emergence of a new Greek state. For nearly a century thereafter, Greek policy remained preoccupied with the many Greeks still under Ottoman rule after the postwar settlement.

Phase One of the Struggle

The precipitating factor in the Greek War of Independence was the revolt of the brigand Ali Pasha, the most infamous of the local Ottoman authorities who profited from the weakening control of Constantinople over its empire. Called the Lion of Ioannina (a city in northwest Greece), Ali rebelled against Sultan Mahmud II by building a sizeable and wealthy personal fiefdom that threatened the sultan's rule in the southern Balkans. In 1820 Mahmud's decision to curb Ali ignited a civil war that provided the opportunity for the Filiki Etaireia and its leader Alexandros Ipsilantis to launch a Greek uprising.

As it developed, the revolution was pursued by various groups with a multiplicity of goals and interests throughout the region, united by a crude plan of action. Hostilities were to begin in and focus on Moldavia and Wallachia to the north, where Ipsilantis and his army of 4,500 men were located. Once these areas had been liberated, the rest would follow. Shortly after Ipsilantis crossed the Prut River from Russian Moldavia into Ottoman territory in March 1821, the uprising spread throughout much of the peninsula. A second front opened within weeks, when Bishop Germanos of Patras raised the flag of revolution at a monastery in the Peloponnesus. The rapid defeat of Ipsilantis in the summer of 1821 shifted the war permanently to the south.

From the beginning, the cohesiveness of the Greek revolution was limited by class differences. The chief goal of the

Greek upper classes was to rid society of the Turks, the military classes sought independent enclaves for themselves in imitation of Ali Pasha, and the lower orders simply desired to escape taxation, increase their property, and move up the social scale. Diaspora Greeks also returned home with dreams of a resurrected democratic past. Keeping these competing and disparate interests together proved one of the greatest challenges of the war.

The first of the war's two phases, from March 1821 to December 1823, was largely a successful insurgency. During this period, the Greek forces were able to capture many major strongholds of the Peloponnesus and establish a strong presence in central Greece. Victories on land were coupled with successes at sea, most notably the sinking of the flagship of the Ottoman navy in November 1822. Total casualties in the first phase have been estimated at 50,000, many of whom were civilians massacred by both sides.

In spite of the rebels' early victories, political stabilization eluded them. After an initial congress in 1821, which formed a government under a new constitution, factionalism soon led to the creation of rival governments. In April 1823, the Second National Congress selected a new government, under the presidency of Petrobey Mavromihalis, which became the third body claiming legitimate rule over the Greek people. The lack of political unity, which at times degenerated into actual civil war, was to prove very costly.

The Greek War of Independence touched a chord in Western Europe. Figures such as the British romantic poet Lord Byron found a "noble cause" in the Greek struggle against the Ottoman Empire. Philhellenes, as these sympathizers came to be called, played a critical role in the war. The conflict attracted the physical, monetary, and moral support of a variety of West European idealists. The Philhellenes raised money to support the insurgents, and they focused the attention of the outside world on the conflict until the powers of Western Europe decided to intervene.

Phase Two of the Struggle

The second phase of the war spanned the years 1824 to 1828. When a counteroffensive by the Porte overcame the feuding Greek forces in 1825, the rebels lost the advantage they had gained in the first phase. In the mid- to late 1820s, the sultan enlisted the assistance of Mahomet Ali, the ruler of Egypt, to launch a two-pronged attack. The sultan's forces marched from the north while the army of Mahomet Ali established a base at Messini on the south shore of the Peloponnesus and then advanced northward. Caught between two superior forces, the Greek armies relinquished all the gains made in the first years of the war. The fall of the fortress at Mesolongion in the spring of 1826 gave the Ottoman forces control of western Greece and of the Gulf of Patras; the fall of Athens later that year restored all of central Greece to Ottoman control. At that point, with the Balkan conflagration close to extinction, the powers of Western Europe intervened.

Western Intervention

In European Great Power politics after the final defeat of Napoleon in 1815, maintenance of the status quo was the first priority. In such an atmosphere, the attention of the Great Powers (primarily France and Britain) could be drawn most quickly by situations that disrupted their common economic interests. Indeed, in 1823 the war in Greece had already begun curtailing commerce in the eastern Mediterranean, but the European powers realized that the defeat of the Ottoman Empire would leave a power vacuum over a very large, strategically important region. Therefore, they moved cautiously to ensure an advantageous position after the anticipated collapse. These calculations balanced Britain and France against Russia, the third Great Power, whose proximity to Ottoman territory had long caused fears in London and Paris that the Russian Empire might reach the Mediterranean Sea.

The involvement of Egypt in 1825 was a turning point because Egyptian control of the Peloponnesus was unacceptable to the French and British. Thus motivated, the Great Powers, with Britain taking the lead, began to search for a diplomatic solution. In the summer of 1825, the British-sponsored Act of Submission set the conditions for a Greek state that would be an autonomous part of the Ottoman Empire but under the protection of Britain. Two years later, the Treaty of London stated that France and Britain would intervene militarily if the Porte refused to negotiate a satisfactory settlement after its military success in the second phase of the war. The combined British and French fleets eventually decided the issue by destroying the Turco-Egyptian fleet at the Battle of Navarino in October 1827. Navarino created the conditions for a new Greek state. The exact boundaries, nature, and disposition of that state remained to be determined, but nonetheless by the spring of 1828 a free Greece had been established.

The Presidency of Kapodistrias

The Assembly of Troezene, convened by the insurgents in May 1827, elected Ioannis Kapodistrias president of the fledgling state and he took up the post in May 1828. Kapodistrias had enjoyed a long and fruitful career in the foreign service of the Russian Empire, at one point holding the rank of privy councillor to Tsar Alexander I. Because he had not been associated with any Greek faction during the war for independence and because the Great Powers knew and trusted him, Kapodistrias seemed an ideal choice as president at this crucial juncture.

Kapodistrias faced enormous problems, however. The Ottoman Empire had not given up hopes of maintaining control of Greece, so hostilities continued in 1828. Within Greece, political factions continued to control what amounted to private armies. Much of Greece lay in ruins, and the new state had no money with which to continue the struggle. Finally, Kapodistrias responded to incessant opposition to his Westernizing initiatives by an enlightened despotism that violated the constitution under which he had been elected. His brief rule was ended by assassins in 1831. The fate of Greece was more than ever in the paternalistic care of Britain, France, and Russia.

Two pacts, the Treaty of Adrianople (September 1829) and the Treaty of Constantinople (July 1832), vouchsafed the existence of an independent Greek state by placing it under British, French, and Russian protection, defined its boundaries, established its system of government, and determined its first ruler—Otto, son of Ludwig I, king of Bavaria. In 1832, then, Greece came into existence. A pale realization of the lofty "New Byzantium" visualized by the eighteenth-century Greek intellectuals, it was a tiny, foreign-ruled, and utterly dependent entity. Nonetheless, for the first time in history the Greek nation existed as a unitary state.

The Rule of Otto

The reign of Otto included the installation of a wide variety of Western institutions, many of which were ill-suited to Greek society and political tradition. The factionalism of the revolutionary period continued and eroded the king's authority. Corruption flourished, and Otto finally was deposed by a combination of popular rebellion and coups.

Otto's Early Years

The second son of Ludwig, Otto of Wittgenstein was seventeen years old when he ascended the throne of the newly formed kingdom of Greece. His reign traditionally is divided into two segments, the first from 1832 until 1844 and the second from 1844 until Otto's abdication in 1862.

Formidable problems faced Otto and the three regents appointed in 1833 to assist him. The agricultural infrastructure on which the economy was based lay in ruins. At least two-thirds of the olive trees, vineyards, and flour mills had been destroyed, and only about 10 percent of Greece's sheep and goat flocks remained. Many villages were devastated, as were several of the most important commercial centers. Destitute and displaced, the rural populace looked to their new king for relief. Several groups that had supported the war for independence now demanded compensation. The military leaders who had led and financed the war wanted land, power, and pay for their men. Shipowners demanded indemnity for their substantial losses in naval battles. The soldiers who had fought the war wanted regular pay, land, or both. The peasants wanted land. Satisfying all these claims was impossible.

Greece's persistent fiscal crises were exacerbated by the fact that the fertile agricultural areas of Thessaly and Macedonia, the major ports of Thessaloniki and Smyrna, and the island of Crete remained outside the kingdom (see fig. 6). In spite of the expertise and connections that the Greeks of the diaspora brought with them as they migrated to the new kingdom, manufacturing and trade remained underdeveloped. The only feasible internal source of revenue was a tax on agriculture, the growth of which was most fundamental to the country's prosperity. Thus, land and loans given to peasants to expand cultivation were soon reclaimed in the form of taxes. The government borrowed repeatedly from Greeks abroad, from foreign banks, and from other European states, incurring formidable debts and establishing a pattern that has endured throughout the modern epoch (see The Economic Development of Modern Greece, ch. 3).

In spite of such obstacles, Greece revived from the devastation of eleven years of war. Athens, the new capital, added a

royal palace and mansions to house the political elite who flocked there. Resettlement in the countryside allowed agricultural production to rebound. The merchant marine recovered from its wartime losses, Greek merchants once again handled much of the seagoing freight of the Mediterranean, and ports such as Siros, in the Cyclades, and Patras, on the northwest Peloponnesus, began to flourish once again.

Political stability proved elusive in the first phase of Otto's rule, however. In imposing Western models, Otto and his advisers showed little sensitivity to indigenous traditions of politics, law, and education. The political system established in 1834 preserved the social schisms that existed during the war and promoted new ones. The kingdom was divided administratively into ten prefectures, fifty-nine subprefectures, and 468 counties. The leaders at all three levels were appointed by the king. Only a small oligarchy, the *tzakia*, had a role in this process at the county level. Such absolute power alienated the Greeks who had fought the war in the name of republicanism. Armed bands were reorganized to further the political aims of their wartime leaders, and violent uprisings occurred annually between 1835 and 1842.

Otto's Roman Catholicism added further fuel to the political fire. In 1833 the patriarch of Constantinople established an autocephalous Orthodox Church of the Kingdom of Greece with Otto at its head. He, however, showed no inclination toward conversion.Tensions came to a head in 1843, when a bloodless military coup soon forced Otto to permit the writing of a new constitution.

After the First Constitution, 1844–62

The second period of Otto's rule began in March 1844, when in the aftermath of the military coup, Otto convened a national assembly to draft a constitution. When the assembly finished its work that spring, a new system of government was established. Otto would henceforth rule as a constitutional monarch. A bicameral legislature would be elected by all property-holding males over twenty-five. In theory Greece became one of the most democratic states in Europe. Otto, however, retained the power to appoint and dismiss government ministers, to dissolve parliament, to veto legislation, and issue executive decrees.

Instead of promoting political parties, parliamentary democracy spawned a new factionalism based on the patronage of

prominent individuals. The politics of personality was exemplified by the career of Ioannis Kolettis, who was appointed prime
minister under the new system in 1844. Kolettis managed parliament and achieved a virtual monopoly of administrative
power by use of lavish bribes, intimidation, and a keen sensitivity to public opinion. Kolettis also originated the Megali Idea
(Great Idea), the concept that Greeks must be reunited by
annexing Ottoman territory adjacent to the republic. Otto's
inability to fulfill the Megali Idea was a major cause of his
downfall.

Irredentism was the single idea that united the disparate factions and regions of Greece following independence. The
Megali Idea influenced all of Greek foreign policy through the
nineteenth century. As early as the late 1830s, Greek insurgent
movements were active in Thessaly, Macedonia, and Epirus,
and by 1848 Greece and the Porte were on the brink of war
over raids by Greek privateers into Ottoman territory.

The Crimean War appeared to offer an opportunity for
Greece to gain major territorial concessions from the sultan.
Expecting that Russia would defeat the Ottoman Empire in this
war, Otto sent Greek troops to occupy Ottoman territory in
adjacent Thessaly and Epirus under the pretext of protecting
Balkan Christians. However, Britain and France intervened on
the side of the Porte, and in 1854 British and French occupation of the port of Piraeus forced Otto to relinquish his "Christian cause"—a humiliation that drastically curtailed his power.
Radical university students narrowly failed to assassinate Queen
Amalia in 1861, and a military revolt in 1862 was only partially
suppressed. Finally, in another bloodless coup later that year,
Otto was forced to abdicate the throne.

The Age of Reform, 1864–1909

In 1864 a constituent assembly promulgated a new constitution that vested sovereignty in the Greek people and specified
precisely the monarch's powers. A single-chamber parliament
with full legislative powers would be elected by direct, secret
ballot. Because the king retained substantial powers, however,
the choice of a new monarch remained an extremely important issue.

The Constitution of 1864

Otto's successor had to be uniquely noncontroversial. Prince
Albert, son of Queen Victoria of Britain, was selected by 95 per-

cent of Greeks voting in a 1862 referendum, but France and Russia rejected this outcome because it would give Britain direct control of the Greek throne. The eventual choice was Prince William, second son of the future King Christian IX of Denmark and brother of the future queen consort Alexandra of Britain. The prince would reign as George I until his assassination in 1913.

Greece's constitutional reforms seemed to yield little political change. Powerful personalities maintained their fiefdoms through patronage networks, although issues such as industrialization and government planning opened a new split between the growing liberal urban middle class and conservatives of the old *tzakia* elite.

The most significant element of Greek political culture in the second half of the nineteenth century was the political clubs that proliferated. Such clubs of professional men and landowners fostered coherent political discourse and linked members of parliament with local power brokers. They also mobilized support for parliamentary candidates representing the political views of the clubs' members. Large landowners, for example, guaranteed the votes of their laborers on behalf of local patrons. Artisan associations and mercantile guilds such as the Athens-based Guild of Greengrocers, also provided vehicles for political acculturation and mobilized electoral support. This patchwork of clubs and guilds was the starting point of political factions and other fluid political groupings that lay at the base of Greek parliamentary democracy as it was practiced under the 1864 constitution.

In spite of the new constitution, the political system was deeply flawed. From 1865 to 1875, seven general elections were held, and eighteen different administrations held office. King George could and did create and dismiss governments if legislation or a budget failed to pass, so political leaders constantly juggled competing interests to keep fragile ruling coalitions together. Often the king asked leaders of minority parties to form governments while more significant legislative figures were overlooked, actions that were a recipe for political gridlock as well as a mockery of the democratic process.

The Trikoupis Reforms

The politician Kharilaos Trikoupis began to address the problem of gridlock in 1869. After Trikoupis wrote a newspaper article identifying the king's toleration of minority governments in 1874 (and after the writer's arrest for treason), the king agreed that a government could be formed only by the leader of the strongest party in parliament. If no party could obtain the pledged support of a plurality, then the king would dissolve parliament and call for a general election. The result of this reform was a relatively stable twenty-five-year period at the end of the century, in which only seven general elections were held.

Trikoupis and his arch-rival Theodoros Deliyannis were the dominant political figures of the last quarter of the nineteenth century—Trikoupis the Westernizer and modernizer, Deliyannis the traditionalist and strong advocate of irredentism. Trikoupis saw Greece as needing to develop economically, become more liberal socially, and develop its military strength in order to become a truly "modern" state. During his terms as prime minister in the 1880s (altogether he served seven terms, interspersed with the first three of Deliyannis's five terms), Trikoupis made major economic and social reforms that pushed Greece significantly to develop in these ways.

Trikoupis emphasized expansion of Greece's export sector and its chief support elements—the transportation network and agricultural cultivation. In the last decades of the 1800s, agricultural reforms, which were only moderately successful, aimed at increasing the purchasing power of the rural population as well as fostering large estates that could raise production of export commodities and improve Greece's chronic balance of payments deficit. However, land-allotment patterns failed to raise most peasants above the level of subsistence farming, and foreclosures of peasant properties created large estates whose single-crop contributions made the Greek agricultural export structure quite fragile.

Between 1875 and 1895, steamship tonnage under Greek ownership rose by a factor of about sixteen. Industrialization, especially textile production, also developed under the paternal eye of the Trikoupis government. Between 1875 and 1900, the steam horsepower of Greek plants increased by over 250 percent. In addition, by greatly expanding public education, Trikoupis fostered a new cultural climate that drew on Western trends in dress, architecture, art, and manners.

The only engine to drive such reform programs was extensive foreign loans. By 1887 some 40 percent of government expenditures went to servicing the national debt. Trikoupis levied taxes and import tariffs on numerous commodities, increased the land tax, and established government monopolies on salt and matches.

The sustained deficits incurred through the 1880s set up an economic collapse in the 1890s. When the price of currants, the chief agricultural export, collapsed in 1893, the national economy collapsed as well. By 1897 Greece was bankrupt, and its age of reform, which yielded many beneficial and permanent changes, had ended.

Attempts at Expansion

The irredentism of the Megali Idea, which had remained a strong force in Greek society since independence, gained new momentum from the liberation of territory surrounding Greece and from changes in Great Power policy in the second half of the nineteenth century. The results were conflict with the Ottoman Empire in Crete and with the Slavs in Macedonia, along with territorial gains in Thessaly and Arta.

In 1866 the first of three revolutions began on the strategically crucial island of Crete. Omission of Crete in the formation of the kingdom of Greece remained a sore point, and the island's status became more problematic as the fate of the Ottoman Empire assumed a greater role in Great Power relations. Although all the powers wished to prevent occupation of Crete by a rival, European solutions to Mediterranean crises repeatedly left Crete to the sultan, merely pressuring him to improve conditions for the Orthodox population of the island.

In the 1860s, however, the Great Powers agreed to the unification of Italy and the transfer by Britain of the Ionian Islands to Greece. As the Orthodox population and nationalist sentiments grew on Crete and King George openly supported the Cretan reunification factions, these changes also reinforced Greek advocacy of claims to Crete. The result was a guerrilla rebellion on Crete that received wide support from the Greek government and people.

Although the Cretan rebels found considerable public sympathy in the West, efforts by Russia and Serbia to profit from the Ottoman Empire's distraction in Crete brought diplomatic pressure from Britain and France. By 1869 Serbian and Russian support of the rebellion had softened, and the Ottoman fleet had used a blockade of Crete to its advantage. At the Paris peace talks of 1869, Greece agreed that Crete would remain part of the Ottoman Empire, with the stipulation of significant changes in the government of the islanders and in their legal status in the empire. However, Cretan unification remained a key issue for the next forty years.

Greece's first major territorial gains were the regions of Thessaly and Arta in the central mainland. In 1881 the Ottoman Empire ceded most of those regions to Greece as a byproduct of the complex negotiations of the Congress of Berlin to end the Russo-Turkish War of 1877. A combination of intense Greek lobbying and Turkish intransigence led to Great Power support for a bilateral treaty transferring the two regions from the Ottoman Empire to Greece.

A second territorial issue of bitter and long-standing importance was the disposition of Macedonia, a territory in which every nationalist group in the Balkans claimed a vital interest. Beginning in the late nineteenth century, efforts to impose either Greek or Slavic culture in Macedonia led to terrorist violence and atrocities and a perpetually volatile situation. Perceiving Macedonia as an essential element of the Megali Idea, Greece held vehemently to its claims, first against the Ottoman Empire and then against other Balkan nations. Elements of this policy remain in force today.

The Venizelos Era

Eleutherios Venizelos was the most influential Greek politician of the first half of the twentieth century, and he left a permanent mark on the country's social and economic life. A Cretan lawyer with a brilliant intellect, Venizelos worked tirelessly for reunification of Crete with Greece in the 1890s; then he burst into national politics when the leaders of the Goudi coup, conducted in 1909 by disaffected military officers, chose him to direct a new civilian government away from the military and financial disasters of the 1890s.

The Rise of the Liberal Party

The first years of the 1900s witnessed mass demonstrations against social conditions and a chaotic upheaval of new political factions, but no strong party or leader emerged. Venizelos became leader of the new Liberal Party, which drew support from nationalist professionals, workers, and merchants and tried to fill the needs of all those classes. In 1910 and in 1912, the Liberal Party won two national elections, making Venizelos prime minister and passing reform legislation at a frantic pace. New state bureaucracies were established, and the powers of the governmental branches were substantially reworked by constitutional amendment. Social laws established workers' rights and simplified taxes while Venizelos built military support by expanding and reequipping the army. The first years of Venizelos's power stabilized Greece's finances and stemmed the massive social unrest that had promised major upheaval.

The Balkan Wars, 1912–13

The Balkans soon were convulsed in a major regional war, from which Greece emerged victorious and with its territory substantially enlarged. At the heart of the Balkan Wars were three issues: the disposition of Macedonia, the problem of Crete, and liberation of the countries still under Ottoman control, especially Albania.

Some Macedonians wanted full unification with Greece, others wanted a separate Macedonian state, and still others wanted Macedonia to be included in a Serbian or Albanian or Bulgarian state. This issue was appallingly divisive, and the choice often was literally a matter of life or death. Guerrilla fighters and propagandists entered Macedonia from Greece and all the other countries of the region. Athens actively supported the irredentist movement in Macedonia with money, materials, and about 2,000 troops. Thessaloniki became more of a Greek city as non-Greek merchants suffered boycotts and left. Greece's lack of access to this key port heightened tension with the Slavic neighbors.

Under these circumstances, all the Great Powers became more involved in the Macedonian problem in the first decade of the twentieth century. Britain pressured Greece to curb guerrilla activities. When the Young Turks took over the government of the Ottoman Empire with a reformist agenda in 1908, a short period of cordial negotiations with the Greeks was chilled by reversion to nationalist, authoritarian rule in Constantinople. New Ottoman intransigence over Crete and Macedonia combined with Venizelos's demand for complete reunification to raise the prospect of war in 1910.

Nationalism in the Balkans was the final element of the war that erupted in 1912. Early that year, a mutual defense pact between Serbia and Bulgaria divided northern Macedonia between those two countries. In response Athens signed bilateral pacts with both neighbors. Essentially, the three Balkan powers thus agreed to cooperate militarily against the Porte, but they did not agree on the vital question of how to distribute territory surrendered by the Ottoman Empire.

The Balkan powers initiated the First Balkan War by marshaling over 1 million troops and then declaring war on the Turks in October 1912. Venizelos's military modernization paid rich dividends. Within a matter of weeks, the Greek army took Thessaloniki and besieged Ioannina to the west. The armies of all three allies fought, mainly to gain a favorable position in a postwar settlement. In the May 1913 Treaty of London, the Ottoman Empire ceded all its European possessions to the Balkan allies, with the exception of Thrace and Albania, the latter of which became independent.

Because the Treaty of London made no division of territory among the allies, and because Greece and Serbia had divided Macedonian territory between themselves in a bilateral agreement, Bulgaria attacked both, initiating the Second Balkan War. Greece and Serbia won victories that ensured major territorial gains at the Treaty of Bucharest in August 1913.

The addition of southern Epirus, Macedonia, Crete, and some of the Aegean Islands expanded Greece by 68 percent, including some of the richest agricultural land on the peninsula, and the population nearly doubled. The major Greek cities of Ioannina and Thessaloniki were reclaimed. Although more than 3 million Greeks remained in Ottoman territory, the Balkan Wars had brought the Megali Idea closer to realization than ever before. When King Constantine was crowned following the assassination of King George in Thessaloniki in March 1913, national morale had reached a high point.

World War I and the National Schism

The division of Europe into competing alliance groups, with the Triple Entente (Britain, France, and Russia) on one side and the Triple Alliance or the Central Powers (Germany, Austria, Italy, and eventually the Ottoman Empire) on the other, had ramifications throughout the complex diplomatic and ethnic relationships of the Balkans. In Greece the war that arose between those alliances sharpened the outlines of two opposing styles of government and foreign policy. The resulting bitter schism remained in Greek politics and society for decades after the end of World War I.

Greece and the World War I Alliances

Amid the European alliances of 1914, Greece found itself in

a quandary. It had a number of reasons for opposing the Central Powers. First, the unredeemed Greeks of the East were cause for opposing any alliance that included the Porte. Second, Bulgaria, still a rival for territory in Macedonia, had aligned itself with the Central Powers. Third, treaty obligations bound Greece to Serbia, which was in a territorial dispute with the Austro-Hungarian Empire over Bosnia. Finally, the Entente powers had earned Greek loyalty by supporting Greek national aspirations since the struggle for independence. On the other hand, Queen Sofia of Greece was the sister of Kaiser Wilhelm of Germany, and the German military establishment had considerable influence among Greek military leaders, many of whom had been trained in Germany. When World War I erupted in the summer of 1914, these interests came into direct conflict, and Greece was compelled to choose a side.

King Constantine, whose sympathies were clearly with the Central Powers, believed that Greece's interests could best be served by maintaining Greek neutrality. Prime Minister Venizelos, on the other hand, was staunchly pro-Entente. His position was reinforced in January 1915 when Britain promised to award Asia Minor (including all of modern Turkey) to Greece if Greece would lend military support to the Serbs and to the proposed British and French invasion of the Turkish mainland at Gallipoli (Geliboli). And Venizelos, believing that the Entente would win the war and make good on its offer, resigned as prime minister when Constantine and the Greek general staff opposed alliance with the Entente. The dispute over national policy finally brought about a constitutional crisis that came to be known as the Ethnikos Dikhasmos, or the National Schism.

The Crisis of Wartime Leadership

The parliamentary election of June 1915 gave Venizelos and the Liberals a majority of seats, but the king refused to recognize the result and withheld approval of the new government until August. In this critical period, Serbia's military position deteriorated, and Bulgaria used the opportunity to declare war on Serbia and reverse the Bulgarian losses of the Second Balkan War. In this process, Sofia also claimed Macedonia and Thessaloniki. Venizelos demanded that the army be mobilized according to the terms of the mutual defense treaty with Serbia. Constantine reluctantly agreed, but only if Greece itself were attacked. Then, without informing the king, Venizelos allowed the French and British to establish a northern front for their Gallipoli attack by landing troops in Macedonia. Before Constantine could react, Venizelos escalated tensions further by orchestrating a parliamentary declaration of war on Bulgaria, which also meant a declaration of war against the Central Powers. A war motion won by a thirty-seven-vote margin, heightening the conflict between Constantine and Venizelos.

Technically, the Greek constitution gave the monarch the right to dismiss a government unilaterally, but the general understanding was that the constitutional provision would only be used when the popular will of the nation was in doubt. Nevertheless, Constantine forced Venizelos to resign once again, dissolved the new parliament, and announced a new election for December 1915.

The Schism Worsens

Together with the vast majority of the electorate, the Liberals boycotted the vote, depriving the newly elected government of all valid popular support. Through the rest of 1915 and 1916, relations between the Liberal and monarchist factions continued to deteriorate as the two sides adopted more rigid and radical positions. Popular opinion vacillated. For example, when French and British troops landed in Macedonia in December 1915 despite the protests of the king, most Greeks supported Constantine's position that the maneuver by the Entente Western Allies violated Greek sovereignty. But when monarchist military leaders allowed eastern Macedonia to fall to the Central Powers in May 1916, public opinion was outraged. Greek national opinion was becoming increasingly unclear.

By mid-1916 Greece stood on the brink of civil war. In Thessaloniki a clandestine pro-Venizelos military organization, the Ethniki Amina (National Defense), launched a coup against the government, with support from the British and French. In October Venizelos returned from Crete to lead the provisional government in Thessaloniki and form a new army to support the Entente. By the end of 1916, the British and French had recognized the provisional government and had blockaded most of Greece to force concessions from Constantine, who feared that Venizelos would topple him. For 106 days, no goods were imported or exported at central and southern Greek ports. Near-famine conditions developed in some areas. Under the leadership of Ioannis Metaxas, former aide-de-camp of

Constantine and future dictator of Greece, a reactionary paramilitary unit, the League of Reservists, was founded. The
league undertook a systematic campaign of terror and violence
against Venizelists in Athens and against anyone who did not
support the monarchy. Once a pattern of violent, sectarian
reprisals had begun, it would prove very hard to stop.

Greece in World War I

The Allied blockade eventually rendered the king's position
untenable. In June 1917, when the British and French threatened to bombard Athens if Constantine remained, the king
passed his crown to his second son Alexander and left Greece,
although he did not formally abdicate. Venizelos was now free
to throw full Greek support behind the Allied cause.

After Greece declared war on the Central Powers in July
1917, ten divisions of the Greek army fought with great valor
along the Macedonian front. In 1918 they routed German and
Bulgarian positions and pushed the front line northward. Germany and its allies soon capitulated, and Greek troops were
among those who marched triumphantly into Constantinople.
At the cost of splitting the nation, Venizelos had brought
Greece into the war on the victorious side. To justify the cost of
this result and heal the wounds caused by the National Schism,
he returned to the Megali Idea.

The Catastrophe in Asia Minor

Venizelos went to the Paris peace talks armed with the assur-
ances he had received from the Allies during the war and
focused exclusively on territorial aggrandizement for Greece.
The peace that emerged seemed to promise full realization of
the Megali Idea. In the event, shifts in domestic and international politics led to a disastrous conflict with the successors of
the Ottoman Empire.

Venizelos showed all of his considerable diplomatic skills at
the peace talks. He wooed the United States president, Wood-
row Wilson, and Britain's Prime Minister David Lloyd George.
Venizelos quickly offered the services of the Greek military as
policing agents and as peacekeepers in occupied territory. Foreign leaders were indebted to the wily Venizelos for this assistance, but the offer fostered domestic discontent. The Greek
armed forces had been mobilized almost continuously since
1912, and the nation was becoming war weary. Also, Venizelos
neglected urgent domestic issues as he put all of his energies

into winning the peace talks. He would eventually pay for this neglect.

After two years of intense negotiations, Greece stood on the verge of fulfilling the Megali Idea. The 1919 Treaty of Neuilly had awarded Bulgarian territory in western Thrace and Macedonia to Greece. The Treaty of Sèvres, signed with Turkey on August 10, 1920, gave Greece the Aegean Islands, hence command of the Dardanelles, and the eastern half of Thrace except for Constantinople. The Treaty of Sèvres also established a new territory around the city of Smyrna (called Izmir by the Turks) on the west coast of Asia Minor—a region long coveted by Greek nationalists. In accordance with the principle of national self-determination, all Greeks in Asia Minor were encouraged to move there. The Smyrna protectorate was to be administered by Greece but remain under the aegis of Turkey. After five years, a plebiscite would determine which country would have sovereignty. The outcome of such a vote had already been decided in 1919 by the stationing of Greek troops at Smyrna to solidify Greek control.

When Venizelos announced in triumph that Greece now occupied two continents and touched on five seas, the irredentist dream seemed to be coming true. The dream soon turned into a nightmare, however. As he prepared to return to Greece from the talks in France, Venizelos was shot by monarchist assassins. He survived, but he was already out of touch with events in Greece, and his extended convalescence isolated him even more from the domestic scene. Two months after the attack on Venizelos, King Alexander died, leaving the exiled Constantine as the only claimant to the throne. A war-weary electorate then expressed its dissatisfaction with the heavy-handed Liberal government by resoundingly vanquishing the Liberals in the elections of November 1920.

Repudiated by the nation at the moment of his greatest triumph, Venizelos went into self-imposed exile. A broad anti-Venizelist coalition took power and immediately scheduled a plebiscite on the restoration of Constantine. Following a landslide approval that was clearly rigged, Constantine returned to the throne amid popular rejoicing in December 1920.

Royalist Foreign Policy Revisions

These developments brought several important consequences. First, royalists avenged the purges inflicted on them in 1917 by mounting counterpurges against Venizelists in the bureaucracy and the military, perpetuating the wounds of the National Schism. Second, the conservatives attempted to outdo the fervent nationalism of the Venizelists by adopting an even more aggressive position toward Turkey. Third, because many of the commitments made to Greece were personal ones between Allied leaders such as Lloyd George and Wilson—who themselves would soon fall from power—and Venizelos, the removal of the Cretan statesman from power considerably weakened those agreements. The result was that Allied support for Greek expansion waned.

The Asia Minor Offensive

In the winter of 1921, the Greek government decided on a military confrontation with the Turkish nationalist movement led by Mustafa Kemal (later known as Atatürk), which was growing in strength and threatening the Smyrna Protectorate. In March Athens launched a major offensive. The Greek army pushed eastward into Asia Minor along a broad front. At one point, the Greek line extended across much of Anatolia. Through 1921, the Greek army met only success, but Kemal retreated skillfully to avoid major defeat. Constantine himself visited the front line, and his younger brother George remained there as a member of the high command. But Greece was now increasingly isolated from its wartime allies. Britain and the United States urged caution and offered to mediate a solution. France and Italy openly supplied arms to the Turks. When Britain and the United States withdrew loans to protest hostilities, Greece's cash resources, and soon ammunition and supplies, were seriously depleted. Internally, the Greek army was fraught with divisions between Venizelists and royalists.

The Retreat from Smyrna

The overextension of the Greek lines proved disastrous. Kemal lured the Greek army ever deeper into the rugged heartland of Anatolia. When he judged that the Greek position was untenable, Turkish forces shattered the Greek line with a major counteroffensive. Kemal then isolated and destroyed the segments of the Greek army, chasing the remnants back to Smyrna. While soldiers, sailors, and journalists from around the world watched from ships anchored in the bay, the Turkish forces burned and sacked the great city of Smyrna, killing about 30,000 Greeks. The Megali Idea went up in smoke on the shores of Asia Minor.

The Interwar Struggles, 1922–36

The disastrous military defeat at the hands of the Turks ensured that the National Schism would define Greek politics and keep society divided through the next two decades. In that time, political stability was rare, except for the successful return of Venizelos between 1928 and 1932. By 1931, however, world economic crisis brought a new set of internal conflicts.

The Treaty of Lausanne, 1923

The Greco-Turkish War had serious and lasting consequences. Two problems immediately faced Greece. The first was the establishment of a legitimate government, and the second was the need to cope with the flood of Greek refugees from the territory that had been lost.

The first problem was addressed quickly when a small, dedicated band of military officers formed a Revolutionary Committee in 1922. Under pro-Venizelos colonels Nikolaos Plastiras and Stilianos Gonatas, the committee landed 12,000 troops at Lavrion, south of Athens, and staged a coup. They demanded and received the resignation of the government and the abdication of King Constantine. George, Constantine's elder son (who had refused the crown when Constantine left in 1917), was crowned as king, and the coup leaders began purging royalists from the bureaucracy and the military.

The next step was to assign blame for the catastrophe. At a show trial, Dimitrios Gounaris, who had been prime minister at the beginning of the war, and seven of his government officials became national scapegoats when they were charged with high treason; six were executed, although their worst crime was incompetence. The executions increased the ferocity of the rift between Venizelists and anti-Venizelists, and the military became an independent political force.

The Plastiras government turned to Venizelos to negotiate an acceptable peace with Turkey. In the Treaty of Lausanne signed in 1923, Greece relinquished all territory in Asia Minor, eastern Thrace, and two small islands off Turkey's northwest coast. At Lausanne Greece and Turkey agreed to the largest single compulsory exchange of populations known to that time. All Muslims living in Greece, except for the Slavic Pomaks in Thrace and the Dodecanese, and Turkish Muslims in

Thrace, were to be evacuated to Turkey; they numbered nearly 400,000. In return approximately 1,300,000 Greeks were expelled to Greece. The determining factor for this shift was religion, not language or culture. Also included in the treaty was protection of Orthodox Greeks and Muslims as religious minorities in Turkey and Greece, respectively.

The Treaty of Lausanne essentially established the boundaries of today's Greece, turning the country into an ethnically homogeneous state by removing almost all of the major minority groups. It also ended once and for all the possibility of including more ethnic Greeks in the nation, the Megali Idea. And, by instantly increasing Greece's population by about 20 percent, Lausanne posed the huge problem of dealing with over 1 million destitute refugees.

The Refugee Crisis

Even before 1923, a torrent of refugees was making its way to Greece. After the ethnic exchange, Greece's poor fiscal situation was strained past its limits by the refugees' need for food and shelter. Tent cities sprang up around Athens and Thessaloniki. Most refugees had fled with only the few items that they could carry; many had nothing at all. A disproportionate number of them were women, children, and elderly men because the Turks had detained young Greek men in labor camps. Massive foreign aid organized by the League of Nations was a major contribution toward alleviating the most immediate needs of the refugees. Eventually, refugee neighborhoods developed around Athens and its port city of Piraeus. Many of these enclaves still retain a distinctive identity today. Other refugees were settled in areas of Macedonia and Crete from which Muslims had departed. The hellenization of these regions included the introduction by new Greek settlers of tobacco farming, which became an important factor in Macedonia's agricultural economy. Many of the newcomers who settled in the cities were professionals or entrepreneurs, who helped to invigorate the industrial sector of Greece. The manufacture of cigarettes, cigars, carpets, and textiles grew dramatically, primarily because of the Asia Minor Greeks. Nevertheless, for many years the general economic condition of the refugee population was grim, and many suffered from discrimination and cultural isolation after leaving Asia Minor.

Political Turmoil in the 1920s

During most of the 1920s, Greece was racked by political turmoil. Only under duress did the military release its grip on the political power it gained in 1922, and the National Schism was reflected in the two factions of the military—so coups and attempted coups occurred quite regularly between 1923 and 1936 (except for the period 1928–32). When the Plastiras government gave way to a democratically elected regime led by Venizelos in 1924, stability seemed within reach. But after assessing the serious splits that had now appeared in his own ranks, most notably over the issue of maintaining or abolishing the monarchy, Venizelos again withdrew into exile. At that point, in March 1924, the monarchy was rejected overwhelmingly in a plebiscite, and Greece was declared a republic— although a republican constitution did not emerge until 1927.

The change of government form could not stem the political unrest, however. Between 1924 and 1928, ten prime ministers held office, two presidents were deposed and one resigned, and eleven military coups occurred. This was one of Greece's darkest periods, culminating in 1926 in the ouster of the military dictatorship of General Theodoros Pangalos and the installation of an "ecumenical cabinet" that dealt with the hopeless deadlock of Venizelist and anti-Venizelist factions by representing all political parties in the executive branch. This unique arrangement lasted until 1928; it produced the republican constitution of 1927, which vested many of the monarch's former powers in a presidency and added a second legislative chamber.

The Second Venizelos Golden Age

In 1928 Venizelos emerged from exile once more to lead his party to win 71 percent of the seats contested in the parliamentary elections. As before, his presence galvanized political support and opposition—but this time Venizelos fashioned an effective parliamentary coalition based on the old Liberal Party and refugees, and he presided over four years of economic growth and political stability.

In spite of a strong parliamentary base, Venizelos had to negotiate treacherous waters as prime minister in order to control the hard-line antiroyalists, most of whom were conservative in other respects, and placate old-style Liberals, leftists, and refugees, an important support group that increasingly was leaning to the left. The conservative Populist Party provided the main opposition, and the central issue separating the two major parties in this period was the constitutional question.

Venizelos was able to implement a number of changes, most of them funded by external loans. He introduced numerous reforms aimed at improving Greek agriculture: land reclamation schemes, agricultural credit programs, and price supports for agricultural produce. The highway and railroad infrastructures were improved and expanded. Protective tariffs were raised to make indigenous products more competitive in the domestic market. Public housing projects were erected and made available to poor Greeks, especially refugees. A British loan of more than £1,000,000 was contracted for the building of public schools (see From 1909 to World War II, ch. 3).

Venizelos also scored some notable successes in foreign policy. The most important of these was his rapprochement with Atatürk, culminating in the October 1930 Treaty of Ankara, by which Greece and Turkey officially recognized their respective territorial boundaries and accepted naval equality in the eastern Mediterranean. Venizelos also normalized relations with neighbors Albania, Bulgaria, Italy, and Yugoslavia.

The Crises of the 1930s

The world financial crisis of 1930 and 1931 initiated a period of political chaos in Greece. The national economy was now based on export of luxury agricultural goods such as tobacco, olive oil, and raisins—commodities whose international demand fell sharply during the hard times of the Great Depression. Payments from Greeks overseas dropped at the same time. Having lost most of its foreign-exchange sources, Greece experienced difficulties in servicing its large foreign debt in the early 1930s.

Because Venizelos did not address the economic dilemma effectively, his fragile political coalition began to unravel. Unable to maintain control, Venizelos relinquished power in mid-1932. Elections that fall divided power almost equally between the Liberals and the Populists, and the latter failed to form a viable government. Chaos and military purges resulted from this deadlock, and Plastiras attempted a military coup in 1933. After the failed coup and an unsuccessful attempt to assassinate Venizelos, the bitterness of the old disputes rose to the surface of public life. In 1935 the failure of another coup, in which Venizelos was directly implicated, completely destroyed his public image. Discredited, Venizelos retired to Paris, where he died in 1936.

The Populists clearly won the parliamentary elections of 1935, aided by the Venizelists' decision to boycott the vote in protest at the imposition of martial law. The unstable Populist government soon toppled, however, and in October a rump parliament declared the restoration of the monarchy and rigged a plebiscite in which 97 percent of votes called for the return of King George to the throne. When he returned to Greece in November 1935, George attempted to repair the National Schism by pardoning all participants in the Venizelist coup of 1935.

The Metaxas Era

The National Schism continued to divide Greek politics and society in the mid-1930s. King George chose General Metaxas to head a new government in 1936, and Metaxas's dictatorial regime finally restored public order. The cost was an extended period of one-party government and repression of human rights that set the stage for more bitter political divisiveness after World War II.

Metaxas Takes Power

The elections of January 1936, which the Populists hoped would finally legitimize their position, instead brought another deadlock between the Populists and the Liberals. This time, however, the political balance was even more precarious because the fifteen votes won by the Communist Party (Kommunistikon Komma Ellados—KKE) gave it the power to swing ballots in parliament.

In this atmosphere, General Ioannis Metaxas emerged as a political force. Metaxas, always a foe of Venizelos and a participant in several coup attempts, had been a minor character on the extreme right of the Greek political spectrum in the 1920s. During that time, he had cultivated a close relationship with the royal house. After his return to the throne in 1935, King George searched frantically for an anticommunist political leader strong enough to bind together a working coalition and control the leftist factions but not strong enough to lead a coup against the throne. The search led the king first to appoint Metaxas minister of war and then prime minister, whereupon

Metaxas immediately pressured parliament into a five-month adjournment.

In May 1936, labor unrest and massive strikes cast doubt on the government's ability to maintain public order. Metaxas used the opportunity to declare a state of emergency, dissolve parliament for an indefinite period, and suspend human rights articles of the constitution. These actions, conducted in August, made Metaxas dictator of Greece. He modeled his regime on the fascist governments of Adolf Hitler and Benito Mussolini. Political parties and trade unions were abolished, strikes became illegal, political opponents were arrested, and press censorship prevailed. Metaxas sought to reduce labor unrest by raising wages and improving working conditions in industry and by raising agricultural prices and absorbing farmers' debts. By 1938 per capita income had increased drastically, and unemployment was dropping. Metaxas dismantled the old patronage system based on royalist and Venizelist party loyalties. Ironically, by sweeping away political parties the rightist dictatorship created a political vacuum in which the constituency of the Greek leftists, especially the communists, grew larger.

Metaxas's "Third Hellenic Civilization" (the first being ancient Greece and the second the Byzantine Empire) lacked the broad base of popular support enjoyed by the dictatorships of Hitler and Mussolini—Greek fascism was not a mass movement, nor was it based on a coherent ideology or racist dogma. In general, the Greek public neither supported nor actively resisted the authoritarian paternalism of Metaxas.

The Metaxas Social and Foreign Policies

In extolling the virtues of self-sacrifice for the public good, Metaxas sought to reshape the national character. He established a variety of national organizations such as the National Youth Movement to foster those virtues in Greek citizens. For the working classes, he instituted a coherent program of public works and drainage projects, set wage rates, regulated hours of labor, guaranteed the five-day work week, and passed other measures aimed at making the workplace safer. The bureaucracy and the military were revamped and streamlined.

The price of such a program was deprivation of freedom. The secret police became all powerful; communists and other leftists were subjected to especially brutal repression. Over 30,000 persons were arrested and incarcerated or exiled on political grounds, and torture was routinely used to extract confessions or accusations that others had acted against the state. A new form of the National Schism, now left versus right, was being created as the old one lapsed.

The main dilemma for the Metaxas regime was foreign policy. Metaxas saw his fellow dictators in Germany and Italy as natural allies, and Germany made major advances into Greek markets in the late 1930s. But Greece's national security remained closely tied to Britain, whose fleet remained a dominant force in the eastern Mediterranean. Moreover, as Italian policy developed in the 1930s, Mussolini's plans for a "new Rome" obviously conflicted with Greek ambitions to control the Aegean and the Dodecanese Islands and exert influence in Albania. Italian expansionism in the region placed Metaxas and Mussolini on a collision course. As war approached in Europe, Metaxas found it increasingly hard to walk the fine line between the Allies and the Axis powers.

Mussolini's persistent provocations settled the issue. In October 1940, Italy demanded that Greece allow Italian occupation of strategic locations on Greek soil. Although Metaxas's resounding refusal plunged Greece into war, it also significantly improved Greece's national self-esteem.

The Terrible Decade: Occupation and Civil War, 1940–50

The decade of the 1940s was the most devastating and deadly in Greek history. In that period, the horrors of foreign military occupation were followed by the ravages of the Civil War. The events of this decade left wounds that remain unhealed more than fifty years later.

The German Invasion of 1941

Initially the war against Germany and Italy went very well for Greece. The nation rallied behind Metaxas, and men of all political persuasions joined the military. Under the leadership of General Georgios Tsolakoglou, the Greek army in Epirus drove the Italians out of Greece and through most of Albania by early December. For many Greeks, this campaign was an opportunity to liberate their countrymen across the Albanian border in "Northern Epirus." The campaign stalled in cold weather, then it lost its leader, Metaxas, who died in January 1941. The British, who at this time had no other active ally in the region, provided air and ground support. But poor coordination between the allied forces made Greece vulnerable to a massive German attack in the spring of 1941, which was intended to secure the Nazi southern flank in preparation for the invasion of Russia. Under the German blitzkrieg, the Greek and British forces quickly fell. Most of the British force escaped, but Tsolakoglou, trapped between the Italian and the German armies, was forced to capitulate. Athens fell shortly afterward as the second element of the German invasion force rushed southward. King George II, his government, and the remnants of the Greek army fled to Crete. Crete fell the next month, however, and George established a government-in-exile in Egypt.

By June 1941, Greece had been divided among Bulgaria, Germany, and Italy. The Germans controlled all the most critical points: Athens, Thessaloniki, Crete, the Thracian border zone with Turkey, and a number of the Aegean Islands. The Bulgarians were given Thrace and most of Macedonia, which they proceeded to rule with an iron hand. The Italians occupied the rest of Greece. From the outset, however, the Germans effectively controlled the country, ruling harshly through the collaborationist governments of Tsolakoglou and later Ioannis Rallis. The German plundering of the nation's resources for the war effort combined with a British naval blockade to cause food shortages, massive inflation, and finally a devastating famine that killed as many as 100,000 people in the winter of 1941–42.

Resistance, Exiles, and Collaborators

The brutality of foreign occupation did not strangle the will to resist. Intermittent, spontaneous acts of resistance during the summer of 1941 led eventually to the formation of a more united effort. In September, the National Liberation Front (Ethnikon Apeleftherotikon Metopon—EAM) was formed to coordinate resistance activities. A secondary aim of the organization was to ensure free choice of the form of government that would follow liberation.

In the five-part coalition of EAM, the old constitutional disputes between monarchists and republicans resurfaced, providing the KKE an opportunity to dominate the organization from its inception. The KKE also took a dominant position in subordinate organizations, such as the combat arm of EAM, the National People's Liberation Army (Ethnikos Laikos

Apeleftherotikos Stratos—ELAS). The KKE's position was possible for a number of reasons. First, in the 1930s the Metaxas regime had driven the communists into precisely the type of underground resistance activity needed to fight the Nazis. Unlike traditional Greek parties (including its allies in the EAM), the KKE was a close-knit, well-organized group with a definite ideology. Also, the communists projected a vision of a better future at a time of great suffering, appealing especially to people who had lacked privileges in Greece's traditional oligarchical society. Finally, the firm stand of the Greek communists on native soil compared well with the actions of the old politicians and the king who had fled to the safety of London and Cairo.

Thus, although the vast majority of EAM and ELAS members were not communists, most were ready to follow the communist leadership. Other resistance groups, such as the National Republican Greek League (Ethnikos Dimokratikos Ellinikos Stratos—EDES), existed, but EAM and ELAS played the largest role in resistance activities. Monarchist elements of society generally withheld support from resistance groups.

Little coordination occurred between the government-in-exile and resistance forces in occupied Greece. Some exile groups even counseled against resistance movements because of the brutal reprisals threatened by the occupiers against the civilian population. In fact, in 1942 the escalation of sabotage, strikes, and mutinies by resistance groups did increase the severity of reprisals. The Germans decreed that fifty Greeks be killed for every German soldier lost, and entire villages were destroyed. The puppet occupation government formed security battalions manned by collaborators, many of whom were die-hard monarchists and thus opposed to the resistance movements because of old constitutional issues. Removed from such terrors at home, the government-in-exile rapidly lost legitimacy.

One of the war's many tragedies was the destruction of the Greek Jewish population. Before the war, Athens, Ioannina, and Thessaloniki had vibrant and sizeable Jewish communities. From Thessaloniki alone, 47,000 Jews were sent to Auschwitz, and by the end of the war Greece had lost 87 percent of its Jewish population.

Under the leadership of Athanasios Klaras, who took the nom de guerre Ares Veloukhiotis, ELAS carried out a number of successful sabotage missions beginning in mid-1942. The

British special operations forces provided arms and experts, who together with fighters from ELAS and EDES struck a major blow against Germany by destroying the railroad line between Thessaloniki and Athens where it spanned the Gorgopotamos Gorge in central Greece. This action severed a vital supply line from Germany to Nazi forces in North Africa. But Britain failed to achieve long-term coordination of Greek resistance activities with conventional operations and other resistance groups in the eastern Mediterranean because of Prime Minister Winston Churchill's steadfast support for the Greek monarchy. By the end of 1942, Greek resistance activity was distracted by internal conflict over the eventual postwar direction of national government. ELAS began a second campaign, this one aimed at ensuring communist domination of resistance activity.

Resistance and Allied Strategy

In the summer of 1943, the British adopted a new strategy in the eastern Mediterranean. To distract Hitler from the main theater of European invasion planned to cross the English Channel in 1944, the British enlisted the cooperation of ELAS in simulating preparations for a major invasion in the Mediterranean. The strategy had credibility because of Britain's attempted invasion of the Ottoman Empire at Gallipoli in World War I. Although all resistance movements were to participate in the plan, ELAS was especially crucial because it controlled the largest army and occupied the most territory. Accordingly, in July 1943 Britain agreed to give ELAS additional support if ELAS would end its campaign against rival resistance groups.

However, in August a disastrous series of meetings in Cairo among guerrilla leaders, the king, and the government-in-exile removed all prospects of cooperation. The resistance leaders demanded guarantees that a plebiscite on the monarchy be held before the king returned to Greece, and that the postwar government include ELAS members heading the ministries of interior, justice, and war. Britain, whose main goal was ensuring continued stability and British influence in the postwar eastern Mediterranean, continued its pattern of intervention in Greek politics by supporting George's refusal of both demands. From that point to the end of the war, the government-in-exile and the EAM resistance were opponents rather than allies.

The immediate result of the Cairo meetings was the onset of civil war between ELAS and EDES in October. Forced to choose, the British stepped up arm shipments to EDES while cutting off the supply to ELAS. This maneuver proved ineffective because the surrender of the Italian forces in September had provided ELAS with enough arms and munitions to be independent of outside supply. Having stabilized its position militarily, EAM declared the formation of a Political Committee of National Liberation (Politiki Epitropi Ethnikis Apeleftheroseos—PEEA) with its capital in the heart of liberated Greece.

The British, alarmed at the prospect of a communist takeover after the war, took steps to resist validation of the PEEA. In October 1944, Churchill and Soviet leader Joseph V. Stalin agreed (without the knowledge of any Greek faction) that postwar Greece would be in the British sphere of influence and that the Soviet Union would not interfere. In return, Churchill conceded Soviet control of postwar Romania.

EAM and Greek Society

Many Greeks rallied to the PEEA as a new alternative to the government-in-exile. For many people in the mountainous liberated areas of Greece, EAM/ELAS rule had established order, justice, and a tranquil communal life that prewar governments had failed to provide. The resistance movement offered women, in particular, new personal empowerment in their participation as warriors and workers. Peasants and working-class men also found unacceptable the prospect of going back to the old ways.

Another group also rallied to the call of the PEEA. The Greek military units that had escaped the Germans were assembled in the Middle East under the name Middle East Armed Forces (MEAF). Most soldiers and sailors, unlike their officers, were EAM sympathizers, and mutinies and strikes occurred in the MEAF between 1942 and 1944 as news of the communist resistance was received. In the spring of 1944, the formation of the PEEA stimulated a "grand revolt" by republican and communist enlisted personnel seeking recognition of a PEEA-sponsored government of national unity.

Liberation and Its Consequences

The grand revolt led to a change in the leadership of the Greek government-in-exile. Georgios Papandreou, who had strong republican and anticommunist credentials, was appointed prime minister of a government of national unity organized in Lebanon. The purpose of the appointment was to attract noncommunist antimonarchists away from EAM to a staunchly anticommunist, pro-British government. In August 1944, after initially rejecting the minor posts allotted to it in the Papandreou government, EAM bowed to Soviet pressure and accepted the terms of the Lebanon agreement. The Germans began to withdraw from Greece in October. Although ELAS's control of the Greek countryside would have made a grab for power easy, in this period resistance forces confined their activities to harassing the German withdrawal.

Papandreou and the national government entered Athens on October 18. The euphoria of liberation swept all before it, and for days the streets were filled with rejoicing citizens. Beyond their joy, however, fear and mistrust abounded, and many key issues remained unresolved. As before the war, the constitutional schism still divided Greeks.

The Lebanon agreement called for the 60,000 armed men and women of ELAS, with the exception of one elite unit, to lay down their arms in December, with the aim of creating a new national force based on the MEAF. In late November, however, Papandreou demanded total demobilization of ELAS, a step the resistance leadership would not take. The leftist factions were already quite suspicious of the failure of Papandreou and the British to actively pursue and punish Greek collaborators, many of whom the Nazis had recruited by citing the threat of a communist takeover. By December, amid rising tension and suspicion on both sides, EAM called a mass rally and a general strike to protest the government's high-handedness. When police forces opened fire on demonstrators in Athens, a thirty-three-day street battle erupted between police and British troops on one side and ELAS fighters on the other. Although EAM was not prepared to seize power and fighting did not spread outside Athens, the potential for wider hostilities was clear. The Battle of Athens ruined some parts of the city and left as many as 11,000 dead.

When Churchill visited Greece to assess the situation, he became convinced that the constitutional issue had to be resolved as expeditiously as possible. Under strong British pressure to improve his image with the Greek people, King George agreed to the appointment of the widely respected Archbishop Damaskinos of Athens as his regent in Greece. In a concession to the opposition, Papandreou was replaced as prime minister by the old Liberal, General Plastiras.

In February 1945, a semblance of peace was restored with the Varkiza Agreement, under which most ELAS troops turned over their weapons in exchange for broad political amnesty, a guarantee of free speech, the lifting of martial law, amnesty for all "political crimes," and the calling of a plebiscite on the constitutional question. The Varkiza Agreement initiated what became known on the political left as the White Terror. Rather than prosecuting collaborators, the Ministry of Justice and the security apparatus, together with vigilante bands of anticommunists, ignored the political amnesty for the next two years, continuing the struggle of the collaborationist security service against resistance figures with known leftist connections. But now the latter had little public support, as most of Greek society went on an anticommunist crusade against which the KKE, forsaken by Stalin, could do little. Wartime heroes were executed for killing collaborators, and judges and tax collectors of the PEEA went to jail for unauthorized representation of the Greek government. Right-wing death squads and paramilitary groups embarked on a campaign of terror and assassination against leftists. Both communist and noncommunist EAM/ELAS members went underground for their own safety. A series of weak governments proved incapable of stemming the escalating sectarian violence.

The Resumption of Elections

Themistoklis Sophoulis, another of the Liberal old guard, formed a government at the end of 1945; then he announced that in March 1946 a national election would precede by two years the promised plebiscite on the monarchy. This decision inverted the order of the two national ballots agreed upon in the Varkiza Agreement. The leftist parties, claiming that fair and impartial elections were impossible in the prevailing climate of violence and repression, called a boycott of the election. When war-weary Greeks went to the polls, their choice was limited by the decay of traditional parties under Metaxas. The election, which was marred by low turnout and considerable fraud, gave power to the People's Party, a loose coalition of the old Populist Party with Metaxasists, monarchists, and anticommunists. The new leader of the government was Konstantinos Tsaldaris, a nephew of the prewar Populist leader.

The Tsaldaris regime renewed the persecution of the left, removing civil servants and university professors from their posts because of their politics and accelerating the manhunts of right-wing bands. In 1946 over 30,000 men and women were interned in concentration camps or exiled. The country drifted ever closer to open civil conflict. Far ahead of schedule, Tsaldaris demanded a plebiscite on the monarchy. Rather than waiting until 1948, as had been announced by Sophoulis, he called for the referendum in September 1946. A highly suspect vote, which included coercion if not outright rigging, restored the monarchy by 68 percent to 32 percent. For many Greeks, the restoration represented a betrayal of everything they had fought for. Although there was widespread opposition to the idea of a communist government, there also was deep antipathy to the monarchy in general and especially to King George, who had been tainted by his closeness to Metaxas. On the verge of civil strife, the KKE resumed recruiting and began reassembling the nucleus of ELAS warriors who had fled into the mountains.

Civil War

In December 1946, Markos Vafiadis announced the formation of a communist Democratic Army of Greece (DAG), the successor of the ELAS. The DAG never exceeded 28,000 fighters, compared with about 265,000 troops in the national army and national police force at the end of the war. The Civil War commenced in earnest during the winter of 1946–47. Vafiadis adopted a strategy of guerrilla warfare, utilizing hit-and-run tactics to harass the national army and its allied groups. DAG forces scored some notable successes, but they were unable to capture any major towns. Like almost all internecine conflicts, the Civil War was marked by brutality on both sides. Villages were destroyed and civilians killed. The atrocities of the war left lasting scars on the nation's consciousness.

By the spring of 1947, Britain no longer was able to meet Greece's escalating demands for money and supplies, so the role of external patron was assumed by the United States. With the Greek case specifically in mind, Harry S. Truman set out in March 1947 a policy of global containment of communist expansion that came to be known as the Truman Doctrine. Truman pledged United States support to all free peoples under the threat of communist takeover. Under that policy, the United States made US$400 million in aid and military assistance available to Greece. United States advisers and military personnel under General James van Fleet came to Greece to train and supply the national army and the security forces.

Although the disproportionate size of the forces had made the outcome of the Civil War inevitable, the DAG's mistakes hastened its fall. After Vafiades was ousted by KKE chief Nikos Zahariadis in mid-1947, the DAG made a disastrous shift from guerrilla tactics to conventional, set-piece battles. Outgunned and outmanned, the DAG was pushed northward into the mountains.

In mid-1949, Yugoslav leader Josip Broz Tito inflicted another costly blow by closing the supply routes through Yugoslavia as part of his policy to conciliate the West. As the situation deteriorated, forced conscription of men and women and compulsory evacuation of children eroded the DAG's popular base of support. The Civil War ended when the last DAG mountain stronghold fell at the end of August. Thus, in addition to the more than 500,000 killed in World War II, during the Civil War 80,000 more Greeks lost their lives, 700,000 more became refugees, and the national economy was left in ruins.

Reconstruction and Retribution, 1950–67

After World War II and the Civil War, Greece was in a political and economic shambles. With massive United States aid, however, new growth began almost immediately. Then, under Alexandros Papagos and Konstantinos Karamanlis, leaders of new conservative coalition parties, political conditions stabilized and the economy experienced an extended growth period (see Postwar Recovery, ch. 3).

The Marshall Plan in Greece

In 1949 the Greek Ministry of Welfare listed 1,617,132 persons as indigent; destitute, despondent, and directionless, they looked to Athens for assistance. Another 80,000 to 100,000 had fled their homeland voluntarily or been resettled forcibly in various parts of the communist world; the largest such settlement was at Tashkent in Soviet Central Asia. The German occupation and the Civil War had left the countryside devastated, the economic infrastructure largely rubble, and the government broke. The most pressing need, then, was the material reconstruction of the country, which required continuation of the large-scale United States aid commitment. In the early days of the Cold War, the West gave priority to reinvigorating Greece because of its strategic location. In a bipolar world, Greece's international orientation was preordained.

As part of the European Recovery Program (commonly called the Marshall Plan), an American Mission of Aid to Greece (AMAG) was established to assist and oversee the nation's economic recovery. Millions of United States dollars poured into Greece. As part of the agreement between Greece and the United States, members of the AMAG were given wide-ranging supervisory powers that quickly led to the formation of parallel administrations—one Greek and one American. Greece had become, for all intents and purposes, a client to the United States.

Initially the bulk of foreign aid went into military expenditures; thus, while other parts of Europe were rebuilding their civilian industrial infrastructures, Greece was forging a military apparatus whose sole function was to contain communist expansion. With the cessation of the Civil War in 1949, the focus of aid spending shifted to civilian priorities. The national currency, the drachma (for the value of the drachma—see Glossary), required stabilization because bouts of hyperinflation during the war years had rendered it valueless. Faith had to be restored in the monetary system. Exports had to be revived. And, of course, the core of Greek agriculture and industry required rebuilding. Greece (especially Athens) came to resemble a giant work site with building construction everywhere; new roads were built and old ones refurbished; and hydroelectric stations were built to power new industry. In 1953 the drachma was devalued in order to make Greek products more competitive. Other measures were taken as well to attract foreign capital to Greece. These policies ushered in a new phase of growth in the early 1950s. However, massive dependence on foreign aid came at the price of foreign dependence in international relations.

Civilian Politics Resume

In February 1950, martial law was lifted in preparation for the first general election since 1946. The social upheavals of wartime enfranchised parts of society previously excluded from political participation; women, emancipated in some ways under the PEEA, were to receive the right to vote in 1951. In the elections of 1950, no fewer than forty-four parties, most of them centered on individual politicians rather than political principles, contested the 250 seats in parliament. Tsaldaris and the Populists won a plurality of only sixty-two, giving the balance of power to a group of center-right parties: the Liberals, led by Sophocles Venizelos, the son of the former prime minister, the National Progressive Center Union under General Plastiras, and the Georgios Papandreou Party. These three parties agreed to form a coalition government with Plastiras at the helm.

In the elections of 1951, called because no stable coalition emerged from the 1950 elections, two new organizations appeared. The royalist Greek Rally Party, under Field Marshal Alexandros Papagos, commander of the national army when it defeated the DAG, included a broad spectrum of Greek society and was modeled on the French Rally Party of Charles de Gaulle. The popularity of Papagos, who had reinstated the autonomy of the Greek military during his tenure as its commander, enabled Greek Rally to eclipse the Populists by garnering 114 seats to the Populists' two. The United Democratic Party, a front for the banned KKE, won ten seats although many of its candidates were in prison. Based on their combined 131 seats, the Liberals and the Center Union formed another shaky centrist ruling coalition. At this point, Greece felt the sharp edge of dependency on the United States. Threatening to withdraw aid, the United States ambassador urged that the electoral system be changed from proportional to simple majority representation, a move that would favor Papagos's conservative Greek Rally Party. Politicians reluctantly made the change. The elections of 1952 gave Greek Rally 247 of 300 seats in parliament, beginning a decade of dominance by the right. This episode also set a pattern of political parties altering voting laws while in office to ensure future electoral success.

The Papagos administration took advantage of its parliamentary majority to unite conservatives and begin to improve Greece's economic situation. Devaluation of the drachma spurred exports and attracted additional capital from the West. Papagos also improved Greece's international security by joining the North Atlantic Treaty Organization (NATO) in 1952 and by entering the Balkan Pact with Turkey and Yugoslavia in 1953. The latter agreement soon dissolved, however, when Yugoslavia's relations with the Soviet Union improved. Stimulated by Greece's new status as a NATO ally of Turkey, Papagos began negotiations with Britain and Turkey over the status of Cyprus, a British crown colony and the home of the largest remaining Greek population in territory adjacent to Greece. When those talks failed in 1955 amid anti-Greek riots in Istanbul and political violence stirred by the Greek-Cypriot National Organization of Cypriot Fighters (Ethniki Organosis Kyprion Agoniston—EOKA), relations between Greece and Turkey entered three decades of hostility.

The Rise of Karamanlis

Papagos died in office in 1955. During his tenure, an obscure politician, Konstantinos Karamanlis, had risen quickly in the Greek Rally Party. In the Papagos government of 1952–55, Karamanlis was a very effective, although autocratic, minister of public works. When Papagos died, King Paul surprised observers by choosing Karamanlis to form a new government. The forty-eight-year-old Macedonian reorganized the Greek Rally Party as the National Radical Union (Ethniki Rizopastiki Enosis—ERE) and proceeded to hold power until 1963.

During the Karamanlis years, the economy continued to grow by most statistical indicators, although it remained under state control and did not develop in new directions. Growth was especially fast in construction, shipping, and tourism. The state bureaucracy, the largest employer except for agriculture, became bloated, inefficient, and politically entrenched in this period. The service sector was the fastest growing element in the Greek economy. Overall, the standard of living of the majority of Greeks improved markedly in the 1950s in comparison with the sufferings of the previous years. Between 1951 and 1964, average per capita income quadrupled, and prices remained stable.

In the same period, Greeks flocked to cities in numbers unseen since 1900. Athens was the favorite destination of rural citizens seeking to improve their economic position. When the high expectations of Greece's shifting population were not realized, however, the postwar consensus that had supported the right began to crumble.

In foreign relations, the two dominant issues of the immediate postwar era, the Cold War and Cyprus, remained critical for Greece. Karamanlis was firmly convinced that Greece's fortunes lay with the West and that Greece must become "European." Karamanlis wanted to move closer to Europe than membership in NATO alone, so in 1962 he won associate status for Greece in the European Community (EC) with the promise of full membership in 1984. He also established close personal contacts in Washington, receiving an official visit from the United States president, Dwight D. Eisenhower, in 1959. No other United States president visited Greece until 1990.

The other overriding issue of the day was Cyprus. The postwar climate of British decolonization had led to expectations that Cyprus, whose population was 80 percent Greek, might become free to join with Greece. There were two obstacles: Cyprus's strategic importance to Britain and the Turkish population on the island. For Britain, Cyprus had a special role in protecting British oil supply lines from the Middle East. In 1954 Britain's foreign secretary, Anthony Eden, had stated simply that, because of that factor, Britain would never relinquish Cyprus. The sizeable Turkish population on the island meant that Turkey also had a stake in the future disposition of the island, if Britain were to agree to a change in its status.

In 1955 the EOKA campaign of violence and terrorism aimed at disrupting British rule and uniting Cypriot Greeks with Greece. After years of conflict and delicate negotiations, the interested parties finally reached a settlement in 1959. The island would be independent and ruled by a joint Greek and Turkish government formulated roughly according to the size of each population. The president would be Greek, the vice president Turkish. Greeks were awarded 70 percent of seats in parliament, with the Turkish minority holding veto power; 60 percent of the army was to be Greek. Britain retained one airfield and one army base, and Greece and Turkey were able to station military advisers on the island. The three nations jointly guaranteed the security of the island, and each had the right to intervene to defend it. The establishment of even temporary peace on Cyprus was a major accomplishment, but this solution was not popular in Greece.

Electoral Shifts to the Left, 1958–63

Karamanlis's role in compromise talks with Turkey began a process of weakening in the ERE's electoral support that continued into the early 1960s. At the same time, elder statesman Georgios Papandreou's coalition profited from public disaffection with Karamanlis to revive the center-left after decades of suppression.

The first sign of deterioration in the conservative party's position came in the 1958 parliamentary elections. The ERE lost seats as the United Democratic Left (Eniea Dimokratiki Aristera—EDA), ally of the outlawed communist party, gained the second-highest vote total. Seeking validation of his pro-Europe policies and the Cyprus treaty, Karamanlis asked for new elections in 1961. His ERE party recovered somewhat from the 1958 result by obtaining 51 percent of the vote and 176 seats in parliament. Former Prime Minister Georgios Papandreou and his Center Union (Enosis Kentrou—EK), in association with some smaller centrist parties, finished second with 34 percent of the vote and won 100 seats. The EDA finished third with 15 percent and 24 seats.

The 1961 elections were marred by widespread allegations of tampering and corruption. Army and police units, alarmed by the high procommunist turnout in 1958, openly intimidated voters, especially in areas known for their left-wing sympathies. Although Karamanlis likely played no role in the voting irregularities, Papandreou found an issue to rally the people: he charged electoral fraud and demanded that the elections be declared void. When they were not, he committed himself to a "relentless struggle" to ensure free and fair elections in Greece.

Many people had grown weary of the stifling of the left, which had continued since the end of the war. Many leftists were still in prison, internal security forces continued to wield great influence, and advancement in the civil service and the military remained dependent on political affiliation. In short, people were tired of the suppression of personal freedoms. In the early 1960s, political violence increased, as exemplified by the 1963 assassination of EDA deputy Grigorios Lambrakis by thugs connected to the security forces (an event dramatized in Costa Gavras's film *Z*).

Karamanlis felt his support deteriorating both to the left and to the right. He clashed with King Paul and Queen Frederika on a number of issues, especially the relationship between the monarch and the military. Karamanlis also became convinced that the power of the military was inappropriate for a democratic state. Once more the constitutional question regarding the role of the monarchy was rising to the surface of Greek political life, and, as in the past, it inevitably involved the armed forces as well. Finally, in early 1963 Karamanlis yielded and tendered his resignation. Upon its acceptance, he went into self-imposed exile in Paris.

The Junta

A number of developments between 1963 and 1967 led to a successful military coup. Social conditions declined despite economic growth. Crowding into cities gave rise to renewed demands for social welfare and better income distribution. The emigration that had commenced in the late 1950s continued into the 1960s (about 452,300 Greeks left between 1963 and 1967). And labor groups were much more militant than they had been at any other time in the postwar period.

Conditions for Overthrow

Another development centered on Cyprus. In 1963 the demand of Cyprus's president, Archbishop Makarios III, for a reduction in the powers of the Turkish minority caused fighting to break out on the island, and all-out war loomed when Turkey threatened an invasion to defend Cypriot Turks. Only the forceful intervention of the United States president, Lyndon B. Johnson, prevented an invasion in early 1964. The United Nations peacekeeping forces that entered Cyprus to prevent war at that point have remained on the island since that time. The Cyprus conflict convinced many in the military of the need to step up war readiness.

The third event was the succession of the inexperienced twenty-four-year-old Constantine II to the throne upon the death of his father Paul in March 1964. Just one month before, the Center Union had won a resounding victory, garnering 52.7 percent of the popular vote and a majority 173 seats in parliament to push the right out of power. Thus the military was deprived of both its royal patron and its connection with the majority party. In the eyes of the right, such changes meant that public order was deteriorating at the same time that war with Turkey seemed imminent.

Instability in the Papandreou Regime

Papandreou's Center Union government enacted a number of far-reaching social and political reforms. Prominent among them was the release of all political prisoners. To deal with the economic crises, Georgios Papandreou appointed his son Andreas, the former chairman of the Economics Department at the University of California at Berkeley, as minister of the economy. Many in the Center Union resented this move. Rising stars in the party such as Konstantinos Mitsotakis felt especially slighted by the appointment. The younger Papandreou, who held far more radical views than his father, soon became involved with a group of left-leaning military officers known as Aspida. The right viewed these developments suspiciously.

Placard celebrating overthrow of national government by military junta, April 21, 1967 Courtesy Sam and Sarah Stulberg

Cabals formed in the army as once again rightist military men assumed the role of "protectors" of the nation. To regain control of the armed forces, Georgios Papandreou forced the resignation of his minister of defense and sought the king's approval to name himself minister of defense. The constitutional question again came to the forefront when Constantine refused the request. In this case, the question was who controlled the military, the king or the prime minister, and the clash of personalities between the two men exacerbated the conflict.

Papandreou resigned in disgust in July 1965. In the succeeding months, a series of caretaker governments came and went, leaving the ship of state adrift. Constantine eventually called for elections in May 1967, and an overwhelming Center Union victory seemed certain. Fearing a purge of hard-line right wingers from the military, a group of junior officers put Operation Prometheus into action in April 1967, and the government of Greece fell into the hands of the junta of the colonels.

The Accession of the Colonels, 1967

The leaders of the self-styled "Glorious Revolution" were two colonels and a brigadier general, whose regime came to be known simply as "the junta," or "the colonels." Supporters of the coup were predominantly officers from lower-class backgrounds who had achieved status through career advancement in the armed forces. Fearful of losing their posts because of their involvement in right-wing conspiracies, they acted out of self-preservation, under the flimsy pretense of forestalling a communist takeover and defending Helleno-Christian civilization in general. The junta succeeded because of the political leadership vacuum at the time and because they were able to strike quickly and effectively. By seizing the main lines of communication, they presented an unsuspecting nation with a fait accompli.

Initially the colonels tried to rule through the king and the existing political system. But, gaining the cooperation of very few politicians, they soon began to arrest all those who showed signs of resisting the takeover, consolidating as much power as possible in their own hands. Andreas Papandreou, for example, was arrested for his connection to the Aspida group; he was released only under intense international pressure. As the methods of the colonels began to resemble those of the Metaxas dictatorship, Constantine organized a countercoup in December 1967, then fled into exile when his plan failed.

Colonel Georgios Papadopoulos, one of three officers who led the coup, rose to the top of the regime and remained there until November 1973. The junta's aims and policies were a curious mixture of populist reforms and paternalistic authoritarianism backed by propaganda and terror. The overarching, proclaimed intent of the military government was to purge Greek society of the moral sickness that had developed since the war. Their more frivolous social policies included the banning of miniskirts and mandatory short hair for men. The regime lacked a base of popular support and remained in power through terror. A formidable secret police apparatus monitored society, using torture and committing other human rights violations that were widely reported by international organizations. In the first three years, the main targets of this policy were known supporters of the communists, but many centrist figures also were arrested.

The regime's brutality made it an international pariah. The only foreign dignitary of note to visit Greece during this period was the Greek-American United States vice president, Spiro Agnew. Greece withdrew from the EC in 1969 to avoid suspension of its association agreement. Nevertheless, Greece's NATO allies confined themselves to verbal condemnation because the regime fulfilled every geopolitical requirement, anchoring the alliance's defenses in the unstable eastern Mediterranean. The United States broke off full diplomatic relations only briefly after Constantine's exile; although military aid to Greece decreased between 1967 and 1973, in 1972 the United States negotiated permanent access to Greek port facilities for its Sixth Fleet.

The Junta Falls

Because the reign of terror was effective in Greece, resistance to the colonels formed mainly abroad. Prominent among the anti-junta groups was the Panhellenic Liberation Movement led by Andreas Papandreou. Such organizations kept international attention focused on the actions of the junta, but it was the regime's own ineptitude and lack of legitimacy that led eventually to its downfall.

The two immediate causes of the fall of the colonels were the Greek student movement and events in Cyprus. In the autumn of 1973, large-scale student demonstrations, motivated by repression at universities, deterioration of the economy, and a drastic increase in inflation, began open defiance of the junta's ban on public assemblies. When students occupied the National Polytechnic University of Athens and began clandestine radio broadcasts calling for the people of Athens to rise up against tyranny, the junta responded by calling in the army in November 1973. Tanks crushed the gathering brutally. The incident exposed the regime's lack of control over society and showed the public that resistance was not futile. The junta lurched even farther to the right when Dimitrios Ioannides, former head of the secret police, overthrew Papodopoulos and replaced him at the head of the government.

Believing that a major nationalist cause would rally the people behind him, in 1974 Ioannides induced a confrontation with Turkey over control of recently discovered oil deposits in the Aegean Sea. He also intensified his ongoing attempts to undermine Makarios by supporting Greek Cypriot terrorist activity. In July, when junta-inspired Cypriots engineered a coup against Makarios, Turkey immediately invaded Cyprus under its rights as a guarantor of the security of the republic established in 1960. Ioannides received little response when he called for full mobilization of the Greek military, which had already shown disaffection by scattered revolts. Thus the Cyprus crisis made clear that the regime's most fundamental base of support was crumbling. At this point, Greek military leaders and politicians collectively decided that only former Prime Minister Karamanlis possessed the ability and the level of popular support needed to dismantle the dictatorship and restore democracy to Greece. Four days after the Turkish invasion of Cyprus, Karamanlis arrived from Paris and took up the task.

Karamanlis and the Restoration of Democracy

Karamanlis faced the formidable task of clearing the wreckage left by the seven years of military rule. There were two major domestic missions: the restoration of a full range of political parties and reestablishing the military as a positive force. A new constitution and a legitimate referendum on the monarchy were the main legislative priorities, but the new role of the military remained more controversial in the 1970s.

The Electoral Triumph of the ND, 1974

Legalization of the KKE was a symbolic step toward finally ending the tensions that had simmered under the surface of Greek politics since the Metaxas regime. In an uncertain climate, Karamanlis scheduled elections for November. Karamanlis's newly formed party, New Democracy (Nea Demokratia—ND), swept into power with 54 percent of the vote and 219 seats in parliament. Surprisingly, the Panhellenic Socialist Movement (Panhellinion Socialistiko Kinima—PASOK), which Andreas Papandreou founded on the basis of his anti-junta resistance group, the Panhellenic Liberation Movement, received nearly 14 percent of the popular vote with a platform opposing Western alliances and the monarchy.

The Center Union, the only major precoup party to appear on the 1974 ballot, gained 21 percent of the vote—but it was soon to be a spent force. The United Left Party (Enomeni Aristera), a coalition of the pro-Moscow and anti-Moscow communist factions that had separated in 1968, received 9 percent of the votes. Now other political questions loomed; most important of these were the fate of the monarchy and the disposition of the junta and its followers.

Dealing with the Monarchy and the Military

Karamanlis staged yet another referendum on the monarchy (the sixth since 1920), in an effort to settle finally the rancorous debate that had poisoned Greek politics throughout the twentieth century. In December 1974, a majority of 70 percent of Greek voters opted to abolish the monarchy. Not coincidentally, this margin was nearly identical to the figure attained in the only other legitimate vote on the monarchy, that of 1924, which had established the interwar republic.

Punishing the junta and reforming the military and the civil service were more delicate operations. Karamanlis wanted to avoid a repetition of the military retributions of the 1920s and to preserve relations between the civilian government and the military. Accordingly, the three top leaders of the junta received death sentences that were later commuted, as did Ioannides. However, none of the more than 100 civilian ministers who had served the junta was convicted of a criminal offense. Many people serving in the military and the police were tried and convicted, and universities were purged of junta sympathizers.

The Constitution of 1975

In 1975 a new constitution was promulgated to establish Greece as a republic with a political structure modelled on that of France (see The Branches of Government, ch. 4). The constitution invested great power in the president, who is obligated to choose as prime minister the leader of the party gaining the most seats in parliamentary elections. Until the constitution was amended in 1986, the president could veto legislation, dissolve parliament, and call for a direct vote of no confidence in parliament (see The Presidency, ch. 4). The sharp escalation of executive authority was controversial, but Karamanlis declared strong presidential powers necessary to deal with extraordinary episodes of Greece's political conflict. The five-year administration of Konstantinos Tsatsos, the first president under the new constitution, passed without his using the considerable powers that had been given to his office.

Cyprus and Relations with the United States

Cyprus continued to dominate Greek foreign policy in the mid-1970s. From the Greek standpoint, the unresolved status of the island was chiefly the doing of the United States, and a substantial anti-Western backlash colored Greek foreign policy during that period.

Since the invasion of 1974, Turkish troops have remained on the island. Although a cease-fire was negotiated in Geneva in

August, talks broke off almost immediately, and the Turkish army began to expand its zone of occupation to a line that included 37 percent of Cypriot territory. Karamanlis, however, was intent on avoiding armed conflict, for which Greece was unprepared, and talks resumed shortly thereafter. In 1975 a Turkish Federated State of Cyprus was declared in the northern part of the island, and negotiations continued intermittently for another two years. A 1977 agreement divided the island provisionally, but no lasting, workable solution was achieved. In 1994 the fate of Cyprus remained a pressing issue that continued to impair relations between Greece and Turkey (see Assessing the Turkish Threat, ch. 5).

The Greek public reacted to the Turkish presence on Cyprus with resentment toward NATO and the United States. In the view of many Greeks, the benefits of membership in a West European security organization were meaningless if the alliance could not stop a NATO ally from invading a country such as Cyprus. In protest Karamanlis withdrew Greece from military structures of NATO, a status that remained until 1980. Greece held the United States and its foreign policy establishment particularly responsible for the Cyprus invasions because of its failure to prevent Turkish action or to compel Turkey's withdrawal after the fact. In 1975 the United States Central Intelligence Agency was still widely held responsible for aiding the junta's accession and supporting its regime. This hostility was partly a backlash against the dependent relationship of postwar Greece to the United States, partly the result of resentment for United States support of the junta.

In blaming the United States for events in Cyprus, Greeks also overestimated the United States' leverage over Turkey. Tension increased in 1976 when the United States, having repealed partially its arms embargo, exchanged US$1 billion in military equipment for military installations in Turkey. Greek protests resulted in a similar agreement with Greece, worth US$700 million, and the establishment of a seven-to-ten ratio that became the standard formula for United States aid apportionment between the two countries.

In the late 1970s, two new issues exacerbated animosities between Greece and Turkey. The first involved the control of the northern Aegean. Each side claimed (and still claims) large areas of the region on the basis of offshore territorial rights. Because the boundaries between mainland Turkey and the Greek islands in the Aegean are so close, the six-mile offshore limits often overlap (see fig. 2). Control of the continental shelf became much more critical with the discovery of oil in the region. On three occasions since the late 1970s, Greece and Turkey have nearly gone on to war over this issue. Other sources of irritation were the question of air control over the Aegean, Greece's attempts to extend its six-mile limit to the twelve-mile limit used elsewhere, and the two countries' treatment of their respective Greek and Turkish minorities. The end of the Cold War greatly diminished the incentive for cooperation against communist neighbors, emboldening both countries to take more independent stands over regional issues.

Domestic and Electoral Politics, 1975–77

The period of domination by the ND included concerted attempts at national reconciliation. Economically, Karamanlis pushed for closer integration with Europe, a policy rewarded in 1981 with full membership in the EC. The ND government practiced statist capitalism, meaning that the state had an intrusive and direct role in determining economic policy at the same time that it tried to foster a free-market system. The primacy of the state in economic affairs was evident in all areas, from prices and wages to labor law. In postjunta Greece, the debate has centered on the degree, rather than the existence, of government intervention in the economy.

Karamanlis called an election in 1977, a year earlier than required by the constitution. A particular goal of this strategy was to obtain validation of his government's foreign policy initiatives. The major surprise of the 1977 election results was the rise of Andreas Papandreou and PASOK. ND's share of the vote fell to 42 percent (172 seats) while PASOK's share rose to 25 percent (93 seats). The Center Union dropped into a distant third place (12 percent and 15 seats), barely ahead of the KKE (10 percent, 11 seats). PASOK's success came largely at the expense of the declining Center Union, which split into factions shortly thereafter. ND's losses had multiple causes. Some ND supporters moved to a new far-right party, and the political equilibrium that Karamanlis had achieved since 1974 removed some of the urgency with which Greeks had supported him in the previous election. ND lacked a clear ideology; instead, the charisma of its leader was its chief rallying point.

At the same time, PASOK's message had increasing resonance with the people. In his rhetoric, Papandreou crafted a skillful mix of nationalism ("Greece for the Greeks") and socialism ("PASOK in government, the people in power"). PASOK promised a "third road" to socialism and a middle way in foreign policy, restoring national pride by breaking the bonds of foreign dependency and reorienting Greece with the nonaligned countries. PASOK's structure also gave it a base of grass-roots support that other parties lacked. Besides its strong central committee, PASOK had local party offices and cadres in towns and villages across Greece. This system proved very effective in organizing support and validating the claim that the party was not based, like the others, on networks of patronage. And, perhaps most importantly, PASOK's slogan of "change" struck a cord with the Greek people's search for a new way forward after forty years of conservative rule.

The Rise and Fall of Papandreou and PASOK

By the elections of 1981, electoral momentum had shifted away from an uninspired ND to the promise of change offered by a newly moderate PASOK. For the next eight years, Papandreou applied his program to society and the economy, with mixed results.

In 1980 Karamanlis elevated himself to the presidency, leaving the lackluster Georgios Rallis as the incumbent prime minister in the next year's elections. In the elections of October 1981, PASOK and Papandreou swept into power with 48 percent of the popular vote and 172 seats in parliament. The ND, which could not match Papandreou's charisma or the novelty of PASOK's program, finished a distant second with 36 percent of the vote and 115 seats, and the KKE came in third with 11 percent and thirteen seats.

Between the 1977 and 1981 elections, PASOK and its leader had continued the move away from an initial image as a Marxism-based, class-oriented party, in order to reassure centrist voters. The "privileged" class against which Papandreou ran in 1981 had shrunk considerably to a small number of Greece's wealthiest citizens. The societal results of the "change" were left deliberately vague. The election result meant that, for the first time in Greek history, an explicitly left-wing party held the reigns of government. The transformation from authoritarian rule to democracy was finally complete (see The Return of the Left, ch. 4).

The PASOK Domestic Program

As it exercised power for the next eight years, PASOK did oversee considerable change in some areas. The new government brought in a sweeping domestic reform program under Papandreou's "Contract with the People". Many initial reforms were long-overdue and cost little. New laws legalized civil marriage, abolished (in theory) the dowry system, eased the process for obtaining a divorce, and decriminalized adultery. Other laws enhanced the legal status of women (see The Role of Women, ch. 2). The university system was overhauled, giving more power to staff and students (see Education, ch. 2). A comprehensive national health service was introduced, for the first time making modern medical procedures available in rural areas (see Health Care, ch. 2).

Some of PASOK's reforms met considerably less success, especially in government and economic reform. The pervasive blanket of smog over Athens, instead of being banished as promised, became thicker in the early 1980s (see Pollution Problems, ch. 2). An attempt to decentralize local government foundered because local administrative bodies had no financial base (see Local Government, ch. 4). And, after PASOK reforms initially gave trade unions greater freedom of action and improved labor relations, circumstances soon caused Papandreou's labor policy to reaffirm state control over labor-union activity. The selective socialization of key means of production, which was to emphasize worker participation and improve productivity, led instead to increased state patronage for inept companies and continued state control of unions (see The Structure of Employment, ch. 3).

Papandreou also attempted to further the national reconciliation by officially recognizing the role of the resistance during World War II, by granting rights of residence in Greece to those who had fled to communist countries after the Civil War, and by ending all public ceremonies that celebrated the victories of the National Army over the DAG. Only Greek refugees were allowed to return, however, excluding a large number of Macedonian Slav members of the DAG.

The greatest challenge to PASOK in the 1980s was managing the economy. The main problem was paying for social programs in the PASOK platform while keeping Greece militarily strong. In keeping with his campaign promise, Papandreou initially raised middle and low incomes, instituted price controls, and introduced tax incentives on investments, giving the state an even larger role than it had had under the ND regime. But by 1985, the annual inflation rate had risen to 25 percent, which led to devaluation of the drachma in what was presented as an austerity plan. The budget deficit still grew, eventually reaching 10 percent of the gross national product (GNP—see Glossary). The public debt that spiralled out of control in the late 1980s continues to be a serious deterrent to economic growth in Greece in the 1990s (see The Public Sector and Taxation, ch. 3).

PASOK Foreign Policy

In foreign policy, PASOK proved far more moderate in power than it had been as an opposition party. Although Papandreou's strident anti-American rhetoric caused friction with the administration of United States president Ronald W. Reagan, PASOK was willing to compromise on specific issues such as continuation of United States bases in Greece, after vigorous negotiations. Despite his theoretical nonalignment and conciliation of bêtes noires of the West such as Muammar al Qadhafi of Libya, Saddam Husayn of Iraq, and Yasir Arafat of the Palestine Liberation Organization, Papandreou balanced Greece's international position by keeping Greece in NATO and the EC.

In its policy toward Turkey, the PASOK government stood firm. In 1982 Papandreou became the first Greek prime minister to visit Cyprus, signaling strong support for the Greek population of the divided island. In 1984 he mobilized the Greek military for war when Turkish batteries opened fire on a Greek destroyer. And in 1987, he once again brought Greece to the brink of war when Turkey threatened to send an oil exploration vessel into Greek territorial waters. In 1988 a thaw resulted from a meeting between Papandreou and Turkey's President Turgut Özal in Davos, Switzerland, where new avenues of bilateral communication and consultation were arranged. Soon thereafter, however, the "spirit of Davos" was strained again by disputes over the treatment of minorities, air space, and access to Aegean oil.

Scandal and Decline

Papandreou's fortunes began to turn during the summer of 1988. In August he underwent major heart surgery, but he refused to yield the reins of power. The opposition mocked his technique as "government by fax." A further complication was the announcement that Papandreou intended to divorce his American wife of thirty-seven years—herself a very popular figure in Greece—in order to marry a thirty-four-year-old airline stewardess who had gained influence in Papandreou's entourage. The family rift caused by this announcement damaged the cohesion within PASOK because Papandreou's sons occupied key positions in the party.

But it was a financial scandal that rocked the political world of Greece most violently. In November 1988, a shortfall of US$132 million was discovered in the Bank of Crete some months after bank chairman Georgios Koskotas, a Greek-American millionaire entrepreneur under investigation for large-scale financial crime, had fled the country (see PASOK's Second Term, 1985–89, ch. 4). In the months that followed, alleged connections between Koskotas and the PASOK government, and even with Papandreou himself, brought the resignations of several ministers and demands for a vote of no confidence in the government. Papandreou, whose second four-year term was to expire within months, held onto power.

Electoral Stalemate

As he awaited PASOK's inevitable losses in the elections of June 1989, Papandreou adjusted the electoral system to make it more proportional and hinder formation of a majority by a rival party. The strategy succeeded in part. Under the leadership of Papandreou's old rival Konstantinos Mitsotakis, ND won 44 percent of the vote, but it fell six seats short of a majority. A short-lived conservative-communist coalition government was formed. In a matter of months, a second election also failed to produce a clear victor that could form an effective government. Finally, in April 1990, ND won a narrow majority of seats and formed the government. Papandreou and the socialists were finally out of power after almost ten years.

In the 1990s, the critical challenges that Greece faces all have deep roots in its history. The end of the Cold War again raises the question of Greece's rightful position in global geopolitics—a question that has been answered in quite different ways as time has passed. As European integration continues apace, rumblings are heard from the richer, northern European nations about the economic burden placed on them by confederation with the poorer members to the south, especially Greece (see International Economic Policy in the 1990s, ch. 3).

Closer integration in the European Union (as the European Community was renamed in December 1993) also stimulates new contemplation from within of Greece's differences and commonalities with Western Europe, the civilizations of which were enormously enriched by contact with Greek culture in the past. Through most of the modern era, however, the nations of the West (including the United States) have been protectors, invaders, or persistent sources of interference in the internal affairs of Greece, a nation lusting for past glory and independence but unable to recapture them. At the end of a uniquely chaotic century, Greeks sought the internal stability that would allow them again to offer the world the best of their culture.

*   *   *

A number of good introductory publications are available in English. Richard Clogg's *A Concise History of Greece* serves as the best starting point. Clogg's earlier *A Short History of Modern Greece* is a valuable companion volume. C.M. Woodhouse's *Modern Greece: A Short History* and Campbell and Sherrard's *Modern Greece* are dated but still useful. *A Profile of Modern Greece in Search of Identity* by Kourvetaris and Dobratz provides a more holistic but flawed picture of the development of Greece in the modern era, and the misnamed collection of essays *Background to Contemporary Greece*, edited by Marion Sarafis and Martin Eve, contains a few very insightful articles. The essays collected by scholar Robert Browning in *The Greeks: Classical, Byzantine, and Modern* provide a solid introduction to the history of Greece from the first millennium B.C. Barbara Jelavich's two-volume *History of the Balkans* places Greece in the historical context of its region. The history and anthropology sections of the forthcoming bibliographical guide on modern Greece, to be published by the Modern Greek Studies Association, will prove invaluable for further investigation of Greek history. Finally, that association's *Journal of Modern Greek Studies* remains the flagship journal in the field, and it should be consulted for the latest developments in the study of modern Greece. (For further information and complete citations, see Bibliography.)

Chapter 2. The Society and Its Environment

Griffon statue that guarded the temple of Apollo at Delphi

GREEK SOCIETY HAS DEVELOPED over a period of nearly 3,000 years, with only few interruptions, in a physical and geographical environment that contributed unique qualities and facilitated widespread dissemination of the elements of its civilization. Despite centuries of occupation by Roman and Ottoman empires, the Greeks maintained an unusually homogeneous ethnicity that today includes only very small minorities. Greece's ethnicity is reflected in the 97 percent of Greeks professing membership in the nation's established church, the Orthodox Church of Greece.

The homogeneity of Greek social traditions, which combine to represent the sense of "Greekness" that unites the nation, has overcome regional diversity. Historically, populations have been divided by mountains and the sea, as well as class differences. Until the second half of the twentieth century, the majority of Greeks tilled the land and led a quite separate existence from the urban elite.

For all of Greek society, the fundamental social unit is the nuclear family, membership in which is the most important element in individual identity. Although urbanization and Westernization have modified that institution in recent decades, ties of kinship, patronage, and ritual kinship still cut across classes and unite rural and urban Greeks. Urbanization and Westernization have also changed the traditional role of women, expanding their range of acceptable activities to include most of the areas formerly reserved for men. Social changes already underway were ratified as law after the Panhellenic Socialist Movement (Panhellinion Socialistiko Kinima—PASOK) came to power in 1981 with a platform of modernizing and secularizing social relationships. Although the program met substantial resistance from the church and elements of secular society, the changes and compromises that emerged have speeded the transformation of traditional society.

Since World War II, the Greek population has urbanized to a dramatic extent, predominantly in Athens and Thessaloniki, and social services have kept pace unevenly with that movement. Health services and social welfare programs are state run, but insurance and delivery are fragmented among several agencies and organizations. Education is very highly respected in Greek society, and its broad availability has steadily increased the middle class since the 1800s. The state monopoly over education at the university level has encouraged students to complete their educations outside Greece, however, because the number of university places has not kept pace with population growth. The curricula of primary and secondary schools have been modernized from the centuries-old forms of classical education only in recent decades.

Greece's physical environment, dominated by its mountains and the sea, has set the conditions under which society and the economy developed. Topographic and climatic regions vary from mountainous, isolated Epirus in the northwest to the sunny, windswept Cyclades Islands in the southern Aegean Sea. The sprawling metropolis of Greater Athens, containing over one-third of Greece's population, lies on a coastal plain at the southeastern tip of the Greek mainland. Rapid postwar industrialization and inadequate planning have created crisis conditions in air and water quality and land usage, most notably in the large metropolitan areas. Effective management of environmental problems has proved difficult, however, for both government and nongovernment agencies.

Physical Environment

The territory occupied by the Greek nation comprises the southern tip of the mountainous Balkan Peninsula and an intricate complex of smaller peninsulas and islands that define the northeast corner of the Mediterranean Sea. Because of this combination of physical features, the topography of Greece is extremely complex and varied. Including all its offshore territory, Greece occupies 131,957 square kilometers. It is bounded on the north by the Former Yugoslav Republic of Macedonia (FYROM—the name internationally approved in 1993 for that entity after its 1991 declaration of independence) and Bulgaria; on the northwest by Albania; on the east by Turkey and the Aegean Sea; and on the south and west by the Sea of Crete, the Mediterranean Sea, and the Ionian Sea (see fig. 2).

Geographical Regions

The sea is the most consistent influence on the physical environment of Greece. The elaborately irregular Greek coastline, one of the longest in the world, includes about 15,000 kilometers of shore. No point on the mainland is farther than 100 kilometers from the water, and Greece includes more than

2,000 islands—of which about 170 are inhabited. Crete (Kriti), the largest of the islands, is the southernmost point of the nation with a significant population.

The second major physical feature, mountains, cover more than three-quarters of Greece's surface area. Although their general pattern is from northeast to southwest, the mountains and the basins between them form irregular barriers to movement across the peninsula. In Greece's early history, the isolating effect of the mountains encouraged populations to develop lasting traditions of independence because of their lack of communication with the outside world.

Beginning in ancient times, the sea endowed Greece with a seafaring tradition; the best-known work of classical Greek literature, Homer's *Odyssey*, describes a long and dangerous voyage assumedly made across the eastern Mediterranean from Asia Minor. Sea travel has promoted contact among populations in Greece and with other peoples, but its exposed peninsula has also made Greece vulnerable to attack from the sea.

Drainage patterns in Greece are affected by the large percentage of land surface covered by rock, by the steepness of the young mountains in the north, which form gorges with narrow, twisting, and fast-moving rivers, and by the deep indentations of the coastline, which shorten the course of rivers across the land mass. The short Greek rivers have irregular seasonal levels that make them unreliable for navigation and irrigation. The three major rivers of Greece—the Vardar (called the Axios by Greeks), the Struma (called the Strimon by Greeks), and the Nestos (called the Mesta by Bulgarians)—primarily drain other countries to the north and northwest.

The topography of both the mainland and most of the Greek islands is dominated by mountains; Greece has more than twenty peaks higher than 2,000 meters. The most important mountain range is the Pindus (Pindos), which extends from north to south in the center of the peninsula at an average elevation of about 2,650 meters (see fig. 7). The highest mountain in the range is Mt. Olympus (Olimbos), legendary home of the gods, which is 2,917 meters high. A southern extension of the Dinaric Alps of the former Yugoslavia and Albania, the Pindus Range consists of several rugged, parallel ridges, the longest of which extends from the Albanian border in the north to the Gulf of Corinth in the south. Geologically, the range extends across the Gulf of Corinth into the Peloponnesian Peninsula and southeastward to form the islands of the southern Aegean Sea. The northern part of the range offers magnificent scenery of jagged peaks and picturesque gorges. The continuous settling and shifting of this comparatively young mountain range makes the entire region, from Epirus on the Albanian border south to Crete, prone to earthquakes. The Pindus is sparsely populated and generally not cultivated, but upland pasturing of sheep and goats is common.

Traditionally, Greece is divided into nine geographic regions that are differentiated by topography and regional tradition but not by political administration. The six mainland regions are Thrace, Macedonia, and Epirus to the north, and Thessaly, Central Greece, and the Peloponnesus farther south. The three island regions are the Ionian Islands off the west coast, the Aegean Islands in the Aegean Sea between the Greek mainland and Turkey, and the island of Crete, which is considered a separate region.

Thrace

Greek Thrace (Thraki) is often distinguished as Western Thrace to differentiate the Greek portion of the large ancient region that is now divided among Greece, Bulgaria, and Turkey. The area of Greek Thrace is 8,578 square kilometers. The eastern border with Turkey is formed by the Maritsa River (called the Evros by Greeks and the Meric by Turks), which flows southward into the Aegean Sea after flowing eastward across southern Bulgaria. The Nestos River flows from southern Bulgaria to define the regional border between Thrace and Macedonia to the west. No major rivers flow through Thrace.

Most of northern Thrace is dominated by the southern tier of the Rhodopes (Rodopi) Mountains, most of which lie in Bulgaria. The Thracian Plain runs along the shore of the Aegean Sea and along the Maritsa Valley to the east. This alluvial plain is cut into three parts by plateaus extending southward from the Rhodopes to the Aegean Sea. The three plains are the most agriculturally significant area of Thrace, and the region's three provinces are defined by their location.

The plain in Evros, the easternmost province, is a traditionally productive agricultural area, enriched by the fertile soil of the Maritsa Valley and by abundant water from the Maritsa and its tributaries. The plains in the other two Thracian provinces, Rodopi and Xanthi, also feature rich soil that is especially favorable for tobacco cultivation.

Unlike Greece's other maritime regions, most of Thrace's coastline is smooth, broken only at the mouth of Lake Vistonis, which is actually a bay of the Aegean Sea located on the boundary of the provinces of Rodopi and Xanthi. The lake is the spawning area for commercially important fish species. The mountainous and sparsely populated island of Samothrace, about sixty kilometers offshore in the Aegean Sea, is administered as part of the province of Evros. The statue that became known as the Winged Victory of Samothrace, now a treasure of the Louvre Museum in Paris, was discovered on the island.

Thrace was the only region of Greece in which Muslims were allowed to remain according to the population exchanges prescribed by the Treaty of Lausanne in 1923. Today the Muslim population is concentrated in the provinces of Rodopi and Xanthi. Most of the region's residents are ethnically Greek, however, and many descend from Greek refugees who returned from Turkey in the Greek expatriation phase of the Lausanne agreement (see The Interwar Struggles, 1922–36, ch. 1).

Macedonia

Immediately to the west of Thrace, Macedonia (Makedonia) is the largest region of Greece, including thirteen provinces and the Monastic Republic of Mt. Athos, an autonomous area. Like Thrace, Macedonia is the Greek portion of a geographically larger area that now is politically divided among three countries. Besides the Greek region, the term Macedonia has included southwestern Bulgaria and FYROM, which until 1991 was the southeasternmost constituent part of Yugoslavia. Greek Macedonia extends westward from the Nestos River to the Albanian border. The southern border is the Aegean coastline, and the northern border is determined by the mountain ranges that extend from Bulgaria and former Yugoslavia. The most notable topographic feature is the Khalkidiki Peninsula, which extends three fingers of land southeastward into the Aegean Sea. Mt. Athos rises over 2,000 meters from the eastern peninsula and has provided seclusion for a legendary monastic community for more than a millennium.

The terrain of Macedonia is primarily rugged mountains interspersed with fertile river valleys and an extensive coastal plain defined by the Vardar River, which empties into the Aegean Sea after flowing southward from FYROM. The valleys of the Vardar and the Struma rivers, and the Plain of Drama in the far east, are Macedonia's agricultural centers. Greece's second-largest city and second-largest port, Thessaloniki (Salonika), is located between the Khalkidiki Peninsula and the mouth of the Vardar. West of Thessaloniki is a plain drained by the Vardar and Aliakmon rivers; the latter arises in the Pindus Mountains near the Albanian border and meanders eastward to form a swampy delta shared with the mouth of the Vardar just to the east. The delta then empties into the Gulf of Thermaikos, the northwesternmost extension of the Aegean Sea. The largest Macedonian island is Thasos, northeast of the Khalkidiki Peninsula.

Thessaloniki is located on the natural harbor of the Gulf of Thermaikos. The harbor ranks Thessaloniki second in importance as a Greek port, after the Piraeus complex south of Athens. In the postwar industrialization process, Thessaloniki's harbor came to serve new manufacturing complexes in the interior, and the city regained the commercial importance it had during the Middle Ages. Beginning in the 1950s, the city was redesigned and modernized. The Salonika Trade Fair is an important commercial event in the eastern Mediterranean.

The city was founded in 315 B.C.; its Christian community was the recipient of the epistles of Saint Paul to the Thessalonians that form two books of the New Testament of the Bible. Because it contains numerous sites of Hellenistic and Byzantine church buildings, Thessaloniki has become a center for the study of ancient architecture. The city belonged to the Byzantine Empire in two different periods, between which it was sacked and occupied by several tribes and kingdoms. The Ottoman Turks took Thessaloniki from Venice in 1430. In the late 1400s, the city was an important refuge for Jews driven from Spain, and it remained the center of Greece's Jewish population until the Nazi occupation virtually extinguished it. In modern times, Thessaloniki was the initial headquarters of the Young Turk movement in 1908, before becoming part of the Greek kingdom in 1913. It was a World War I base of Allied operations against Turkey as well as the capital of the breakaway pro-Allied government of Eleutherios Venizelos (see World War I and the National Schism, ch. 1).

The island of Thasos has rich mineral deposits that supported a prosperous community. The island changed hands frequently in the first millennium B.C. Its minerals long ago exhausted, Thasos became a tourist resort in the 1970s. Offshore oil deposits have been exploited in the 1980s and early 1990s.

Epirus

Southwest of Macedonia and bounded on the north by Albania, Epirus also is the Greek portion of a larger territory, which extends into southern Albania. An extremist irredentist movement has sought recovery of "Northern Epirus" from Albanian control (see The Balkans, ch. 4). Epirus is bounded on the south by the Gulf of Amvrakikos, site of the Battle of Actium where Octavian defeated Mark Antony to determine control of the Roman Empire (see Greece in the Roman Empire, ch. 1). Dominated by the main Pindus Range, which runs north and south and reaches an altitude of 1,800 meters, Epirus has been isolated from the rest of Greece by the lack of natural passageways running east and west. Because there are no major river valleys or basins between its steep, constricted ridges, Epirus is also a poor agricultural region, suitable mainly as pasture. Some grains are grown in the northern plains. The central mass of the Pindus Range forms the border between Epirus and Thessaly, the region to the east. The main river of Epirus is the Arakhthos, which flows southward out of the mountains and into the Gulf of Amvrakikos.

Through most of its history, Epirus either consisted of isolated villages (during the era of city-states elsewhere), or it was occupied by the Romans or the Turks. Periods of federation and self-governance occurred immediately after the death of Alexander the Great and in the thirteenth century. The populace of Epirus played an important role in the Greek War of Independence (1821–32). The northern part of present-day Greek Epirus was ceded to Greece by the Ottoman Empire in 1881; southern Epirus became part of the kingdom of Greece in 1913. The main city, Ioannina, is a regional agricultural and commercial center.

Thessaly

Thessaly (Thessalia) occupies the east side of the Pindus watershed, extending south of Macedonia to the Aegean Sea. The northern tier of Thessaly is defined by a generally southwest-northeast spur of the Pindus Range that includes Mt. Olympus, close to the Macedonian border. Within that broken spur of mountains are several basins and river valleys. The easternmost extremity of the spur extends southeastward from Mt.

Olympus along the Aegean coast, terminating in the Magnisia Peninsula. The peninsula envelops the Gulf of Pagasai (also called the Gulf of Volos), which forms an inlet of the Aegean Sea. According to legend, Jason and the Argonauts launched their search for the Golden Fleece from that peninsula. Thessaly's major river, the Pinios, flows eastward from the central Pindus Range just south of the spur, emptying into the Gulf of Thermaikos.

The Pinios River flows through the northern edge of the most important topographical feature in Thessaly, the central plains. The Pinios has several tributaries that originate in a delta configuration that encompasses the entire plain to the south of the main river. The alluvial soils of the Pinios Basin and its tributaries make Thessaly a vital agricultural area, particularly for the production of grain, cattle, and sheep. Modernization of agricultural practices in the mid-twentieth century has controlled the chronic flooding that had restricted agricultural expansion and diversification in the low-lying plains. Thessaly is the leading cattle-raising area of Greece, and Vlach shepherds (of Romanian origin) shift large flocks of sheep and goats seasonally between higher and lower elevations.

The population center of Thessaly is the Greater Volos metropolis, a shipping center combining the cities of Volos and New Ionia with six smaller towns at the northern end of the Gulf of Pagasai. The nearly landlocked gulf provides a natural harbor at Volos for shipping the agricultural products from the plains just to the west and chromium from the mountains of Thessaly. The Northern Sporades (Vorioi Sporades) archipelago, administered by Thessaly's Magnisia Province, forms a series of islands, three of which are inhabited, extending eastward into the Aegean Sea from the Magnisia Peninsula.

Thessaly never had an independent existence. It was fragmented and isolated from the main political developments of the classical period to the south; then it was occupied by the Macedonians and Romans, who were followed by a variety of tribes and peoples until the Ottoman Turks took control in 1393. The Ottoman Empire ceded most of Thessaly to Greece in 1881, the remainder in 1913.

Central Greece

South of Thessaly and Epirus, the region of Central Greece extends from the Ionian Sea on the west to the Aegean Sea on

Women in village costume,
Metsovon, Epirus
Courtesy Sam and Sarah
Stulberg

the east, encompassing the southernmost territory of mainland Greece. (Some geographers combine Thessaly and Epirus in their description of Central Greece.) The region includes the island of Euboea (Evvoia), which extends 180 kilometers from northwest to southeast parallel to the east coast of the mainland, separated from the mainland at the city of Khalkis, north of Athens, by a very narrow waterway. The island, which is the second largest in Greece, is formed by an extension of the Pindus spur from the Magnisia Peninsula to its north. Euboea's mountains are interspersed with fertile valleys that produce olives, grapes, and grains, although there are no major rivers. The east coast, which faces the Aegean Sea, is rocky; the island's only harbors face the Vorios Evvoïkos and Petalion gulfs between Euboea and the mainland.

The mainland portion of Central Greece forms a "foot" extending southeastward from the Gulf of Amvrakikos, the inlet that defines the northern border of Central Greece on the Ionian seacoast. The main range of the Pindus Mountains extends southward into the western part of Central Greece. The Pindus Range is extended by the Parnassian Range, which is close to the mainland's southern shore and rises to 2,457 meters at Mt. Parnassus, mythical home of the Muses. The Helicon (Elikon) Range, which includes the historic city of Thebes

(Thivai), extends the Parnassian Range southeastward toward Athens.

The main rivers of the region are the Kifisos, which forms an east-west valley as it flows from the southern Pindus into the Gulf of Vorios Evvoikos west of Khalkis, and the Akheloos, which empties into the Ionian Sea after flowing southward from the mountains of Epirus. In the district of Boetia (Voiotia), between the Gulf of Corinth and Euboea, the Kifisos and the Asopos rivers form two extensive fertile plains where grain, tobacco, grapes, and olives are grown.

Athens

The province of Attica, which has been settled at least since 3,000 B.C., is where the classic Greek Attic dialect originated. Attica includes the capital, Athens (Athinai), which is surrounded by the largest metropolitan area in Greece, and Piraeus, Greece's chief port. Greater Athens includes forty-one municipalities and fifteen communes (see Local Government, ch. 4). It is the hub of Greece's import and export activity and the center of the largest industrial complex in the country, featuring a wide variety of light and heavy manufacturing enterprises. Average personal income for Athenians is higher than the national average.

The earliest known buildings in Athens were constructed about 1,200 B.C. Classical Athens, the city that existed from the fifth century until the third century B.C., is recognized as the cradle of Western civilization. It was home to the great generation of Greek playwrights that included Aeschylus, Aristophanes, Euripides, and Sophocles, to the philosophers Aristotle, Epicurus, Plato, Socrates, and Zeno, and to the sculptors Myron, Phidias, and Praxiteles. Under the rule of the great statesman Pericles, Athens reached the pinnacle of its golden age in the middle of the fifth century B.C.

In 86 B.C., Athens was conquered by the Romans, under whom it continued to flourish as a center of learning and fine architecture and sculpture. Although the Germanic Heruli tribe destroyed most of the city in A.D. 267, Athens continued as an important center of Greek scholarship until the Roman emperor Justinian closed its renowned schools of philosophy in A.D. 529. From that point, Athens assumed minor status, and Constantinople became the focus of Greek culture.

The seventh through the tenth centuries were the darkest period for the city. Some activity then revived in the centuries that followed, before Athens was captured by the Crusaders in 1204.The Ottoman Turks captured the city in the fifteenth century, turning the Parthenon, the main temple built for the goddess Athena in the fifth century B.C., into a mosque. That conversion meant that the building had served three religions within three centuries after having been an Eastern Orthodox church under the Byzantine Empire and a Roman Catholic church after 1204. Athens was fully liberated from Turkish rule only when it was chosen as the new capital of the kingdom of Greece in 1833.

When Greece gained its independence, Athens was a market town with a population of a few thousand, built on and around the Acropolis, the 150-meter hill that was the center of the ancient city. In the decades that followed, Athens gradually returned to the central cultural, economic, and political role that it had enjoyed in classical times. By 1900 the population was about 180,000 and Athens was linked with the thriving port of Piraeus, on the Gulf of Saronikos to its southwest. The city's rapid population growth in the twentieth century has been largely because of immigration—from Turkey in the population exchanges of the 1920s and from Greek rural areas throughout the century.

The Nazi occupation of 1941–44 and the Civil War that followed in 1946–49 destroyed much of the city's infrastructure and most of the central city. Athens experienced a second phase of disorganized growth as it rebuilt after the Civil War. Rapid industrialization and population shifts, accompanied by widespread housing and highway construction, occurred without any plan for land utilization or transportation structure. (This problem was not new, however—travelers in the third century B.C. were already complaining about the complexity of the street pattern.) In the mid-1990s, Athens remained a complex, overcrowded central city.

The Peloponnesian Peninsula

The Peloponnesian Peninsula, also called simply the Peloponnesus, is a mountainous landmass connected to Attica, easternmost province of Central Greece, by an isthmus only six kilometers wide at its narrowest point. The isthmus is cut by the Corinth Canal, which allows marine traffic to move between the Aegean and the Ionian seas north of the Peloponnesus via the gulfs of Corinth and Patras. The canal, originally planned by the Roman emperor Nero in the first century A.D. and completed in 1893, shortens this voyage by 325 kilometers.

The Pindus Range continues southward from the mainland across the peninsula, extending into each of the three peninsulas that are the southernmost points of the Peloponnesus. Between the mountains is the Plateau of Arcadia (Arkadia). Lowlands extend along the western and northern coasts, along inland river valleys, and in spring-fed mountain basins. Alluvial plains in the east and south are fertile, but agriculture requires irrigation. Most of the peninsula's rivers are dry in summer.

All the population centers of the Peloponnesus, except for Tripolis in the mountains, are on the periphery of the peninsula. Sparta, once the most powerful polis in Greece, is several kilometers inland on the plain of the Evrotas River. Corinth, another major polis of classical times (and the origin of the word *currant* because of its role in exporting that crop), is now a relatively unimportant small city on the northeast coast. The largest city is Patras (Patrai), an important industrial, commercial, and port city on the northern coast. The other major port is Kalamai in the southwest.

Crete

The largest island in Greece and the fifth largest island in the Mediterranean, Crete is 243 kilometers long and varies in width from twelve to fifty-six kilometers. It is located about seventy-five kilometers southeast of the easternmost peninsula of the Peloponnesus. The island's topography is dominated by rugged mountains that rise from the sea to form a rocky southern coastline. The slope downward to the northern coast is more moderate, forming a coastal plain and several natural harbors. The highest point is Mt. Ida (Idi), 2,456 meters high, roughly in the center of the island. The central east-west spine of mountains breaks into four segments; the major flatland is the Mesara Plain in the south-central region. That region and several upland basins provide agricultural land that has seasonal flooding. Crete has six rivers, whose flow varies greatly according to the season, and there is one fresh-water lake.

The center of the ancient Minoan civilization and the scene of many episodes of Greek mythology, Crete was settled in about 6300 B.C. (see The Origins of Civilization: 3200–1050 B.C., ch. 1). Although the Minoan civilization ended about 1200 B.C., Crete's location in the eastern Mediterranean made it a natural link in the transfer of cultures from the Near East

Slate-roofed houses in the Pindus Mountains
Courtesy Sam and Sarah Stulberg

into Greece during the millennium that followed. After several centuries of Venetian rule, Crete was taken over by the Ottoman Empire in 1669. After Greece gained its independence, reunification of Crete with Greece became a burning international issue in the nineteenth century. After several uprisings against Ottoman rule and autonomous status between 1897 and 1913, Crete became part of Greece.

Although Crete historically yielded copper, iron, lead, and zinc, only gypsum and limestone are extracted in modern times. An estimated 20 percent of the land is totally unproductive, and 48 percent is used for grazing. The major agricultural products are olives, grapes, carob, almonds, and citrus fruits. The capital city, Heraklion (Iraklion), an important tourist center and port, is twice as large as the next largest city, Khania.

Heraklion has been severely damaged several times by Crete's frequent earthquakes.

The Ionian Islands

The Ionian Islands extend from the coast of southern Albania to the northwest coast of the Peloponnesus. The group, combined by administrative rather than geographic logic, includes many uninhabited rocks and islets as well as four large islands—Corfu (Kerkira), Leucas (Levkas), Cephalonia (Kefallinia), and Zacynthus (Zakinthos)—each of which, together with the smaller islands surrounding it, is governed as a separate province. Altogether, the Ionian Islands comprise 1.8 percent of Greece's land area.

The largest island, Cephalonia (746 square kilometers), is due west of the Gulf of Patras, which separates the western Peloponnesus from the mainland. Mountainous and rocky, Cephalonia and its smaller neighbor Ithaca (Ithaki) grow mainly olives and currants. Thirty centuries ago, Ithaca was the homeland to which the legendary Homeric voyager Odysseus sought to return after the Trojan War.

Corfu is the northernmost of the main islands, lying off the coast of Albanian Epirus and Greek Epirus. Corfu, with an area of 593 square kilometers, is dominated in the north by a mountain range that virtually severs its northern coastal plain from the territory to the south. The fertile southern lowland is cultivated intensively to grow olives, figs, citrus fruits, and grapes.

Settled by colonists from Euboea in the eighth century B.C., Corfu had a sporadically independent existence during the city-state era, participating on various sides in the wars among city-states in the fifth century and fourth century B.C. In the two millennia that followed, the strategic location of Corfu between Greece and Italy caused it to change hands many times; the capital city, Kerkira, contains a citadel built by the Venetians in 1550. The island was finally ceded by the British to Greece in 1864.

The third-largest and southernmost island, Zacynthus (402 square kilometers), lies off the northwest coast of the Peloponnesus. The island has a wide, fertile interior plain that provides more cultivated land than the other Ionian islands; currants are the main crop. The plain is enclosed on the east and west by limestone hills, which form steep seaside cliffs on the western shore.

Zacynthus, which was named after an ancient chief of Arcadia in the central Peloponnesus, was colonized by people from the Peloponnesus in the fifth century and fourth century B.C. The island was used as a base by the Athenians, then the Romans. After being sacked repeatedly by Vandals and Saracens and being fought over by Italian city-states between 1185 and 1484, Zacynthus was held by Venice until 1797. The years of British occupation ended with the cession of the Ionian Islands to Greece in 1864.

Leucas, smallest of the major Ionian Islands (303 square kilometers), hugs the coast of the southern Greek mainland, north of Cephalonia. The island's inland terrain is hilly, and the population is concentrated in the valleys and forests close to the east coast. The coastal lowlands are the main agricultural area, although higher basins farther inland also have fertile soil. The main crops are olive oil, red wine, and currants. A number of severe earthquakes have damaged populated places on Leucas in the nineteenth and twentieth centuries. A smaller island, Meganisi, lies off the southeastern shore and is administered together with Leukas.

Leucas was first colonized by Corinthians in the seventh century B.C. They dug a canal across the marshy isthmus that originally connected Leucas with the mainland. In the second century B.C., the Romans then built a stone bridge to reestablish the connection. Rome made the island's capital, Levkas, a free city in A.D. 167, but the island was subject to periodic invasions and changes of jurisdiction during the millennium that followed. In 1718 Venice gained control of the island; then France and Britain alternated possession in the nineteenth century until Leucas was ceded to Greece in 1864. A modern canal was dug across the isthmus in 1903.

The Aegean Islands

The Aegean Sea extends from Crete northward to the shores of Macedonia and Thrace, connecting with the Black Sea to its northeast through the Dardanelles Strait, the Bosporus Strait, and the Sea of Marmara, which lies between the two straits. This configuration means that the Aegean Sea is the only route from the ports of Russia and Ukraine into the Mediterranean and to the rest of the world. The term *Aegean Islands* technically includes Crete and all the islands in the Aegean Sea between Greece and Turkey. Turkey possesses only two small islands at the northeastern end of the sea. Rights to the seabed and the continental shelf adjoining the islands and the Turkish mainland became a major issue between the two countries in the 1980s (see Turkey, ch. 4).

The islands are geological extensions of the mountains of the Greek mainland, forming regional clusters in the Aegean Sea. (They once formed a land bridge from the mainland to Asia Minor.) The Northern Sporades, off the east coast of the Greek mainland, are administratively part of Thessaly. The Cyclades (Kiklades) are a larger, denser group of twenty-four islands southeast of the Peloponnesus and directly north of Crete. Most of the islands in this archipelago are dry, rocky, and infertile, but two—Naxos (the largest) and Siros (location of the provincial capital, Ermoupolis)—have enough fertile land to grow fruit and vegetables. Naxos has fertile and well-watered valleys as well as the highest elevation among the island group, 1,007 meters. The mostly uninhabited island of Delos (Dilos) around which the Cyclades rotate according to legend, is the mythological birthplace of the god Apollo; it has become an important archaeological site and tourist attraction.

East of the Cyclades and closest to the Turkish coast are the Dodecanese (Dodekanisos) Islands, an archipelago including fourteen inhabited and eighteen uninhabited islands that were held by Italy until 1947. (The composition of the group has varied over time, as indicated by the name, which means "the twelve islands"—referring to the inhabited portion of the group.) Except for the two largest islands, Rhodes (Rodos) and Cos (Kos), the islands are deforested and have poor drainage.

Rhodes, the largest and easternmost of the island group, has an area of 540 square kilometers. Lines of hills run parallel from northwest to southeast, perpendicular to a ridge that follows the entire northwest coast, reaching an elevation of 1,200 meters. The inland valleys and coastal plains offer rich land for pasturage and grain cultivation.

A part of the ancient Minoan civilization, Rhodes was an important commercial center under Dorian tribes from the mainland around 1,000 B.C., then again in classical times. A bronze statue of the sun god Helios, often called the Colossus of Rhodes, stood at the harbor entrance of the capital city, Rodos, and was one of the seven wonders of the ancient world. An earthquake toppled it in the third century A.D. In the classical period, Rhodes was independent, shifting its loyalty among Athens, Sparta, and Persia. Its most notable role in subsequent history was as an island fortress of the Christian Knights Hospitallers against the Turks between the early fourteenth and early sixteenth centuries. In the twentieth century, tourist trade has made Rhodes prosperous. The island produces mainly wine, grain, and fruit.

Cos has a limestone ridge along its southern coast and a fertile lowland, watered by springs farther inland, along the northern coast. The central lowland also produces fruits, vegetables, olives, and tobacco. The coast provides one usable harbor.

The islands of Samos and Ikaria are located just north of the Dodecanese group; together with a small island group, the Fournoi, between them, they form a single province. Samos is unique among the Greek islands because it is covered with trees; its fertile farmland produces olives and grapes. Ikaria and the Fournoi lack fertile land. The island of Chios (Khios), midway up the Turkish coast, is mostly mountainous, but fertile plains in the south and east allow cultivation of fruit and grapes. Lesbos (Lesvos), Lemnos (Limnos), and Ayios Evstratios are the three northernmost Aegean islands. Lesbos, third largest of the Greek islands, has rugged inland terrain with well-irrigated coastal lowlands and foothills where olives are the chief crop. Lemnos, equidistant between the easternmost spur of the Khalkidiki Peninsula and the Turkish mainland, has comparatively flat terrain, but water is scarce and the island is best suited to raising sheep and goats rather than agriculture.

Climate

The dominant condition of Greece's climate is the alternation between hot, dry summers and cold, damp winters typical of the Mediterranean. But considerable local variation results from elevation and distance from the sea. Generally, continental influences are felt farther north and in the center of the mainland. The main climatic regions of Greece are the mainland mountains, Attica (the southeasternmost part of the mainland) and the Aegean, the west including the Ionian Islands, and the continental northeast.

In winter low-pressure systems reach Greece from the North Atlantic, bringing rain and moderating temperatures but also drawing cold winds from the eastern Balkans over Macedonia and Thrace as they pass into the Aegean Sea. The same low-pressure systems also draw warmer winds from the south, creating an average January temperature differential of 4°C between Thessaloniki (6°C) and Athens (10°C). Cyclonic depressions provide the lowlands of the west and the south with mild winters and little frost. Beginning in late fall and continuing through the winter, the Ionian Islands and the western mountains of the mainland receive abundant rain (snow at higher elevations) from the west, whereas the eastern mainland, shielded by the mountains, receives much less precipitation. Thus the average annual rainfall of Corfu off the west coast is 1,300 millimeters; that of Athens on the southeastern mainland is only 406 millimeters.

In summer the influence of low-pressure systems is much less, allowing for hot, dry conditions and an average sea-level temperature of 27°C in July. Summer winds have a moderating effect along the coast, but very dry, hot winds have a parching effect that causes drought in the Aegean area. The Ionian and Aegean islands are especially warm in October and November.

Elevation has an appreciable effect on temperature and precipitation at all latitudes, however. At higher elevations in the interior, some rainfall occurs year-round, and higher mountains in the southern Peloponnesus and on Crete are snow-capped for several months of the year. The mountains of Macedonia and Thrace have colder continental winters influenced by winds channeled through the river valleys from the north.

The Environment

In the years after World War II, several factors placed severe stress on Greece's natural environment. Expansion of industrial activity, the rapid increase in motor vehicles, the influx of foreign tourists, and uncontrolled land use have lowered air and water quality and depleted Greece's already limited pristine regions. In response, over the past two decades Greek governments have passed many laws and general policies, but Greece generally has lagged behind other West European countries in environmental protection.

Pollution Problems

Athens has become known for poor air quality. During the city's frequent severe incidents of *nephos* (smog), many citizens require medical care for circulatory and respiratory ailments. Athens's climatic conditions favor formation of photochemicals that trap pollutants close to the ground, partly because the reconstruction activity that began after World War II has proceeded without a comprehensive plan for traffic and industrial

Peasant woman carrying firewood; sign, common in Greek countryside, says "Dumping of trash and construction materials strictly prohibited." Courtesy Sam and Sarah Stulberg

location. The same conditions contribute to air pollution in Thessaloniki, but to a lesser degree. More than half the total vehicles in Greece are in the Athens and Thessaloniki areas, and their number doubled between 1983 and 1992.

Sulfur dioxide, contributed chiefly by industrial effluents, has severely damaged stone buildings and monuments in Athens and Thessaloniki and generated acid rain that has caused some deterioration to forests in Epirus, Macedonia, Central Greece, and around Delphi, east of Athens. According to estimates, the Parthenon, the best-known of Greece's remaining architectural monuments from classical times, has sustained more atmospheric damage since 1970 than it did in its first 2,000 years of existence.

The largest single source of sulfur dioxide pollution, the oil-burning electric power station in the industrial center southwest of Athens, was closed in 1994 except for emergency power supply. Other heavy polluters are the chemical, textile, and nonmetallic mineral industries established in the Athens region during the boom of the 1970s. Fuels used by Greek industries generally have a slightly higher sulfur and lead content than those used in other European countries, but central heating plants use high-sulfur oil. Winds also transport sulfur dioxide from industrial centers in neighboring countries. Air quality over the major Greek islands has remained good, except for a few population centers such as Heraklion on Crete.

Water pollution has likewise become a serious problem because of industrialization and development policies. Greece has shared in the general deterioration of water quality in the Mediterranean Sea in recent decades. In addition, Greece has drained many lakes completely to generate hydroelectric power or to expand agricultural land. Several animal species have disappeared from Greece as a result of habitat alteration caused by this process. An extended drought (1987–93) diminished both water quantity and water quality in rivers and lakes, causing chronic water shortages in the largest cities and limiting the growth of natural vegetation. Harbors and lakes adjacent to industrial centers, especially the Gulf of Saronikos south of Athens, upon which about half of Greece's industry is located, receive large quantities of untreated industrial waste and municipal sewage. Experts describe the inner gulf as nearly devoid of life. The same type of urban pollution occurs in Thessaloniki's Gulf of Thermaikos. Altogether, about fifty urban centers deposit sewage into the seas surrounding Greece. Ships pump out their bilges and oil as well. In 1994 only 10 percent of the Greek population was served by wastewater treatment plants and, in spite of Greece's extensive coastline, it produced only 0.1 percent of the world's catch of fish.

Since 1970 drastic increases in agricultural application of chemical fertilizers and pesticides have added a new source of runoff pollution. Rivers farther from industrial regions have remained relatively clean, but the diversion of the Akheloos River for hydroelectric power generation in the southwest corner of the mainland was expected to have a drastic ecological effect beginning in the 1990s.

Greece's soil, naturally poor in organic matter, has been degraded further by uncontrolled use of fertilizers and by soil erosion. (Erosion is hardly a new problem, however—Plato described the erosion of Greece's hills 2,400 years ago.) Together with chronic droughts, erosion has caused accelerating desertification in many agricultural areas (see Agriculture, ch. 3). Vegetation has also been stripped by overgrazing and the clearing of steep slopes for construction projects. About one-third of Greece's irrigated farmland suffers from saline deposits. The agricultural fields of Thessaly and Macedonia, on the other hand, do not have salinization or erosion problems.

Environmental Policy

The crises that became visible in the 1970s and closer integration with Western Europe have brought a proliferation of environmental legislation. By 1990 over 800 issue-specific environmental laws and decisions were in force, but few comprehensive laws tied them together into policies that could be enforced nationally. Among major international environmental agreements, Greece is a signatory of the 1987 Montreal Protocol on ozone-depleting substances and the International Tropical Timber Agreement of 1983; the nation did not sign the Convention on International Trade in Endangered Species (CITES); it signed but did not ratify the United Nations Convention on the Law of the Sea (UNCLOS).

The constitution of 1975 gives the state authority over Greece's environment and natural resources. The National Council for Physical Planning and the Environment, established in 1976, has concentrated on industrial planning rather than environmental issues. The authority of the Ministry of Environment, Town Planning, and Public Works, which was formed in 1980, has varied under different administrations and has suffered from internal contradictions when the ministry is assigned large public works projects. Meanwhile, all ministries whose activities affect the environment have maintained independent environmental departments not answerable to the environmental ministry.

The basic principles of Greece's environmental policy are set forth in the 1986 Law On the Protection of the Environment. The law, which provides for no autonomous environmental regulatory agency, requires nearly 100 implementation decisions by government agencies—many of which had not been enacted by 1994—before going into full effect. The unwieldy nature of the bill has promoted bureaucratic obstructions at many points prior to approval.

The first set of standards for atmospheric pollution in Athens emerged in 1982 as part of a United Nations-sponsored pollution control project that had been initiated by the military junta (see The Junta, ch. 1). The standard traffic limitation measures in the central city, allowing private vehicle access only on odd or even days, are tightened when pollution indexes are especially high, which happened only nineteen times between 1982 and 1989. Heavy fines are levied for violation of the access law. A large pipeline, designed to carry industrial waste from the Athens region to biological treatment facilities, was eight years behind schedule in 1992, casting doubt on the likelihood that the treatment facility would be built.

Land-use policy is a very controversial issue in Greece. The need for new landfills is urgent because landfills are crucial to the solid-waste management program, but agreement on sites has been extremely rare. Experts consider an industrial decentralization policy especially urgent to end random construction of new plants and to prevent further concentration in the urban centers of Athens and Thessaloniki. Some financial disincentives to further construction in Athens are in place, as are financial incentives to construction elsewhere. But no overall policy is in effect.

Greece has been lax in enforcement of the environmental guidelines of the European Community (EC) and its successor, the European Union (EU), affecting Greece's international waters. Three EC directives on water-resource protection and the international water management conventions of Ramsar and Verni are not followed by Greek authorities.

Environmental politics in Greece are characterized by strong special-interest groups and a relatively weak environmental movement that began in 1972. The Greek political tradition of close patronage relationships between government figures and private citizens of influence has distracted administrations and fragmented public pressure on environmental issues. This phenomenon was most obvious in the mid-1980s, after the Panhellenic Socialist Movement (Panhellinion Socialistiko Kinima— PASOK) had been elected on a platform promising significant environmental improvement. In that period, a series of ambitious reforms was defeated by special-interest pressure, and by 1984 PASOK had forsaken the bulk of its environmental platform for the duration of its 1981–89 tenure (see Political Developments, 1981–94, ch. 4).

Policies attacking industrial pollution are resisted by the Association of Greek Industrialists and well-organized groups of small industrialists, both of which carry considerable influence with the economic ministries and the leaders of both major parties. Innovations, such as lower tariffs on fuel-efficient imported vehicles and development of alternative mass transportation, meet the opposition of economic ministries that gain much revenue from taxes on vehicles. Well-organized Greek automobile dealers also have a stake in continued use of privately owned vehicles.

Ministries responsible for infrastructure projects and the construction industries that carry them out oppose land-use and conservation policies. Stefanos Manos, an industrialist and a pioneer of environmental planning as a minister in the government of Konstantinos Karamanlis in the late 1970s, was forced to resign in 1979 because his program would have required building projects to include services such as sewers and roads. In 1982 industry pressure ended a major PASOK urban reconstruction program, replacing proposed stricter standards with more lenient ones that exacerbated the problem of uncontrolled urban land use. In the New Democracy (Nea Demokratia—ND) administration of Konstantinos Mitsotakis (1990–93), the policy of stimulating economic activity further strengthened ministries and enterprises involved in building the country's infrastructure. In this period, the Ministry of Environment, Town Planning, and Public Works was not able to reconcile conflicts between environmental and economic interests because government agencies resisted transferring their environmental responsibilities.

Regional groups started mobilizing to promote environmental protection in the mid-1970s. Beginning in 1973, a number of major regional efforts were incorporated into national political agendas and thus achieved many of their goals. In the 1980s, demonstrations began in Athens (including one in 1986 after the Chernobyl nuclear power plant disaster in the Soviet Union), and the ideological basis of organizers became more sophisticated. Nevertheless, in the early 1990s Greece's environmental social consciousness remained quite fragmented and localized, and efforts by "green" groups to achieve representation in the Assembly have been marginally successful at best.

In the early 1990s, progress in environmental protection in Greece was the result of increasing media attention to escalating problems; also of pressure from the EC and the EU to uphold national and international obligations and pass environmental legislation; of major decisions made by the Council of State, the highest administrative court in the nation, overturning anti-environmental government policies; and of the activity of a small group of autonomous nongovernmental environmental organizations. Those organizations have mobilized citizens in response to specific issues such as the 1991 proposal to ease industrial location policy by the Ministry of Environment, Town Planning, and Public Works and the continuing need for urban smog control. Fishing interests organized an especially successful organization, Helmepa, to oppose water pollution. Activist groups have brought legal proceedings successfully before the Council of State and agencies of the EU.

Demography

Most of the dramatic postwar changes in the size and location of the Greek population had ended by 1990. Birth rates are low in Greece, as in the rest of Europe, and the average age of the population is expected to continue rising in the foreseeable future. Emigration, a traditional part of Greece's demographic pattern, remains steady at a quite low level, but political events in Albania and the former Soviet Union have posed serious dilemmas in immigration policy.

Population Characteristics

At the time of the 1991 census, the population of Greece was 10,264,156, an increase of 524,000 (5.4 percent) since 1981. In 1991 population density was 78.1 persons per square kilometer—a misleading statistic because much of Greece's mountainous territory is uninhabited (see fig. 8). The birth rate has been shrinking steadily since its peak of 20.3 births per 1,000 inhabitants in 1951; between 1984 and 1991, the rate decreased from 12.7 to 10.1 births per 1,000 persons, placing Greece at or below the average growth level of nearly all other Western industrialized nations. Males, whose average life expectancy of seventy-five years is five years less than that for females, make up 49 percent of the population.

In 1990 approximately 59,000 marriages took place in Greece. Of the women who married that year, most (40 percent) were in the age-group between twenty and twenty-four, while 26 percent were between twenty-five and twenty-nine. Of the men, 38 percent were between twenty-five and twenty-nine, and 22 percent were in each of the age-groups immediately younger and older. In 1991 some 6,351 marriages, or 0.6 percent, ended in divorce. Of the 102,229 births recorded in 1990, some 7 percent were to women aged fifteen to nineteen, 31 percent to women between twenty and twenty-four, and 34 percent to women between twenty-five and twenty-nine.

In the early 1990s, demographic forecasts predicted that the population would remain virtually stable in the period between 1990 and 2010; however, the demographic characteristics of the population were changing dramatically. In 1990 the working-age population (people between ages fifteen and sixty-four) numbered 6,703,000, or 66 percent of the total. An expected rise of over 600,000 in the elderly population (from 14 percent to 20 percent of the total) would shrink the percentage of working-age Greeks to 64 percent by 2010. In the same period, young adults (ages fifteen to twenty-four) were expected to drop from 15 percent to less than 11 percent of the total. Greece is therefore participating in the general European trend of aging populations and fewer individuals entering the workplace, but in 1991 Greece's ratio of thirty-one elderly people per 100 working-age citizens was the highest in Western Europe.

Since World War II, the population of Greece has shifted noticeably into the geographical axis defined by Athens in the south and Thessaloniki in the north. The highest rates of migration occurred between 1950 and 1967, a period of major change in all of Greek society (see The Social Order, this ch.). As people flocked to Athens in greater numbers than at any time since the late nineteenth century, the average annual growth rate of the capital exceeded 4 percent between 1951 and 1956 (see table 2, Appendix). After the hardships of World War II and the Civil War, the government's promise of new economic opportunity, centered in Athens, attracted many villagers. Between 1955 and 1971, an estimated 1.5 million farmers left their land. In the 1960s, the share of agricultural workers in the work force dropped from 53 percent to 41 percent (see table 3, Appendix).

As the first members of rural families established lives in the city, they formed the basis for a type of chain migration. In 1960 an estimated 56 percent of the inhabitants of Greater Athens were postwar migrants. The trend slowed somewhat in the 1960s and 1970s, but in those decades Athens grew by 37 percent and 19 percent, respectively, and Thessaloniki grew by 46 percent and 27 percent, respectively. Migration to Athens came mainly from southern Greece and the islands, that to Thessaloniki from the north of the country. By 1981 cities with more than 10,000 people contained 56.2 percent of the population, towns of 2,000 to 10,000 people contained 11.9 percent, and the remaining 31.9 percent lived in villages or rural communities.

In 1991 the population of Athens, the largest city, was 748,000, but the population of Greater Athens, including its

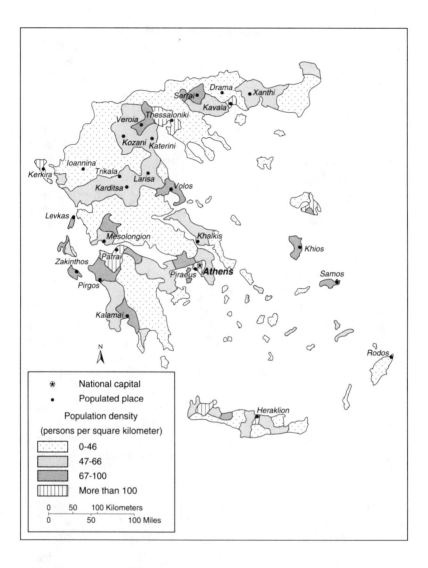

Figure 8. Population Density, 1994

port city of Piraeus, was 3.1 million. The second largest city, Thessaloniki, had 396,000 people in 1991, but only four other cities, Patras, Heraklion, Volos, and Larisa, had populations over 100,000.

Emigration and Immigration

The long tradition of emigration from the Greek mainland

began in the eighth century B.C., when Greeks began to colonize the shores of the eastern and western Mediterranean Sea and the Black Sea. Overpopulation, foreign trade, and self-improvement have remained the primary incentives for emigration through the last 2,700 years, although specific political and economic factors have varied.

The Greek diaspora, or dispersion of Greeks to other parts of the world, occurred in phases determined by historical events. In the fifteenth century, the fall of the Byzantine Empire to the Ottoman Turks triggered large-scale emigration to avoid foreign domination. In the later centuries of Ottoman rule, however, Greeks moved around the Mediterranean to take advantage of favorable trading conditions that became available as far away as Odessa and Marseilles (see The Ottoman Era, ch. 1). Later waves of emigration followed the appearance of new markets in Egypt and Asia Minor in the nineteenth century, the destruction caused by World War II and the Civil War of 1946–49, and the economic woes of the mid-1960s. Conversely, major immigrations occurred after independence was won in 1832, with the population exchange of the 1923 Treaty of Lausanne, and when the restriction of minority rights drove out the Greek émigré communities in twentieth-century Russia, Bulgaria, Turkey, and Egypt.

Before 1890 Greek emigrants went mostly to other areas of the Mediterranean. In the twentieth century, however, the favored destinations have been Australia, Canada, and the United States, in all of which sizeable Greek communities have developed. The number of United States citizens with Greek ancestry has been estimated as between 1 million and 3 million.

Between 1944 and 1974, nearly 1 million persons emigrated from Greece, a far higher number than those who immigrated. Beginning in the 1960s, over two-thirds of long-term Greek emigrants went to Western Europe, mainly as guest workers. As many as 80 percent of those workers went to the Federal Republic of Germany (West Germany) in the 1960s and the early 1970s. In 1973 about 430,000 Greeks were working in West Germany. After 1974, however, emigration began dropping sharply, finally stabilizing at a rate of a few thousand persons annually. After a flurry of immigration in the late seventies, mainly as a result of the return of Civil War political refugees and most of the West European guest workers, the return of Greeks to their homeland from Western Europe also stabilized at a rate of 3,000 and 5,000 persons per year.

In the early 1990s, about 500,000 foreign citizens were living in Greece, of whom about 300,000 were working or seeking employment. Thus nearly 5 percent of the total population and 7.5 percent of the workforce was foreign. Substantial portions of some national groups, especially Albanians and Egyptians, were in the country illegally. Since 1987 about 37,000 persons of Greek origin who formerly lived in the Soviet Union entered Greece. An estimated 500,000 ethnic Greeks remain in the former Soviet Union, returning to their homeland at a rate of 2,000 to 5,000 per year in the early 1990s.

Since the early 1970s, the population of legal foreign workers in Greece has remained steady at about 30,000. Until the mid-1980s, illegal employment of foreigners was confined mainly to seasonal work in agriculture and tourism; after sharp increases in the last decade, however, the number of illegal foreign workers is estimated to be almost ten times greater than that of legal foreign workers. Little social conflict has resulted from this change, however, because illegal workers most often solve seasonal and unskilled labor shortages rather than competing with Greeks for more desirable jobs.

Current government policy is to aid Greek citizens to return from abroad and to accept Greek immigrants from the former Soviet Union. In general, Greece does not encourage naturalization of immigrants, however. It cooperates with other EU countries to develop common migration policies and to reduce illegal immigration.

The case of Albania presents unique problems for the makers of immigration policy. Under Albanian communist regimes, the status of the Greek minority in Albania, estimated variously between 59,000 and 400,000 in 1989, was a troublesome issue between the two countries. The chief disputes concerned the number of Greeks in Albania and the extent of their freedom of expression, religion, and culture. Although tension lessened in the late 1980s, the large-scale flight of Greeks (and Albanians) from postcommunist Albania into Greece presented a new version of the previous ethnic tension.

Ethnic Minorities

The population of Greece is quite homogeneous, with an estimated 98 percent of Greek descent. The largest minority groups are Albanians, Armenians, Bulgarians, Roma (Gypsies),

Macedonian Slavs, Pomaks (Muslim Slavs from Bulgaria), Turks, and Vlachs (a Romanian group). The Muslim population, estimated at about 120,000, is concentrated in Thrace (Greece's easternmost land region) and the Dodecanese Islands off the southwestern coast of Turkey, because the Treaty of Lausanne (1923) repatriated all Turks from Greece except for those in Thrace and the Dodecancese Islands. In the early 1990s, the Albanian population fluctuated and caused international tension as illegal refugees entered Greece to escape Albania's unstable conditions.

The Social Order

As late as 1980, an estimated two-thirds of murders or attempted murders in Greece were inspired by a male's need to uphold family honor in the face of public humiliation caused by the victim (see Crime, ch. 5). Although many of the superficial aspects of traditional social behavior, relationships, and roles have changed, especially in the cities, modern Greek society still retains elements of a much more traditional set of values, such as the protection of a family's reputation. Nevertheless, since the nineteenth century upward mobility has been unusually common in Greece; because the ideal of generational improvement has been widely distributed, Greece's class system has been much more flexible than that of other European countries.

The Family

The family is the basic social unit of all strata of Greek society, whether rural or urban. For an individual not to marry or to remain separate from his or her family is viewed as unusual behavior. Sons and daughters still live with their families until they marry, bypassing the Western tradition of living independently between those two stages of life. Families play a large role in selection of a mate, although the traditional arranged marriage is now less frequent than in previous generations. In rural areas, tradition calls for courtship to be a time when society examines a young woman's conduct to evaluate her character. A potential groom and his family still consider a woman's reputation, health, age, and appearance, although the elements of reputation have changed since the 1960s. Until the late 1960s, modesty and innocence, the chief ingredients of a young woman's honor, were demonstrated by her dress as well as her behavior. By 1970, however, young women commonly dressed in fashionable West European styles, and chaperones were no longer required.

The basic household, or nuclear family, includes a husband, wife, and their unmarried children. This unit may also include a parent or another family relative, and in some regions a young married couple may live with the parents of one spouse until they can gain financial independence. In village tradition, the groom takes his bride to live at least for a short time with his parents; they may remain in that house or one in the same village, creating an extended family. In the Cyclades Islands and the Dodecanese Islands, the wife's parents and village are the traditional destination of the newlyweds. The same pattern has been adapted to city life, where the wife's parents may provide housing for in-laws from several areas of Greece.

The primary purpose of marriage is thought to be to produce children, without whom the couple would not be happy. The second goal is preservation and augmentation of the family property from the previous generation. In rural areas, the nuclear family is a source of agricultural labor. Other forms of family enterprise, such as fishing and small businesses, receive similar benefits from offspring.

The Role of Women

In some ways, the traditional roles of women in Greek society have been differentiated by class. Until the end of World War II, the economic basis of most of society was either agriculture or fishing, activities that were simply passed down through generations, together with the social structures that made them work best. The common view historically was that women were basically inferior, sexually dangerous, and vulnerable. Accordingly, women were expected to exercise authority over others only informally and in specific parts of the extended family and society.

In the traditional standards for peasant women, honorable behavior, or *philotimo*, required caring for the family and remaining in a domestic context where they were submissive to the opinions and demands of men. The actual ingredients of that cultural code of honor varied somewhat among regions and even among villages. In general, however, women were taught to restrain sexual impulses because failure to do so would tempt men into improper conduct. Straying from this code brought shame to the woman and social derision to her husband, if the woman were married, because he would be expected to control his wife. Marriage and motherhood transformed a woman's image from that of modest virgin to the dominating force in the household and among her children. Within the private sphere of the family, the opinions of the wife and mother received great respect as she evaluated the behavior of her husband and children. Her role was especially important in protecting the family's honor.

In both urban and rural society, motherhood remains an important ideal, grandmothers still play an important role in child rearing, and women continue to be the chief social links and organizers of rites of passage—in spite of the variations that urbanization has introduced into the structure of such relationships. Rural life provides a closer-knit social and family grouping, whereas urban wives see their relatives less often and have fewer close bonds with the informal support system composed of neighbors. The faster pace of social change in the cities also shrinks the common ground of understanding between mothers and daughters.

The Westernizing influence of the nineteenth century brought noticeable changes in the external lifestyle of women in the Greek oligarchy. But, as women imitated the wives of Western monarchs and diplomats, they lost the fundamental economic role and the practical skills possessed by women in rural Greek society. Some experts argue that this development actually reduced the image of women in the Westernized elite, turning them into social ornaments. At the same time, however, the basic prescription for modest virginity before marriage and fidelity and demure behavior after marriage persisted in the elite as it did in the lower classes.

The active participation of women in the Greek resistance movement of World War II brought about fundamental changes in their relation to men in Greek society. Then, in the postwar years, urbanization, industrialization, and the consequent growth of the middle class led to massive changes in Greek society, and Western alliances internationalized the outlook of Greeks. Women received the right to vote in the early 1950s, and a new class of female wage earners grew rapidly in economic and bureaucratic fields. The growth of participation was slower in politics.

In two notable periods, military governments attempted to crush women's movements in Greece. In the 1930s, the regime of Ioannis Metaxas had repressed the League of Women's

Rights. The last concerted effort to reassert the traditional norms, values, and behavior for women occurred between 1967 and 1974 under the military regime of Georgios Papadopoulos. The Papadopoulos regime's demands for subservience by women, the institution of dress codes for women, and the prohibition of mixed social events for students yielded a sharp increase in women's demands for equality and liberation when the regime was toppled in 1974.

Despite the repression of women's rights groups, women played an active role in opposition to the military regime, and the Greek feminist movement expanded and diversified during that period. The feminist dialogue already prominent in Western Europe and North America spread gradually into Greece in the 1970s, although women's organizations often lost their autonomy as they and their agendas became subordinate to the leftist political parties that gained strength at the same time (see The Return of the Left, ch. 4).

The pressure brought by women's movements, combined with economic needs, broadened general support for major social legislation by the first PASOK administration (1981–85) of Andreas Papandreou. Accordingly, the Family Law of 1983 made equality of the sexes the law of the land. Until that time, the husband had formal authority within the family, in representing the family to the world outside the home, and in acting as host and main provider. The 1983 law replaced these familial relationships with even distribution between the spouses of decision-making authority and obligations to contribute to family needs. The husband no longer could legally administer a wife's property or forbid her to work. Naturally, legislation in such private matters had only a gradual impact in a highly traditional society.

The decriminalization of adultery was another legislative reform of the early 1980s that had resonance in the structure of Greek society. The overturned adultery statutes, whose application followed the traditional sexual stereotypes by falling predominantly on women, had called for fines or imprisonment. Legalization of abortion, a process that had begun in the late 1970s with expansion of the conditions under which the law permitted abortion, brought conflict with the Orthodox Church and conservative elements of secular society. Abortion on demand at state expense was legalized in 1986. The number of legal abortions rose from 180 in 1985 to 7,338 in 1989.

Between the end of World War II and the mid-1980s, as more women moved to cities and finished rearing their families while still young enough to work, women's participation in the Greek work force increased dramatically. Between 1977 and 1987, the share of women in the work force increased from 32 percent to 43 percent (although growth in that figure stopped for a period in the mid-1980s). The female work force in 1987 included almost 45 percent in agriculture, 22 percent in industry, and 34 percent in the service sector. Experts differed sharply, however, as to whether a given job was now more open to a person of either sex or whether more women-only jobs had merely been created during that period. Women's participation was encouraged by the legal requirement of twelve to sixteen weeks of maternity leave at full pay, a rule strengthened in 1992 by the EC's requirement that all member countries offer at least fourteen weeks with at least statutory sick pay.

The educational advancement of women paralleled their entry into the work force in the 1980s. The share of female university students grew from about 30 percent in the 1970s to about 53 percent in 1989, although a disparity remained between the sexes in the numbers holding university degrees in the late 1980s. In 1990 Greece lagged in availability of part-time postsecondary education programs, which affected women more than men.

Women have moved into Greek government circles gradually, although more rapidly than in most other Western countries. The three PASOK administrations, which took office in 1981, 1985, and 1993, respectively, each had a female minister of culture (for most of that time, the actress Melina Mercouri) and several female deputy ministers; in 1993 the Ministry of Justice of the Mitsotakis administration was headed by a woman. In the 1980s and the 1990s, the ministries of culture, health, welfare, and social security and foreign affairs usually had at least a female deputy minister. The first woman was elected to the national legislature, the Assembly, in 1954, and since that time many women have been elected to that body. A political party, Synaspismos, was led by a woman for several years in the 1980s. And in 1994, the leader of the Communist Party of Greece (Kommunistikon Komma Ellados—KKE) was a woman.

Religion

An estimated 97 percent of the country's population identi-

fies itself as belonging to the Greek branch of the Eastern
Orthodox Church of Christ, commonly known as the Orthodox Church of Greece. The Greek church became autocephalous (independent of the patriarchate in Constantinople) in
1833, shortly after Greek independence, but a close relationship remains among most branches of Orthodoxy (see Out of
the Ottoman Empire, ch. 1). In many respects, church and
state are not separate in the Western sense in Greece. In spite
of reforms in the 1980s and a loss of some influence since
World War II, the Orthodox Church remains the officially
established religious institution of the country, and from that
position it exerts considerable influence in secular matters (see
Church and State, ch. 4). The largest non-Orthodox religious
groups in Greece are Roman Catholic, Protestant, and Muslim.

The Orthodox Church of Greece

An important aspect of Greek culture is the close connection between "being Greek" and "being Orthodox," which is
based on long historical tradition. In the Byzantine Empire
(A.D. 330–1453), the emperor was called God's vice-regent and
his empire a model of heavenly order. Given this status, the
emperor could preach and receive communion like a priest
and convene church councils. Under the Ottoman Empire
(1453–1821), the patriarch of Constantinople exercised wide-
ranging secular powers over Orthodox Christians in Greece
and elsewhere in the empire (see The Nature of Ottoman
Rule, ch. 1).

The constitution of 1975 describes the Orthodox Church as
the "established religion" of Greece. The seemingly minor
change from the previous constitutional term *state religion* was
considered a significant recognition of religious plurality when
the new constitution was adopted.

The official status of the church confers special privileges
and obligations. For example, the president of Greece must be
affiliated with the church; he or she is sworn in according to
the rites of the church; and major church holidays are also
state holidays. Most top positions in the military, the judiciary,
and public schools are de facto restricted to Orthodox candidates. Although the constitution stipulates freedom of religion,
it also forbids all religious groups to proselytize among Orthodox believers unless they have specific permission. Although
Greek law in general neither defines proselytization nor
enforces the prohibition, foreigners and Greeks affiliated with

Roadside prayer shrine,
Epirus
Courtesy Sam and
Sarah Stulberg

Ninth-century Byzantine
cathedral of Saint
Eleutherios, Athens
Courtesy Bernice Huffman
Collection, Library of
Congress, Washington

some non-mainstream religious sects occasionally have been imprisoned for religious activities construed as violating the constitution. Catholics, Jews, and Muslims have not received such treatment, however.

The church depends on the state for financial and legal support: the state pays the clergy, subsidizes the church budget, and administers church property. (In the 1980s, the church turned down an opportunity to gain greater economic independence by reorganizing its finances to pay the clergy directly.) Religious education is mandatory for Greek Orthodox children in public primary and secondary schools, and the state subsidizes religious studies at institutions of higher learning. The church is supervised by the Ministry of Education and Religious Affairs.

The institutionalization of Greek Orthodoxy as the official state religion gives the church a powerful voice in political policy making and the organization of society. The church also has a vested interest in preventing social reform that would weaken the established social order and blur the identification of "Greekness" with Orthodoxy. Its defense of traditional values has been especially strong on issues such as the role of women; particularly in rural areas, the attitudes and values of women are predominantly defined by church doctrine.

In 1981 the socialist PASOK government led by Andreas Papandreou came into power promising to reform antiquated aspects of Greek society. The separation of church and state was one element among PASOK's proposals. In subsequent years, the church objected strongly to separation and forced capitulation or compromise on most issues. The conservative ND, Papandreou's main opposition, had given only tepid support to the separation of church and state prior to 1981, but, beginning with the 1981 election, the ND changed its position to one of strong opposition to separation and to the rest of PASOK's social reforms.

The only successful PASOK proposal that directly affected the church was the legalization of civil marriage ceremonies. Until 1983 the church had recognized only religious marriages and forbidden the marriage of Orthodox believers to nonbelievers. Seeing the socialist legalization of civil marriage as a threat to the foundations of society, the church used its influence in the Ministry of Education and Religious Affairs to force a compromise in the Family Law of 1983. The original legislation would have made civil marriage the only legally recognized form, with religious marriage merely an optional ceremony. The compromise made both forms legal. Since that time, about 95 percent of marriages in Greece have occurred in the church; a large share of the civil ceremonies involved a partner not of the Orthodox faith.

The ownership of church property was another controversial issue of the 1980s because the socialists proposed transferring fallow farmland owned by the church through a state agency to agricultural cooperatives for cultivation. This suggestion, originally made by the military dictatorship in the late 1960s, was finally abandoned in the early 1980s because of the hostility it aroused from the church toward the government. In 1987 the minister of education and religious affairs, Antonis Tritsis, revived the proposal—purportedly not as an effort to weaken the connection between the church and Greek nationhood, but to increase the church's participation in civil society. Although large numbers of lay intellectuals and some church officials supported the idea initially, the public and most of the church hierarchy saw it as an attack on church prerogatives. Under strong pressure from that constituency, supporters in the church withdrew, and the emasculated bill that was passed never was enforced.

Lay theologians traditionally have played a large role in the intellectual base of the Orthodox Church, and the relation of church and state is a frequent topic of their voluminous writings. In 1994 the church found itself in transition, symbolized by conflict over the choice of a successor to the ailing primate, Archbishop Seraphim of Athens. At this critical point, progressive and conservative factions in the hierarchy disagreed over the church's future role: the former advocated a greater direct response to the needs of people; the latter defended the church's special status, arguing against the loss of authority that such a change might incur. In this controversy, the lay theologians played a more marginal role than they had in past policy discussions of such magnitude.

The church is divided administratively into the Monastic Church of Greece, which has seventy-eight dioceses; the semi-autonomous Church of Crete, with eight dioceses; four dioceses in the Dodecanese Islands; and the self-governing monastic community of Mt. Athos, which has constitutionally guaranteed autonomy. The church is governed by a Holy Synod consisting of all the diocesan bishops, who convene once a year under the chairmanship of the archbishop of Athens, who is automatically the primate. For day-to-day administration of the church, a supreme executive body of twelve bishops is chosen from the Holy Synod. They serve a one-year term under the primate, who serves as the synod's thirteenth member.

The Church of Crete is made up of seven metropolitans (dioceses) and the archbishopric of Crete in the capital, Heraklion. The church is administered by a synod of the seven metropolitans, presided over by the archbishop; it is under the ultimate spiritual and administrative jurisdiction of the patriarch of Constantinople (whose title retains the former name of Istanbul) rather than the primate of Greece. In 1994 the leader of the Church of Crete was Archbishop Timotheos. The four metropolitan sees of the Dodecanese Islands and the Monastic

Republic of Mt. Athos are also administratively dependent on the patriarch of Constantinople, but the constitution gives Mt. Athos special protection. Mt. Athos is administered by a council of twenty monks, one from each monastery.

Although the *millet* administrative system of the Ottoman Empire made the patriarch of Constantinople politically responsible for the entire Orthodox population in the empire, the church never had a single figure wielding the level of power and authority possessed by the pope in the Roman Catholic Church. The realm of the patriarch of Constantinople is officially called the Ecumenical Patriarchate of Constantinople, and it is the patriarch who has represented Orthodox believers in discussions with the Vatican about possible reunification since the Second Vatican Council in the early 1960s. No appreciable rapprochement is expected soon, however.

The patriarch, who is an ethnic Greek but must reside in Istanbul and be a citizen of Turkey, may not interfere in the affairs of the fifteen autocephalous churches into which Orthodox Christianity is divided. As primate of the Greek church, the archbishop of Athens differs from the pope in relying on consensus and popular approval of his decisions on administration and doctrine, rather than on the doctrine of infallibility. Orthodox doctrine, including that of the Greek branch, emphasizes the communality of its bishops and the direct preaching and performance of pastoral duties by bishops within their comparatively small dioceses. Like the other autocephalous churches, the Greek branch has its own liturgical language, but it shares with them the sacraments, doctrine, and traditions handed down from the early church as the correct, hence orthodox, practice and belief.

Orthodox practice differs from that of other Christian religions in other ways. Orthodox babies are baptized with a threefold immersion; then they are confirmed as members of the church immediately, making them eligible to receive Holy Communion. The Anointing of the Sick is practiced not only for the dying but also for the ill because the sacrament is believed to bring healing and the forgiveness of sins, a manifestation of the Orthodox belief in the unity of body and soul.

Of the major religious festivals on the Orthodox calendar, which are called the Twelve Great Feasts, eight honor Christ and four honor the Mother of God. Easter, the Feast of Feasts, is the most joyously celebrated holiday. The four major periods of fasting are at Lent, Christmas, Assumption, and the Fast of the Apostles. Church buildings are normally in a cross-in-square configuration with a dome and an icon-covered screen separating the sanctuary from the rest of the church. In traditional churches, worshipers stand throughout services, and seats are located only along the walls; however, many churches in Athens now provide seating throughout.

Orthodox clergy include married and celibate priests. Married men may become priests, but marriage is not permitted after ordination, and only unmarried priests may move up past the rank of priest. The majority of priests, especially outside urban areas, have primary or secondary education and a modicum of religious training. Most urban priests have at least studied theology at a seminary; priests and bishops in larger cities normally have degrees in theology from universities in Athens or Thessaloniki.

The village priest is the traditional preserver of Greek culture and traditions, and as such he usually enjoys high respect among his parishioners. In poorer parishes, peasants often went into the priesthood for economic advancement, and in many cases a married rural priest continued his secular trade after ordination. By the 1980s, however, the social prestige of the priesthood had dropped, so children received less encouragement to enter that profession. Increasingly university graduates in theology became teachers of religion in secondary schools rather than entering the priesthood. Observers listed the reasons for this trend as the lack of intellectual functions in the priesthood (priests do not regularly give sermons, and few become theologians) and the higher pay received by teachers.

The monastic tradition has always been an important part of Orthodoxy. Unlike Roman Catholic monks, who may teach and do social work, Orthodox monks devote themselves to prayer, painting icons, studying, and producing manuscripts. The ascetic life is seen as an alternative to the martyrdom that monks formerly suffered under religious persecution. The monks are divided into those living as hermits, those living in monasteries, and those living in loosely linked settlements under a single spiritual director. The best-known example of the last category is Mt. Athos, where a spiritual enclave has existed since A.D. 959. In 1990 Mt. Athos, where no female is allowed, had twenty monasteries, of which seventeen were Greek, one Bulgarian, one Russian, and one Serbian. The overall number of Greek monks declined in the 1980s, although Mt. Athos continued to attract young, better-educated monks.

The church plays a different role in Greek cities than in villages. Average church attendance in the cities, where parishes are larger and more impersonal, is lower than in villages. Overall attendance has been estimated at between 20 and 25 percent. (Weekly churchgoing is not obligatory in the Orthodox Church as it is in the Roman Catholic Church.)

For villagers time is marked by the religious calendar, and the local church is the focal point of the community. Because the village priest is a figure familiar to all and lay committees have an input in administering church affairs, identification with village churches is closer than with urban churches. Whatever their location or pattern of public religious observance, many Greeks maintain a corner at home with icons, a special lamp, holy oil, and holy water. Many people have special relationships with saints whose intercession they ask in times of crisis. Superstition and pagan beliefs are still interwoven in religious practices in some rural areas.

Other Religions

In 1992 four Roman Catholic archdioceses were functioning in Greece, including two directly responsible to the Holy See in the Vatican, four dioceses, and the Apostolic Vicariate of Thessaloniki. An estimated 51,380 Roman Catholics lived in Greece at that time. The largest populations are descendants of Venetian settlers in the islands, where three of the four archdioceses are located. These three are the archdioceses of Rhodes; of Corfu, Zacynthus, and Cephalonia in the Ionian Sea; and of Naxos, Andros, Tinos, and Mykonos in the Aegean Sea. Two other Catholic churches, the Uniate Rite and the Armenian Rite, also have small parishes in Greece.

The main Protestant group is the Greek Evangelical Church (Reformed), which has thirty churches with an estimated total of 5,000 adherents. In the seventeenth century, Orthodoxy was influenced strongly by Calvinism, the predominant theology of the West European Reformed churches, and during that period of shifting religious politics several attempts were made to join Orthodox and Protestant churches. Today the Orthodox Church of Greece is in communion with the Church of England but not with the Roman Catholic Church.

Greek law recognizes a chief mufti as religious head of the Muslim population, which numbered about 132,000 in 1975 and included only Sunni (see Glossary) Muslims. Some 83 percent of Greece's Muslims are Turkish speaking; the other 17

One of the Meteora monastery group, Thessaly, atop a rock pinnacle
Courtesy Sam and Sarah Stulberg

percent are Pomaks and Gypsies. The Turkish Muslims are concentrated in Thrace and the Dodecanese Islands, where government funds maintained 205 mosques and two seminaries were functioning in the early 1980s. Alleged confiscation of Muslim religious property has been an issue of confrontation with the Greek government.

Before World War II, Greece had a Jewish population of about 75,000, with the largest concentration in Thessaloniki, where the Jews played a key role in the city's rich cultural and commercial activity. An estimated 60,000 Jews in Thessaloniki were either executed or sent to the concentration camp at Auschwitz by the Nazis during the occupation; in the early 1990s, Greece's Jewish population was estimated at about 5,000. The Central Board of the Jewish Communities of Greece, located in Athens, is the main administrative body of Judaism.

Language

Greece is linguistically homogeneous; only an estimated 2 to 3 percent of the population does not use Greek as the primary language. Because of this uniformity, the national census omitted the category of mother tongue after 1951. Modern Greek is spoken on the mainland, on most of the surrounding islands, in the Greek community of Istanbul, in most of Cyprus, and in some villages of Calabria in southern Italy. The most frequently used other languages are Turkish, Slavic Macedonian, Vlach (a Romanian dialect), Albanian, and Pomak (a Bulgarian dialect). Greek is a direct descendant of an Indo-European language spoken by civilizations in the northeastern Mediterranean for centuries before Christ.

The Greek language, in its several variations, has been used to record each step in an unbroken literary tradition stretching almost 3,000 years—a role that no other European language has been able to play (see table 4, Appendix). Modern Greek retains many of the linguistic qualities, and a high degree of unity, from its original stock. In spite of this continuity, the chief linguistic problem for Greeks has been a dichotomy between usage of the spoken language and the traditional literary language. That divergence continues, with three forms in varying degrees of use.

Koine, which means common, developed from an Attic dialect and became the spoken language of Greece at the time that Alexander the Great consolidated his empire (see The Fire from Heaven: Alexander the Great, ch. 1). The New Testament, the writings of the early Christian church fathers, and all of Greek literature for about ten centuries were written in this language. As Koine underwent internal modifications and influences from other languages in the Byzantine period (until 1453), scholars preserved the Greek that had been used by the classical writers beginning with Homer, in a purer form known as Attic Greek.

The dichotomy between Koine and classical Greek grew even wider when a new feeling of national identity arose in the late eighteenth century. Language became a political issue as people debated which form of Greek would be most appropriate for the independent state that they contemplated founding. In the opinion of some people, the classical roots of Attic Greek best represented the Greek nation but for others the use of Koine in official Constantinople gave that form a more recent claim to acceptance. A third group favored a modified form of demotic Greek, the modern spoken language, because they equated nationhood with the practice of the majority of Greeks.

Modern demotic Greek is based on the version of the spoken language used in the Peloponnesus. The language's evolution in the Byzantine period is imprecisely known because its use was restricted to speech and informal documents that generally were not preserved. Elements of demotic Greek had begun appearing in some poetic works in the fourteenth century, but until almost the end of the nineteenth century only Crete and Cyprus used it for serious literature or translations from Western languages.

In this situation, the nationalist Adamantios Korais (1748–1833) suggested a compromise between Attic and demotic Greek. Therefore, a new, artificial Greek, called Katharevousa (from *katharos*, meaning pure), was devised and accepted as the official language of the newly independent Greek state. Katharevousa, which was an attempt to recover elements of classical Greek, remained the official state language until 1976. Although the new form gained in intelligibility among the emerging state elite in the nineteenth century, a renaissance of the spoken language occurred at the same time. Katharevousa had the effect of homogenizing Greek dialects, and a number of literary figures such as Alexandros Papadiamandis produced notable works of literature in Katharevousa. In 1888 Ioannis Psicharis, a scholar of the speech of the common people and the leader of the demotic movement, wrote the first serious book in demotic Greek.

Although demotic Greek had been used in primary education almost continuously since 1917, Katharevousa remained the standard language of secondary and university education until 1976, when a law replaced it with demotic, or standard modern Greek. Use of Katharevousa was enforced especially stringently during the military dictatorship of 1967–74. After 1976, however, the practices of government agencies, which previously had used Katharevousa, varied widely because some, most notably the courts, lagged behind the others in adopting demotic Greek. Thus a single government document originating from more than one agency could contain more than one language style. Although the previous mixture of styles had disappeared from newspapers in the early 1990s, Greeks still needed to know Katharevousa because of its survival in many older books, laws, government publications, and church documents.

A number of local dialects comprise the third form of Greek in active use, although the dialects became more standardized after the introduction of Katharevousa. The greatest variation from standard Greek is shown in Tsakonian, which is spoken in the mountains of the Peloponnesus, and in the dialects closely matching those spoken by Greeks in southern Italy and Turkey. Each of the other, more common dialects is distinguished by one or more specific variations in sound and inflection patterns. Of that group, Old Athenian, the language of Athens until independence, is now used on the southern coast of Attica and on the island of Euboea. The northern dialects are spoken in the northern parts of the mainland and of Euboea and in the northern Aegean Sea. And the dialects of Crete, Cyprus, Rhodes, Chios, and other islands show another set of characteristics. Generally speaking, class and regional variations from standard Greek in pronunciation, construction, and vocabulary are less distinctive than are the differences between provincial English and French and their respective "standard" forms.

Education

The Greek culture, with its roots in classical civilization, has always placed high value on education. Especially in the postwar period, the urbanization of the Greek population has been closely connected with the desire for education, which since the nineteenth century has been considered by much of society as the key to upward social mobility and a better life.

Historical Background

The education system established shortly after Greece gained independence was the result of a combination of the French Elementary School Law of 1833, the Bavarian system of secondary education, and the pre-World War I German university system. Between Greece's independence in 1832 and the early 1990s, many elements of that system survived with very little change under a great variety of political leadership. The major factors in this stability were the obligatory use of Katharevousa, the artificial official state language; poor funding of education; centralization; and the influence of the Orthodox Church of Greece on secular schools. Until 1976 employment in business and the civil service required fluency in Katharevousa, creating a vicious cycle that sustained the language in schools spite of its distance from spoken, or demotic, Greek (see Language, this ch.).

In the twentieth century, a half-dozen reform programs failed to make a significant impact on the system's reliance on traditional subjects and teaching methods. In 1974 the collapse of military rule and the Karamanlis government's quest for membership in the EC began a wave of new legislation aimed at closing the gap between Greece and other European countries, especially in the realm of technical education. Touching all levels of Greek education at varying depths, the reforms continued through the 1970s. The 1976 reform changed the number of compulsory years in the basic schooling cycle from six to nine and revamped the technical education program. The 1977 reform made technical education more widely available, with the aim of increasing the ratio of graduates with practical rather than academic expertise. Adult education was also decentralized in 1976. In the 1970s, there was a new emphasis on mathematics, the physical sciences, analytical thinking rather than rote learning, and individualized teaching.

Meanwhile, the rapid urbanization of the 1950s through the 1970s put new strains on the schools. As the rural population decreased, schooling in many remote areas deteriorated further because normal classes could not be filled from the local population. And the urban influx at the other end of the process forced many city schools to operate double shifts—especially once attendance became compulsory in the *gymnasia* (sing., *gymnasium*), the initial stage of secondary school.

The first PASOK government, which took office in 1981, increased education's share of the national budget by almost 50 percent in its first four years. The PASOK program also centralized primary and secondary education under the Ministry of National Education and Religious Affairs (the word *national* was dropped from the ministry name after 1993), standardized curricula and teaching methods, and assigned inspectors to ensure compliance. In the 1990s, demand for modernization of the Greek education system has accelerated as membership in the EC (now the EU) and continued urbanization have placed more emphasis on reaching West European standards.

Education Administration

The education system is highly centralized, in keeping with its French and German models. The Ministry of Education and Religious Affairs approves all decisions on curricula, hiring practices, examinations, and standards. The Center for Educational Studies and Inservice Training advises the ministry on curriculum development. The country is divided into fifteen administrative regions for education, each of which is subdivided into 240 districts headed by inspectors who monitor curriculum application. Universities, all of which are financed by the state, are governed internally by a faculty senate, but all policy decisions must be ratified by the Ministry of Education and Religious Affairs.

Primary and Secondary Education

Article Sixteen of the 1975 constitution states that "the goal of education is the moral, intellectual, professional, and physical development of their [the students'] national and religious consciousness so that they become free and responsible citizens." To accomplish this goal, nine years of education, normally accomplished from ages six through fifteen, are free and compulsory. Of the compulsory years, the first six are in primary school, the next three in a *gymnasium*; an additional three secondary years (in a college-preparatory *lyceum*—pl., *lycea*) are optional but also free of charge. Students on the college-preparatory track may choose a classical or a scientific option, the latter of which is also offered by technical schools.

All state schools are coeducational, and since 1976 instruction in secondary schools has been in demotic Greek rather than the formal Katharevousa. (This change was made in primary grades in 1964.)

Preschool is also free for children between the ages of three and one-half to five and one-half years, an option taken up mainly in urban areas. Urbanization increased preschool enrollments in the 1970s and the 1980s, although fewer than half the children in that age-group attended in 1992 (see table 5, Appendix). After the reform of 1976 added the formerly optional first three years of secondary school to the compulsory program, enrollment in the first stage of secondary school increased sharply. But enrollment in the optional secondary stage dropped during that period because the reform of 1977 channeled many students out of the college preparatory line into secondary technical institutions.

Following its reorganization in 1977, the technical and vocational training system offers three options: a technical *lyceum*, a public or private secondary school, or a postsecondary center for higher technical and vocational education. The technical *lycea* offer programs in chemical, electrical, mechanical, or metallurgical engineering; business administration; architectural design; social services; and agriculture. Graduates can then attend a higher vocational training school or seek employment in their specialty. The 1977 reform also sought to raise the status of all technical schools by including nontechnical curricula and upgrading their standards for examinations and faculty credentials. Promotion to the *lyceum* is automatic for graduates of the *gymnasium*. The Panhellenic Examinations are administered in two stages, at the end of grades eleven and twelve, to determine eligibility for university enrollment.

In 1989 some 93 percent of children in the primary school age range were enrolled in school, and 87 percent of children in the secondary range were enrolled. A total of 13,229 preschools and primary schools had an estimated enrollment of 976,444, and 3,468 secondary schools enrolled 843,732 students. Fewer than 10 percent of primary and secondary students attend private schools. Religious schools do not exist because religious instruction is compulsory for Greek Orthodox students in public schools. In 1989 the male-to-female ratio in primary and secondary schools was fifty-two males to forty-eight females.

The University System

Article Sixteen of the Greek constitution prohibits the operation of private institutions of higher learning. The cultural rationale behind that position is that education should not be commercialized at any level, nor should its availability be determined by the workings of the marketplace. In the early 1990s, the legalization of private institutions of higher education, urged by many education experts, was blocked by a PASOK government that was averse to opening a traditional bastion of state control to privatization. In practice, this situation has meant that the full burden of supporting Greece's system of universities and higher technical schools falls on the state budget, hence ultimately on the Greek taxpayers. It also means that the supply of higher education does not respond to increased demand except insofar as a government makes a conscious policy adjustment.

The high social status conferred by a university education causes enormous demand for the relatively small number of places in the university system. This trend sharpened in the early 1990s; in 1994 about 20,000 university slots and 20,000 technical college slots were contested among about 140,000 secondary school graduates. Although the number of university acceptances had increased after the reforms of the late 1970s and the early 1980s, the number of applicants increased at a much faster rate during that period. The economic stimulus of EU membership was a major factor in continuing that trend into the 1990s.

Because of their limited funding, Greek universities offer very few programs beyond the bachelor's degree, and faculty have little incentive to do advanced research. The ratio of faculty to students is also quite high in most universities. The highly politicized administration of Greek universities was based on a "chair" system that put groups of associated departments under the control of senior faculty and discouraged innovative teaching methods. A 1983 law was passed to democratize university administration by replacing the system with American-style departments and giving junior faculty and student representatives a voice in policy making. The restructuring was achieved despite stiff resistance from entrenched senior faculty. Another measure established a National University Council to advise the government on higher education policy and an Academy of Letters and Sciences to set university standards.

The intense demand for higher education has had several results. Students with sufficient means attend as much as two years of supplementary private schooling in specialized *frontisteria* (sing., *frontisterion*), either during their last two secondary years or after graduation, to prepare them for entrance examinations. (The quality of these expensive private schools is quite uneven; statistics show that on the average they make only a marginal difference in test results.)

Many of those students who are not accepted by a Greek university go abroad to study—the largest number to Italy and significant numbers to Britain, France, Germany, and the United States. In the mid-1980s, Greece had the highest ratio of foreign to domestic university enrollment in the world. The increasing numbers of Greek students at foreign universities

The Athens Academy, national research center for science and the humanities
Courtesy Press and Information Office, Embassy of Greece, Washington

drained funds from the domestic economy, and a significant number of students established careers abroad, depriving their homeland of their expertise. In the 1990s, foreign universities began to open branches in Greece, where Greek students could begin study programs that must be completed at the parent institution abroad, increasing the "brain drain." The sale of fraudulent university degrees also was a frequent occurrence in the 1990s.

Private postsecondary institutions called "Laboratories of Liberal Studies" now offer three- and four-year programs. Graduates of these programs have been absorbed readily by private industry, despite the fact that their credentials are not the equivalent of university degrees. In 1989 some 194,419 students were enrolled in postsecondary institutions. In 1994 the

Greece: A Country Study

largest universities were the National and Capodistrian University of Athens, the Aristotle University of Thessaloniki, the University of Crete, the University of Thrace, the University of Ioannina, the University of Patras, the National Polytechnic University of Athens, the University of the Aegean (with facilities on several Aegean islands), and the University of Macedonia. In addition, programs in archaeology and Greek studies are offered by American, British, French, German, Italian, and Swedish colleges, primarily for visiting students of those nationalities.

Adult education programs are directed by provincial and local authorities under the general policy guidelines of the Ministry of Education and Religious Affairs. In the provinces, a central goal of adult education is to combat illiteracy, the rate of which was estimated at 6.8 percent of the population in 1990. The rate for females, however, was over four times higher than that for males, reflecting the higher dropout rate of females from secondary school. The rapid spread of primary education in the postwar years reduced Greece's adult illiteracy rate from 72 percent to 10 percent between 1951 and 1981.

Health And Welfare

The health care system of Greece has reformed and grown significantly since 1980, but resources and personnel have been distributed unevenly among geographical regions and within the medical profession. In the early 1990s, indicators for life expectancy and incidence of major diseases were as good as or better than the average for nations of Western Europe.

Health Conditions

In 1991 the infant mortality rate was estimated at about nine deaths per 1,000 live births, an improvement from the 1987 figure of eleven and from the 1960 figure of forty. New specialized facilities outside Athens and Thessaloniki were responsible for a significant improvement in neonatal care in the late 1980s and early 1990s.

In 1992 the death rate in Greece was nine per 1,000 persons. The major causes of death, in order of incidence, are heart disease, malignant tumors, cerebrovascular disorders, accidents, and respiratory diseases. Through November 1991, there were 52.8 cases of acquired immune deficiency syndrome (AIDS) reported per 1 million population, the lowest rate in Europe.

136

By mid-1994, some 916 cases were reported. Of that group, 11 percent contracted AIDS through medical procedures, 5 percent were identified as drug users, and 52 percent were homosexual or bisexual. In mid-1993 the Center for Control of Special Infections, the center for AIDS research in Greece, estimated that 10,000 to 15,000 people in the country were carrying the AIDS-related human immunodeficiency virus (HIV), and that the 9,000 to 13,500 new cases of AIDS expected in the following seven years would place a serious burden on the national health system.

According to a 1994 report, the proportion of drug users in the Greek population doubled in the previous decade. The most frequently used drug is marijuana. Drug use increased most significantly among women and members of the lower class. According to a 1993 survey in Thessaloniki *lycea,* about 10 percent of students between ages fifteen and seventeen had experimented with a narcotic; the most prevalent substance was marijuana. A 1991 report indicated that over half the people detained in prison were taking drugs in prison. The number of drug-related deaths in Greece remained stable in the early 1990s, between sixty-six and seventy-nine per year (see Narcotics Sales; Narcotics Abuse, ch. 5).

In the same decade, tobacco and alcohol use declined, although the proportion of the population using alcohol remained quite high, and about half the adult population, regardless of class, smoked daily. The group with the highest proportion of smokers was males between ages twenty-five and thirty-five.

The major infectious diseases are influenza, pulmonary tuberculosis (resurgent since the mid-1980s), viral and infectious hepatitis, intestinal infections, and chicken pox. Isolated cases of malaria were reported in the early 1990s.

Health Care

In the 1970s, Greece's expenditures for health care were lower than the average for Western nations, about 2.4 percent of the gross domestic product (GDP—see Glossary) for the first half of that decade. Publicly supported health facilities and private medical practices coexisted, and many doctors practiced in both areas. The distinction between public and private treatment was unclear, and members of public plans often received care in both sectors. The public system, in which the patient-to-doctor ratio was very high, generally provided poor service for

Harbor at Patras, northwest Peloponnesus
Courtesy Sam and Sarah Stulberg

which patients had to endure long waits. Often patients in the public system, which nominally ensured free treatment, made informal payments to doctors to receive better care. (Private health care insurance did not exist in that period.) By 1984 such payments made up an estimated 51 percent of Greece's total health expenditures.

By the late 1970s, the poor infrastructure, lack of reliable care, and necessity of informal payments aroused public dissatisfaction with and distrust of the state health system. In 1976 a government study identified major problems, including the lack of coverage for the poor, uneven geographical distribution, lack of coordination among government health agencies, and poor organization of finance and coverage in the public health insurance. The report also exposed the vast underground economy of the health system's informal payments, and it proposed three approaches for overall reform.

Opposition from the medical profession and politicians killed reform legislation in 1980. In 1983, however, the introduction of a National Health Service coincided with similar steps in other nations of southern Europe and heralded major restructuring of the legislative basis for the health care delivery system. Under the new program, the Ministry of Health, Welfare, and Social Security combines the subordinate functions of environmental health, occupational health, nutrition, and health education, formerly divided among other ministries. A Central Health Council, composed of professional experts and consumers, advises the ministry on policy matters. Devised by the Papandreou government, the plan defined the basic structure of the existing national health system.

The plan sought to place all health care under the state, to ensure equality of health care delivery, and to decentralize the health planning apparatus by establishing health councils in fifty-two designated health districts. Another goal was reducing reliance on informal direct payments for treatment. Although the plan allowed existing private practices to remain, fee restrictions forced many out of business. To establish a full-time corps of physicians in the state system, doctors were prohibited from dividing their time between public and private facilities. New training programs were established to increase the supply of nurses. A major omission in the 1983 program was reform of the health care financing and insurance system; this aspect remains essentially as it was before 1983. In the mid-1980s, government expenditures on health care increased to between 4.5 and 5 percent of GDP.

The conservative ND government that took power in 1990 made some changes in the laws governing the National Health Service. To improve the choices available to patients, new private hospitals and clinics again were permitted, and many restrictions on private-sector care were abolished. Physicians in the public sector again could have supplementary private practices. The last provision was reversed when Papandreou returned to power in 1993.

Full evaluation of the performance of the reform program since 1983—particularly in the areas of equity, access, and quality of care—has not been possible because Greek governments have not consistently publicized specific goals, and there is no mechanism to assess performance.

Public health services are funded by the state budget, together with mandatory contributions by employers and employees. In 1991 the official total expenditure on health care reached 5.3 percent of GDP—a low figure by Western standards—with about 70 percent of the total coming from public funds. However, another 1991 estimate, taking account of the continuing high rate of private expenditure, was 7.8 percent of GDP. The health insurance of all but 2 percent of Greek citizens comes from about 370 government insurance organizations, the services and costs of which vary greatly and none of which fully reimburses hospital costs. Many of the firms have accumulated huge deficits in the 1980s and 1990s.

In 1991 Greece had 138 public and 252 private hospitals, equipped with 35,773 and 15,500 beds, respectively. The ratio of beds to population, 5.1 to 1,000, was nearly the lowest among West European nations; according to the standards of the World Health Organization, Greece should have about 20,000 additional beds. The concentration of hospital beds in Athens, which has a surplus, has meant shortages elsewhere and requires that patients travel to Athens for treatment. In an average year in the early 1990s, about 78 percent of admissions are to public hospitals, in which the average occupancy rate is 75 percent, the average stay nine days. All public hospitals also offer outpatient and emergency care, the latter free of charge.

The number of doctors has increased dramatically since 1960, producing a surplus by 1980. The 1991 ratio of doctors to population, 3.4 per 1,000, was among the highest in Western Europe. However, most doctors work in Athens or Thessaloniki, creating shortages in many provinces. Anesthetists, orthopedists, and psychiatrists are especially lacking outside urban centers. Neither the 1983 nor the 1991 reform remedied this distribution problem. All of Greece has a shortage of professional nurses. In 1991 some 25,300 nurses were working in public hospitals, but only about one-third had full professional qualifications. All the major health care specialties experience shortages of nurses. Other trained health professionals, especially physical therapists, are also in short supply, as are support personnel such as occupational therapists and social workers. Personnel shortages in clinics were blamed for decreased vaccination availability since the mid-1980s. Wealthier Greeks often travel to hospitals in Britain, Germany, and Switzerland for major surgery.

Social Welfare

A very complicated system provides social welfare in Greece. The many social security organizations in existence afford a great variety of benefits and provisions. This situation resulted from haphazard planning and information input when the system was being established, from disproportionate influence by certain groups of potential beneficiaries, and from the large number of self-employed workers in the economy. By 1984 some 650 carriers were dispensing old-age, survivor, and disability pensions and health benefits through private, private supplementary, and lump-sum payment programs. The system is under the jurisdiction of the Ministry of Health, Welfare, and Social Security (covering work injuries, sickness, medical benefits, and pensions) and the Ministry of Labor (providing unemployment and family allowances). The legislation prescribing benefits for Greek citizens is the Social Security Law of 1981.

The system is financed primarily by contributions made by employers and through the payroll deductions of employees. Government subsidies also support the coverage of certain types of workers. In 1992 employer and employee social security contributions were virtually equal; the former totaled 13.8 percent of national tax revenue, the latter 14.2 percent.

Membership in pension and health coverage programs is primarily determined by occupational group and industry. Despite the large total number of carriers, three large systems cover about 85 percent of non-civil service workers. The most extensive carrier is the Social Insurance Administration (Idryma Kinonikon Asfaliseon—IKA); the other two major programs are the Agricultural Insurance Organization (Organismos Georgikon Asfaliseon—OGA) and the Tradesmen's and Craftsmen's Fund for the Self-Employed (Tameio Emporikon Viomihanikon Epihiriseon—TEVE). Workers not in the civil service or covered by one of the smaller companies are required to enroll in an IKA program. In general, IKA covers blue- and white-collar workers; the OGA, which is funded entirely by taxes, covers the rural population; and the TEVE covers small business and merchants. A government-operated fund covers civil servants (about 5 percent of the work force) and military personnel, and small funds cover specific professions such as the law, banks, and public utilities.

The IKA programs, the most comprehensive of the three, provide old-age, disability, maternity, funeral, sickness, medical, and workers' compensation benefits. Remaining coverage types—unemployment, military service, and family allowances—are provided by the Manpower Employment Organization. Most funds provide cash benefits for lost income because of illness or accident, maternity, spa treatment, and death and funeral expenses.

In the 1980s, the amount of employer and employee contributions varied greatly among the major funds, although the funds provided similar coverage; legislation passed in 1992 aimed to equalize contributions among the occupational groups. The workers' contribution level of IKA was raised, to 7.5 percent of salaries, and between 1993 and 1996 all other funds covering salaried workers will be required to match that level. Contributions to funds for self-employed professionals generally remained at a lower level than those of salaried workers. Other reforms have aimed at covering unprotected workers, ensuring equal coverage of the sexes, and providing for the increasing number of retirees (see Population Characteristics, this ch.). An Employee Auxiliary Insurance Fund has been established to provide coverage to groups such as miners and municipal workers previously outside the system.

The problematic development of Greece's social welfare system reflects the larger social context. Elements of traditional prescriptions for social interaction are still present as Greece moves closer to the influential West. In education, health care, environmental protection, women's rights, and even religion, the forces of reform continue to erode old familiar institutions. The main dilemma is how to find a recipe for modernization that will honor the best traditions of the past.

*   *   *

A number of valuable studies describe Greek social life, especially in its rural aspect. John K. Campbell's *Honour, Family, and Patronage* and Juliet Du Boulay's *Portrait of a Greek Mountain Village* are among the best. *The Metamorphosis of Greece since World War II* by William H. McNeill shows all of Greek society during an important period of change. Two chapters of *Urban Life in Mediterranean Europe: Anthropological Perspectives*, edited by Michael Kenney and David I. Kertzer, study the development of Greece's urban society. Two articles in *Greece in the 1980s*, edited by Richard Clogg, describe the Orthodox Church of Greece and the Greek education system. T.R.B. Dicks's *The Greeks: How They Live and Work* surveys all aspects of Greek society and its background.

The role of women and the Greek education system are described, respectively, in "Gender and Social Change in Greece: The Role of Women" by Adamantia Pollis and in "Education in Socialist Greece: Between Modernization and Democratization," by Constantine Tsoucalas and Roy Panagiotoponlou, both in *The Greek Socialist Experiment*, edited by Theodore C. Kariotis. Two publications of the Organisation for Economic Co-operation and Development (OECD), the annual *Trends in International Migration* and chapter 11 of *The Reform of Health Care Systems: A Review of Seventeen OECD Countries*, provide current information on health and demographic trends. Environmental conditions and policies are described in two recent journal articles: "The Politics of Greek Environmental Policy" by Dimitris Stevis (in *Policy Studies Journal*), and "The State of the Greek Environment in Recent Years" by Basil D. Katsoulis and John M. Tsangaris, in *Ambio*. (For further information and complete citations, see Bibliography.)

Chapter 3. The Economy

Highway bridge over Alfios River, Peloponnesus

GREECE IS A SMALL COUNTRY with not many more than 10 million people. Its territory, which is dominated by large mountain ranges and an extensive coastline, offers the natural resources on which the traditional economic activities of agriculture, herding, and fishing were based. In the era after World War II, the Greek economy underwent significant transformation. Manufacturing and services emerged as major areas of economic activity that in the mid-1990s combined to account for 85 percent of the gross national product (GNP—see Glossary). The transformation is also reflected in the composition of the Greek population. Whereas in 1940 over 50 percent of the population lived and worked in agricultural areas, only about 25 percent of the population remained rural in the mid-1990s.

Per capita income in Greece has grown substantially in the postwar decades. From about US$500 in 1960, it had increased to about US$6,500 in 1992. By international standards, Greece can be characterized as a country of medium-level development. Its per capita income places Greece above only Mexico and Turkey among the member nations of the Organisation for Economic Co-operation and Development (OECD). On the other hand, Greece's average per capita income exceeds that of most non-OECD countries in the world, including the East European and Central European countries emerging from centrally planned economic systems.

Domestic economic growth in Greece was impressive in the early postwar period, but growth had virtually stopped by the early 1990s. Although the present economy shows many areas of dynamism and profitable investment opportunities, the overall condition is one of stagnation. In recent years, the public sector of the Greek economy has posed particularly difficult and chronic threats to economic stability by generating high deficits and accumulating public debt. These conditions have created macroeconomic imbalances and have forced the implementation of stabilization policies by successive governments. Of necessity, stabilization policies have involved restrictive monetary practices, income restraints, and increased tax burdens—all measures that tend to stifle economic growth. These actions have helped to reduce price inflation significantly, supplying at least one condition for future economic evolution, although the rate of inflation in 1994 remained above levels usually regarded as acceptable by developed countries.

Certain areas of Greece's industry and service sectors are making impressive progress that bodes well for the long-term future. Especially encouraging is growth in food products, textiles, light telecommunications equipment, banking, and business services. Some Greek exports have shown significant growth in the early to mid-1990s. Greek financial markets have gained strength, and private economic initiatives in neighboring Balkan countries undergoing transition to a market economy have flourished. In the mid-1990s, Greek investments enjoyed a high rank among all foreign investments in Bulgaria, Romania, and Albania.

Its small size and its geographic location have always made Greece an economically extroverted country heavily dependent on international economic relations. Since the early 1960s, Greece's major economic alliance has been with the European Community (EC—see Glossary), which has been known as the European Union (EU—see Glossary) since late 1993. Since gaining full membership in the EC in 1981, Greece has practiced free trade with its European partners, adjusting to community requirements for the free movement of capital and labor among member countries. As one of the less-developed members, Greece also has received substantial European grants for agricultural support, various infrastructural investments, and training programs. Greece has participated in EC/EU deliberations on the key issues of adding new member countries and closer integration of participating economies.

Public policy has required that substantial efforts be made in two areas in the mid-1990s. First, heavily regulated sectors such as transportation and telecommunications are being liberalized in order to streamline operation of the market economy and allocation of resources in Greece. Second, the government actively seeks the improvement and extension of economic and social infrastructures in transport, communications, education, and social services. These efforts will be greatly boosted by the Second Community Support Framework (the so-called Delors Package Number Two), a program adopted by the EC in 1993 to distribute its structural funds among member nations whose per capita income is below 75 percent of the community's average. When the program began, those countries were Greece, Ireland, Portugal, and Spain. Under the package, between

1994 and 1999 Greece is to receive US$25 billion to US$30 billion for infrastructure, training, and other initiatives. The utilization of these funds for new domestic capital formation offers the hope of renewing economic growth in Greece.

The Economic Development of Modern Greece

Only in the 1950s did Greece begin its transformation from a largely agricultural economy to one based primarily on services and industry. Progress was slowed, however, by the lack of a domestic entrepreneurial class willing to invest in industry. Government economic policy therefore relied heavily on foreign investment, state intervention played a large role in economic planning, and tourism became a vital part of postwar expansion. After almost three decades of steady growth, the Greek economy began to stagnate in 1979, beginning an era of struggle to resume growth while avoiding high inflation.

The Nineteenth Century

During most of the nineteenth century, the most important changes in the Greek economy were in the agricultural sector. The introduction and extensive cultivation of cash crops for export was the most significant innovation in the more fertile regions of the country. The earliest such crop was currants, which were introduced mainly in the Peloponnesus. Much later, tobacco was introduced as an export crop in more northern areas of the country. In the less fertile areas, subsistence farming predominated well into the second half of the twentieth century.

The profitability of export crops depended largely on Greece's merchant marine fleet, which had developed during the last decades of Ottoman rule around 1800. In that period, international treaties and political conditions were conducive to increased commercial movement in the eastern Mediterranean. After independence was achieved in 1832, domestic commercial growth was a further stimulus to expansion of the merchant fleet. Expanding trade in Greek agricultural products provided the impetus for development of the first Greek financial networks and a variety of domestic economic infrastructures.

The establishment of the National Bank of Greece in 1841 was an important development in the country's financial base. Endowed with the power to issue bank notes and able to deal in both domestic and foreign currency, the National Bank fostered the gradual unification of a national market, by making a uniform national currency available from its branches all over the country. This development greatly facilitated internal and external trade, domestic saving, availability of credit, and inflows of capital from abroad. By the 1870s, the National Bank was emerging as the country's major economic institutional force.

Other parts of Greece's economic infrastructure did not appear until the latter part of the nineteenth century, predominantly during the several terms of Prime Minister Kharilaos Trikoupis. In the 1880s and 1890s, paved roads, the first network of railroad lines, the opening of the Corinth Canal, and the construction or rehabilitation of several seaports contributed greatly to the development of an internal market in Greece, as well as to the movement of Greek products to foreign markets. The first manufacturing plants also appeared in Greece during Trikoupis's tenure, in conjunction with the large infrastructural projects of the period. Before 1900, however, industrial growth was hindered by economic crises, the instability of the agricultural export economy, and government debt.

From 1909 to World War II

Eleutherios Venizelos, who became prime minister in 1910, thoroughly revamped Greece's economic and social institutions, although his modernization programs were interrupted by a series of wars between 1912 and 1922. The 1923 Treaty of Lausanne provided for the exchange of Greek and Turkish minorities, dramatically enlarging Greece's population. The institutional reforms of Venizelos, the new skills brought to Greece by refugees from Asia Minor, and increased domestic demand promoted another period of growth and industrialization. At the same time, refugee resettlement in Macedonia and Thrace introduced more productive agricultural practices (see The Interwar Struggles, 1922–36, ch. 1).

The last Venizelos administration (1928–32) was another era of modernization in Greece's economic institutions. Financial reform included establishment of the Agricultural Bank of Greece and the Bank of Greece, which replaced the National Bank as the bank of currency issue. These institutional changes aimed mainly at improving resource allocation and national policy making; however, they did not make the benefits of eco-

Site of Roman agora, center of economic and social activity, Athens
Courtesy Bernice Huffman Collection, Library of Congress, Washington

nomic growth available to wider segments of the population. Widespread poverty persisted despite growth.

In 1931 the onset of the Great Depression ended Greece's interwar growth, which had not lasted long enough to bring about a permanent improvement in Greek economic structures. Greece had continued to depend to a large extent on agricultural exports and emigrant remittances for its foreign exchange. The decline of international trade and incomes in the 1930s hurt the Greek economy by reducing its foreign-exchange earnings. A new period of economic stagnation, together with persistent urban poverty, stimulated sharp class conflicts, which fostered the growth of Greek communist militancy, widespread labor unrest, and finally the imposition of a fascist dictatorship in 1936.

The Nazi occupation and plunder of Greece between 1941 and 1944 devastated Greece's economy and suspended the foreign trade and agricultural output on which it depended heavily. The Nazis also forced the Greek treasury to pay huge amounts of "occupation expenses," which caused hyperinflation when new money was printed to meet the obligation. The stratification of wealth caused by hyperinflation and black markets during the occupation seriously hindered postwar economic development.

Postwar Recovery

The postwar reconstruction efforts of the Marshall Plan (formally the European Recovery Program) and new economic cooperation in Western Europe provided no immediate benefit to Greece, which underwent a bloody civil war from 1946 until 1949. A new round of destruction of wealth, inflation, and economic instability lasted until the early 1950s. Significant amounts of United States aid went to Greece during this period under the Truman Doctrine and later under the Marshall Plan, establishing a long pattern of dependency on Western benefactors. Total United States aid to Greece from 1947 to 1977 amounted to US$5 billion. In the early postwar years, most of the aid was in the form of grants for outright military assistance or given in connection with military requirements and war-related economic needs.

The Civil War ended in 1949, but economic stabilization was achieved only in 1953. The starting point of postwar recovery was a package of domestic economic measures passed in 1953, which included a 50 percent currency devaluation, laws for the protection of foreign investment, and banking regulations to control inflation and speculation. Extensive public investments in infrastructure (roads, seaports, airports, and electric and telecommunications networks) were undertaken under the leadership of Konstantinos Karamanlis, first as minister of public works (1952–55) and then in his first term as prime minister (1955–63). The 1953 program began twenty years in which Greece would achieve high growth rates, effective industrialization, export expansion, urban growth, and significant— although uneven—prosperity for its population.

The period from the late 1950s to the late 1960s has been characterized as the era of the "Greek economic miracle," during which the gross domestic product (GDP—see Glossary) grew at the fastest rate in Western Europe, averaging 7.6 percent annually throughout the 1960s. Industrial production grew at an average annual rate of 10 percent over the same period, exceeded in Western Europe only by Spain's performance. In the 1960s, manufacturing exports surpassed agricultural exports for the first time in Greece's history, partly because of large foreign investment in industry that boosted capital-intensive manufacturing activities. The most significant projects in this category were a refinery and petrochemical complex of Standard Oil of America and an aluminum complex built by the French company, Pechiney Ugine Kuhlmann. Other development in shipyards, chemical plants, pharmaceuticals, metallurgy, and electrical machinery was also undertaken, associating the largest investments in Greek manufacturing with foreign ownership.

Economic growth, industrialization, and urbanization caused social tensions in the 1960s associated with the inequitable distribution of new wealth. Neither the centrist government of Georgios Papandreou (1964–65) nor the military junta that took power in 1967 was able to ameliorate conditions. The military dictatorship simply favored specific economic interests, notably large tourist enterprises, urban real estate and construction, and shipowners. The basic weaknesses of the Greek economy, including social inequities and the lack of competitiveness in the country's new manufacturing sector, remained untreated. They would resurface in acute form with the world economic crisis of the early 1970s.

The first energy crisis and the international monetary turmoil following the Arab-Israeli War of 1973 had an adverse effect. When exports could not cover the higher cost of foreign oil, a large deficit resulted in the Greek balance of payments, and the domestic economy suffered serious inflationary pressures. Such economic problems increased popular resistance to the dictatorship and contributed to its collapse in mid-1974.

Economic Policy after 1974

The end of the period of growth became obvious after the reestablishment of democracy in Greece in 1974. For both internal and external reasons, the democratic governments that followed the junta were unable to restore growth. Thus, for example, the average annual growth rates of the GDP, which had been 7.6 percent in 1961–70, dropped to 4.7 percent in 1971–80 and then to 1.4 percent in 1981–90. Clearly the "Greek economic miracle" had come to an end.

Greece's return to its association with the EC after ties had been severed during the dictatorship was a major institutional event in the restoration of democracy. In 1981 Greece became a full member of the organization. It was the tenth member in the economic alliance of European nations and the first of the Mediterranean "new democracies" to join the community (Spain and Portugal followed in 1985). Upon achieving membership, Greece began a gradual adjustment of its legislation and elimination of its protectionist policies, leading eventually to full liberalization of trade and the movement of capital and labor. Greek trade was greatly reoriented as a result. In 1980 about 48 percent of Greek exports and 40 percent of imports were destined to, or originated from, EC countries. By 1991 these percentages had risen to 64 and 62 percent, respectively.

The democratic governments of the 1970s and 1980s faced the accumulated internal problems of economic institutions and the social modernization that had been either neglected or suppressed by the junta. On the agenda of social modernization were labor legislation, social insurance, education reform, and the provision of health care—elements without which the growth of a modern economy would be impossible. On the economic front, postdictatorship governments had to tackle the deficit-ridden balance of payments, the damaged competitiveness of Greek industry caused by high energy costs and escalating pressures for higher wages, and a rising inflation rate. The policy requirements for the social and economic problems were frequently contradictory. Modernization of social protection required new public spending and generally expansionary policies, but economic adjustment required income and spending restraints. The internationalization of the Greek economy after 1981 made economic adjustment more urgent.

In response to this situation, the governments of the 1970s and 1980s generally vacillated between emphasizing social modernization and economic adjustment. In the 1970s, the vacillation took the form of a variety of measures for supporting troubled firms in the private sector, taken simultaneously with attempts to stabilize the economy.

The economic crisis of the 1970s had been felt initially by the private sector, where many manufacturing firms joined the ranks of the so-called problematic enterprises that faced failing markets, financial default, and bankruptcy in the decades that followed. Entry into the EC made conditions for Greek industry even harder because the most immediate effect of Greek accession was a removal of protection for domestic industry and a large increase in import penetration, mainly by foreign manufactured goods. For example, throughout the period between 1983 and 1991, about 25 percent of Greece's manufactured goods were exported, while the share of imports in domestic consumption of manufactured products increased from 30 percent to 57 percent.

The crisis conditions of the 1970s eventually penetrated the public sector under both conservative and socialist governments. In the 1980s, the socialist administrations of Papandreou sought to bolster areas of the economy that lagged farthest behind Greece's EC partners by extending welfare protection in a variety of forms. But this policy was not supported by tax reforms that would generate new revenue for public spending, so the deficits and public borrowing that had begun in the late 1970s intensified in the 1980s. A "roller coaster" cycle of pre-election largesse and post-election stringency in public spending has been apparent under both conservative and socialist governments in the 1980s and 1990s. As a proportion of total public expenditure, the budget deficit went from 32 percent in 1981 to 44 percent in 1990.

The crisis in the public sector, with high budget deficits, public borrowing, and an erosion of tax compliance in combination with continuing economic stagnation, created serious economic imbalances that persist in the mid-1990s. Price inflation remained at the high average annual rate of 18 percent throughout the 1980s and the early 1990s, declining to 12 percent by the end of 1993 and to 10.6 percent by the end of 1994. Stabilization policies, briefly implemented in 1986–87 under socialist minister of national economy Konstantinos Simitis, initially reduced inflation and public deficits, but the Panhellenic Socialist Movement (Panhellinion Socialistiko Kinima— PASOK) government continued its pattern of reversals by changing back the policies in 1988 in preparation for a national election.

In 1990–93 the conservative government of Konstantinos Mitsotakis and his National Democracy (Nea Demokratia— ND) party undertook harsher, more persistent stabilization efforts accompanied by a privatization program for state-owned firms and a tax reduction program. Conservative policies were only partially successful, however, because they had the side effect of depressing the economy. Thus, tax revenues failed to increase at the expected rate, pressures for increased public spending remained high as unemployment and social problems worsened, and business prospects did not brighten enough to boost private demand for the state-owned enterprises put on sale in the privatization program.

The PASOK government of Andreas Papandreou, back in power in late 1993, continued to implement stabilization policies, reorienting them by directing its tax reform policy to enforce compliance by undertaxed strata of society, by following a more pragmatic course on privatization to maximize revenue from sales, and by avoiding new indirect taxes that would rekindle inflation. The initial impact of this approach on inflation was positive, dropping the annual rate to a twenty-year low of 10.6 percent. However, the problems of unemployment and industrial decline clearly persist in the mid-1990s.

Despite the problems of the public sector, the Greek economy contains elements of dynamism. Firms in foods, textiles, telecommunications equipment, banking, and business services have made impressive progress in the early 1990s. Greek financial markets have gained volume and liquidity. Private economic initiatives in neighboring Balkan countries in transition to market economies have flourished, and Greek investments rank among the largest in Bulgaria, Romania, and Albania.

The Structure of the Economy

The basic structural features of the Greek economy have been changing since the mid-1970s. Although statistical information is not always up to date, discernible trends indicate the essential movements. The composition of national income and the changing role of international trade, the structure of employment, the operation of Greece's underground economy, and the size and relative weight of the public sector are the main areas in which change is occurring in Greek economic structures.

The Composition of National Income

In 1992 the share of the GDP generated in the so-called primary sector, including agriculture, animal husbandry, and fishing, was about 12 percent. At the same time, the secondary sector—mining, manufacturing, energy, and construction—yielded 26 percent of GDP, and the share of the tertiary sector, including trade, finance, transport, health, and education, was 59 percent. The high share of services is characteristic of the entire postwar period. The relative shares of the three sectors were, respectively, about 18 percent, 31 percent, and 50 percent in 1970.

The service sector long has been considered a residual sector of activity, featuring activities with high underemployment and masked unemployment that absorb resources released by other sectors. Many experts consider this traditional view wrong in the mid-1990s because modern services are having a palpable impact on the Greek economy and on everyday life. In any case, the quantitative as well as the relative weight of the service sector has been growing in recent years. After the service share of GDP remained static in the 1970s, the 1980s showed a distinct trend toward increased participation by services. This trend is consistent with the weakening of industry, which normally releases resources into the service sector. However, it is also consistent with a rise in the standard of living, which normally increases the demand for services. Both factors likely contributed to the rising share of services after 1980. Living standards improved over that period, but domestic manufacturing also suffered a serious loss of its market share to international competition.

Another important recent trend relates to the allocation of national income to investment within the country. The formation of fixed capital as a proportion of GDP has declined steadily in Greece from an all-time high of 27 percent to about 20 percent in recent years. This trend is connected with the slowdown in growth rates and in manufacturing activity; it is also probably related to the redistribution of resources to services, because most demand for fixed investment arises either in the primary or secondary sectors of an economy.

Despite the investment slowdown, the ratio of private savings to GDP has not exhibited any significant change, remaining at about 20 percent. On the other hand, total national saving (including private and public saving), has dropped because Greek public saving has been negative in recent years (see The Public Sector and Taxation, this ch.). High private saving is desirable for the economy because it enables the financing of public sector deficits as well as domestic investment.

The Role of Foreign Trade

It is generally expected that foreign trade plays a large role in a small open economy such as exists in Greece. A measure of the relative weight of trade is the ratio of the sum of exports and imports to the country's GDP. In Greece this ratio grew until 1985, when it reached almost 50 percent, but it declined from that point to about 40 percent in 1992. The decline has been evenly divided between exports and imports. The export decline verifies the weakening competitive position of Greek products in the world market, and especially in the market of the EC/EU. The import decline is simply the outcome of domestic demand being weakened by the austerity policies of the early 1990s. Nevertheless, the Greek economy remains highly internationalized and quite sensitive to developments in foreign trade, as compared with larger economies such as that of the United States, in which the sum of exports and imports is less than 20 percent of GDP.

The high degree of internationalization in the Greek economy is demonstrated by the fact that, besides exports and imports of goods, the nation's foreign economic relations include a large component of so-called invisibles, such as receipts from tourism, international merchant shipping, and emigrant remittances. Generally speaking, these receipts can be considered as revenues from sales of services to foreigners inside or outside the country. In recent years, invisibles have amounted to between 22 percent and 25 percent of GDP. Thus, the degree of internationalization of the Greek economy is even higher than is suggested by trade figures alone.

The Structure of Employment

The structure of employment in Greece corresponds only roughly to the structure of the national product. According to the most recent labor survey (1991), some 22 percent of the employed population worked in agriculture, 28 percent in industry, and 50 percent in services. Comparison with the corresponding percentages for the participation of the three sectors in the national product indicates that agriculture is more labor-intensive than the other two sectors, but productivity is lower in agriculture and there is substantial underemployment in the agricultural labor force.

An analysis of the labor force by sex shows that working men are overrepresented in industry (33 percent of total male employment is in the secondary sector), whereas working women are overrepresented in agriculture and in services (33 percent and 50 percent of female employment is in the primary and tertiary sectors, respectively). In terms of total employment and unemployment, in 1991 approximately 2.3 million men and 1.6 million women were working. In the same year, 109,000 men and 188,000 women were reported as unemployed. Thus, within the nationwide unemployment rate of 7.0

percent, the female population experienced a higher unemployment rate of 11.7 percent. In 1989 (the last year for which such figures were available), the rate of unemployment among persons of both sexes under age thirty was 18.8 percent. Estimates indicate that the unemployment rate in Greece hovered around 9.8 percent in 1993. Experts assume that women and younger workers in general continue to show relatively higher unemployment rates than the national average. Pay rates also differ between men and women. In 1990 among salaried employees in manufacturing and trade, females received compensation averaging 80 percent of compensation given males for comparable work.

An important characteristic of the Greek employment structure is the division of the working population into groups of occupational status. Thus, in 1989 about 5.6 percent of the working population were employers, and 51.4 percent were wage and salary earners. The balance was made up of 28.7 percent who were self-employed and 14.3 percent who were unpaid family members occupied in a family business. The relatively high percentages in the last two categories are typical of a society featuring many very small business firms run on a family basis together with a large service sector.

The large number of individuals employed in seasonal or nonpermanent agricultural and service positions means that it is quite common for people to work at more than one job. Thus, for example, a farmer or an urban craftsman may also provide tourist services in the summer. Double occupations are even encountered among public-sector employees who take second jobs in the evening. Besides creating a certain fluidity in a worker's social role, this tendency complicates the measurement of productivity and unemployment in various sectors of the economy.

Labor Unions

The large component of self-employed persons in the labor force and the predominance of small family businesses have impeded the growth of effective labor unions in Greece. Nevertheless, the Greek labor movement grew along with the process of industrialization, and the movement made its presence felt in the interwar and the postwar periods. Labor organization is centered on craft and trade unions limited to a single community. These local units are usually affiliated with national federations in both given industries and in geographic labor centers.

The secondary organizations combine in turn to form the national labor body, the General Confederation of Greek Workers (Geniki Synomospondia Ergaton Ellados—GSEE). The GSEE's present membership is about 600,000 persons.

The GSEE has long suffered from political interference by parties in power and in opposition. Although the socialist governments of the 1980s took some steps to strengthen the independence of unions, they also continued the tradition of political interference in practice. The strength of the trade unions in the mid-1990s is mostly in employee federations in banking and in public utilities companies, state-owned enterprises, teachers' associations, and associations of transportation and other municipal workers. In the early 1990s, the GSEE played the important role of negotiating national labor agreements with employers' associations (and the government on occasion), establishing the framework for pay increases and other labor benefits for the country as a whole. Thus, in its capacity as national labor representative, the GSEE has taken an important role in issues affecting the management of the economy and the development of human resources as a part of the economy's endowment.

The Underground Economy

Multiple occupations are linked to the growth of an underground economy in Greece. As in many other national economies since the 1970s, Greece's underground economy includes a variety of economic activities outside the reporting and taxation systems of national government. In a country such as Greece, with a large service sector and a multitude of very small enterprises, the proliferation of unreported, untaxed, and unregulated activities is a natural occurrence. Estimates of the Greek underground economy have ranged from 35 to 50 percent of the officially reported economy, meaning that actual incomes and employment exceed official figures by the same percentages. Avoidance of taxes and social security payments has cut the costs of small enterprises and entrepreneurs, whose survival is threatened by economic crisis and international competition. Although the underground economy provides income and employment to otherwise unemployed labor, its operation obstructs the modernization of the country's fiscal system and the development of internationally competitive production capabilities in the economy.

The Public Sector and Taxation

The shape of the Greek public sector was already established in the nineteenth century. From the inception of the modern Greek state, provision of public-sector jobs was a preferred way for politicians to grant favors (see The Civil Service, ch. 4). Public-sector jobs also provided opportunities for upward mobility in an economy whose development potential was unrealized until a very late stage. Beginning about 1974, several factors have contributed to growth of the public sector. Greek governments responded to the economic crisis of the 1970s with a variety of policies that increased government spending in order to protect the public from the consequences of the economic downturn. This response was intensified by the need for democratic consolidation when the military dictatorship ended in 1974. It was enhanced further in 1981 when the first socialist government in Greek history brought with it a programmatic goal to modernize the Greek system of social protection.

Beginning with the socialist administrations of the 1980s, public-sector growth has been the subject of intense political debate. The center of that debate is the appropriate percentage of GDP that public expenditure should occupy. After remaining at about 25 percent of GDP in the late 1960s and early 1970s, public expenditure began climbing after the mid-1970s. By 1980 it had reached 30 percent; then by 1985 it exceeded 40 percent. For the years 1990–93, the figure remained steady between 42 and 45 percent of GDP (see table 6, Appendix).

The basic components of this accelerating outlay are primary expenditures such as the purchase of goods and services, pensions, subsidies, and interest payments on the public debt. Because of the accumulation of public debt on large deficits that have persisted since the late 1970s, between 1980 and 1992 interest expenses grew quite rapidly from less than 2 percent of GDP in 1980 to 11.4 percent of GDP in 1992. On the other hand, since the late 1980s primary expenditures have stabilized at between 35 and 38 percent of GDP. Thus, about half of apparent growth in the public sector, as compared with GDP, comes from the Greek state's bulging interest expenses. About 75 percent of this interest expense is service of domestic debt, held by Greek residents and denominated in drachmas (for value of the drachma—see Glossary). Thus, this expenditure is a transfer payment within the country, from taxpayers to the creditors of the state, through the mediation of the state.

Primary expenditures have risen mainly in the category of social transfer payments such as pensions, welfare payments, subsidies to social security organizations, and supports to failing firms that were justified in the name of maintaining employment and labor income.

On the other side of the ledger, public revenues have grown significantly over the last two decades. From about 22 percent of GDP in 1970, they had risen to almost 33 percent by 1992. That year, according to the National Statistical Service, primary expenditures were nearly 36 percent of GDP, so had there been no public debt, the Greek budget would have been close to balance.

The problem of enhancing public revenues is paramount for Greece's fiscal future. Contrary to the practice in most European countries, Greek tax revenues come primarily from indirect taxation (sales, excise, and, mainly, value-added taxes), and only secondarily from direct taxation (income, corporate profit, and property taxes). In 1992 corporate and individual income taxes contributed about 17 percent of total tax revenues, social security contributions added another 28 percent, and indirect taxes on goods and services amounted to 45.5 percent of tax income. The largest component of indirect tax revenues is the value-added tax (VAT—see glossary), which was instituted in 1987 to comply with the tax harmonization policies of the EC.

The low yield of direct taxation in Greece is not the outcome of low tax rates. Rather, it is due to low income tax compliance. Tax enforcement is problematic in a country with a high percentage of self-employed workers and a large service sector. For many years, salaried employees and pensioners have paid the largest share of direct taxes, when in fact these categories of the working population are not the wealthiest or the most able to shoulder the tax burden. In addition, Greek tax collection is riddled with inefficiency, lax enforcement, and even corruption—factors that have survived numerous reform efforts.

A new set of tax reforms was passed in 1994 to broaden the tax base and make the tax burden more equitable. The top income tax rate was cut to encourage those with higher incomes to participate. A "profession tax" now sets a minimum taxable income for every member in prescribed levels of each profession, and tax inspectors can examine personal financial records to establish tax liability.

Aside from the government and its agencies, the Greek public sector includes a variety of enterprises in various sectors of the economy. Some of these concerns enjoy monopoly status, such as the Public Power Corporation (Dimosia Epicheirisi Ilektrismou—DEI), the Greek Telecommunications Organization (Organismos Tilepikoinonion Ellados—OTE), and Olympic Airways, which alone operates domestic air travel. Other public-sector enterprises, most notably national banks and manufacturing companies owned by them, coexist with private firms in their field of activity.

The growth period of the public sector also included extension of public ownership to troubled private firms, usually through state-controlled banks. In the late 1980s, the government began the process of privatizing or liquidating these firms. In the early 1990s, minority blocks of shares were issued to privatize in part two large public utilities, DEI and OTE— although the cancellation of an open bidding process on the shares of the latter in 1994 signaled a possible reversal of such privatization plans. In addition, the monopoly status of several public enterprises is undergoing gradual change. Competition in domestic air travel, alternative forms of energy generation by private agents, and mobile telephone communications are examples of activities in which private entry has already begun or is being considered in the mid-1990s.

Virtually all current observers of the Greek economy agree that the public sector must be streamlined if the country is to experience a new round of development. Because many of the mid-1990s problems of the public sector result from earlier crises in private companies that were inherited by the state, the prescription for long-term improvement includes private-sector assistance in the cleanup of public-sector problems. This requirement means that the Greek political agenda will continue to include effective tax reform and an end to subsidies for many types of private enterprise.

Wages, Prices, and Inflation

As Greece entered the 1990s and the requirements of EC membership grew stricter, inflation remained a central problem for economic policy makers. In 1990 the annual inflation rate was 20 percent; after four years of austerity policies, the rate had declined to 10.6 percent at the end of 1994. At that point, experts believed that private-sector confidence in the government's anti-inflation policies had been boosted, making future reductions in the inflation rate likely.

The implementation of the EU's convergence program in the mid-1990s will mean strong anti-inflationary efforts as well as harsh fiscal adjustment to reduce government deficits (see International Economic Policy in the 1990s, this ch.). Minimizing the differential of inflation rates between Greece and the other EU countries is crucial in establishing a stable nominal exchange rate for the drachma and participation for the drachma in the EU's Exchange Rate Mechanism (ERM), the currency stabilization mechanism in which all EU member countries except Greece participated in 1994. Greek foreign-exchange policy has involved moderate and gradual devaluations timed to dampen rather than accelerate inflation. Thus, on average the Greek currency has been devalued in the last few years by less than the differential inflation between Greece and its main trading partners. Another crucial factor in inflation policy has been balancing interest rates at a level high enough to restrict the flow of money but low enough to encourage borrowing and investment. In spite of government monetary restrictions, in late 1994 an official EU evaluation projected a 1995 inflation rate of 9.5 percent for Greece, which the EU described as an unsatisfactory reduction from the overall 1994 level of 11.1 percent.

The government traditionally had fixed prices and profit margins, especially under the influence of organized commercial lobbies. Between 1988 and 1992, the average prices of consumer goods rose by between 69 percent for durable goods and 118 percent for clothing (see table 7, Appendix). In the same period, total wholesale prices more than doubled. Beginning in 1990, however, EC requirements have gradually promoted free competition. In 1992 the government abolished controls on profit margins and price controls on most products, including imported petroleum and petroleum products. The result was an overall decrease in prices in 1992. Legislation in 1993 abolished some remaining restrictions.

Between 1985 and 1992, average wages of workers in manufacturing increased by 179 percent. Until 1990 the government played a direct role in establishing wages in private as well as state-owned enterprises. The nationwide Automatic Indexation Scheme and government norms for wage increases destroyed jobs by forcing artificial wage levels on enterprises in poor fiscal condition. Beginning in 1991, however, free collective bargaining has become the rule, and since that time the government has not interfered in wage settlements in private enterprises. Wage arbitration also moved noticeably from the national to the local and enterprise level in the 1990s, promoting labor market flexibility. Although the government did not raise public-sector wages or pensions in 1992–93, the overall rate of wage increases did not subside during that period. The 1995 plans for meeting EU convergence standards included a 6 percent limit on wage increases that year, together with tight hiring restrictions to constrict wage outlays in the public sector.

Industry

The productivity rate of traditional industry remains very important to the Greek economy, even as the service sector appears to be the primary source of growth. In spite of prolonged stagnation in manufacturing, experts believe that the industrial sector can be a source of effective increases in human productivity and labor skills, innovation, and efficient organization for the production of services themselves. In the early 1990s, some industries made significant advances in these areas, spurring hopes that the entire sector would revive.

Greek manufacturing, and industrial activity in general, underwent great expansion in the 1960s, but the sector has been slowing ever since and has virtually stagnated in the early to mid-1990s. In view of the importance of the industrial sector in a country of medium-level development such as Greece, experts consider this current inertia one of the root causes of the country's economic problems.

Energy

The energy sector has exhibited significant growth in Greece. Between 1982 and 1992, total energy consumption grew from 16.1 million to 22.9 million tons of oil equivalent (Mtoe), an increase of 42 percent. Of 1992 consumption, 8.2 Mtoe came from coal, 13.8 Mtoe from oil, 0.8 Mtoe from hydroelectric generation, and 0.1 Mtoe from natural gas. The country depends on imports for a significant portion of its energy. In 1992 domestic energy production amounted to 8.6 Mtoe (an increase of 54 percent over the preceding decade), whereas net imports amounted to 15.6 Mtoe.

In 1991 Greek hydroelectric stations produced slightly more than 10 percent of the power generated domestically, liquid-fuel-burning thermoelectric stations produced about 23 percent, and coal-burning thermoelectric stations produced about 66 percent. Greece has no nuclear power plants. Between 1980 and 1991, electricity production increased by 48 percent. Expansion of coal-burning stations accounted for more than the net increase because production from the other two sources declined during that period. Thus, the use of domestically available coal for electricity production has been intensified over this period.

Domestic production of fuel consists mostly of coal. With known reserves of about 3 billion tons, production in 1990 amounted to 51.9 million tons, nearly double the amount in 1980. Crude petroleum is extracted in the offshore Prinos Field, near the island of Thasos in the northern Aegean Sea. Production of crude was 6.7 million barrels in 1989, down from about 9.5 million in 1985. Between 1982 and 1992, Greek oil production dropped by 33 percent, and further declines are expected because reserves are rapidly being depleted. The largest refinery is the Aspropyrgos Refinery near Athens, which has a capacity of 110,000 barrels of oil per day.

The distribution of electricity consumption among sectors of economic activity in 1992 was as follows: industrial consumption absorbed 27 percent, transportation absorbed 42 percent, and other uses such as agriculture, commerce, and municipal installations accounted for 31 percent. Classified another way, in 1990 industry used 33 percent, transportation used 30 percent, and households and commercial establishments used 37 percent. Between 1982 and 1992, industrial consumption grew by less than 5 percent, transport consumption by 49 percent.

Electricity production in Greece is the domain of the state-owned DEI. A limited amount of private electricity production is allowed, but most of the power in this category is consumed by the generating enterprise or sold to the DEI. In 1991 less than 3 percent of Greece's total electricity production of 32,786 gigawatt hours was produced outside DEI facilities. The country's power generation capacity stood at 9,446 megawatts in 1991.

The DEI is implementing a large-scale, ten-year program of investments and modernization, which is projected to cost US$5 billion. The program will involve the construction of new thermoelectric and hydroelectric capacity, the development of

Small hydroelectric dam, Peloponnesus
Courtesy Sam and Sarah Stulberg

environment-friendly forms of energy generation such as wind and geothermal sources, extensive automation of generation and load distribution centers, and other technical improvements.

The use of natural gas is meager in Greece. A major project, long in the planning stage, is extension of a pipeline from its present terminus in Bulgaria to deliver Russian natural gas to Greece. The project will be funded by the Second Community Support Framework of the EU. The project will allow the replacement of oil currently used for power supply by many consumers. Such an adjustment will reduce environmental pollution, especially in urban areas. The main 520-kilometer pipeline will be supplemented by urban distribution networks in Thessaloniki and the Athens metropolitan area. The projected cost of this project is about US$2 billion. After years of delay, in September 1994 Greece signed new protocols with Russia for supply and with Bulgaria for pipeline construction between the Bulgarian port of Burgas and the Greek port of Alexandroupolis, on the Aegean Sea. The line is seen as a foundation of new industrial development in northern Greece.

Construction

Construction of buildings, especially houses, is an important part of the Greek economy that has long been a primary form of fixed investment. In 1991 more than 5 percent of GDP was produced by the construction industry (see table 8, Appendix). However, the construction of dwellings represented 23 percent of total fixed investment in the country that same year. In 1989 the construction sector generated 6.5 percent of total employment. In 1989 private construction built the equivalent of 67.3 million cubic meters of space, compared with 49.3 million cubic meters in 1985. In both years, about 43 percent of this activity took place in urban areas. Public construction of buildings, totaling 2.8 million cubic meters in 1989, was minor compared with private construction.

Given the important role that construction of private housing has traditionally played in the economy, together with the political significance of housing supply, economic policy makers have favored construction activity as a way to boost incomes, employment, and domestic demand. Thus, the construction sector has been a long-time political favorite that receives tax advantages. In the climate of deficit reductions and tax reform dominating the mid-1990s, however, the increased taxation of construction is being seriously contemplated.

An important part of the activity of the construction sector is large public works projects. The construction sector will receive major benefits from large-scale infrastructure projects contemplated in the second half of the 1990s. Among those projects are an upgraded Athens metropolitan railroad system, a US$3 billion project already under construction; a new Athens airport whose total projected cost is US$4 billion; and major bridges such as the Riou-Andirriou connection northeast of Patras, which is projected to cost US$500 million. Seaport and highway construction is also included in infrastructure expansion plans. Under the terms of EU financing for these major projects, bids for their construction must be opened to international competition. This requirement means that the Greek construction industry will rapidly open up to international competition and to international joint ventures.

Mining

Mining and quarrying represented only 1.8 percent of GDP in 1991 and 0.6 percent of total employment in 1989. Despite the small size of the mining industry, however, its importance lies in the significant mineral wealth of Greece. Lignite has an important role in electricity generation. Bauxite, the raw material for aluminum production, is also found in abundance in Greece, with known reserves of 1 billion tons. There are also substantial deposits of ferronickel ores, magnesite, mixed sulfurous ores, ferrochrome ores, kaolin, asbestos, and marble. Recovery of metallic ores remains concentrated in the hands of a few large companies. In 1988 there were sixty-two mining operations, employing 2,696 persons, an average of forty-three workers per company. Quarry production, on the other hand, is fragmented among many small enterprises. In 1988 some 945 quarries were in operation, employing a total of 6,362 persons, an average of about seven persons per establishment.

Among the main mineral ores being mined, 1990 production was as follows: 4.3 million tons of asbestos, 2.5 million tons of bauxite, 2.1 million tons of nickel ore, 697,000 tons of magnesite, and 177,000 tons of chromite. A portion of this production is exported in raw form, but beginning in the 1980s, concerted efforts have been made to develop domestic processing capability.

Bauxite processing has been a major element of industrial metallurgy development projects in Greece. A major investment by the French Pechiney group in the 1960s was the first important step in the processing of Greek bauxite and the production of alumina (semiprocessed aluminum ore) and aluminum. In the mid-1980s, Greece signed an agreement with the Soviet Union for construction of a large alumina plant with a ten-year buyback arrangement for a large part of the plant's output. After the agreement was revised and the plan delayed, Greece again is actively pursuing this project in the mid-1990s. The plant's projected production capacity is 600,000 tons a year, making it the major user of Greek bauxite.

Manufacturing

Manufacturing provided almost 18 percent of GDP in 1991, making up the largest portion of the secondary sector's contribution to national production. In that year, fixed investment in manufacturing represented 16 percent of the nation's total fixed investment. In 1989 manufacturing provided about 19 percent of the country's employment, including 21 percent of jobs among males and 17 percent among females.

For several years up to 1994, the contributions of manufacturing to the GDP, to employment, and to investment—respectively, 18 percent, 13 percent, and 20 percent in 1985—have remained at approximately the same levels. In general, manufacturing production has stagnated since 1980. For example, given a base value of 100 for 1980 production, the values for ensuing years are 101 in 1985, 103 in 1988, and 101 in 1991.

The manufacturing category includes a variety of subsectors and activities. In 1990 the four largest subsectors accounted for 43 percent of total value added in manufacturing; in order of importance, these were foodstuffs, textiles, chemicals, and processed nonmetallic minerals. The same four subsectors have been the leading contributors since 1977, when they totaled 45 percent of overall manufacturing value added. Computers, computer software, and motor vehicles are manufactured by a few smaller firms. Besides state-owned military equipment firms, two Athens-based private companies make armored fighting vehicles and helicopters for the military, as well as satellites and launch vehicles, and the Greek Arms Industry (Elliniki Viotekhnia Oplon—EVO) is by far the largest private military supplier (see Defense Enterprises, ch. 5).

In terms of employment, the leading manufacturing subsectors are foodstuffs, textiles, clothing and footwear, and transportation equipment (including shipyards), which contributed a combined 51 percent of total manufacturing employment in 1988. The same four subsectors were the leading providers of employment in 1978, when they contributed 48 percent of total manufacturing employment. It is clear from both the structure of value added and the structure of employment that the manufacturing sector's composition has remained largely immobile over the last fifteen years.

Between 1980 and 1991, the four subsectors showing the greatest growth in productivity rate, in order of growth performance over the whole period, were paper with 62 percent, beverages with 45 percent, rubber and plastics with 36 percent, and chemicals with 27 percent. The four subsectors showing the greatest declines in production over the period were leather and fur, down 41 percent; clothing and footwear, down

Goat herd on a country road, Epirus
Courtesy Sam and
Sarah Stulberg

Selling artichokes and
quinces, western
Peloponnesus
Courtesy Sam and
Sarah Stulberg

30 percent; metal products, down 26 percent; and wood and cork products, also down 26 percent. In general, the steepest declines are found in the more traditional industries, although growth has been distributed between traditional industries and those employing advanced technology.

The statistical dominance of small and medium-sized enterprises (SMEs) in Greek manufacturing actually increased in the 1980s. Between 1978 and 1988, the percentage of manufacturing employment in establishments employing fewer than five persons rose from 29 percent to 31 percent, and the share of establishments employing fewer than fifty persons rose from 60 percent to 64 percent. The relative weight of small firms in Greek manufacturing is among the highest in the EU. The average number of people in the work force in Greece's largest enterprises, 278 workers, is among the lowest in Europe; by comparison, Sweden's largest firms average 384, Portugal's 600. One disadvantage of this preponderance of small businesses is that small firms have fewer resources for the research and development activities that enhance a country's competitive position. In 1990 Greece and Portugal showed the smallest shares of total business enterprise research and development in the EC, each contributing only 0.1 percent compared with Germany's 35 percent and France's 22 percent.

At the same time, the SMEs have made a major contribution to employment expansion in Greek manufacturing enterprises. Between 1978 and 1988, about 35,000 new jobs were created in manufacturing, but the contributions of SMEs and larger establishments were quite different. In that period, SMEs created 50,000 new jobs while those firms with more than fifty employees showed a net loss of 15,000 jobs.

The overall contribution of manufacturing to Greek exports has been substantial. In the early 1990s, manufacturing's share in total foreign-exchange earnings from exports of goods has fluctuated between 48 and 54 percent. In 1992 manufactured products earned US$3.1 billion of Greece's total export income of US$6 billion, or 52 percent. The main categories of manufacturing exports are textiles, earning US$1.6 billion; metals and metal products, earning US$595 million; chemicals and pharmaceuticals, earning US$198 million; and cement, earning US$182 million in 1992. Although there are yearly fluctuations in export earnings from one or the other product category, these products have been Greece's leading manufacturing exports since the mid-1980s.

Despite the vital role of manufacturing in total Greek export performance, very few manufacturing subsectors sell a preponderance of their product abroad. In 1991 only the export of leather and fur products exceeded domestic sales; basic metals showed the second-highest ratio with 47 percent of sales outside Greece. Virtually all other subsectors achieved less than one-third of their sales income from exports. These statistics indicate clearly that in general Greek manufacturing firms depend on the domestic market and local demand for their livelihood. Because of this situation, the rapid import penetration that followed EC membership in the 1980s caused serious damage to Greek manufacturing's ability to respond to domestic demand. Between 1983 and 1992, the percentage of imported goods out of total manufactured goods purchased moved from 31 percent to 47 percent.

In the 1970s and the 1980s, the prolonged crisis in Greek manufacturing led to acquisition by the public sector and by public-sector banks of a large number of ailing firms. By 1986 the state-owned Enterprise Reconstruction Organization had taken over forty-four such firms. In the ensuing years, a slow privatization and liquidation of these firms has taken place, and by 1994 almost none were left. Nevertheless, ownership of several ailing firms still remains with bank portfolios, especially in the Bank of Greece and the Industrial Development Bank of Greece.

Foreign investment in Greek manufacturing has not been very large, despite strong incentives legislated by the Greek government as early as 1953 for the enhancement and protection of foreign investment. Total postwar foreign investment in Greece is estimated at about US$8 billion. Especially in the 1960s, a few large foreign investment projects were undertaken in new manufacturing sectors. The prime examples of such projects are the Pechiney Aluminum Plant, the Esso-Pappas petrochemical complex built by Standard Oil of America and Greek-American entrepreneur Thomas Pappas near Thessaloniki, and several shipyards. In more recent periods, foreign investment has concentrated on the acquisition of existing firms under the anticipated new conditions of a unified European market. Large acquisitions of this type have taken place in foodstuffs and beverages. When Greece's major cement company, AGET, was privatized in 1992, a large share of capital and the entire management were acquired by a large Italian concern. In 1988 an estimated 18 percent of total manufacturing employment was under foreign ownership.

Public policy has taken a favorable stance toward manufacturing in the entire postwar era. Incentives that have been applied to encourage manufacturing production, investment, and exports include subsidies, tax breaks, tariff protection, and cheap loans. Greece's EC membership required elimination of direct and indirect protection to Greek firms, hence the phasing out of tariffs and export subsidies. Under EU conditions in the mid-1990s, any favorable treatment extended to Greek firms must also be available to firms from other member countries. In addition, the liberalization of Greece's financial system has eliminated the long-standing practice of regulating interest rates in favor of manufacturing (see Banking and Finance, this ch.).

Incentives to manufacturing are now primarily in the form of grants and subsidies for new investment. Grants are outright capital contributions that can vary from 15 to 55 percent of a project's investment cost, depending on the sector, the export potential, the technology content, and the location of the investment venture. In assessing such investments, the Greek authorities seek to achieve both industrial modernization and geographic decentralization away from the chronic congestion and environmental pollution of Athens and Thessaloniki (see Pollution Problems, ch. 2). Subsidies take the form of interest-rate subsidies, fast depreciation schedules, and special tax allowances. To avoid the proliferation of very small enterprises, recent changes to the law have also encouraged ventures featuring economies of scale.

In the early 1990s, some signs of manufacturing recovery emerged. Exports in sectors such as chemicals began to gain strength in 1993 and 1994. Between 1990 and 1992, manufacturing profits showed hefty annual gains of about 20 percent. The profits have improved the capital structure and raised the equity of manufacturing firms.

Agriculture, Forestry, and Fishing

Agriculture, forestry, and fishing, the components of the primary sector of the economy, contributed about 12 percent of Greek GDP in 1992, compared with 17 percent ten years earlier. A fundamental fact of postwar Greek development has been the sustained shrinkage of the role of the primary sector. Nevertheless, the primary sector, and especially agriculture, remains of much greater importance to Greece than to most other EU countries. (In the EU as a whole, the agricultural sector contributes about 7 percent of GDP). On the other hand, Greek agricultural productivity is estimated to be about half the average for the EU agricultural sector as a whole.

Agriculture

Despite the nineteenth-century transformation of Greece's agricultural sector toward export crops, the tradition of small-scale landholdings fragmented into several work locations has persisted throughout the nineteenth and twentieth centuries. The pattern was reinforced by the application of state land distribution programs that divided national lands to endow landless peasants with holdings of their own. The only exception was in Thessaly, where tenant farmers cultivated cereal crops on large estates until the early twentieth century.

Consistent with the primary sector's declining role in the economy, employment has also declined. In 1981 some 972,000 persons were employed in the sector, representing 27.4 percent of national employment, as compared with 22 percent in 1991, when only about 873,000 persons were employed in the primary sector. Over that decade, about 10 percent more of the female work force than of the male work force remained employed in the primary sector, however. A major reason for this disparity is that in agricultural areas second occupations are available predominantly to men, while women remain tied more closely to their agricultural pursuits.

Greece's total utilized agricultural area is close to 3.7 million hectares, of which 59 percent is in the plains and 41 percent is in mountainous or semimountainous areas (see fig. 7). Two-thirds of the land under cultivation is used for crops, and about one-quarter for tree plantations. The remainder is used for vegetables, pasturage, and vineyards (see fig. 9). In 1990 the number of individual agricultural holdings was estimated at 924,000. Thus, the average area per holding is slightly less than four hectares. By contrast, the average holding in the EU as a whole is fourteen hectares. A similar comparison applies to hectares per working person in agriculture. In Greece, land area per agricultural worker is five hectares, whereas in the EU as a whole it is fourteen hectares. In 1987 about 24 percent of all holdings were less than one hectare in size, and another 67 percent were between one and ten hectares. Only the remaining 9 percent exceeded ten hectares. The small size of holdings

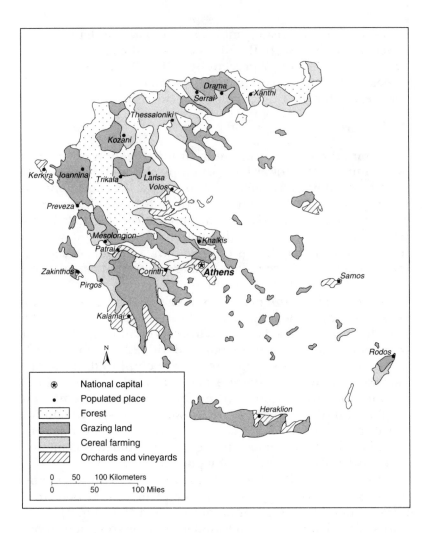

Figure 9. Land Utilization, 1994

in Greece is a major cause of lower agricultural productivity compared with other EU countries. The economies of scale offered by modern farming methods have a limited impact on small plots of land.

Differences in landscape and climatic conditions have led to differences in cultivation methods in various regions of Greece. Thus, for example, at the end of the 1980s, in Thessaly and Macedonia 85 percent of cultivated land was arable cropland.

In Crete, on the other hand, two-thirds of utilized agricultural areas were vineyards and tree plantations. In the Peloponnesus, almost two-thirds of cultivated land was arable cropland, and one-third was used for vineyards and tree plantations.

Animals and animal production constitute about 30 percent of the total value of Greece's agricultural output. The largest components of Greece's animal population are sheep and goats (estimated at about 14 million head), whose meat and milk, respectively, provide 6.2 and 6.6 percent of the agricultural total. Hogs and cattle numbered about 1 million and 655,000, respectively, at the end of the 1980s. Greek farmers also possessed an estimated 28 million chickens, 1.8 million rabbits, 1.3 million pigeons, and 1.2 million beehives at the end of the 1980s. Whereas most of the animals are evenly distributed among the agricultural regions of the country, about half the cattle are found in Macedonia, where large plains dominate the landscape. Beef and cows' milk account for 5.8 percent of agricultural output, chicken meat and eggs another 5.5 percent, and pork meat 3.5 percent.

The shares of major crops in total agricultural production in 1989 were as follows: industrial plants (mainly tobacco, cotton, and sugar beets) contributed 15.7 percent, cereal grains 10.8 percent, vegetables and fruits 10.5 percent each, olive products 9.7 percent, and grapes 5.5 percent. The last two products, traditional leaders in Greek agricultural exports, have now declined to relatively small parts of total agricultural production value.

The agricultural contribution to export values comes primarily from plant products, especially grains, fruits and vegetables, and tobacco. In 1992 Greece exported more than US$1.5 billion of plant products for consumption or industrial use. The very limited export of animal products is confined mainly to cheese, whose export value in 1992 was US$21 million, and leathers, which earned US$38 million the same year. On the other hand, a large portion of food imports into Greece are meat and milk products, purchase of which cost US$1.4 billion in 1992, 7.2 percent of total Greek import expenditures.

Since the World War II, public policy has supported agriculture strongly, partly because the devastation of the Civil War necessitated immediate reestablishment of populations in agricultural areas to regenerate the food supply. This state support took three forms: income and price supports, special credit conditions, and organizational aid.

Income and price supports, which were mainly administered through a list of national minimum prices for crops, have now been largely eliminated by the subsidy restrictions placed on EU members by the union's Common Agricultural Policy. In 1992 agricultural support funds from the EU to Greece amounted to US$3.3 billion, or 62 percent of all funds flowing from the EU to Greece. Domestic expenditures for agricultural subsidies, supports, and public projects amounted to US$1.9 billion, about 7 percent of the state budget in 1992.

Greek agriculture traditionally received special credit conditions from the Agricultural Bank of Greece, which had been founded in the late 1920s for that purpose. However, the banking liberalization that began in the late 1980s under European directives is reshaping the Agricultural Bank of Greece into a full commercial bank. Moreover, no sector can receive favorable lending terms under the competitive credit conditions that are now taking over the Greek money market. Nevertheless, agriculture remains an important segment of the credit market because the demand for "cultivation loans," which are essentially working capital facilities, remains high. By the end of 1993, agricultural loans accounted for 15 percent of total bank credit outstanding.

Organizational aid to agriculture has taken a variety of forms. Land consolidation programs have been on the agenda for a long time, aiming to overcoming the extreme fragmentation of landholdings. Greece has had a voluntary consolidation program since 1963 as well as compulsory consolidation in coordination with large irrigation projects. However, consolidation, which is essentially a voluntary process, occurs only very gradually. Between 1985 and 1989, the yearly averages of hectares consolidated and villages participating were 11,700 and fifteen, respectively.

The formation of agricultural cooperatives has been another method of streamlining agricultural production and overcoming the limitations of small landholdings and fragmentation. Farming cooperatives were first officially established in Greece in 1915. Eventually the cooperative structure was built up vertically with provincial cooperative unions and a national federation of unions, which still exist. Every Greek government has supported cooperatives, or some aspects of their activities, as part of its agricultural policy. Cooperatives also take specialized forms, such as credit unions and marketing ventures. Under the socialist governments of the 1980s, cooperatives were greatly enhanced. A large portion of agricultural credit was allocated via cooperatives. Investment incentive laws, which were primarily directed to manufacturing and tourism, were also extended to cooperative farming investments, and the direct marketing of agricultural produce was encouraged in order to bypass frequently monopolistic private wholesalers of produce. At the end of the 1980s, some 7,300 local cooperatives were operating with an estimated membership of 940,000.

Forestry and Fishing

Although forests cover an estimated 15 percent of the country's land area, forestry makes a very limited contribution to Greece's GDP. In 1992 the industrial wood, firewood, and resins derived from Greek forests amounted to less than 1 percent of the GDP. Although the value of forest production showed a tendency to increase, the volume of production declined during the 1980s. Greek forests, which had been devastated during the World War II occupation and the Civil War, recovered to some extent in the postwar era. However, forest management, like other forms of land management, has been a very low priority of all postwar governments. Underutilized and overgrown, the forests have been plagued by fires in recent years. In the 1970s, forest fires burned about 78,000 hectares; in the 1980s, some 200,000 hectares of forest were destroyed by fire. The trend is continuing in the 1990s, although since 1985 fire protection efforts have intensified.

Despite its maritime tradition and its extensive coastline, Greece is not a major producer of fish. In 1992 fishing contributed 0.7 percent to the Greek GDP. In 1992 the Greek fishing fleet numbered 21,167 vessels with a total gross tonnage of 118,000. About three-quarters of its capacity was in vessels of less than 100 tons. In 1988 some 16,510 persons were employed in fishing. Fishing output has steadily increased since the 1980s. In 1983 Greek fishing production from all regions amounted to 99,090 tons (live weight). In 1991 output had risen to 148,768 tons (live weight), with a 50 percent increase in volume since 1983. Pollution in the Mediterranean and overfishing in coastal waters have reduced the traditional contribution of coastal output to domestic consumption. Most fish comes from the Mediterranean at large, and about 10 percent of the total in 1992 was caught off the Atlantic coast of North Africa. The three largest fishing ports are Piraeus in the south and the Macedonian ports of Thessaloniki and Kavala in the northern Aegean.

The Service Sector

The Greek service sector is the largest and most heterogeneous component of the national economy. It comprises a considerable variety of activities ranging from street vending and rental of tourist rooms to highly automated telecommunications, sophisticated financial transactions, and public administration. The service sector also probably includes a good portion of the "underground economy." It is therefore possible that the value of its output and its employment level are understated.

Transportation and Telecommunications

Transportation and telecommunications, two segments of the service sector that are vital in supporting all economic activities, are undergoing rapid modernization in the mid-1990s. The transportation system underwent extensive reconstruction and expansion after World War II. However, in some cases geopolitical factors have hindered further expansion of the system. In many respects, Greek telecommunications still lag behind the systems of Western Europe, and topographical and geopolitical factors have hindered expansion.

Transportation

The coastal location of many Greek cities and towns, the multitude of islands, and the rugged terrain of the country's interior have traditionally made sea transport the basic means of linking localities within the country and Greek cities with foreign countries. The five largest Greek cities are all major ports: Athens/Piraeus, Thessaloniki, Patras, Heraklion, and Volos. In all, Greece has 123 ports large enough to handle passengers or freight. Besides the traditionally busy ports of Piraeus, Thessaloniki, and Patras, the ports of Igoumenitsa in the northwest, Volos in the east, and Kavala in the northeast have been gaining importance as transfer points for goods destined for Italy, the Middle East, and the Balkan countries (see fig. 10).

The Greek merchant fleet is among the largest in the world. In 1981 Greek-owned vessels numbered 4,402, totaling 50,909 gross tons. Of that number, 3,932 ships totaling 42,389 gross

tons were registered under the Greek flag, and in that year, Greek-owned ships comprised 12 percent of world shipping tonnage. By 1990 all numbers had decreased. At that point, 2,189 vessels, totaling 24,970 gross tons and representing 6 percent of world tonnage, were Greek-owned. In 1994 the Greek merchant fleet was operating 1,407 vessels totaling 46.4 deadweight tons. In 1990 about 10 percent of Greek-owned ship tonnage sailed under foreign registry. Hard-hit by the international shipping slump in the 1980s, the Greek-registered part of the fleet shrank from a high of 3,972 ships in 1980, when Greece had the second-largest merchant marine in the world.

In the second half of the twentieth century, coastal shipping has declined as a connector of domestic points because of the development of an extensive overland transport network. The great majority of overland transport is by road rather than railroad or air. In the early 1990s, however, the closing of major roadways in the former Yugoslavia, which had provided an overland connection between Greece and Western Europe, enhanced the importance of Ionian ports such as Igoumenitsa, Patras on the northwest shore of the Peloponnesus, and Kalamai at the southern tip of the Peloponnesus.

In 1990 Greece had 38,312 kilometers of roads, of which 9,100 kilometers were classified as national highways and 29,212 kilometers as provincial roads. About 21,000 kilometers of the latter category were paved roads, and 116 kilometers of the former category were classified as express roads. Changing geopolitical conditions in the Balkans and the Black Sea region have affected Greek plans and policies for expanding the existing road network. Nevertheless, Greece plans to spend about US$370 million on its roads and ports between 1995 and 1999, with about 70 percent of that amount coming from the EU's cohesion funds. Among the projects in that program, one is the Via Egnatia, a 740-kilometer road that would duplicate the path of an ancient Roman causeway and link Igoumenitsa in the west with Alexandroupolis in eastern Thrace, before proceeding to the Turkish border. This road is part of the EU's attempt to reverse the decline of the Greek northeast, which is now one of the least-developed regions in the entire European Union. The second project is a 480-kilometer road running north and south in western Greece to link Igoumenitsa with Patras and Kalamai. Both major highways have projected completion dates early in the 2000s.

The Greek rail system is under the administration of the Greek Railroads Organization (Organismos Sidirodromon Ellados—OSE), which was established in 1971. In 1991 the total length of the Greek rail network was 2,503 kilometers, of which twenty-six kilometers was a high-speed electrified shuttle line connecting Athens and Piraeus. The rail system in 1991 was not appreciably longer than it was before World War II. Of the existing rails, 1,565 kilometers are 1,435-millimeter gauge, 887 kilometers 1,000-millimeter gauge, and fifty-one kilometers 750-millimeter gauge. The Athens-Piraeus shuttle uses the broadcast gauge track; the Athens-Peloponnesus line uses 1,000-millimeter track. Throughout the postwar period, the rail system was neglected in favor of road and air transportation. For that reason, much railroad equipment is obsolete, and operation costs are high.

To remedy the railroads' backwardness, beginning in 1978 the chief construction project of the OSE has been modernization of the main line from Athens through Thessaloniki and on to Idhomeni on the border of the Former Yugoslav Republic of Macedonia (FYROM), a corridor that carries more than half of Greece's rail traffic. After domestic funding proved inadequate, in 1990 the EC approved a grant of half the project's total cost, to be matched by funds from Greece's Public Investment Program. At the end of 1993, about 70 percent of the 510-kilometer line from Athens to Thessaloniki had been double-tracked, electrical signals were in operation along the line except in one 134-kilometer segment, and a modern telecommunications system covered the entire axis. In 1990 new diesel locomotives went into operation on this line, cutting transit time from seven hours to six hours, ten minutes. In the planning stage is upgrading of the 220-kilometer Athens-Patras line, which is to be converted to electrified, 1,435-millimeter-gauge track with modern signaling, able to handle speeds of 200 kilometers per hour.

In 1992 the OSE operated 214 diesel locomotives, 106 diesel train-sets, 467 passenger cars, and 10,585 freight cars. Railcars and equipment were supplied by German firms and Hellenic Shipyards of Piraeus.

In 1993 construction began on a twenty-six-kilometer extension of the Athens-Piraeus line, in order to provide Athens with a three-line urban rail system. Construction of a subway system in Athens was halted in 1983 because of lack of funds, and in

1992 mass transit in the city still depended on electrified rail, trolleys, and buses.

In 1991 the Greek railroads carried 12.3 million passengers and 3.5 million tons of freight, over an average distance per trip of 164 kilometers. In 1989 the corresponding load of the interurban bus transport system, also operated by OSE, was 164 million passengers carried over an average distance of thirty-two kilometers. Thus, the pattern of mass-transit passenger use divides between longer distance rail use and shorter distance buses.

In 1989 passenger boats and car ferries on coastal runs transported 11 million passengers. Finally, urban public transport of all forms in 1989 carried an estimated 862.1 million passengers, three-quarters of whom were in the Athens metropolitan area. In the latter, 20 percent of the passenger load is carried by the existing Athens metropolitan rail system, about 10 percent by electrical trolley buses, and the remaining 70 percent by normal buses.

The use of private passenger cars has increased along with the growth of the urban and highway road networks, providing an ever-greater share of total transport service in the economy. There were 858,845 cars in 1980, but their number had doubled to 1,735,523 in 1990, significantly worsening the air quality and traffic congestion in major urban areas. For several years, restrictions have been in force on passenger car circulation in Athens, and are gradually extending to other cities and tourist areas in the summer. To ease severe air pollution in Athens, plans call for harsher restrictions on numbers of cars and their mechanical and exhaust specifications.

Air travel within the country is the exclusive domain of the state-owned Olympic Airways. In 1992 Olympic operated four Boeing 747s, eight A300s, seventeen Boeing 737s, nine Boeing 727s, and twenty-one other aircraft. In 1989 some 6.7 million passengers were transported. Olympic offers domestic flights among the principal cities and islands and overseas to most points in Europe and the Middle East, as well as to Japan, Singapore, Thailand, South Africa, and the United States.

Although the passenger loads of the company have been growing at an average of about 3 percent annually, Olympic Airways has been facing financial difficulties as a result of high costs. A plan to restructure its operation has been negotiated between Greece and the EU, which has undertaken to regulate the national air carriers of member countries.

Thirty-seven airports are in operation, of which the majority are located in the islands and are used by military as well as civilian flights. The two largest international airports are located at Athens (Hellinikon Airport) and Thessaloniki (Thessaloniki-Macedonia Airport). In the early 1990s, Hellinikon Airport handled an average of 6.3 million passengers annually. Other international airports are located at Alexandroupolis, Corfu, Lesbos, Andravida, Rhodes, Cos, and Heraklion. A new international facility is planned at Spata, at the tip of the Attic Peninsula southeast of Athens.

Greece has no navigable rivers. The six-kilometer Corinth Canal, completed in 1893, connects the gulfs of Corinth and Saronikos, thereby shortening by 325 kilometers the west-east voyage from the Ionian Sea to Piraeus on the Gulf of Saronikos. Maximum draught of ships using the canal is 7.1 meters, maximum width 19.4 meters. Three bridges span the canal: one carrying a rail line, two carrying roads.

Telecommunications

The establishment of telecommunications networks comparable to those in Western Europe has been difficult in Greece. Several factors have influenced this situation, which has endured for several decades: unstable and polarized political conditions, the mountainous interior and dispersed islands, and the inefficient monopoly of telecommunications, which are run by the state-owned Greek Telecommunications Organization (Organismos Tilepikoinonion Ellados—OTE).

When the telephone system was nationalized and the OTE was established under the Ministry of Transportation and Communications in 1949, only one Greek in 100 had a telephone line. Development remained slow through the 1970s; then, beginning in 1981, the Papandreou government began a concerted effort to modernize the country's antiquated telephone network by installing automatic digital exchanges in place of older mechanical exchanges. This process began in 1986, but distribution of digital equipment proceeded very slowly into the early 1990s. During the 1980s, Greece's per-line investment was only about 4 percent of the average for the most developed countries in the world, the telephone breakdown rate in that period was fifty-seven per 100 inhabitants, and the average waiting period for telephone installation exceeded four years.

Between 1980 and 1990, the number of automatic exchanges increased from 1,209, with a capacity of 2.5 million

Pizza sign on Santorini (Thira), a favorite tourist destination
Traffic jam on an Athens side street
Courtesy Sam and Sarah Stulberg

lines, to 1,923, with a capacity of 4.1 million lines. In the same period, the number of telephones in operation increased from 2.8 million to 4.7 million. The waiting list was longer in 1990 than in 1980, however, and even high-priority users, such as hospitals and businesses, waited for as long as a year for installation in 1990. In 1992 Greece had 4,722 telephone exchanges and 5.3 million telephones in service.

In the early 1990s, the politicization of the OTE remained a serious obstacle to installation of a modern national communications network. During the socialist administrations of 1981–89, telephone investments were awarded first to regions supporting the party in power, and by 1988 the OTE was the focal point of charges that the government had wiretapped opposition leaders. In 1990 the new conservative government promised that by 1993 about 1.2 million digital lines would be in service and cellular service would be introduced. (At that point, Greece was the only EC country without cellular service.) In the years that followed, bids for cellular and digital equipment procurement brought bitter disputes over suppliers and calls for reform. In 1991 the EC issued special communications standards for Greece because of its slow development.

In the early 1990s, the poor quality of transmissions limited the use of the public network for data transmission. The leasing of modem lines from the OTE is subject to complex regulations and limitations. In 1987 a public-packet switched data network, Hellaspac, began operation. Mobile telephony became the first type of telecommunications not monopolized by the OTE when two private consortia introduced it in 1993. In 1994 the Papandreou government attempted partial privatization of the OTE by selling a minority part of the company's equity capital on the Greek and foreign stock exchanges, but the plan died amid interministerial wrangling and insufficient planning when market prices for the shares appeared much lower than expected. Instead, the government extended the OTE's monopoly over the national telecommunications infrastructure and cable networks until 2003. Although new privatization plans were possible as early as 1995, experts disagreed about the prospects for price reductions, modernization, and the fate of foreign networks in the Greek market without genuine domestic competition in the industry.

Greek Radio and Television (Elliniki Radiofonia Tileorasi—ERT) is the government broadcasting corporation. Since private broadcasting stations were legalized in 1987, breaking the state monopoly of telecommunications, Greek television and radio programming has diversified significantly, although the ERT's broadcasts still reach the largest numbers of listeners. In 1993 about 2.3 million television sets and 4.1 million radios were in operation.

In 1994 the ERT's Greek Radio (Elliniki Radiofonia—ERA) was operating twenty-five medium-wave and eighteen frequency-modulation (FM) radio stations; eleven private radio stations were operating in Athens at that time, and twenty-two additional stations broadcast to regional areas. Four national and regional networks provide domestic radio programming, and an external service, the Voice of Greece, broadcasts overseas in sixteen languages.

In 1994, the ERT's Greek Television (Elliniki Tileorasi—ET) operated three television networks, encompassing forty-seven channels. Of that number, Athens had five, Thessaloniki three, and the Greek islands a total of ten stations. The ET–1 network provides the main service, ET–2 specializes in cultural programming, and ET–3 transmits regional programming from its Thessaloniki facility. Two private television channels that were licensed in 1990 have gained large audiences, and other private entertainment channels had been licensed by 1992. The government networks provide color telecasts through the French Secam color television broadcast system. Several foreign cable channels are received in Greece, but only one, the Cable News Network (CNN), provides regular news coverage.

Tourism

As the most internationalized subsector and one of the major industries of the Greek economy, tourism is a strong earner of foreign exchange. The warm climate, the long, scenic Mediterranean coastline, the many significant archaeological and historical sites, the traditional hospitality of Greeks, and improvements in the local infrastructure have increased the number of foreign travelers attracted to Greece. The tourist residence capacity has grown also. Between 1970 and 1990, the number of beds in tourist accommodations increased from 119,000 to 438,000. Of this residential capacity, 84 percent is located in hotels, of which Greece had 4,659 in 1992. However, the share of motels, furnished apartments, and guest houses has been increasing over the last decade.

Tourist visits followed a moderate growth trend in the 1980s. In the last two decades, Greece's traditional competitors, Spain and Portugal, have been joined by Turkey and the other Balkan countries with beaches on the Adriatic and Black seas. Total nights spent by foreigners in Greece were 30.6 million in 1981 and rose to 34.5 million in 1989. Since the mid-1980s, tourist arrivals have generally fluctuated between 8 million and 9 million persons per year, but in 1994 this number exceeded 10 million. Despite long efforts by Greek governments to extend the tourist season throughout the year, Greek tourism remains concentrated in the summer months. In 1990–91, for example, three-quarters of tourist arrivals took place in the five-month period between May and September.

The vast majority of tourists visiting Greece are European. In 1989 some 92 percent of tourists were European, compared with 88 percent in 1981. In 1991 the largest numbers of tourists in Greece came from Germany and Britain, which together accounted for over 40 percent of the total. Visitors from Yugoslavia, Italy, France, and the Netherlands added another 24 percent. The share of United States tourists in the total dropped significantly, however, from 4.4 percent in 1981 to 2.3 percent in 1989.

The major archaeological sites of Greece remain a strong attraction for tourists. In 1990 the most visited sites were the Acropolis of Athens (1.4 million visitors), the palace of Knossos on Crete (706,306 visitors), the temple of Apollo at Delphi (590,736 visitors), the Epidaurus Theater in the Peloponnesus (540,596 visitors), the palace and treasure of Mycenae in the Peloponnesus (507,161 visitors), and the Acropolis of Lindos on the island of Rhodes (419,187 visitors).

Foreign-exchange earnings from tourism have been increasing since 1983. In 1992 tourist earnings amounted to US$3.3 billion, showing an average annual increase of 5.5 percent since 1983. Tourist receipts have risen at a considerably faster rate than tourist night-stays, indicating that the Greek policy of upgrading the quality of tourist visits has been rewarded by increased per capita spending. In 1992 the amount of foreign exchange earned from tourism equaled 55 percent of Greek merchandise exports for that year, accounting for almost 20 percent of total Greek exports of goods and services.

Besides extending the tourist season, policy makers have sought to promote tourism in the north and west of the country and to enhance luxury tourism. Infrastructure projects for maritime tourism, such as the increased construction of marinas, have been a major priority in recent years. Investment incentives similar to those offered to manufacturing are also extended to tourist projects. In awarding grants and subsidies, state policy has favored Epirus, Macedonia, Thrace, and the eastern Aegean Islands. Support rates also depend on the type of project; luxury hotels and therapeutic treatment spas, sports, and winter tourism resorts now receive preferential treatment.

Banking and Finance

The financial sector's importance in Greece surpasses its proportional contribution to the country' s GDP, which in 1990 stood at about 3 percent. Besides its traditional functions in collecting savings and reallocating them by lending, the financial system in Greece, as in many advanced countries, has begun to perform a variety of other services such as underwriting new security issues, corporate services for acquisitions and restructuring, wealth and portfolio management, and leasing. In the early 1990s, the capital market for securities also has grown quickly, and the volume and frequency of transactions on the Athens Stock Exchange have multiplied.

The bulk of the financial flow in the Greek economy always has moved through the banks. The banking system consists of three kinds of institutions. One is the central bank (the Bank of Greece), which manages and controls the country's money supply and its exchange rate with other currencies. The bank accomplishes these tasks mainly by regulating the liquidity of other banks and by direct interventions in money markets (including the foreign-exchange market). It is also the main supervisory agency for the quality of commercial bank portfolios, and the protection of the monetary system against bank failures. In line with requirements of the 1992 Maastricht Treaty, which standardized the financial organizations of EU member countries, the Bank of Greece must become independent of the government, and the bank must enforce strict limits on government use of the money supply as a source of loans. European central banks also will be jointly responsible for the management of the projected European common currency.

Commercial banks are a second type of financial institution in the Greek system. They are deposit institutions that traditionally have engaged in commercial and industrial lending. More recently, Greek commercial banks have expanded their operations to provide a wide range of wholesale and retail banking services. Their loans include commercial, industrial, consumer, and mortgage credits. They issue credit cards and travelers' checks, buy and sell foreign exchange, and issue letters of credit. They directly engage in securities underwriting. Through their subsidiaries, they also offer brokerage services and own mutual funds of Greek and foreign securities.

A third class of institution is the "specialized credit institution" such as investment banks, the Agricultural Bank of Greece, mortgage banks, and the Postal Savings Bank. The traditional role of these institutions was to offer credit in specifically designated areas. However, banking liberalization and European policies on a unified banking market have forced specialized institutions to diversify their operations. In the 1990s, specialization in a particular area must be determined by market conditions rather than by legislative constraint. The prime example of this change is the Agricultural Bank, which was legally restricted to granting agricultural credit, distribution of which it in turn monopolized. In 1991 the Agricultural Bank became a full-fledged commercial bank, at the same time that other commercial banks were allowed to enter the agricultural credit market. The same conversion occurred with mortgage and investment banks.

Commercial banks operating in Greece include both domestic and foreign institutions. The number of such institutions is constantly increasing. In 1992 twenty-two Greek and eighteen foreign banks were in operation. The foreign banks, which operate in Greece through locally established branches, control about 10 percent of assets and deposits in the Greek banking market. Among Greek banks, the Bank of Greece is by far the largest institution, controlling 29 percent of banking assets and 37 percent of deposits in 1991. The largest among the foreign banks is the New York-based Citibank, which in 1991 controlled about one-quarter of the assets and one-third of the deposits held by foreign banks in Greece.

A number of Greek credit institutions are either directly or indirectly controlled by the state. Some, such as the Industrial Development Bank of Greece, are 100 percent state-owned. A majority interest in others, notably the two largest commercial banks, the National Bank and the Commercial Bank of Greece, is held by employee pension funds that traditionally have been managed by the state. Recent changes in legislation seek to moderate state control by granting a degree of self-management to employee pension funds, and shares in the banks are now traded on the stock exchange. Smaller subsidiary banks, such as the medium-sized Ionian Bank of Greece, are owned by the Commercial Bank of Greece and the National Bank of Greece.

The major assets of commercial banks traditionally included credits and loans to the private sector. Since the late 1980s, however, the heavy borrowing requirements of the state have altered the portfolios of bank assets. Roughly one-third of their assets now are made up of government securities, equal to the share devoted to loans and security holdings of the private sector. The liabilities of commercial banks continue to be dominated by private deposits.

Since 1987 the Greek banking system has undergone almost complete liberalization. Interest rates are now set by market conditions, quantity controls on credit have been long abolished, foreign-exchange transactions and capital movements have been deregulated, and restrictions on entry into banking have been removed. In the implementation stage in 1995 were EU directives on the freedom of bank establishment among member countries, on the free provision of financial services across frontiers, and on common standards for capital adequacy. In short, banking is becoming a modern and very competitive business in Greece.

The Athens Stock Exchange (ASE) has also undergone significant modernization and revitalization since 1987. Legislation enabling the formation of brokerage firms and their participation as members of the exchange, the introduction of an automated trading system, and the establishment of a Central Securities Depository have been the main institutional changes of recent years. In 1993 market capitalization of the shares listed was US$13.5 billion, and the total value of market transactions was US$2.8 billion. Between 1990 and 1993, fifty-seven listings were added, bringing the total number of companies with listed stocks to 150. New capital raised in 1993 through stock issues amounted to US$436 million. Plans call for enhancement of stock-exchange operations by linking of the Athens exchange with peripheral terminals such as Thessaloniki and by encouraging foreign companies—most notably those in the Balkans—to list their shares on the exchange.

In the mid-1990s, government policies in the financial area are mainly directed to the maintenance of competition in banking, and to further strengthening of the role of the stock exchange. The new competition in banking is manifested mainly in the appearance of new products and services such as automated teller machines, whose introduction by market leaders soon forced most banks to follow suit. An initiative has been adopted to establish an automated interbank clearing and payments system in Greece.

The exchange rate of the Greek unit of currency, the drachma, has undergone gradual devaluation (called a "managed float") since 1987 (see Wages, Prices, and Inflation, this ch.). In mid-1994, elimination of Greece's short-term capital movement restrictions and a decisive defense of the currency by the large Greek banks deflected speculation on the drachma that could have resulted in sudden devaluation.

Foreign Trade

In the 1990s, Greece's international economic activity was directed increasingly toward equality with its partners in the EU. At the same time, however, the traditional patterns of foreign trade and trade balances remained quite stable.

The Balance of Payments

Greece's balance of payments has maintained the same characteristics for a long time; specifically, the trade balance (exports minus imports) has traditionally been negative. In the years 1991–93, exports of goods fell short of imports by an annual average of more than US$13 billion. The traditionally positive balance of invisibles, particularly services such as tourism, shipping, and transfers such as remittances from emigrants and payments from the EU, has usually covered most of the trade deficit. In the years 1991–93, invisibles showed an annual surplus of about US$11.5 billion. Finally, the country has usually had a positive net capital flow, which in 1991–93 averaged US$3.5 billion per year. The overall outcome of Greece's international payments was a surplus in 1991 and 1993, but a deficit of US$2.1 million in 1992. On the whole, since 1990 surpluses have exceeded deficits, and the country's foreign-exchange reserves have grown considerably. At the end of 1993, foreign-exchange reserves stood at US$8.7 billion.

Export and Import Structure

One of Greece's important export sectors is the sale of international shipping services, which are a crucial source of foreign exchange. Having reached an historic high of US$1.8 billion in 1980–81, these earnings then declined to US$1 bil-

*Ship passing through Corinth Canal between Peloponnesus
and Greek mainland
Courtesy Sam and Sarah Stulberg*

lion by 1986 before recovering and approaching the US$2 billion level in 1992. In 1992 the foreign exchange earned by shipping equaled one-third the value of Greek merchandise exports and about 13 percent of total exports of goods and services.

In 1992 two-thirds of foreign-exchange earnings from shipping came from shipowners' remittances. The share of sailors' remittances has declined consistently, however, because of increasing utilization of cheaper foreign labor on Greek-owned vessels. Chronic stagnation of the Greek shipping industry in the late 1980s and early 1990s has prevented additional earnings from this source.

Besides shipping, between 1991 and 1993, the largest contributions by invisibles to goods and service export income came from two services: tourism contributed 19 percent, and emigrant remittances added 14 percent. Even before World War I, remittances from the large Greek émigré community began to make a significant contribution to Greece's foreign-exchange earnings. From that time until the mid-1990s, they remained a significant source of foreign currency.

Net receipts from various programs of the EC, which averaged US$4 billion per year between 1991 and 1993, amounted to 25 percent of invisibles. The largest types of expenditures recorded under invisible payments were interest, profits, and dividends transferred abroad, amounting to over US$2 billion and representing about 20 percent of all invisible payments; and expenses for Greek tourism abroad, which averaged US$1 billion in 1991–93, or 10 percent of invisible payments.

Trading Partners

Because Greece's membership in the EC since 1981 has meant abolition of trade barriers of all kinds, the geographic distribution of Greek foreign trade has been increasingly oriented in favor of its partner countries in the EC/EU (see table 9; table 10, Appendix). In 1980 some 49 percent of Greek exports and 43 percent of imports were directed to or originated from countries of the EC. In 1992 EC countries received 62 percent of Greece's exports and supplied 62 percent of its imports. Among EC countries, the main trading partner was Germany, which in 1992 absorbed about 22 percent of exports and supplied 20 percent of imports. Italy was the second largest trading partner, with export and import percentages of 18 and 13 percent, respectively. The next largest export partners, in order of trade value, were France, Britain, Egypt, the United States, and Cyprus. The next largest import partners, in order of trade value, were France, the Netherlands, Japan, Britain, and the United States. In the early 1990s, the greatest trade increases occurred with Bulgaria, Egypt, Japan, China, and the Republic of Korea (South Korea). The sharpest decline occurred with Yugoslavia.

The United States is Greece's largest trade partner outside the EU. In 1992 the United States bought 16 percent of Greek exports and sold 9 percent of Greek imports. In 1992 Greece showed a negative trade balance with the United States of US$867 million. Between 1988 and 1992, trade with the East European and former Soviet nations that until 1991 constituted the Community for Mutual Economic Assistance (Comecon) more than doubled, with exports growing from US$209 million in 1988 to US$568 million and imports from US$599 million in 1988 to US$931 million in 1992.

Greece's main export products are fruit, vegetables, olive oil, clothing, and textiles (see table 11, Appendix). The chief imports are machinery, transportation equipment, food, chemical products, and petroleum and petroleum products (see table 12, Appendix). The last category of purchases caused a trade imbalance with the nations of the Organization of the Petroleum Exporting Countries (OPEC) of nearly US$1.3 billion in 1992; between 1983 and 1992, expenditures for oil imports from OPEC remained relatively steady at between US$1.5 billion and US$2 billion, with steep drops in 1988 and 1989 partly caused by falling world oil prices.

Capital flows into Greece have been both private and public. Most public capital flows are incoming government loans or outgoing repayment of existing loans. Besides the government, the central bank and state-controlled credit institutions also engage in foreign-capital transactions. At the end of 1993, the Bank of Greece estimated that the amount owed directly or guaranteed by the Greek government to foreign creditors was about US$26 billion.

Private capital flows into Greece have been significant in recent years. In the period 1987–92, Greece received long-term net private capital flows for long-term forms of investment totaling US$9.7 billion. Of those, US$4.3 billion was in entrepreneurial capital, and the remainder was in real estate investment.

Since 1989, Greek investment in manufacturing enterprises abroad has accelerated, primarily in the neighboring Balkan countries. Food processing, textiles, other consumer goods, and building materials are the primary sectors of Greek manufacturing investment in Bulgaria. According to official estimates, Greek investment now ranks first among all foreign investment in Bulgaria and is among the leaders in Albania and Romania.

International Economic Policy in the 1990s

In the 1980s and 1990s, the dominant factor in Greece's international economic policy has been participation in the EC (now the EU). EU policies for internal market unification, free capital movements, and movement toward implementation of the Economic and Monetary Union (EMU), set forth in the Maastricht Treaty, form the main axes of Greek policy. The guidelines of Greece's participation in the EMU were set in 1993 when the EC Council of Ministers approved a five-year Convergence Plan. By 1998 the plan calls for Greece to have reduced the annual inflation rate to 4 percent, increased GDP growth from 2 percent to 4 percent per year, reduced the public-sector deficit to 0.2 percent of GDP, and reduced unemployment to 7.7 percent. Some of the goals were modified in 1994.

Having liberalized all restrictions on its trade within the community since the 1980s, Greece has proceeded in the 1990s with the liberalization of capital movements. Remaining restrictions on short-term capital movements were eliminated slightly ahead of schedule in May 1994 when Greece faced a speculative attack against the drachma.

The EMU includes plans for the eventual creation of a single European currency. As countries converge toward the common currency, their ability to conduct national economic policy will be correspondingly reduced. Already, for example, the liberalization of financial markets and the freedom of capital movements has reduced the flexibility of Greece's monetary policy, by requiring that domestic interest rates be aligned with those prevailing in European money markets. Presumably, the loss of national control over this phase of Greece's economic policy will be balanced by large resource transfers that will raise economic levels in real terms for the less developed partners.

Greece's regional economic policy is mainly oriented to newly arising market economies in the Balkans and the Black Sea region. The policy envisions unified infrastructural communications and transportation networks; the implementation of a "drachma zone" in the Balkans to enhance Balkan currency convertibility and introduce the trading of Balkan currencies in the Athens foreign-exchange market; support for Balkan firms in the form of financial services and contributions to EU programs for private-sector initiatives; and export guarantee plans for Greek firms trading with enterprises from formerly socialist economies (see Transportation and Telecommunications, this ch.).

Commercial initiatives in the Balkans and the expansion of Greek activities in the EU have forced considerable adjustment in Greece's domestic economy. After the prolonged slump of the 1980s and early 1990s, the Greek economy entered a period of adjustment in 1991. In that period, conformity to EC regulations had the potential to streamline troublesome aspects of the system by shrinking the influence of the public sector and stimulating privatization. If full-scale participation in the international economy helps Greece tighten its macroeconomic policies and continue structural reform, the long-term prospects of exploiting available resources will improve.

At the end of 1994, the PASOK stewardship of the national economy received mixed reviews. The Greek business community continued to vacillate about committing large amounts of capital to new investment; the government's large debt had increased, although at a slower rate; and few of the planned, large-scale EU-funded infrastructure projects had begun. On the other hand, inflation continued to decline, attaining twenty-year lows by the end of 1994; manufacturing production showed signs of reviving; reformed tax laws were successfully implemented to reduce special-interest bias and increase the rate of revenue collection; and exchange controls were removed completely without endangering Greece's balance of payments or its exchange rate. Expert projections for 1995 included a continued restraint on income and consumption and a continued rise in unemployment. If confidence in the economy were to continue to increase, however, public and private investment would stimulate new growth in the mid-1990s that could overcome Greece's divergences from the European average in growth rate, inflation, and rate of fiscal consolidation.

*   *   *

Invaluable current information and statistics on economic policy and trends are provided by the Economist Intelligence Unit's quarterly *Country Report: Greece* and the Organisation for Economic Co-operation and Development (OECD) annual *OECD Economic Survey: Greece.* General descriptions of Greece's telecommunications and media systems are available in *The World's News Media,* edited by Harry Drost, and Eli M. Noam's *Telecommunications in Europe.* Economic development in the postwar period is discussed in *The Economy of Greece, 1944–66* by Wray O. Candilis and in Nicos P. Mouzelis's *Modern Greece: Facets of Underdevelopment. Greece and Yugoslavia* by Nicholas V. Gianaris describes the historical development of the economy of those countries and economic policies in the 1970s and 1980s. In his *The Development of the Greek Economy, 1950–1991,* George A. Jouganatos places an econometric analysis of postwar economic events in the context of political events. A broad review of Greek economic evolution in the twentieth century can be found in *The Greek Economy in the Twentieth Century* by Andrew F. Freris. *Greece, the New Europe, and the Changing International Order,* edited by Harry J. Psomiades and Stavros Thomadakis, provides an extensive analysis of issues pertaining to Greek membership in the European Community. The National Statistical Service of Greece publishes a *Monthly Statistical Bulletin* that includes economic indicators. The most current information can be found in the London daily *Financial Times* and in the monthly economic supplements of the Foreign Broadcast Information Service's *Daily Report: Western Europe.* (For further information and complete citations, see Bibliography.)

Chapter 4. Government and Politics

Greek flag flies on windmills along a causeway, Rhodes

THE TWENTIETH ANNIVERSARY of the fall of the military junta dictatorship, in July 1994, afforded Greeks an opportunity to assess their country's progress since that event. Most political observers found that concrete gains had been made and that democracy had been consolidated. Although the political system of Greece still includes serious flaws, the democratic transition of 1974–94 has often been cited for the efficiency with which it has dealt with political problems lingering from the tumultuous past and put in place checks and balances that should resolve future dilemmas.

Foremost among the past problems were the final disposition of the monarchy and the legalization of the communist party. By resolving both of these questions within one year after the junta's fall in 1974, Prime Minister Konstantinos Karamanlis removed two of the major deficiencies of the post-World War II political atmosphere that had made the accession of a military dictatorship possible in 1967 (see The Junta, ch. 1). The immediate result of World War II had been the three-year Civil War that left Greece with a stunted parliamentary system characterized by a meddling monarch, pervasive domestic surveillance tactics, and interventionist foreign allies throughout the 1950s and early 1960s.

Preparing Greece's political system for long-term stability was a formidable task. After seven years of political isolation ended in 1974, the government of Karamanlis's party, New Democracy (Nea Demokratia—ND), tried to recover the economic momentum that had propelled a rapid political evolution in the late 1950s and made possible the liberal agenda of Prime Minister Georgios Papandreou in the mid-1960s. The junta had separated Greece from the successful path being followed by its European neighbors, leaving the capitalist system that emerged from the early 1970s unprepared for the mounting social and political demands that it encountered.

The legalization of all leftist parties and the establishment of a presidential republic cleared the way for consolidation of the new democratic gains. The expanded political spectrum led to vigorous calls for further democratization and modernization, goals most eloquently expressed by Andreas Papandreou's Panhellenic Socialist Movement (Panhellinion Socialistiko Kinima—PASOK). Founded in 1974 from a nucleus of antijunta activists and Papandreou's close personal supporters, PASOK came to power in 1981, with change as its byword. PASOK's rapid rise confirmed that government power could now pass in orderly fashion from one party to another of quite different ideology.

The PASOK election also began a jarring and controversial era of sociopolitical transformations. Central features of that period were a climate of openness and a palpable sense of political disorientation. PASOK's fiery rhetoric fostered high public expectations that were frustrated by a deepening economic crisis and by PASOK's unfocused long-term political agenda.

To sidestep harsh domestic economic realities in the 1980s, the government used flamboyant diversionary tactics that made Greece appear unstable to its friends and allies. PASOK's first term brought new segments of society, which until that time had not been heard in policy discussions, into the political mainstream. However, by the middle of PASOK's second administration, this process was halted when the state could no longer afford to satisfy mounting interest-group demands. Experts saw PASOK's losses to the conservatives of Karamanlis in 1989, following a period of malaise and scandal, as the death knell of the party. Unhappily, the ND failed as badly as had PASOK, so the voters again turned to Papandreou in 1993. But neither the ND nor PASOK successes at the polls showed that the political system had evolved beyond a civilized exchange of power between two dominant parties. Greek parties had not yet become instruments for popular participation in the increasingly urgent process of reforming and modernizing national institutions—tasks that experts believe a national party must keep central in the electorate's attention.

The Constitutional Framework

Greece is a parliamentary republic whose president is the head of state and whose prime minister is the head of government. The governmental and political system is based on the constitution of 1975. The latest revisions to the constitution, all of which had the purpose of curtailing presidential powers, were ratified in June 1986. Historically, the most frequent reason for changing the constitution had to do with the continuing dispute over whether monarchy or republic were the proper form of government for Greece. This conflict was a major source of political tensions for almost 150 years.

The 1975 constitution was drafted by a popularly elected legislature following the ouster of the last military dictatorship (see Karamanlis and the Restoration of Democracy, ch. 1). The document provides the basis for a republican form of governance, reflecting the overwhelming popular vote in the referendum of December 1974 to abolish the monarchy. According to the constitution, sovereignty rests with the people. Governmental structure and functional responsibilities are broadly divided into three branches: executive, legislative, and judicial. These branches are to operate under the principle of checks and balances. The presidency of the republic is placed above the three branches and above partisan politics as well. The 1975 document limited the authority of the president in order to prevent a concentration of power in his hands, but it also left some important political initiatives within the definition of the office's power. On the other hand, the thrust of the 1986 amendments to the constitution was to ensure that the president would remain a strictly titular head of state.

A full range of human rights is protected under the constitution, which states that all persons residing within Greek territory may enjoy, "full protection of their life, honor, and freedom, irrespective of nationality, race, or language and of religious or political beliefs," unless otherwise disallowed by international law. Every adult citizen has the right to participate in the social, economic, and political life of the country. The state and all its agents are directed to ensure that individual rights and liberties are exercised fully. The state may, for its part, call on all citizens "to fulfill the duty of social and national solidarity."

The specification of basic rights and liberties includes freedom of speech, of the press, of peaceful assembly and association, and of travel; economic freedom and property ownership; privacy of correspondence and the inviolability of the home; due process of law; and the prohibition of retroactive legislation. Also guaranteed are the right to petition the state for redress of grievances and the right to employment, to social security and housing, to education, and to health care.

Traditionally, the Orthodox Church of Greece has maintained a close link with the state. The special status of the church is acknowledged in the constitution, which declares, "The prevailing religion in Greece is the Eastern Orthodox Church of Christ." Nevertheless, the freedom of religious conscience is declared inviolable, and "all known religions" are to be free, and their rites of worship are to be performed unhindered. They are also to be protected by law to an extent not prejudicial to public order or to moral principles. Nevertheless, the constitution provides special status for the Orthodox Church by prohibiting proselytization by all other religions. Instances of religious persecution have been rare and irregular, so the implications of this prohibition are unclear (see Human Rights, this ch.; Religion, ch. 2).

The constitution states that work is a right, and all workers are entitled to equal remuneration for equal services performed. The freedom of unionism, including the right to strike for higher wages and better employment conditions, is constitutionally protected, but judicial functionaries and members of the state security forces are prohibited from striking. Civil servants and employees of other public corporations may strike, subject to the limitations of the law.

All but the most basic articles of the constitution—such as those defining Greece as a parliamentary republic, those guaranteeing fundamental rights and liberties, and those vesting legislative, executive, and judicial powers in the appropriate branches of government—may be amended. To amend the constitution, a proposal must be introduced into the legislature by at least fifty members of parliament. It must then be confirmed by a three-fifths majority vote of the total parliamentary membership on each of two ballots held at least one month apart. The next session of parliament finally enacts the amendment by an absolute majority vote of the total membership. Constitutional revision is not permitted before the lapse of five years from the completion of a previous revision; this provision is designed to ensure the stability of constitutional order.

Government Organization

Greece is a unitary state based on a system of parliamentary representation. The powers of the state are separated into three branches to prevent their concentration in a single authority. Despite constitutional provisions to strengthen local administration (article 102), in 1994 power still rested largely with the central government. For the first time in October 1994, local elections included direct election of province governors (*nomarchs*). Until that time, governors had been appointees of the national government.

The Presidency

The president is the principal link among the executive, legislative, and judicial branches of the government. He or she is insulated from direct political pressures by virtue of being elected by open ballot (since 1986) of the Assembly (the Vouli). The presidential term is five years, and the maximum number of terms is two.

A candidate for the presidency must have a Greek father, have been a Greek citizen for at least five years, be at least forty years of age, and be entitled to vote in parliamentary elections. To be elected, an individual must receive a two-thirds majority in parliament (200 votes) on the first and second ballots, or, if no such majority is reached, a three-fifths majority (180 votes) on a third ballot. Failure to elect a president on the third round results in the dissolution of the Assembly within ten days and the holding of new elections within forty days. The new Assembly must begin immediately the process of electing a president. In this election, a three-fifths majority is required on the first ballot, an absolute majority (151 votes) on the second, and a simple majority on the third. Should the presidency be vacated at any time, the Assembly must meet within ten days to elect a successor for a full term. If the president is incapacitated, presidential duties are temporarily assumed by the speaker of the Assembly.

In 1985, as Karamanlis's first presidential term was ending and a presidential election approached, the rival PASOK government argued for expansion of the powers of the Assembly at the expense of the president, who was characterized as having excessive prerogatives under the 1975 constitution. The amendments passed in 1986 actually did not change the prescribed functions of the Assembly; instead, they simply shifted powers from the president to the office of the prime minister, leaving the former with largely ceremonial duties.

The presidency still retains numerous ceremonial functions. The president represents Greece in international relations and, with the concurrence of the Assembly, declares war and concludes agreements of peace, alliance, and participation in international organizations. The president also is the head of the armed forces, but actual command is exercised by the government. Much of the president's power in relation to the Assembly is limited by the constitutional provision that most presidential acts must be countersigned by the appropriate cabinet ministers. The president may be impeached if charges against him or her are signed by at least one-third of the members of the Assembly and subsequently approved by at least two-thirds of the total membership. A special ad hoc court, presided over by the chief justice of the Supreme Court, would then try the president.

The Branches of Government

The day-to-day governance of Greece is conducted by three branches of government arranged according to the parliamentary system, with an independent judiciary and an executive branch that serves with the approval of the Assembly (see fig. 11).

The Executive Branch

The executive establishment, or government, consists of the cabinet, which includes twenty-two departmental ministries led by the prime minister. Also included are one cabinet-rank minister to the prime minister and thirty-one alternate or deputy ministers. Ministers, who need not be members of the Assembly, are chosen by the prime minister and their names submitted to the president for formal appointment. Together with the prime minister, ministers are collectively responsible to the Assembly for the formulation and implementation of the general policy of the government; each minister is also individually responsible for all acts undertaken by his office as an agency of government. Cabinet members are free to attend sessions of the Assembly, and they must be heard when they request the floor. The Assembly also may request ministers to appear before it to explain policies or to answer questions.

The cabinet must receive and maintain the confidence of the Assembly; a confidence vote must be held within fifteen days from the date a new cabinet is announced. This vote focuses on what is officially called "the government program"—a broad outline of the government's proposed policies and programs. The Assembly may withdraw its confidence by passing a censure motion, which must be signed by a minimum of one-sixth of that body's membership and be adopted by an absolute majority. Only one such motion may be introduced every six months. Ministers and their deputies who are members of the Assembly may vote on confidence and censure motions. When a government resigns after a no-confidence motion is passed, it is customary for a temporary, nonpartisan caretaker government to be formed to administer the new elections. Unsuccessful censure votes were taken in 1988 and in 1993.

The 1986 constitutional amendments enlarged the legislative capacity of the prime minister and the cabinet. Combined with the absence of internal party controls in both major political parties, this development has rendered executive actions largely unaccountable.

The Legislative Branch

The Assembly is a unicameral body of 300 deputies elected through direct, universal, and secret ballot (see The Electoral System, this ch.). The term is four years except in time of war, when it is extended for the duration. The Assembly convenes on the first Monday in October for an annual session of at least five months. It elects its own officers and a standing committee that determines the order of legislative work. At the beginning of each session, committees are formed to examine bills, with committee membership proportional to party representation in the chamber. In practice, only the law-making committees have performed as a regular part of this system however.

The Assembly generally conducts legislative business in plenary sessions, as required under the constitution when certain subjects are deliberated. The prescribed subjects include parliamentary standing orders and elections; church-state relations, religious freedom, and individual liberties; the operation of political parties; delegation of legislative authority to a cabinet minister; and authorization of the state budget. Plenary sessions may also be requested by the government to consider bills of particular importance for debate and passage.

When the Assembly is in recess, its legislative work (with the exception of subjects specifically reserved for consideration by full session) may be conducted by a legislative section. The Assembly usually divides into two sections, equal in size and proportionally representative of the strength of the political parties in the legislature. The jurisdiction of each section corresponds to the jurisdictions of roughly half the government ministries. A bill passed by a section has the same status as one adopted by the full Assembly.

Bills may be introduced by the government or by a member of the Assembly. In practice, however, the vast majority of laws passed originate with the government. To pass a bill in plenary session of the Assembly requires an absolute majority of those present, which must not be less than one-quarter of the total

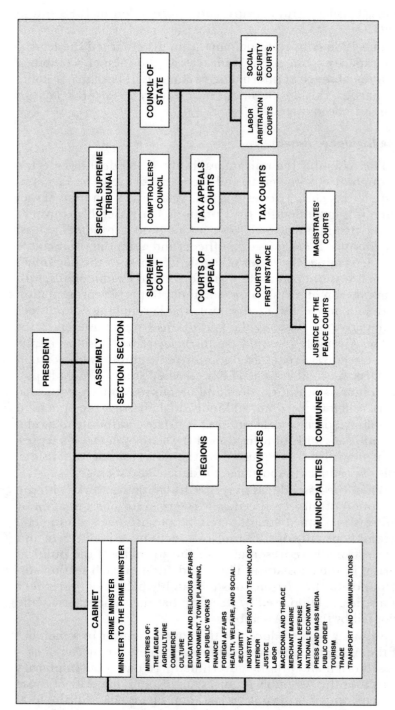

Figure 11. Government Organization, 1994

membership. Passage of a bill by a section requires approval by a majority of those present; the majority must be at least two-fifths of the total sectional membership. A bill rejected by either a section or by the plenum cannot be reintroduced in the same annual session.

The Judiciary

The current legal system of Greece is based on a combination of codified Roman civil law and French and German models, all of which in turn owe much to classical Greek precedents. Greek philosophy in general and the Greek-based tenets of rationalism and natural law in particular contributed significantly to the evolution of Roman law. Later, the eastern, or Greek, part of the Roman Empire played an important role in preserving Roman law after the collapse of the empire in the west in A.D. 476.

Justice is administered by an independent judiciary, which is divided into civil, criminal, and administrative courts. Judges enjoy personal immunity, and they are subject only to the constitution and the law in discharging their constitutional responsibilities. Judges and other judicial personnel are appointed, promoted, and transferred formally by presidential decree, based on the prior decisions of a self-policing Judicial Council. Lower-level judges, including those in the courts of appeal, serve until sixty-five years of age, and those in the highest courts serve until seventy-five years of age. In each case, criminal conviction, a grave breach of discipline, disability, or professional inadequacy are grounds for dismissal.

The Judicial Council comprises the presidents of the three highest courts of the land: the Supreme Court for civil and criminal justice, the Council of State for administrative cases, and the Comptrollers' Council for fiscal matters. Other members of the Judicial Council are chosen by lot from among those judges or councillors who have served in the high courts for a minimum of two years.

The lowest courts in the civil and criminal court structure are the justice of the peace courts and the magistrates' (or police) courts, which are responsible for minor civil and criminal cases. Above this level are the courts of first instance, which handle the bulk of civil and criminal litigations. More serious cases are tried before juries. Juvenile and commercial cases also may be tried by the courts of first instance. Twelve courts of appeal hear appeals from the courts of first instance. In exceptional cases, such as those involving major crimes, the appellate courts may function as courts of original jurisdiction. The Supreme Court hears appeals from the courts of appeal on questions of law. All court sessions are public unless a court decides that publicity would prejudice public morality or would endanger the safety of litigants or witnesses. Felonies and crimes against the state are decided by mixed juries that combine the functions of judge and jurors. Administrative cases are initially adjudicated by special courts, such as labor arbitration courts, social security courts, and tax courts of first instance. There are also tax appeals courts.

State finances, which also fall under the administration of the judiciary, are overseen by the Comptrollers' Council. The comptrollers audit the expenditures of central and local government agencies as well as public corporations, and they present an annual financial report to the Assembly. The comptrollers also rule on public pension disputes and try cases involving the liability of civil and military officials alleged to have caused financial loss to the state by fraud or negligence.

At the pinnacle of the judicial system is the Special Supreme Tribunal, comprising the presidents of the Supreme Court, the Council of State, and the Comptrollers' Council; four councillors of the Council of State; four members of the Supreme Court chosen by lot every two years; and, in some cases, two law professors also chosen by lot. The tribunal hears cases involving parliamentary election disputes, the results of public referenda, and jurisdictional disputes between courts and government agencies. The ultimate authority for judicial review, the Special Supreme Tribunal, also interprets and rules on the constitutional validity of laws in cases where the Council of State, the Supreme Court, or the Comptrollers' Council have rendered conflicting judgments. The ruling of the tribunal is irrevocable. Constitutional interpretation in all other cases is a matter for the legislature, not the judiciary.

Under this arrangement, the relative infrequency of conflicting interpretations on matters of constitutionality is because of the traditional self-restraint of the judiciary as a whole. Only in recent years has the Supreme Court been activist as it has ruled on a considerable body of new legislation regulating environmental and city planning practices. Beginning in 1982, the Greek judiciary sometimes was accused of corruption and political bias. Although the truth of such accusations was unclear, the PASOK administrations of the 1980s proclaimed their intention of reforming the judicial system in order to eliminate corruption. However, few real changes resulted from that resolution.

In May 1994, a new law passed under PASOK sponsorship caused considerable controversy. The law, which introduced a new system of internal review and control within the judiciary, has met with strenuous opposition from the Supreme Court president and justices. Opponents denounced the government's tactics as interventionist, unconstitutional, and partisan. Among others, the minister of justice was accused by judges of promoting the new law to gain future political influence over the judiciary. After initial opposition, however, in the second half of 1994 dissenting judges began softening their previous position toward the new law, and full compliance was expected.

Local Government

Traditionally, local government has been popularly viewed as the exclusive domain of the wealthy elite; the concept of popular involvement in local affairs was remote at best and failed to take any firm root in Greek governance. In 1982 the PASOK government, which had promised to foster administrative and economic independence at the local level, enacted a bill called Exercise of Government Policy and Establishment of Popular Representation in the Provinces. This legal framework was intended to transfer from the central government to provincial and local bodies the authority to make decisions on matters pertaining to provinces, municipalities, and communes.

PASOK's early initiatives on decentralization had lost momentum by the mid-1980s, however. The ND administration that succeeded the PASOK government in 1989 made no significant attempt to relax the hold of the central government on local affairs. Upon returning to power in 1993, PASOK renewed the promise of decentralization. The local elections of October 1994 included for the first time the popular election of province governors, who previously had been appointed in Athens. The democratic election of these officials did not guarantee the degree of authority or autonomy they would enjoy.

The 1994 local elections were seen as an especially important barometer of national party vigor at a time when the strength of the opposition ND and the ruling PASOK was approximately equal and a national election was possible within six months. ND candidates were elected mayor in Athens and Thessaloniki, and the PASOK mayor of Piraeus was reelected by a slim margin. Overall, both the ND and PASOK gained higher percentages of the vote than they had in the most recent national elections, the June 1994 choice of delegates to the European Union (EU—see Glossary).

Greece is traditionally divided into nine regions, the boundaries of which are based on geographical, historical, and cultural factors (see fig. 7; Geographical Regions, ch. 2). The Greater Athens area is sometimes designated as an unofficial tenth region. Although used for statistical purposes, the regions have no administrative significance. They are, however, the basis for subdividing the nation into fifty-two provinces or prefectures, which are the main subnational administrative units and the principal links between the central and local government.

Besides the duties of local administration, the province governor or *nomarch* functions as the principal agent of the central government, with responsibility to coordinate the activities of ministerial field offices within his or her jurisdiction. The governor is assisted by a provincial council, which is composed of the mayor of the province's capital, two representatives drawn from the municipalities and communes, representatives of mass organizations for farmers, workers, professionals, and employers, and selected members of public corporations. For consultation on local matters of shared interest, two or more provincial councils may hold joint meetings with senior officials of the central government ministries.

The bottom level of local government in 1994 consisted of 359 municipalities and 5,600 communes, or wards. Usually a municipality is a town encompassing a population exceeding 10,000 inhabitants, and a commune has 5,000 to 10,000 persons. Municipalities and communes elect councils headed by a mayor and a president, respectively; the mandate of these councils is renewed every four years, with elections coinciding with local elections at the next highest level. The membership of the local councils varies from five to sixty-one deputies, depending on population.

The Mount Athos Peninsula, the site of a monastic center of the Orthodox Church of Greece since A.D. 959, has constitutionally guaranteed autonomous status apart from the regular administrative structure of Greece. Mount Athos, officially the Monastic Republic of Mount Athos, includes twenty monasteries governed by the Ecumenical Patriarchate of Constantinople. Nevertheless, the state is represented there by a governor, whose duty it is to ensure that public order and safety are maintained and that the charter of autonomy is faithfully implemented.

The Civil Service

Government administration is entrusted to a network of public personnel within a vast civil service bureaucracy. Entry into the civil service is generally by competitive examination supervised by a board of civil servants, but government ministries sometimes avoid the regular recruitment channel and engage personnel by contract. In the latter case, recruitment depends on the discretion of each minister and hence is highly conducive to political favoritism. Specialists are hired through a noncompetitive procedure at higher salaries than otherwise would be possible. After several years of service, contract personnel often acquire civil service tenure.

Civil service personnel are organized into three categories. Personnel in category A are university graduates who perform administrative and executive functions. Category B is for high-school graduates who perform clerical duties. There are no educational requirements for personnel in category C, who are accepted without examination or other tests of skill. Promotion from a lower category to category A is automatic upon receipt of a university degree. In most cases, civil service tenure is lost only because of major political upheavals or dismissal for misconduct or incompetence. Mobility among ministries, or even among directorates and bureaus within a ministry, is minimal, and it is not unusual for a civil servant to spend an entire career working for the same office.

Inefficiency and favoritism have caused the general public to criticize the civil service and to attach little prestige to it. Despite periodic attempts to rationalize the goals and the methods of the system, public administration is probably the single most visibly inefficient sector of the Greek governmental process. Although a School for Public Administration provides the prospect of more efficient top-level personnel, the staffing of bureaucratic jobs continues to rely on anachronistic practices.

Since 1974 both ruling parties have offered programs to deal with the glaring inefficiencies of the civil service, especially in the area of personnel recruitment. In the 1980s, PASOK and ND administrations passed about a dozen laws altering the procedures of the state bureaucracy. However, the impact of this legislation seemed meager apart from broadening the immediate political influence of the governing party.

Continued reliance on subjective criteria and personal connections in state agencies may be rooted in Greece's experience of administrative repression under right-wing governments during the early stages of the Cold War—a pattern that cultivated in Greek citizens a deep distrust for formal criteria such as exams, inspectors, and objective qualifications. Political parties are still able to sidestep rules in order to enhance their influence. Especially just before national elections, parties in power have routinely expanded their voter base by recklessly overstaffing the civil service ranks. This practice creates a short-term impression of social well-being by reducing unemployment. Such a policy reinforces negative effects of clientelism, upon which prewar parties relied in creating their constituencies (see The Interwar Struggles 1922–36, ch. 1). Since 1974 government spending on such short-term boondoggles has also inflated Greece's spiraling public debt. In 1990, employment in the public sector was estimated at nearly 30 percent of the total in Greece, including all enterprises under state control (see The Public Sector and Taxation, ch. 3).

The Electoral System

Except during the junta regime of 1967–74, the electoral process has provided a relatively stable, if ill-used, structure for the exercise of democratic choice in postwar Greece. Elections are based on direct, universal, and secret ballot. Parliamentary and municipal elections are held every four years unless the dissolution of the Assembly necessitates an interim election. Voting is compulsory for all citizens aged eighteen and above, and nonvoters are subject to legal penalties.

The 300 members of the Assembly are elected from fifty-six local constituencies, which are represented by from one to thirty-two seats according to their population. Candidates are elected under a unique "reinforced" proportional representation system. Since the 1974 election, 288 members of the Assembly have been chosen directly on the basis of constituency votes; these members must belong to a particular constituency and must compete for election. The remaining twelve seats are occupied by "national deputies," elected at large from party lists in proportion to the popular vote the parties receive. These deputies thus represent the entire country. Their posi-

President Konstantinos Karamanlis and government officials at
religious ceremony, Christmas 1994
Courtesy Press and Information Office, Embassy of Greece, Washington

tion in the Assembly is largely honorary, although they have all
the same functions as directly elected members.

In one form or another, the reinforced proportional representation system has been in force in national parliamentary
elections for over forty years. The formula under which the
October 1993 elections were held was the product of the seventeenth revision of the electoral system since the 1920s. Virtually
every Greek government has modified the prevailing electoral
scheme to optimize its own prospects in forthcoming elections.

Not surprisingly, the electoral system that results from this
process is consistently biased in favor of larger parties. The
ostensible justification for such a distortion is that the imbalance helps to preserve stable party politics and, more important, stable one-party governments.

A parliamentary majority can be achieved and a government
formed even if the winning party fails to secure a simple majority of the popular vote. This outcome is made possible by
awarding extra representation (essentially a bonus) to the
larger parties that obtain more than a minimum percentage of
the national vote. The various reinforced systems applied since

the 1920s vary only in the relative advantage that each version has bestowed upon the top two or three parties.

The electoral system under which PASOK won the October 1993 elections illustrates these points. The 47 percent of the popular vote obtained by PASOK resulted in that party's gaining 57 percent of the seats in the Assembly. In 1990 the incoming ND party anticipated that the next elections would continue its plurality with a reduced margin over the second party (PASOK). Therefore, Prime Minister Konstantinos Mitsotakis increased the bonus of the largest party (and, under some circumstances, of the third-ranking party, as well) at the expense of the second-ranking party. The new electoral system also stipulated that a party would need at least 3 percent of the national vote to gain parliamentary representation. As it turned out, the ND fell victim to its own miscalculations when PASOK outpolled the ND by 7.6 percent in 1993. Thus, Mitsotakis's change gave PASOK a substantial working margin in the Assembly when PASOK's 47 percent of the vote yielded the party 170 seats in the Assembly to the ND's 111. By contrast, the previous version of reinforced representation had yielded the ND only 152 seats in 1990 after it received exactly the same 47 percent share of the popular vote. Already in mid-1994, PASOK was considering another modification of the formula.

The reinforced proportional representation system has always been opposed by small parties, especially those on the left, to whom reinforcement had been an exclusionist instrument that minimized representation between the 1950s and the 1970s. Beginning in the 1950s, one of the principal demands of the left in Greece has been the adoption of a straight proportional representation system that would reflect the popular will more accurately in the Assembly (see Political Developments, 1981–94, this ch.).

As the fear of communism receded in the 1980s and 1990s, PASOK and the ND reached a de facto consensus in favor of a system that would make representation more in proportion to the ballots cast but still would significantly favor the largest parties. In the 1990s, the principle of reinforced proportional representation appears to be a less urgent issue than it was in the 1980s. Since the return of civilian elections in 1974, the electoral system has provided relative political stability; of the eight national parliamentary elections held since that time, only the two held in 1989 failed, despite reinforcement, to produce a one-party majority government in the Assembly.

Another electoral issue is whether the parliamentary candidates on a party's list should be nominated according to the preference of voters or according to a ranking determined by party leaders. Although it allows more direct public control of election results, the preference vote system is seen as undermining party discipline and enabling locally influential politicians to buy votes through the maintenance of patron-client networks. The existing election law calls for the preference vote, but in 1994 the leaders of both the major parties leaned toward strengthening discipline in their respective parties by installing a system based on the rank list.

Political Developments, 1981–94

The 1980s and early 1990s saw the return to power of a left wing that had been forcibly isolated from the mainstream of Greek politics since the early 1930s. That period also saw the failure of the left's most radical policies, followed by a hesitation among the electorate between the left and the center, both of which failed to solve Greece's most pressing problems.

The Return of the Left

In 1981 PASOK's triumph over the ND, which had governed Greece since the overthrow of the military junta in 1974, was a watershed event in Greek politics, about which much has been written. The victory and the proclamation of a grand new plan of government were greeted with elation by the party's most ardent supporters, and with fear and apprehension by many conservatives. By the end of PASOK's first four-year term in 1985, the strong feelings of both groups had largely dissipated. With the exception of some important pieces of social legislation and a massive influx of new faces into the top levels of government, PASOK had proved incapable or unwilling to make the dramatic transformation that it had promised.

Papandreou's populist economic policies resulted in an accelerating public debt and an unabated annual rate of inflation in excess of 20 percent. Despite occasional outbursts of anti-American rhetoric that generated frictions with Western allies, Greece remained firmly committed to the much-maligned North Atlantic Treaty Organization (NATO— see Glossary) alliance. And, far from being a modernizing force, PASOK had managed to make the civil service and the large, debt-ridden public companies even more inefficient and unwieldy, through the massive hiring of employees that swelled the ranks of supernumeraries in these organizations.

PASOK's Second Term, 1985–89

Sensing public disenchantment, PASOK abandoned the slogan of change and mounted a largely negative electoral campaign, arguing that it needed more time to implement its program and raising the specter of a return to power of a vengeful right. This strategy worked extremely well. In spite of an aggressive and massive campaign effort by the ND, in 1985 PASOK obtained 46 percent of the vote—a drop of just over 2 percent from 1981—and a comfortable parliamentary majority with 161 Assembly seats. The ND increased its 1981 share of the vote by 5 percent and its parliamentary representation by thirteen seats. The ND claimed these figures gave the party a moral victory, but the elections were nevertheless a bitter disappointment. The negative campaign tactics appeared to have been particularly effective in some key major city districts in Athens and Thessaloniki, where communist voters apparently abandoned their party to vote for PASOK, averting a victory by the conservatives.

In October 1985, just five months after the elections in which he had promised better days to come, Prime Minister Papandreou abruptly changed course. Alarmed by skyrocketing deficits, public debt, and inflation and seeking to satisfy the European Community (EC—see Glossary) conditions for low-cost loans to Greece, he announced an austerity program under the direction of Konstantinos Simitis, a former minister of agriculture whom Papandreou's had appointed minister of the national economy. In the painful two-year period that followed, some confidence was restored in the Greek economy at the cost of a rapid devaluation of the drachma (for the value of the drachma—see Glossary); significant reductions in public borrowing, consumer demand, and industrial production; and a fall in real wages of almost 12 percent (see The Structure of Employment; Wages, Prices, and Inflation, ch. 3).

The austerity program also cost PASOK considerable popularity. Especially alarming for Papandreou were the local elections of 1986, in which the ND scored large gains in communities throughout the country and, more important psychologically, managed to elect mayors in the two largest cities of Greece—Athens and Thessaloniki—as well as Piraeus. In mid-1987, Papandreou unceremoniously dismissed Simitis and, with national elections looming, the austerity policies were abandoned. PASOK resumed its strategy of seeking public approval by public-sector hiring, which reached massive proportions in the months before the 1989 elections. In the same period, public borrowing increased from 13.5 percent of the gross national product (GNP—see Glossary) in 1987 to 21.8 percent in 1989.

The Decline of PASOK

In early 1989, PASOK modified the reinforced proportional representation structure to reduce the likelihood that the first-ranking party could gain an absolute majority of seats in the Assembly—a clear indication that PASOK expected to lose the election to the ND.

The most important political events between 1988 and the mid-1989 elections, however, were the serious illness of Papandreou and scandals and allegations of corruption within the PASOK government. In August 1988, the prime minister underwent multiple heart bypass surgery, following which he was constantly in frail health. His personal life also underwent a major change when he divorced his well-liked American-born wife of many years and, in the summer of 1989, married Dimitra Liani, a flight attendant some thirty-five years his junior.

Of the many scandals that emerged in Greek politics in the late 1980s, by far the most notorious was the so-called Koskotas affair. In 1986 Georgios Koskotas, an émigré who had spent several years in New York City, became governor and main stockholder of the privately owned Bank of Crete in Athens. During the next two years, Koskotas spent huge amounts of money building a large publishing empire that included major Athens newspapers and the most popular soccer team in Greece. Koskotas finally overstepped his financial limits in mid-1988 when several publicly owned companies, in an apparently orchestrated move, transferred their accounts to his bank at below-market interest rates. At about the same time, the Assembly passed a law that clearly eased matters for Koskotas in dealing with judicial inquiries. Under growing pressure and with his empire collapsing, Koskotas finally fled the country in early 1989 and was captured in the United States. Koskotas then confirmed from his United States prison cell the repeated allegations in the Greek press that he had paid PASOK large sums of money, some of which had gone directly to a close aide of the prime minister.

Coalition Government, 1989–90

All opposition parties called for "cleansing" in the June 1989 elections, which nevertheless included an orgy of mudslinging from both left and right. PASOK alleged that some ND leaders, including Mitsotakis, also had dealt with Koskotas. The elections were a clear victory for the ND, which obtained 44 percent of the vote and 145 seats. A coalition of the left, which included the pro-and anti-Moscow branches of the Communist Party of Greece (Kommunistikon Komma Ellados—KKE) and smaller groups, running under the name Synaspismos (Coalition), also made its best showing of the postjunta years, gaining 13 percent of the vote and 27 seats. Given the circumstances, however, PASOK also did remarkably well, depriving the ND of a clear majority in the Assembly by gaining 39 percent of the vote and 125 seats.

Mitsotakis struck an unusual bargain with the two branches of the KKE to achieve a governing majority. The three parties formed a coalition government that would prepare the country for new national elections in the fall of 1989 while simultaneously pursuing the cleansing process in public life. The KKE agreed to join the coalition on condition that Mitsotakis not be appointed prime minister. Accordingly, the new government was led by ND deputy Tzannis Tzannetakis, a former naval officer, and KKE members were appointed to several ministries, including the Ministry of Justice. In a political system with a traditionally huge gulf between the right and the left, the notion of the ND governing together with the communists was truly novel. This coalition marked a major step toward national reconciliation and the legitimation of the communist party within the body politic.

After a hasty investigation and a number of emotional and tense parliamentary sessions in July and August 1989, the ND-KKE majority voted to indict Papandreou and several of his close political lieutenants for involvement in the Koskotas affair and also for illegal wiretapping activities. Both allegations were categorically denied by Papandreou. Under the law, the ex-prime minister and his associates would be tried by a special court of twenty-five judges, presided over by the chief justice of the Supreme Court.

In November 1989, Greece held its second national elections of the year, using the same system of reinforced proportional representation as in June. Papandreou, anticipating that the ND would be able to form a majority government this time, pleaded with the Synaspismos leaders to join PASOK in entirely eliminating the reinforcement of parliamentary representation, fulfilling a long-standing aspiration of the left. However, KKE leaders, who had spent many years battling for exactly this type of electoral system, instead stood by their earlier promise to Mitsotakis that they would not seek to change the electoral law.

The ND won the second 1989 elections with 46 percent of the vote, but its 149 seats fell two short of a parliamentary majority. The biggest surprise of the election was the performance of PASOK, which most political observers expected to have a disastrous showing. Indeed, the election may be seen as the greatest political triumph in PASOK's history: with its leader in poor health and facing trial for corruption and other offenses and virulent attacks from the right and the left (both trying to deal PASOK a decisive blow), the party still obtained nearly 41 percent of the popular vote, an increase of 1.5 percent over its showing earlier in the year. The patronage that PASOK had dispensed before the June election was not available to it in November, meaning that the party depended more heavily on its own merits.

Synaspismos, by contrast, suffered a major defeat in November 1989, losing almost 20 percent of their previous national vote, most of it in the large cities where they had done particularly well in June. One explanation was that Synaspismos supporters felt betrayed by the close cooperation with the right under the Tzannetakis government and returned to the PASOK fold in November. Many voters apparently saw the KKE attack on PASOK as politically opportunistic, and the rush to indict the ailing Papandreou may have also generated sympathy for the him as the victim of a political conspiracy.

No party was able to form a government, and, with the KKE unwilling to enter another right-left coalition, Mitsotakis and Papandreou joined KKE leader Kharilaos Florakis in temporary support of a government of national unity, led by the respected octogenarian former governor of the Bank of Greece, Xenophon Zolotas. At a time of swift economic deterioration, the notion of a grand coalition of the ND, PASOK, and the KKE generated much popular relief initially. However, it soon became clear that constant bickering among the factions and deep animosity between Papandreou and Mitsotakis would undermine the government of national unity. In April 1990, yet another election was held.

Greece: A Country Study

The ND Returns to Power

The elections of 1990 finally produced the parliamentary majority (a bare 152 seats) that Mitsotakis had been seeking since 1984. After nine years, the ND had regained sole power; Mitsotakis then served as prime minister for the next three and one half years, through October 1993.

The second major political event of 1990 was the Assembly's election, with the concurrence of PASOK, of Konstantinos Karamanlis to his second term as president. Coming five years after Papandreou had unexpectedly denied Karamanlis a second term in the presidency, this event was viewed as a vindication of Karamanlis and the capstone of a long and distinguished political career.

The new ND government promptly presented a medium-term economic recovery program designed to cut inflation (which had again reached 20 percent per year) by more than half (the target was 9.9 percent by the end of 1993), to reduce state expenditures and public employment, and to increase revenues by a variety of means including a crackdown on tax evasion, the privatization of many government-owned companies, and the sale of public land.

The EC strongly endorsed this program as a step toward stabilization of the national economy. However, indecisiveness and internal disagreements within the ND hampered implementation in the government's first two years. Government policy was pulled in opposite directions: free-market advocates wanted to move rapidly toward reducing the overwhelming dominance of the public sector in the country's economy, whereas a more moderate group argued for more cautious reform of the state system in order to preserve the social safety net.

In practice, both factions of the ND were usually overcome by large numbers of populists who simply wanted to enjoy the spoils of victory after nine years in opposition and to share their wealth with loyal party supporters. Thus, despite preelection promises to freeze appointments to the civil service and to public-sector companies, the ND contradicted its own economic recovery program by adding considerable numbers of its own supporters to patronage appointments. Clientelism and patronage became as integral to this "reform period" as it had been under the second PASOK administration of 1985-89.

The early 1990s also saw the continuation of trials of PASOK figures on corruption and other charges. By far the most

224

The Assembly in session
Courtesy Press and Information Office, Embassy of Greece, Washington

important of these procedures was the special court trial of Papandreou and three top associates for involvement in the Koskotas affair. The trial, which lasted several months, was followed eagerly by Greek television viewers. The chaos of that trial was a public demonstration that the politicized Greek judicial system was incapable of dealing effectively with cases involving malfeasance by elected officials. Neither the government nor the judiciary attempted to bring Papandreou personally before the court, and Koskotas, the state's star witness, produced none of the evidence he claimed to have against Papandreou. The trial ended with Papandreou's acquittal by a narrow margin. After the Koskotas trial turned into a public relations disaster, the ND government retreated and canceled Papandreou's wiretapping trial.

The threat of privatization and the ND's austerity program triggered waves of strikes by public employee unions in 1991 and 1992. Particularly aggressive were the employees of the Public Power Corporation (Dimosia Epicheirisi Ilektrismou—DEI), who disrupted the electricity supply, and those of the Urban Transportation Company of the Athens region, who engaged in violence against nonstriking fellow employees.

Although the public showed little sympathy for the strikers, the government responded quite passively to their activities.

In 1991 the disarray in the ND government was partly corrected by the appointment of Stefanos Manos as minister of national economy. Under Manos, free-market advocates gained control of the ND's economic policies. A new austerity program was announced, together with an aggressive privatization program centered on the sale of most of the state-owned Greek Telecommunications Organization (OTE—Organismos Tilepikoinonion Ellados) to private investors (see Transportation and Telecommunications, ch. 3). Manos pursued these plans assiduously throughout the remainder of the ND's term in office, but he achieved very few of his ambitious goals. Manos was stymied by governmental ineffectiveness, dissension in ND ranks, and the premature collapse of the Mitsotakis government. The austerity program, which seemed to penalize wage earners most heavily, was also very unpopular and certainly contributed to the heavy losses that the ND suffered in the 1993 national elections.

Paralleling PASOK's embarrassments in 1989, the Mitsotakis administration also fell prey to allegations of scandal and corruption. Prominent among them was the affair of AGET, a large Greek cement company sold to the Italian Ferruzzi conglomerate, which in 1993 was implicated heavily in the government corruption scandals of Italy. Mitsotakis, his daughter, and a close military associate were accused of illegally wiretapping political opponents. In August 1994, the cement company affair and the wiretapping case were both under investigation by special parliamentary committees and by judicial authorities.

As a result of all these difficulties, the ND government was staggering by the end of its third year in office, and Papandreou was calling for new elections. The downfall of the government, however, was the festering feud between Mitsotakis and Antonis Samaras, who had been the first minister of foreign affairs in the Mitsotakis administration. Samaras had been forced to resign his post because of his radical nationalist position on the Macedonia issue (see The Balkans, this ch.). Then, in June 1993, he announced the establishment of a new party, Political Spring (Politiki Anixi—PA). About three months later, a Samaras ally in the Assembly withdrew his support of the government, ending the ND's tiny majority and forcing new elections in October 1993.

The Elections of 1993

The ensuing campaign was perhaps the most negative in postjunta Greek politics. Rather than presenting coherent platforms, the two major parties ran extremely derogatory campaigns, evoking voters' fears about the dire consequences of electing their opponents. In a desperate tactic that apparently backfired with voters, the ND also stressed Papandreou's frail health and limited stamina. Sympathy also was generated for Samaras when the ND labeled him a traitor for his policy in Macedonia. Under these conditions, Papandreou made a political comeback that very few people believed possible four years earlier. The performance of PASOK (47 percent of the vote, 170 seats) surprised many international observers who had consigned Papandreou to history. Swing voters in 1993 (unlike 1981), were probably more motivated by the dismal performance of the ND than by a hope that PASOK somehow held the answers to the critical economic, social, and foreign policy problems facing Greece.

The defeat of the ND precipitated a change of leadership in the party, as Mitsotakis resigned in favor of Miltiadis Evert. At the same time, the ND repudiated its recent experiment with "neoliberalism." The formation of the PA undoubtedly shifted many votes away from the ND in 1993; indeed some 75 percent of all PA voters in 1993 had voted for the ND in 1990. It is not at all clear, however, that these voters would have supported the ND and not PASOK in 1993 if the PA had not formed.

Other major losers in 1993 were the KKE and the new version of Synaspismos, which now included only the anti-Moscow branch of the KKE and splinter leftist parties. The KKE lost to the PA its long-standing position as the third-largest party in Greece; Synaspismos fell below the 3 percent threshold for eligibility to send deputies to the Assembly. By contrast, the PA began its political existence with momentum as a new force with substantial support.

Despite the continuing polarization of voters between PASOK and the ND, the negative tone of the campaign clearly disenchanted large numbers of the electorate. In June 1994, this reaction was confirmed by the results of the elections for Greek representatives to the European Parliament (the governing body of the EU, for which the political parties of member nations submit candidates as they do for domestic representation). The combined vote for PASOK and the ND barely exceeded 70 percent, compared with the 86 percent the two parties had totaled in the October 1993 national elections.

Prospects for Political Change

In the summer of 1994, new national elections appeared possible in the spring of 1995 because of an unprecedented situation. The five-year presidential term of Karamanlis was due to end in May; if the Assembly failed to elect a new president by then, a new Assembly would have to be elected. In mid-1994, Papandreou had hinted broadly that he would seek the presidency as the crowning achievement of his political career. Because he was unlikely to garner the required 180 Assembly votes, a Papandreou candidacy would be problematic (see The Presidency, this ch.). Papandreou's withdrawal from consideration in November did not eliminate the prospect of a deadlock over the presidency, however, because several prominent candidates, including Mitsotakis, were likely to provoke strong opposition. Experts expected considerable political maneuvering over this issue in the first months of 1995.

The next elections would mark the first occasion since 1984 that the two major parties would not be headed by Mitsotakis and Papandreou, the two men whose personal rivalry defined and polarized Greek politics in that period. They would also force PASOK finally to confront the question of existence without Papandreou. Most importantly, the elections had the potential for a major realignment of political forces: they would give a more definite indication of the PA's strength, they could signal the end of Synaspismos, and they likely would require both the ND and PASOK to present new images to the Greek electorate.

Political Parties

Greek political parties traditionally were based largely on personal connections and personalities, lacking real organizations with mass membership and tending to appeal to narrow segments of the electorate. Greeks pursued their own contacts—usually through a patron-client relationship—to promote their individual interests, rather than developing and pursuing common interests through mass political organizations or interest groups.

PASOK was the first mainstream party to apply discipline and organizational work to the process of party politics. Early in its first term, the PASOK government also enacted a law to provide state subsidies to the parties to minimize the undue influences that private funding exerted on the operation of political parties. In the 1980s, the other parties, most notably the ND, were somewhat successful in emulating PASOK's organizational techniques. By the mid-1990s, Greek parties generally had become more mass-based and issue-oriented as they moved toward the model of West European political systems. This evolution was eased by the urbanization and industrialization that Greece had experienced for the previous forty years (see Demography, ch. 2).

Nevertheless, clientelism still pervades Greek politics in the mid-1990s. PASOK, which had made the abolition of *rousfeti* (personal favors arranged by politicians for their constituents) one of the principal themes of its message of change, itself became one of the most accomplished practitioners of mass clientelism in modern Greek history. In the early to mid-1990s, repeated allegations of corruption and misuse of public funds are indications that the corrosive party practices of the 1980s are still in force.

The Panhellenic Socialist Movement

The Panhellenic Socialist Movement (Panhellinion Socialistiko Kinima—PASOK), which has alternated in power with the ND for more than twenty years, was founded in 1974 by Andreas Papandreou and enjoyed a meteoric rise in popularity that led to its massive electoral victory in 1981. PASOK's initial success has been attributed to three factors: Papandreou's charismatic personality; the party's unique, well-articulated, locally based internal structure; and a clear leftist and reformist ideological orientation that in many ways matched the electorate's readiness for change at that time.

PASOK began as an attempt to create a modern populist party that rejected the traditions of personalism and clientelism. The new movement brought into the body politic a new group of people who seemed to reinvigorate the political system. PASOK is a cadre party, organized geographically, with the local party members and organizations as the basic units. Local party organizations elect representatives to provincial assemblies, which are run by a provincial executive committee of eleven to fifteen members serving eighteen-month terms. These local functionaries perform the key organizational and mobilizing activities and serve as the intermediaries between the national and local party levels. In addition, trade union, agricultural, youth, and professional organizations (some of which have considerable power) are affiliated with the party and are represented in the party's congress.

The PASOK party congress is the highest organ, which in theory determines party policy and controls the central committee and its disciplinary council. The congress consists of members of the Assembly, of the party central committee, and of the disciplinary council, as well as representatives of local, provincial, and affiliated organizations. In practice, the congress meets seldom; its major function is to provide symbolic democratic legitimacy to decisions made at the centers of true power, the central committee and its executive bureau.

The eighty-member central committee includes twenty members of the Assembly and sixty members elected by the party congress in consultation with the party's president (who has been Andreas Papandreou since the party's inception). The central committee meets at least once every three months. It elects an executive bureau composed of nine members (including the PASOK president) that meets twice weekly to develop policies in its role as the effective ruling body of the party. Papandreou has always exercised iron-fisted control over the ideology and the policy of the party's executive organizations, but he has allowed them much latitude on tactical and organizational matters and the operation of election campaigns.

PASOK has also made a concerted effort to instill party discipline and ideological coherence, which were previously unknown among noncommunist Greek parties. The nine-member disciplinary council, elected by the Party Congress, ensures the compliance of the general membership, and a separate four-member disciplinary committee oversees the activities of the party's parliamentary deputies. Discipline is strict, and a number of dissenters, including some deputies, have been expelled from the party.

Ideologically, PASOK has undergone a massive transformation since its creation, partly in response to Papandreou's own evolution, partly as a matter of practical necessity. The Marxist economics and rhetoric, the strident anti-Americanism, and the opposition to any affiliation with the EC, which marked the first party platforms in the mid-1970s, were gradually abandoned in the two decades that followed.

The general economic policies of the PASOK government that took power in October 1993 did not differ significantly from those of its ND predecessor. PASOK did not challenge the trend toward partial or total privatization of some public-sector companies, although the pace of implementation has been slower in specific cases than under the ND. In foreign policy, the PASOK administration has pursued avidly a close relationship with the administration of President William J. Clinton, making good United States relations a cornerstone of Papandreou's foreign policy (see The United States, this ch.). And the current PASOK government is at least as pro-European as its ND predecessor had been, enthusiastically supporting the EU. Overall, in the mid-1990s the party differed little in rhetoric, and even less in policy, from the social democratic parties of Western Europe.

In mid-1994, as Papandreou appeared ready to seek the presidency in 1995, intraparty bickering increased, and the struggle to succeed him became overt. At that point, six individuals, three "loyalists" and three "reformists", seemed likely contenders for the future leadership of PASOK. The "loyalists" were: Akis Tsohatzopoulos, who then held the powerful position of secretary general of the party; Kostas Laliotis, minister of environment, town planning, and public works; and Gerasimos Arsenis, minister of national defense. The "reformists" (so called because of their insistent calls for modernization, as well as a tendency to deviate somewhat from the party line and criticize Papandreou's policies) were: Vasso Papandreou (no relation to the prime minister), a PASOK deputy and former commissioner of the EC; Theodoros Pangalos, minister of transport and communications, who was highly praised for his handling of the Greek term of presidency of the EU in 1994; and Konstantinos Simitis, simultaneously minister of commerce and minister of industry, energy, and technology. Although all six contenders were long-time associates of Papandreou, he was said to favor one of the loyalists, who also enjoy much support among party members. On the other hand, in late 1994 the reformists were believed to enjoy growing support among rank-and-file PASOK supporters and uncommitted voters.

Experts believed that a radical realignment of forces at the top level of Greek political power was a possible outcome of the leadership struggle. If, for example, one of the loyalist candidates gained power in PASOK, some PASOK reformists might bolt the party in favor of a scheme that would bring together a coalition of pro-European moderates from the ND, PASOK, and Synaspismos. The main basis for such uncertainty was Papandreou's domination of PASOK; his future absence would have an unpredictable impact on both the internal cohesion and the electoral fortunes of the party.

New Democracy

New Democracy (Nea Demokratia—ND) is the other major pole around which postjunta Greek politics has evolved. The ND was founded in 1974 by Konstantinos Karamanlis. It was largely a revival of his National Radical Union (Ethniki Rizopastiti Enosis—ERE), which had dominated Greek politics from 1955 to 1963. The ND won large parliamentary majorities in both 1974 and 1977, and Karamanlis had remained prime minister until his election to the presidency in 1980. He was succeeded as the party's head and prime minister by Georgios Rallis, a long-time associate and a moderate. After the ND was defeated badly in the 1981 general elections, the party replaced Rallis with the more conservative Evangelos Averoff-Tositsas, another long-time Karamanlis loyalist. But in 1984 Averoff resigned his position after a poor party showing in that year's elections to the European Parliament. He was replaced by Konstantinos Mitsotakis, a moderate conservative and the long-time political arch-rival of Andreas Papandreou. Mitsotakis had joined the ND only six years earlier after playing important roles in various centrist parties.

In 1965 the defection of Mitsotakis and other senior ministers from Georgios Papandreou's Center Union government had caused a furor and was partly responsible for setting off a sequence of events that led to the colonels' coup and the imposition of military rule in 1967. Since that time, Georgios Papandreou's son Andreas has vilified Mitsotakis for his act of "treason," and Mitsotakis has never enjoyed personal popularity in Greek politics. However, in 1984 the ND saw Mitsotakis as the only politician who could rival Andreas Papandreou in terms of personality, toughness, and political adroitness.

Mitsotakis remained ND leader until immediately after the October 1993 elections, when he stepped down following the party's defeat. During his nine years as party chief, he controlled the ND by promoting personal supporters to key party positions. This preoccupation with personal allegiance, which sometimes made Mitsotakis dependent on friends and associates with dubious qualifications, generated strong resentment among party loyalists. These forces gradually coalesced around Miltiadis Evert, the scion of a well-known Athenian family and a long-time party stalwart. In the early 1990s, the relationship between Mitsotakis and Evert grew increasingly cool and occasionally deteriorated to open hostility.

Evert voiced strong opposition to some of the bolder liberalization steps adopted by Mitsotakis's economic "tsar," Stefanos Manos, arguing in particular for the preservation of the "safety net" that protects Greek workers and employees from economic displacement. An open break nearly occurred when Manos attempted to privatize the OTE during the summer of 1993, and Evert threatened to bring down the government unless the privatization plan were halted. Although Evert won his point, the ND's one-vote majority collapsed shortly thereafter.

During the ensuing electoral campaign, the ND's internal divisions remained obvious to the nation. Under growing pressure from within the party, Mitsotakis promised to step down if the ND were defeated. In November 1994 Evert was overwhelmingly elected the new leader of the ND.

Evert became the first member of the post-Civil War generation to lead one of the two major Greek parties. At the same time, the leadership of the conservative movement in Greece reverted to favoring greater state control of economic resources. Evert's ascendancy also ended the polarizing and vituperative personal rivalry of Papandreou and Mitsokakis, which had occupied center stage for the previous ten years. Evert was fifty-four—young by Greek political standards—when he became the leader of the ND. He had risen through the party ranks from the youth organization of the ERE to hold several ministerial positions and the mayoralty of Athens. He enjoys a reputation for personal integrity and for decisiveness, a quality implied by his nickname, "Bulldozer," which also alludes to his considerable physical size.

Evert's first ten months leading the ND were not easy. He attempted simultaneously to restore party unity, take control of the party's apparatus, and signal a new style of leadership. Toward the first objective, he immediately appointed Ioannis Varvitsiotis, his main opponent in the contest for the party leadership in November 1993, as party vice president. Then, in the summer of 1994, Evert created a party political council as a top-level policy-making committee, to which he appointed the most prominent ND parliamentary delegates, including Manos and Andreas Andrianopoulos, two of his most vocal critics in the party. To gain party control, he replaced many Mitsotakis appointees in the ND headquarters, and he used the April 1994 party congress to consolidate his leadership position.

To convey a sense of change and renewal to voters, Evert also tried to distance the ND from Mitsotakis personally. Evert was noticeably slow in defending his predecessor against charges of corruption and wiretapping before parliamentary committees and judicial authorities, angering the many Mitsotakis loyalists within the party. In mid-1994, the Evert and Mitsotakis factions also struggled for control of the ND's influential youth organization.

The June 1994 elections for the European Parliament were a setback for Evert. Although PASOK's share of the vote fell to 38 percent from its 47 percent share in the October 1993 national elections, the ND was not the beneficiary. On the contrary, the ND lost nearly 7 percent, achieving its lowest share in a national vote in its twenty-year history. The Mitsotakis faction, which had taken little part in the campaign, nevertheless blamed Evert for the party's poor showing.

The ND's most notable organizational success has been the Youth Organization of the New Democracy (Organisia Neon tis Neas Demokratias—ONNED), a vigorous and often fractious youth group that has been instrumental in recruiting new blood into the party, mobilizing public support, and occasionally challenging the constituent influence of powerful local politicians. The party has fared well in university student elections in the 1990s, as well as in organizing support in labor unions and professional associations.

Since the mid-1980s, the main ideological struggle within the ND has been between moderate reformists and neoliberals and free-market advocates who have called for a vigorous reversal of state intervention in the economy, accelerating privatization, and encouraging innovation and competition. The centrist domination has been evident in the party's conciliation toward the left in its consistent support of progressive social legislation. Experts believe, however, that a large part of the ND's grassroots supporters are to the right of the party's leadership in this respect.

Political Spring

In July 1994, the former ND minister of foreign affairs, Antonis Samaras, formed a new party, Political Spring (Politiki

Anixi—PA). Samaras, seen as a likely successor to Mitsotakis until a bitter feud with the prime minister over the Macedonia issue, finally left the party in protest against the government's Macedonia policy. As he ran on the PA ticket in the October 1993 election, Samaras gained public sympathy from the name-calling campaign that the ND mounted against him. After struggling early, the PA received nearly 5 percent of the popular vote, becoming instantly the third largest party in Greece and electing ten deputies, including Samaras, to the Assembly.

After the election, Samaras maintained a high profile by criticizing the failures of both major rival parties. Not surprisingly, the PA became the self-appointed guardian of the hard-line position on the Macedonia issue. The party stated repeatedly that Greek acceptance of any form of the word "Macedonia" in the name for the nation that had been the southeastermost republic of Yugoslavia would amount to treason. The party has advocated a similarly tough stand on disputes with neighboring Albania (see Foreign Policy, this ch.).

In the elections for the European Parliament in June 1994, the PA benefitted further from continuing voter disaffection with PASOK and the ND, gaining nearly 9 percent of the vote. Beyond its strongly nationalistic positions on foreign affairs, the PA has not yet articulated clearly its ideology and economic policies. Most of them, however, are quite similar to those of the ND. Although the PA claims to represent a coalition of forces from all sides of the political spectrum (and indeed, has managed to attract to its ranks a few figures from the left), the majority of its constituency seems to be decidedly conservative: in a summer 1994 poll of PA voters, more than 95 percent of respondents identified themselves as either right-wing, right-of-center, or center, in approximately equal numbers. The PA's strongest support is in Athens, Thessaloniki, and regions such as the southern Peloponnesus and northern Macedonia containing large concentrations of royalist and ultraconservative voters.

In the late summer of 1994, the PA stood at a crossroads. With little discernible difference between its positions and those of the ND (other than the approach to Balkan affairs), the party was increasingly perceived as simply a vehicle for the personal ambitions of Samaras. Under these conditions, the ND's electoral fate might determine that of the PA. If the ND seemed to have poor prospects in the next national elections, the PA might attract wavering and discouraged voters from the larger party. If, on the other hand, the ND had a promising position as the elections approached, Samaras might come under intense pressure to avoid splitting the conservative vote by forming an electoral coalition or actually merging his party with the ND.

Communist Parties

Formed in 1918 with strong support from the Bolshevik Party in Moscow, the communist party never gained more than a small minority in elections, but its presence often had a profound impact on government policies and the policies of the West toward Greece.

Background of the KKE

Formerly called the Socialist Workers' Party, the Communist Party of Greece (Kommunistikon Komma Ellados—KKE) had strong ties with Moscow from its inception, and it was a loyal member of the Communist International (Comintern). Most of its support came from refugees from Turkey and linguistic and ethnic minorities. In the interwar period, the KKE participated in elections, but it polled only 9 percent of the vote in 1935. Nevertheless, that vote was a major influence in the imposition of an anticommunist military dictatorship under Ioannis Metaxas in 1936; from then until 1974, the KKE was outlawed.

Between 1940 and 1944, the KKE formed the backbone for Greece's wartime resistance movement, a role that for the first time made it a popular party (see Resistance, Exiles, and Collaborators, ch. 1). During the war, an estimated 25 to 30 percent of the population was associated with one or another of the KKE's auxiliary organizations; however, the period of the Civil War (1946–49) cost it most of its popular support. The party leaders and much of the party membership fled to Eastern Europe; those that remained in Greece operated through surrogate parties: first the Democratic Front, then the United Democratic Left (Eniea Dimokratiki Aristera—EDA), which was disbanded by the military junta in 1967. In 1974 the civilian government of Karamanlis legalized the KKE after the ouster of the junta.

In 1968 the KKE split into two separate wings. The origin of the split lay in the 1950s and early 1960s, when the EDA served as the forum for communist activity within Greece. Over time a gap developed between communists who had remained in

Greece and those who had fled abroad, and in 1968 this gap was the ground for the formation of the KKE-Interior and the KKE-Exterior. The fundamental difference between the branches was that in the 1970s the KKE-Exterior, the larger faction, retained its leadership and loyalty to Moscow while the breakaway KKE-Interior was following the independent Eurocommunist parties of Western Europe as its models. The schism was formalized with the restoration of democracy and the legalization of the KKE-Interior in 1974.

Since that time, the two parties have grown completely apart as they developed different ideologies, internal structures, and constituencies. Tactically, however, their relationship has been more complicated. The two have formed electoral coalitions— first in the national elections of 1974, then in the elections of 1989 and 1990 under the name Synaspismos. Following the disastrous results of the 1990 elections, the parties embarked on completely divergent paths, seemingly heralding a final break. Together with several allied leftist groups, the KKE-Interior retained the name Synaspismos. Therefore, the KKE-Exterior is now referred to simply as the KKE.

Evolution of the KKE

Between the dissolution of the Center Union following the 1977 election and the PA's ascendancy in 1993, the KKE was the third largest party in Greece. The best performance of the KKE standing on its own was the 11 percent of the vote achieved in 1981. (In coalition with the KKE-Interior under Synaspismos, a high of 13 percent was reached in the June 1989 elections.)

Following the dissolution of the Soviet Union and the collapse of the Warsaw Pact (see Glossary) alliance in 1991, the KKE has become a more marginal player. In the 1993 elections, its 4.5 percent share of the vote made the future look bleak. The KKE has shown no signs of changing traditional communist dogma to project an image attractive to a large number of younger voters. Its constituency remains primarily traditional left-wing voters in some sections of the working class and the refugee population centered in the largest cities, in parts of Thessaly in north-central Greece, and on some of the Dodecanese and Ionian islands.

The KKE is organized according to the standard Soviet model: control of local party cells is centralized in the highest party organization, the politburo, which is headed by the secretary general of the party. The politburo is elected by the central committee, which meets every six to eight months. The committee in turn is elected by the party congress, held every four years, which is in principle the highest policy-making authority. In practice, power within the party is highly concentrated in the politburo. In the 1980s, the party's mass organizations lost much of their strength among university student organizations and labor unions. The most notable loss has been in Greece's major trade union organization, the General Confederation of Greek Workers (Geniki Synomospondia Ergaton Ellados— GSEE), which until the mid-1980s was heavily influenced by the party.

Synapismos

Synaspismos (SYN—Coalition), the party that has finally emerged from the union of KKE-Interior with several other leftist groups, has a small number of hard-core adherents but a much larger number of potential sympathizers. Thus, the party does much better in local elections and in elections for the European Parliament (seen by some Greek voters as an opportunity to express their real preferences), than in the national parliamentary elections, which, because of their impact on people's daily lives, are often perceived as a choice between the lesser of two evils, PASOK or the ND.

In 1981 Synaspismos received only 1 percent of the vote for the Assembly, but over 5 percent of the vote for the European Parliament. In 1993 SYN obtained only 2.9 percent of the vote in the national elections, narrowly missing the 3 percent required to send any deputy to the Assembly. Then, in June 1994, it secured two of the twenty-five Greek seats in the European Parliament by gaining over 6 percent of that vote.

SYN has adopted a strongly pro-European stance. Domestically, it advocates administrative reform and modernization, as well as moderate economic policies—policies not much different in late 1994 from those practiced by PASOK and advocated by Evert's ND. On foreign policy, SYN is clearly the most conciliatory party on the Macedonian issue and on relations with other Balkan nations, often warning against the dangers of unbridled nationalism. Its frequent inability to speak with a single voice accounts for much of the party's failure to establish itself as a viable alternative in the minds of many Greek voters. But its most fundamental problem is that, more than any other party, SYN is in direct competition with PASOK for issues and supporters on the moderate-left of the spectrum. Experts believe that the end of Papandreou's tenure in PASOK could enhance SYN's role in representing that constituency, depending on the effectiveness of Papandreou's successor. SYN would be most likely to come to power as a member of a broad government coalition with centrist and center-left reform parties.

Other Parties

More than thirty small parties contested the October 1993 national elections. Their combined share of the total vote was approximately 1.5 percent, and many of them obtained fewer than 1,000 votes in the entire country—a result typical of post-1974 Greek elections. In general, these small parties are concerned mainly with specific, narrow interests (for example, the Party of Greek Hunters), and they are often geographically limited and ideologically ambivalent.

To the left of the KKE, a number of splinter Marxist, Maoist, and anarchist groups have consistently participated in national elections and obtained minuscule support. On the far right, several attempts were made before the mid-1980s to field a viable slate of candidates. In 1974 a projunta grouping obtained 1 percent of the vote. In 1977 the National Front, a coalition of junta supporters, ultraconservatives, and royalists mounted the most serious right-wing challenge of the postjunta years, obtaining nearly 7 percent of the total vote and seating five deputies in the Assembly. In 1981 the Progressive Party, led by Spyros Markezinis, who served in 1973 as prime minister in the junta regime of Georgios Papadopoulos, obtained 2 percent of the vote. Since 1985, however, most of the votes of the far right have gone to the ND or the PA.

The only noteworthy mainstream minority party of the 1985–94 period was the Democratic Renewal Party, which was formed by Konstantinos Stefanopoulos, a widely respected ND politician and long-time Karamanlis loyalist, when he lost an ND leadership contest to Mitsotakis in 1985. Democratic Renewal never has made a significant impact in national elections, but the one deputy it elected in June 1990 made it possible for Mitsotakis to form a majority government by switching his support to the ND. Democratic Renewal was dissolved after another disappointing showing in the elections for the European Parliament in June 1994. Evert has invited Stefanopoulos back to the ND fold, and he may rejoin that party at some point.

The nascent Green Party has failed to attract significant electoral support. One Green deputy was elected to the Assembly in the 1990 elections, but the movement has been fractious, and the mainstream parties have been quick to pay lip service to environmental causes, thus preempting the development of any mass following for the Greens (see Environmental Policy, ch. 2).

Interest Groups

Since the establishment of a modern Greek parliamentary system, the representation of individual interests has relied on direct, one-to-one relations between politicians and constituents. In contrast to other Western democracies, Greek civic culture has not encouraged the development of permanent pressure groups that would foster pluralism by combining individual demands into coherent interest groups. Joining a political party and establishing direct personal contacts with party officials are still considered to be the most effective methods for reaching individual goals.

Even in the latter half of the twentieth century, Greece differs from other industrialized countries by the presence of only a handful of fragile interest groups whose demands are almost always economic and activated on specific occasions rather than displaying a broader conception of the "public good." For example, once a labor dispute has been settled by the government (sometimes following strikes that have crippling effects on the economy), the seemingly intransigent labor organizers relapse into political inertia until the time for negotiating the next wage raise. The role of broader pressure groups, on the other hand, has traditionally been usurped by the ability of the political parties to represent and monopolize meaningful, long-term social issues—and by the willingness of citizens to have politicians carry their message.

This pattern originates in the politics of the protracted Ottoman occupation and in the patterns of political behavior resulting from delayed industrial development. A traditional Greek oligarchy, functioning as exclusive local employers in a predominantly agricultural economy, became the organizational center for the exchange of governmental favors for votes. Until 1900 the virtual absence of competing private employers, such as those that would have emerged in industries, established the state as the ultimate employer through the representation of the state by the oligarchy. As the oligarchy served the government and perpetuated its mechanisms, for that class the state became the exclusive educator and bestower of legitimacy.

As industry grew slowly, the political party system emerged as the natural broker for aggregating interests, as it constantly refined the procedures for the personal exchange of favors. As a result, the political system failed to produce interest groups that would mobilize against the excessive concentration of power in the hands of political parties. Instead, the Greek political parties came to compete constantly for position within each and every interest group that appeared. Over time, personal favors granted by politicians replaced official procedures and became what one observer has termed the "lubricating oil of the system."

The platform of change on which PASOK rose to power in 1981 included a promise to abolish the exchange-of-favors system, which was universally viewed as the source of all political evil. But as PASOK governments ushered in an era of fresh politicians whose power came not from a local or provincial base but from the personal charisma of their party leader, clientelism merely assumed a new populist form. In attempting to enlarge its system of political mass participation and incorporation, PASOK sought to suffuse all cultural and civic domains with its own political spirit. As it continued into the 1980s, this politicization eventually weakened Greece's already feeble institutions of nonpolitical social advocacy. In the 1990s, this tendency caused potentially active advocacy groups such as labor unions, the church, the military, and the mass media—traditional sources of large-scale advocacy in Western democracies—to remain quiescent except for occasional strikes.

Organized Labor

Labor union activities have frequently been subjected to legal restrictions by regimes that considered stable economic conditions the paramount domestic goal. Although the GSEE was established in 1918 and in 1994 comprises some 3,000 unions and fifty-seven federations, it rates low in public esteem, as does the Supreme Civil Servants' Administrative Committee (Anotati Dioikousa Epitropi Dimosion Ipallilon), known as ADEDI (see Labor Unions, ch. 3). In the early 1980s, PASOK attempted to cultivate a healthier activism in the GSEE after that organization's activities had been paralyzed for decades by extreme right- or left-wing dogmatism. By 1985, however, election setbacks were blamed partly on trade-union hostility, and

PASOK responded by packing the unions with party activists. Thus the unions reverted to political control after a largely unconsummated commitment to independent advocacy.

The cultural hostility toward the activity of permanent labor organizations is matched by the public attitude toward the Association of Greek Industrialists (Sindesmos Ellinon Viomikhanon—SEV), the powerful group that represents the interests of private industries. In the late 1980s and early 1990s, however, SEV greatly improved its public image.

Party meddling in the unions and subsequent confrontational tactics became equally flagrant during the ND government that took office in 1990. In the summer of 1992, following the privatization of the Urban Transportation Company, prolonged strikes and social upheaval put the ND administration on the defensive. With the return of PASOK to power in the fall of 1993, renationalizations (socializations) were soon announced, and a fresh wave of confrontations was in full swing by the spring of 1994. Experts believed that plans for increased privatization of state-owned industries, set to begin in the winter of 1994–95, were likely to begin a new phase of active trade unionism.

Church and State

The separation of church and state is a concept that is alien to Greece, because of the unusually close relationship between Orthodox Christianity and the Greek national identity. Historically, the Orthodox Church hierarchy has been a conservative political force that generally has supported the monarchy and opposed communism. Its organization and administration, if not its religious tenets, have been subject to state influence. For this reason, although the church is the only Greek nongovernmental institution built upon the concept of community, it does not contribute to the nation's narrow range of permanent interest groups. The church's politicization has meant frequent instances of internal factionalism. With this situation in mind, the PASOK administrations of the 1980s tried to end the church's reliance on the Ministry of National Education and Religious Affairs, which administers church property and employs all church officials. The goal of such a change was to achieve administrative separation of church and state.

In the 1980s, some indicators showed a decline in the church's capacity to exert influence on the political process. A case in point was the church's failure, despite public opposition, to prevent a PASOK-sponsored Family Law from being enacted in 1983. That law reformed a range of social traditions, for the first time permitting civil marriage and divorce (see The Social Order, ch. 2). On the other hand, in 1987 the government's attempt to confiscate and redistribute church property provoked bitter confrontations that eventually forced the state to back down and a government minister to resign in disgrace (see Religion, ch. 2).

At the end of the ND administration and the beginning of the new Papandreou regime of 1993, the government was embarrassed again by well-publicized church-state wrangling over a political issue. This time a series of episcopal appointments approved by Greece's Holy Synod collided with the vociferous and even violent refusal of incumbents to leave their positions.

The Military in Politics

Unlike Greece's weak, politically impregnable civilian interest groups, the military has had a strong presence as an independent player in Greek politics, although traditionally it has been as factionalized as the rest of society. Originally an aristocratic institution, the military eventually grew into a powerful pressure group, based in the lower classes, whose middle-class aspirations and grievances have had a critical impact on the course of Greek political history at several junctures.

The military has intervened in politics a number of times, usually to install in power the political party of its choice. More rarely, most recently in 1967, it has seized power for itself. The period of junta rule was a disaster for Greece in both domestic and foreign policy, and it had a terrible effect on the public image of the military as an institution. After the inglorious failure of its coup in Cyprus led to the fall of the junta regime in 1974, many observers believed that the military could only play a political role again to save the country from an imminent catastrophe such as an invasion from Turkey. The end of bipolar geopolitics has eliminated the communist threat, but Greece's eastern neighbor remains a perennial concern that necessitates large military and defense expenditures, affording the opportunity for continued political input by the military establishment. The protracted Balkan crisis of the early to mid-1990s highlighted the military's politically sensitive role (see Turkey, this ch.; Assessing the Turkish Threat, ch. 5). Upon his return to office in 1993, Papandreou caused a national controversy by recalling retired general officers with PASOK loyalties and giving them high staff positions—an extension of a practice well established by earlier administrations (see The Command Structure, ch. 5).

The Media

The Greek press is highly politicized and actively competes for readership, at times in a sensationalist and intensely partisan manner. Since the state monopoly of radio and television ended in 1987, the number of independent radio and television stations and channels has grown rapidly. The constitution prohibits censorship and all other government practices hindering freedom of the press. The last remaining vestiges of press restriction were only removed in August 1994, however, fifty-six years after the Metaxas dictatorship first imposed them (see the Metaxas Era, ch. 1).

The role of the media in bringing down the Papandreou government after the Koskotas scandal in 1989 was evidence that the media liberalization of the 1980s had established a new and explosive range of power and patronage relationships. However, the PASOK administration had already devised an institutional response to media power by appointing an American-style government spokesperson to handle daily confrontations with the press. The ND administrations that followed found a spokesperson just as useful. Further confirmation of the new importance of media power came in 1994 when, in addition to the government spokesperson, the second reshuffle of the Papandreou government included a minister of the press among cabinet officials.

The main source of printed news is the Athens News Agency, also known as Athenagence or ANA, which has correspondents in all the larger towns in Greece and some foreign bureaus. Greece has more newspaper and magazine titles per capita than any other country in Europe—120 daily newspapers and about 1,000 weeklies and fortnightlies are published. No daily paper dominates—rather, all the major papers sell between 50,000 and 150,000 copies, providing fierce competition (see table 13, Appendix). All legal political parties have been able to rely on at least one newspaper to spread their views to constituents. Fifteen major dailies appear in Athens alone. Readership averages 150 per 1,000 population. Newspaper ownership is becoming more concentrated, although it is still diverse by European standards.

Initially established under the interwar Metaxas dictatorship, the national radio network remained under government control in the postwar period, becoming an important tool in promoting the strongly conservative and anticommunist views of the state. Although state control of radio never was explicitly set out in law, when television was introduced in 1968 the ruling military junta passed laws giving the government exclusive control of that medium.

In the newly democratic climate that followed the junta's fall in 1974, the public's thirst for political discourse was soon turned into a powerful weapon by governing parties. The prime-time news of all three television networks was dominated by positive portrayals of government and party activities. In 1987, however, Athens mayor Miltiadis Evert, an opposition candidate newly elected in an upset, became the first to exercise the legal possibility of opposition radio broadcasting. He opened an independent station in Athens, and soon hundreds of independent stations had begun broadcasting throughout Greece. In April 1989, Greek courts ruled that the state monopoly of broadcasting violated EC standards, and in October the Assembly legalized private ownership of television stations.

The introduction of privately owned radio and television stations has brought a new attitude from the government toward the mass media. Because state-controlled media outlets are now confronted with severe criticism and competition from media that the state had previously monopolized, the government has consistently attempted to improve the image carried by independent networks. Despite the liberalization of the late 1980s, however, the state-owned Greek Radio and Television (Elliniki Radiofonia Tileorasi—ERT) still dominates radio and television. In 1989 an independent committee was established to administer ERT, to loosen the control exercised since 1975 by the General Secretariat for Press and Information, and to improve programming.

Human Rights

In the twenty years since the restoration of democratic rule in 1974, Greece has compiled a generally positive human rights record in accord with the strong commitment to democracy made by the Karamanlis regime of 1974. However, international human rights organizations have classified incidents of discrimination and unlawful treatment by government authorities as violations of human rights. The most frequently cited situation involves Greek policy toward conscientious objectors. In 1992 about 420 conscientious objectors, mostly Jehovah's Witnesses, were in prison because Greece has no civilian alternative to military service, and unarmed military service lasts twice as long as ordinary service. In 1991 a European Parliament delegation was refused access to the military prison where conscientious objectors were being held. Some Greeks have also been imprisoned for publicly expressing opposition to Greek policies in Macedonia and toward domestic ethnic minorities. Occasional reports of torture and ill-treatment have emerged from Greek prisons in recent years.

Although the population of 120,000 ethnic Turks in western Thrace has had no major conflicts with the Greek majority, in 1991 a human rights report of the United States Department of State referred to a pattern of discrimination against that Muslim community. In 1993 a sizeable demonstration in the town of Xanthi protested the Greek government's choice of a new mufti, the highest official of the Muslim hierarchy in Greece.

Another disturbing note is reported discrimination against non-Orthodox individuals in filling positions in the government, the military, the judiciary, and teaching. An apparent result of the unusually close connection between church and state in Greece, the practice has long been criticized by European human rights groups and the United Nations (UN). In addition, members of minor religious groups have been imprisoned for violating the law against proselytizing. More tolerance has been displayed toward the religious activities of representatives of the mainstream Roman Catholic, Jewish, and Muslim religions, although in late 1994 the Greek Roman Catholic Church protested discrimination by a local public prosecutor.

In 1994 the Ministry of Education and Religious Affairs (the word national was dropped from its title in 1994) established a pilot program against racism and xenophobia in schools near immigrant and Muslim communities, as well as a National Committee Against Racism, Xenophobia, Anti-Semitism, and Intolerance.

Foreign Policy

Greece's geographic position has made inevitable a continuous involvement with close neighbors and the constant attention from great powers with vested interests in the eastern Mediterranean. In the years since World War II, Greek governments have been required to assume positions on local crises such as those in Cyprus and the Balkans while protecting Greece's best interests in the larger context of European geopolitics. The end of the Cold War left Greece with major foreign policy concerns to its immediate north and east.

Historical Background

Throughout its modern history, Greece's strategic location in the Mediterranean and the Balkan Peninsula has been seen as an invitation for foreign intervention in the domestic and external affairs of the country. The policies and actions of foreign powers were mostly dictated by their competition for influence in the region rather than by the likely impact on Greece. While deploring foreign influence, Greeks usually accepted it grudgingly when national security and continued independence were the likely results of such acceptance. Since the foundation of the modern Greek state, however, foreign policy orientation, and especially the attitude toward potential foreign dominance, has been one of the foremost criteria distinguishing one political party from another.

After World War II and the Greek Civil War, the United States emerged as Greece's principal patron, a special relationship that Britain had maintained from the late eighteenth century until about 1950. In the postwar years, foreign involvement became synonymous with United States involvement because of Greece's heavy dependence on the United States for military and economic aid. Such dependence evoked mixed reactions; it was generally popular with right-wing Greek leaders, but it was harshly attacked by communist and other left-wing groups. By the early 1960s, a growing number of moderate and centrist Greeks had come to voice the need for more independence in foreign affairs, but without jeopardizing their nation's close relationships with its Western allies and especially the United States.

Greek assertiveness toward the United States was especially heightened in the years after the junta and the 1974 Turkish military intervention in Cyprus because of alleged United States complicity in the series of events that began with the junta's assumption of power in 1967. In the 1970s, the Greek government sought to renegotiate its United States military bases agreement and to reassess its ties with NATO. Both NATO and the United States had come under heavy criticism in Greek society for their alleged tacit support of the colonels and favoritism toward Turkey. After the return of civilian government in 1974, the Karamanlis administration's foreign policy did not deviate significantly from Greece's pre-1974 posture, except where Turkey was concerned. Relations with arch-rival Turkey remained acrimonious because of unresolved disputes over Cyprus and the Aegean Sea (see Assessing the Turkish Threat, ch. 5).

The PASOK administrations of the 1980s increased anti-Western rhetoric, largely through symbolic gestures favoring Arab and Central European communist states. However, on the level of Greece's membership in the EC and NATO, little or no change was made in the substance of Greece's fundamentally pro-Western foreign policy stand (see PASOK Foreign Policy, ch. 1).

By the end of the 1980s, several developments had led to an almost complete reversal of the climate of strong anti-Westernism of the previous decade. Papandreou's overtures toward the Soviet Union and Arab and Mediterranean states had failed to produce the regional support he had expected to obtain against Turkey and its continued occupation of Cyprus. Moreover, Greece was clearly gaining economic benefits from its participation in the EC, which was also proving useful in penetrating the slowly awakening markets of Greece's Balkan neighbors. By 1989 PASOK was also able to claim that it had restored national pride and fulfilled its campaign promises, as arrangements on phasing out most of the United States military bases in Greece were about to be completed.

The collapse of the Berlin Wall, the ousting of PASOK from power in 1989, and the unprecedented left-conservative coalition that followed it, all but silenced remaining leftist opposition to a solid pro-Western stance. Most decisive in this respect was Greece's signing of the Maastricht Treaty and its enthusiastic membership in the European Union, which was created by ratification of that agreement in 1993. In the summer of 1994, as Greece completed a third, rather successful presidency of the European organization, the country's foreign policy orientation and commitments toward the West were no longer in question.

Nevertheless, distinct underlying differences on strategy and tactics remained among the Greek political parties. Two of them, Synaspismos and the newly established PA, had renewed calls for the creation of a national council for foreign policy, which would be an apolitical source of consistency that would make foreign policy more independent of alternations between ND and PASOK administrations.

In late 1994, however, the PASOK government had achieved a rather broad consensus on Greece's foreign policy priorities: Turkey was universally perceived as the principal threat and regional adversary; membership in the EU and in NATO was viewed as the essential pillar of Greece's position in the world; and a continuing close relationship with the United States was a goal with wide approval. A flare-up in Greek-Albanian relations, the "Macedonian question," the threat of a spillover of hostilities after the fragmentation of Yugoslavia, and the Cyprus stalemate continued to constitute salient problems that colored Greece's relations with Turkey, the most crucial neighbor, and the United States, the key ally.

Greece and the European Community

In his address to the nation on July 24, 1994, to celebrate the twentieth anniversary of the return to parliamentary democracy, President Karamanlis pointed to Greek membership in the EC and then the EU as the single most fateful (and fortunate) move in determining the country's foreign policy orientation and economic development in the last two decades. Shortly thereafter, however, the relationship with the EU was under some strain because of Greece's chronically lagging economy and EU pressures for strict implementation of the economic convergence measures called for by the Maastricht Treaty (see International Economic Policy in the 1990s, ch. 3).

Considerable political friction had also developed between Greece and the EU. In February 1994, Greece's unilateral embargo against the Former Yugoslav Republic of Macedonia (FYROM—as the nations of the world officially recognized that nation) provoked sharp disapproval and the threat of legal measures from all the European allies.

Greece's initial associate membership in what was then the EC was arranged in 1961 by Karamanlis for strictly economic reasons. Then, soon after the end of the military junta in 1974, Karamanlis again steered Greece into the EC associate membership that the junta had relinquished in 1969, this time on unequivocally political grounds. In his view, close association with the economic organizations of the democratic West would institutionalize democracy and make another military coup less likely. The move would also relieve the pressures stemming from Greece's dependency on a single foreign power (the United States) in the bipolar world of the Cold War. (Ironically, PASOK then used the danger of overdependency in its propaganda against maintaining full membership in the EC between 1981 and 1985, by which time the benefits of the relationship had become clear to all.).

By signing the Single European Act in 1985, the PASOK government committed Greece to a broad set of social, environmental, and technological goals set by the EC with the expectation that a single European market could be established in 1992. In the event, the Maastricht Treaty of 1992, which upon its ratification in 1993 established the EU as the basis of the single market, found fervent support from Greece. Being the sole Balkan member of the EU has boosted its leverage against Turkey, and membership has enabled Greece to narrow the focus of its defense and security interests. Greece is also a member of the other major Western political and defense alliances: the Conference on Security and Cooperation in Europe (CSCE—see Glossary), NATO, and the Western European Union (WEU—see Glossary). On occasion, Greece has taken advantage of these European ties in the pursuit of its national interests. Greece has resorted to a battery of political ploys to block the inflow of large EU loans to Turkey, for example, while also calling into question that country's domestic political practices and human rights record. These moves have also had a significant influence on the EU's continued denial of Turkey's applications for EU membership.

Similarly, while presiding over the EU in 1994, Greece sought to block FYROM's entry into the CSCE, without prejudicing the general principle of adding new members to that organization. Another important goal on the Greek agenda was the implementation of economic development projects in Albania and Bulgaria under the EU's interregional program (see Security in the Balkans, ch. 5). Greece felt that improving economies in neighboring countries were in its long-term interest; by 1992 Greece was the largest foreign investor in Bulgaria's manufacturing sector, and it was among the leaders in Romania as well. On the other hand, the massive influx of Albanian refugees into Greece placed serious strain on Greek-Albanian relations in the early 1990s. In early 1994, an incident on the Albanian-Greek border escalated into a severe crisis and forced Greece to reverse its support of the EU Alba-

European leaders at the conclusion of Greek presidency of the European
Union, Corfu, June 1994
Courtesy Press and Information Office, Embassy of Greece, Washington

nian aid program in order to gain leverage over human rights practices in Albania.

In its tenure as head of the EU, Greece successfully conducted negotiations on the future membership of Austria, Finland, Norway, and Sweden, all of which held domestic referenda on that issue in 1994. Experts believed that further involvement in the political networks and federalist institutions of Europe, as opposed to strictly defense-oriented organizations, would benefit Greece's international posture and provide valuable experience in negotiation of economic issues.

Turkey

In late 1994, relations with Turkey remained Greece's most intractable international problem, with strong ramifications in domestic economic and defense planning. For Greece the end of superpower politics and the enlargement of the EU had little effect on the long-standing disputes with Turkey over Cyprus and adjacent sea-lanes and airspace. The end of the Warsaw Pact meant that both Greece and Turkey found themselves competing even more intensively than during the Cold

War for the attentions of their common defensive patron, the United States. Meanwhile, Greece's advantageous position in the EU appeared to intensify Turkish intransigence and complicate any compromise settlement of bilateral conflicts.

After the fall of East European communist regimes in 1991, several of the conflicts and stresses that occurred to Greece's north and west had an effect on its relations with Turkey when Muslim populations, chiefly in Albania and Bosnia and Herzegovina, were threatened. Greece's position as an economic supporter of Serbia, blockaded by NATO because of its role against the Bosnian Muslims, injected additional distrust into relations between Greece and Turkey.

Disputes between the two countries over treatment of minorities date back, however, to the aftermath of the Greco-Turkish War of 1921–22. Following the end of that war, which was a disaster for Greece, the 1923 Treaty of Lausanne prescribed the exchange of large numbers of each state's nationals living within the other country's boundaries (see The Interwar Struggles, 1922–36, ch. 1). The exchange did not include two significant groups, however: Greeks living in the Istanbul area and Turks living in Greek Thrace, across the border from European Turkey. Each community numbered approximately 100,000 in 1923. The treatment of the two ethnic minorities has been an issue ever since.

A partial solution to the establishment of minority rights was achieved in 1968, when Greece and Turkey signed a treaty agreeing to allow the groups to be educated in their own languages. But the press in both countries continued to publish inflammatory articles on the issue, and the groups were the objects of periodic hostility from the indigenous populations of their adopted countries.

Turkey has sought to relocate members of its Greek community to Greece. Whereas in 1965 some 48,000 inhabitants of Turkey claimed Greek as their mother tongue, by 1990 official estimates put the number of Greeks at about 3,000. On the other hand, Greece has not attempted to repatriate its Turkish minority. In 1990 unofficial estimates placed the size of the Turkish population in Greece at approximately 120,000. Some Greeks were reportedly worried that the size of the Muslim community might serve as a justification for future Turkish territorial claims in Thrace, although no hint of such a claim had been observed. Meanwhile, the Muslim minority in Thrace appeared to be generally tolerated by the surrounding Greek population.

In the mid-1990s, Cyprus remained the primary issue that defined and limited relations between Greece and Turkey. Together with Britain, the two neighbors were the guarantors of Cypriot independence under the 1960 treaties. Since the island republic was partitioned de facto in 1974, the Cyprus problem has been a vital national issue for Greece and a critical election-year litmus test of the patriotism of Greek candidates as well as Turkish intentions and policies. Both Greece and Turkey have taken the position that they have the legal right and obligation to render active support to the Cypriots of their respective nationalities—a Greek Cypriot majority and a Turkish Cypriot minority. Since 1974 the UN and Western nations have sponsored numerous talks between the Cypriot communities, but no permanent settlement has been reached.

Essentially, the Greek Cypriots advocate a strong central government, a single constitution, a parliament with representation proportionate to the Greek majority and Turkish minority populations, and substantial autonomy for the bicommunal regions. Seeing such a division of power as prejudicial to their own interests, the Turkish Cypriots demand a federation of the two regions, each with its own constitution and an equal voice in decision making on major intercommunal issues. To protect their minority status, the Turks also demand veto power over majority decisions.

Intransigence on both sides—each accusing the other of failing to negotiate in good faith—hardened the split on the status of the island republic. In November 1983, the Turkish Cypriots unilaterally declared the northern region (about 37 percent of the island) to be an independent Turkish Republic of Northern Cyprus. Greece was quick to condemn the "pseudostate" as a base for aggressive expansionism, declaring that no solution was possible without the withdrawal of Turkish troops.

In the 1980s, despite occasional rapprochement between the two sides and regular Greek-Turkish summits at Davos, Switzerland, PASOK administrations deviated little from the nationalist course of the Karamanlis era. In 1993, after a period of relative inaction under the 1990–93 ND administration, the new Papandreou government announced a "common defense policy" for Greece and Cyprus, to counter the psychological pressure of the Turkish military presence along Greece's eastern borders. At the same time, Greece committed itself to regional "confidence-building measures," to be sponsored by the UN and the United States as part of the Partnership for Peace doctrine advanced by United States president William J. Clinton in 1993.

By late summer 1994, however, the Turkish position in Cyprus had not changed. The UN Security Council Resolution 938 registered strong international displeasure over the twenty-year-old military occupation of the island, and it also noted Turkey's unwillingness to participate in the UN confidence-building program. During the same period, as it was working on the addition of four new members to the EU, the Greek presidency was also promoting full EU membership for Cyprus. In response, Rauf Denktas, the president of the Turkish Republic of Northern Cyprus, complained that UN resolutions did not guarantee the rights of Turkish Cypriots, and that further efforts to include Cyprus in the EU would be viewed as a national threat that would be answered by annexing Turkish Cyprus to Turkey.

The Greek government has also been critical of Turkey for its human rights practices and the treatment of the Kurdish minority in Turkey. In mid-1994, terrorist bombings on the island of Rhodes, believed in Greece to have been carried out by Turkish agents, caused a new wave of suspicion and bitterness between the two neighbors. In the bilateral negotiations of fall 1994, Greece placed its hopes on demilitarization of Cyprus and rapid inclusion of the island into the EU. These hopes were partially founded on a recent decision by the European Court of Justice refusing to recognize products from the Turkish-Cypriot north as coming from a separate state.

The Greek-Turkish conflict involves several additional issues, such as the demarcation of the continental shelf for the purpose of establishing underwater mineral rights. Authority over airspace and air traffic control in the Aegean, militarization of the Greek islands near the Turkish coast, and the deployment of the Turkish Aegean Army in western Turkey are also key concerns.

Greek oil exploration in the Aegean began in 1970 and resulted in small natural gas and oil strikes off the west coast of Thasos, close to the coast of Thrace, in 1974 (see Energy, ch. 3). In 1973, however, Turkey also granted concessions to Turkish oil companies in several parts of the Aegean. Greece regarded some of those areas as within the limits of the Greek continental shelf, entitling Greece to economic rights, if not full sovereignty, over the area. The islands are part of Greece, so Greece applied the 1958 Geneva Convention on the Continental Shelf, which provides that a state has the same seabed rights in its offshore islands as it does in its mainland coast. In short, islands extend a state's continental shelf past the landmass to which they belong politically. Turkey's position was that strict application of this principle would deprive Turkey of a continental shelf in areas where Greek islands are very close to the Turkish coast, thus requiring a special exception in this case. In August 1976, Greece brought the question before the UN Security Council and the International Court of Justice. The council adopted Security Council Resolution 395, urging the Greeks and the Turks to resolve their differences by negotiation, a recommendation reiterated by the court. In mid-1994, the continental shelf issue remained unresolved, and no negotiations had been scheduled.

In late 1994, all Greek political parties regarded Turkey as the principal threat to Greek security. This perception has been used to justify increased emphasis on military spending in the 1990s (see Defense Expenditures, ch. 5). That spending has included deployment of military forces to demonstrate Greek resolve at a time of reduced reliance on NATO—an organization that Greece has decried for its inability to prevent the invasion of Cyprus by another member of the alliance. In 1994, demonstrating the "common defense space" of Greece and Cyprus, the Greek navy executed a series of exercises in Cypriot and international waters, under the close observation of the Turks (see Greece in NATO, ch. 5).

The United States

Since World War II, Greece has had an ambivalent attitude toward its most powerful ally of the period, the United States, mostly because of the role the latter played in the years following the war. United States reorganization of and assistance to the Greek armed forces were generally credited with thwarting a communist seizure of power during the Civil War, and United States economic aid provided under the Truman Doctrine proved the major factor in Greece's postwar economic reconstruction (see The Marshall Plan in Greece, ch. 1). Nevertheless, many Greeks felt that the United States acted more in opposition to the expansionist Soviet Union than in support of Greek prosperity. In the 1960s and 1970s, as Turkey became a major issue in Greek-American relations, most Greeks maintained that United States policy toward Greece was only one aspect of a broader strategic policy aimed at the stabilization of NATO's flank in the Eastern Mediterranean.

Serious strains appeared in Greek-American relations after the 1967 military coup, concentrating the general resentment over Cold War policy on a single issue. Many Greeks believed that a more forceful United States reaction against the colonels' takeover could have prevented the seven years of military dictatorship that followed. Although the United States publicly pressed the colonels to restore democracy and heavy weapons deliveries were halted between 1967 and 1970, no drastic change was made in the execution of United States security policy. The United States continued delivery of light weapons to Greece and advised other Western allies not to impose sanctions on the military regime. Greece's strategic location was a strong influence against destabilizing even a military dictatorship, but Washington's prudence unwittingly deepened the Greek suspicion of United States complicity in junta rule.

A second major source of strain was the Cyprus crisis of 1974, whose impact on Greek-American relations was still reverberating in the mid-1990s. Turkey invaded Cyprus, beginning over twenty years of occupation of the northeast part of the island, in response to an abortive coup against the Cypriot government backed by the Greek junta. As in 1967, most Greeks felt that stronger United States pressure would have prevented a major crisis for Greece, in this case by forcing a Turkish troop withdrawal, or at least ensuring better treatment for Greek Cypriots caught in the Turkish-occupied zone. Under pressure from the United States Congress, the United States soon stopped supplying arms to Turkey, but relations with Greece had already been damaged.

Although the United States had welcomed heartily the return of democracy in July 1974, the postjunta government of Karamanlis withdrew from the military wing of NATO to dramatize its displeasure with NATO's response to the Turkish invasion and Greece's financial and military independence from the United States. Shortly thereafter Karamanlis began talks aimed at recovering full sovereignty over the United States bases in Greece.

A series of bilateral Defense and Economic Cooperation Agreements (DECAs) largely defined relations between the two countries from passage of the first agreement in 1976 until the dismantling of the Soviet empire. Greece withheld

Prime Minister Andreas Papandreou on official visit with United States President William J. Clinton, Washington, April 1994
Courtesy White House Photo Office

approval of the 1976 agreement, however, until it was sure that a defense cooperation pact that the United States had signed with Turkey in the preceding month would not adversely affect the balance of power between Greece and Turkey. When the United States ended its arms embargo on Turkey in 1978, Greece and the United States negotiated an informal understanding that a seven-to-ten ratio would be applied in the United States provision of aid to Greece and Turkey, respectively.

Although many Greeks continued to believe that the United States favored Turkey over Greece in security matters, relations remained generally cordial under the Karamanlis administration. In 1980 the two countries signed an umbrella agreement for cooperation in the economic, scientific, technological, educational, and cultural fields.

During the 1980s, PASOK's new foreign policy included opposition to all military blocs and condemnation of United States support of dictatorial militarist and oppressive regimes such as those of Turkey and Latin America. In an apparent gesture of evenhandedness, PASOK also condemned Soviet intervention in Afghanistan. Papandreou also called for the removal of United States bases from Greece and Greek withdrawal from NATO, but not before the Cold War military alliances were phased out.

In 1983, after resuming negotiations suspended under the previous ND government, the Papandreou government signed a new DECA that provided for the presence of four United States bases through 1988, to be followed by their dismantling some months later. The accord also called for United States assistance in the modernization and maintenance of Greek defense capabilities in such a way as to preserve the military balance between Greece and Turkey using the seven-to-ten formula. The Greeks unilaterally stipulated that Greece had the right to terminate the DECA if in its judgment the United States tilted the balance of power in favor of Turkey. The DECA signatories acknowledged the linkage between national security and economic development, pledging cooperation in economic, industrial, scientific, and technological fields.

The new world order that emerged after 1989 marked a transition in the relations between Greece and the United States. The tensions caused by constant criticism from Papandreou's government in the mid-1980s began to ease when PASOK rhetoric cooled in 1987. The conservative Mitsotakis quickly began mending fences when he came to power in 1990. In July 1990, Mitsotakis made a courtesy visit to Washington, the first official Greek visit in decades. When the prime minister returned, a new DECA was signed. Then, as a token of its moral support for the Persian Gulf War of early 1991, Greece dispatched a frigate to the scene.

According to the 1990 DECA, Greece allows the United States the use of defense facilities at Souda Bay in Crete, a nearby communications network at Heraklion, some secondary communications stations around the Athens area, and facilities on the Ionian island of Leucas. The United States Hellinikon Air Base at Athens's main airport was closed, and its Nea Makri Naval Communications Station near Athens was to be quickly phased out. The treaty also contains numerous economic and administrative provisions related to existing and future installations and personnel.

The reduction of United States military facilities on Greek soil brought a rather smooth resolution to the friction that had existed between the two allies since the early 1950s (see The Role of the United States, ch. 5). For the United States, a lower profile in Greece was consistent with the general downsizing of United States military installations on foreign soil. For Greece, the agreement achieved two important objectives. First, the reductions satisfied the elements of the Greek public that linked the issue of national sovereignty with the United States military presence in Greece. At the same time, Greece's national defense maintained the benefit of the traditional seven-to-ten aid apportionment ratio between Greece and Turkey. Indeed, it was now possible for Greece to argue that, after the end of the Soviet menace, only Turkish intransigence was responsible for making this ratio necessary. The Greek perception of the United States now changed from a superpower that had aided Greece as a policy instrument against the Soviet Union to a defender of Greece's interests.

The withdrawal of United States forces was celebrated when President George H.W. Bush visited Crete in 1992 to recognize Greece's symbolic contribution to the allied Persian Gulf War effort. The tension that had persisted since World War II thus came to a gracious conclusion that maintained the dignity of all sides and yielded a new Greek-United States DECA, reaffirming the existing military assistance formula.

When PASOK returned to power in October 1993, it was clear that the four-year absence had given the party time to revise its thinking about Greece's long-term interests in the post-Cold War geopolitical context. In fact, PASOK's attitude toward the United States had now turned full circle. Soon after taking power, Papandreou avidly sought support from the Clinton administration on the issues of FYROM, Cyprus, and Greek-Turkish relations. In April 1994, a meeting of Papandreou and Clinton in Washington was pronounced a success by both sides, despite the apparent lack of substantive commitments by the United States on the FYROM dispute. In the late summer of 1994, the United States was actively involved with UN efforts to settle the disputes in Cyprus and FYROM and was also watching closely the disturbing turn of events in the relations between Albania and Greece.

The Balkans

In the fall of 1994, Greece prepared for a period of difficult relations with Balkan neighbors far weaker than itself. In the turbulence of the post-Cold War Balkans, only Greece displayed homogeneity, stable democratic institutions, and the multidimensional support of the EU. However, it was unclear whether these attributes would prove sufficient to place Greece in a dynamic and leading role. The festering disputes with Turkey had made Greece defensive and vulnerable at a moment when general Balkan instability created precisely the type of regional vacuum that Turkey might fill by citing its solidarity with the Muslims of southeastern Europe.

Throughout the 1980s, Greece's relations with neighboring Balkan countries had generally continued on the friendly and mutually beneficial course that the Karamanlis government had initiated in the postjunta years. Greece desired stability in an area that had long suffered from conflicting territorial claims and political turmoil. Greece also hoped to win its neighbors' support for its position on Cyprus.

Bulgaria, Romania, and Yugoslavia

In 1976 Greece initiated an inter-Balkan conference on cooperation that was attended by representatives of Greece, Yugoslavia, Romania, Bulgaria, and Turkey. Albania initially refused to take part because of its conflicts with Turkey. Observers noted that Greece and Romania seemed to be the most enthusiastic about inter-Balkan regionalism, perhaps heralding some form of bilateral political cooperation. Turkey and Bulgaria were more hesitant. Turkey's position was that the settlement of bilateral differences had to precede regional cooperation. Similar conferences on economic and technical cooperation followed in 1979 and 1982; the latter meeting led to a 1984 conference on denuclearizing the Balkans.

Friendly and productive relations between Greece and neighbors Bulgaria, Yugoslavia, and Romania continued to be the rule throughout the 1980s and beyond the end of the Cold War. In 1991 brisk trade with Bulgaria was coupled with expanded military cooperation agreements. A series of consultations between the prime ministers of Bulgaria and Greece finally yielded a twenty-year treaty on friendship, good neighborliness, cooperation, and security. In the same year, similar diplomatic exchanges with Romanian leaders resulted in broad agreements on commercial ties and investments, as well as a mutual defense treaty in the same year.

The breakup of Yugoslavia deprived Greece of an important market and a friendly neighbor, as well as easy land access to other European states—in 1990 nearly 40 percent of Greek exports traveled by land across Yugoslavia into Western Europe. Far more important, however, the Yugoslav crisis has reopened old wounds that had been festering from the onset of communist rule in that country until its demise in 1989–90.

Policy Toward Serbia

In mid-1992, the UN responded to Serbian offensives in the former Yugoslav republic of Bosnia and Herzegovina by declaring a full embargo on trade with Serbia by all member nations. The sanctions placed Greece, which had recognized the independence of Bosnia and Herzegovina shortly after its declaration in 1992, in a difficult position. Serbia was an important trading partner with strong religious and historical ties to Greece, and Serbia had supported the Greek position on the FYROM issue. Beginning in 1992, the Mitsotakis and Papandreou governments, fearing that the Bosnian war would spread in a direction that would involve Turkey, Albania, and Greece, undertook a long but fruitless series of peace negotiations with Serbia's president, Slobodan Milosevic, Bosnian Serb leader Radovan Karadzic, and the Bosnian government. Meanwhile, food, oil, and arms were reported moving from Greece into Serbia in violation of the UN embargo. Before, during, and after its 1994 presidency of the EU, Greece was the only EU nation to back the Serbian position that Serbian forces had entered Bosnian territory in response to Bosnian provocations. In early 1994, Greece incurred the displeasure of its European allies by voting against NATO air strikes on Serbian positions. Greece also refused the use of its NATO air bases at Preveza on the Ionian Sea for such attacks and refused to supply Greek troops to the UN peacekeeping mission in Bosnia. In NATO, Greece's position was diametrically opposed to that of Turkey, which supported the Bosnian Muslims.

In December 1994, after official talks with Milosevic in Athens, Papandreou reiterated that the positions of Greece and Serbia on the Bosnia issue were virtually identical. A Milosevic proposal for a confederation of Greece and Serbia with FYROM failed to gain support among any faction in Greece.

The Macedonian Dispute

The dissolution of Yugoslavia also fueled a bitter confrontation between Greece and the neighboring Former Yugoslav Republic of Macedonia (FYROM). Initially fashioned into a republic in the late 1940s under Marshall Josip Broz Tito, the ethnically mixed territory that Tito called the Republic of Macedonia sought international recognition of its independence under terms that many Greeks consider threatening to their territorial integrity. Greece contended that by calling itself *Macedonia,* the new state usurped the glory associated with the Hellenic empire of Philip of Macedonia and his son Alexander the Great (fourth century B.C.). That era has been a proud historical heritage of the large northern Greek region that throughout history has borne the name of Macedonia.

Greece's position has been that the 1913 division of the larger territory of Macedonia never was meant to create ethnic claims by a separate and distinct Macedonian nation. Greece has charged that the newly created state has irredentist and expansionist designs against its neighbors, Greece in particular. Besides the use of the name Macedonia, FYROM has used the ancient Macedonian "star of Vergina," a Greek-treasured symbol of Philip's kingdom, in its national flag. On a more substantive level, the preamble to FYROM's constitution calls on Macedonians everywhere to rise and unite under FYROM's flag—a rallying cry that Greeks find incendiary.

Since September 1991, two different Greek administrations have attempted to convince the international community of the seriousness of FYROM's threat by bringing the dispute before the UN, while at the same time trying to conduct a dialogue with President Kiro Gligorov of FYROM. The UN-sponsored efforts almost came to fruition in the summer of 1993, but hopes for a settlement faded soon thereafter. Meanwhile, on the Greek domestic front, the formation of the nationalist PA party just before the 1993 elections forced all Greek parties to harden their positions on the FYROM issue.

In February 1994, after only a few months of frustrating negotiations, and during its six-month term in the rotating presidency of the EU, the new Papandreou government imposed a trade embargo on all nonhumanitarian goods bound for FYROM via Greek ports of entry. Although all Greek political parties and the general public supported Papandreou's initiative, foreign reactions, especially those of NATO and the EU, ranged from negative to outraged. Dissenting voices inside Greece pointed out that the country's largely symbolic stance had isolated it from its European partners and increased the threat of a generalized conflict in an already explosive situation in the Balkans.

None of these arguments affected the official Greek stand. Two months later, the European Commission (see Glossary) asked the European Court of Justice for an injunction against the Greek embargo as a serious breach of EU law.

Despite the general success of its 1994 EU presidency, Greece did not manage to use that opportunity to advance its position on FYROM. UN-sponsored mediation by veteran United States negotiator Cyrus Vance and, subsequently, by Clinton emissary Matthew Nimetz, succeeded only in establishing that the question of the country's name and its connotations remained the central stumbling block to any agreement.

In late June 1994, the European Court of Justice rejected the European Commission's request for an immediate temporary injunction against the Greek embargo. Although resolution of the case itself was still several months away, this decision restored national confidence in diplomatic approaches. After FYROM president Kiro Gligorov was reelected in November, negotiations resumed, but the participants broke them off almost immediately, and Greece again appealed to the EU for redress.

Relations with Albania

During most of the Cold War, relations between Greece and its northwestern neighbor Albania were tense, mainly because the large Greek minority population (estimated at between 250,000 and 400,000) in Albania was deprived of basic human rights by the Stalinist Albanian regime of Enver Hoxha. Relations with Albania made great strides in the mid-1980s, however, although the two countries were still technically at war under a Greek royal decree issued in 1940.

After 1978, when Albania began friendly overtures to Greece, cooperation in trade expanded steadily. In January 1985, the border between the two countries was reopened for the first time in forty-five years; this event was greeted by both sides as heralding a new era in their relations, although full normalization required another two years.

The fall of the last Albanian communist regime in 1990 was followed by total economic collapse, however; after a short period of liberalization, tensions increased again between the two countries. The key issue was the thousands of Albanian and Greek-Albanian refugees who began pouring into Greece once the Albanian border was opened fully. Greece was unable to stem this flow, which at times exceeded 900 persons per day and reportedly included some criminal elements.

In 1991, in an effort to limit the influx of refugees by improving economic conditions in Albania, the Mitsotakis government signed an interbank agreement granting Albania US$20 million in credits. These funds were largely wasted, however, and five months later, after Albania had joined the CSCE, several international organizations called for an end to relief aid until the money's proper application could be ensured. Albanian president Sali Berisha was accused of corruption and misappropriating loans from the World Bank (see Glossary). After these allegations, as well as renewed charges of human rights violations, Greece, as president of the EU, supported the suspension of some 35 million European currency units (ECUs—see Glossary) that had been earmarked for Albanian aid by the European Community Finance Organization (ECO-FIN). As economic conditions in Albania worsened, Berisha tried to divert public opinion by harassing human rights activists, among whom were the leaders of Omonia, an opposition political party representing the Greek minority in the south of Albania (referred to in Greece as Northern Epirus) that had elected five deputies in the 1991 Albanian parliamentary election.

Meanwhile, refugee traffic at Greece's borders increased until the Greek minority in Albania was reduced to an estimated 35 percent of its former size at the end of 1993. Minor incidents at the Greek-Albanian border became daily occurrences as resentments built up on both sides. In April 1994, two Albanians were killed at a military camp close to the Greek border. Although the killers were never caught, the Greek-Albanian population received the blame. In May six leading members of Omonia were arrested for crimes against the state. The Stalinist-style trial that began in August attracted the attention and concern of European jurists and President Clinton. Meanwhile, the Greek government had started large daily deportations of Albanian illegal immigrants.

Although Prime Minister Papandreou offered to loosen aid restrictions if the trial were ended, the Omonia leaders were convicted and jailed. As Greece vowed to seek redress, Greek-Albanian relations reached another low point, and their future was thrown into uncertainty.

Russia

The process of democratic consolidation pursued by the Karamanlis governments during the 1970s had included among its objectives the steady improvement of relations with the Soviet Union. Several bilateral economic cooperation agreements included large and sensitive projects ranging from the construction of energy plants to arranging for the servicing of Soviet ships in Greece. Regular exchanges of top-level visits, initiated by Karamanlis, continued under the two PASOK administrations in the 1980s.

In the 1980s, Western observers and Greek opposition leaders frequently charged that PASOK's "independent and multidimensional" foreign policy gave the appearance of a pro-Soviet bias. For example, Papandreou described the United States as "the metropolis of imperialism," and in 1983 he praised Polish communist party first secretary Wojciech Jaruzelski as a patriot rather than condemning Jaruzelski's declaration of martial law in Poland.

Explaining these statements, Papandreou argued that he was trying to wean Greece from total dependence on the United States and to end "one-sided alignment with one specific bloc." Although the prime minister's comments clearly irritated Greece's American and European allies, the Greek-Soviet ties established in the 1980s survived the political upheaval that ended the Soviet Union in quite good condition. Russian president Boris N. Yeltsin made a successful visit to Athens in 1993, and in July 1994 a high-level delegation from the Greek defense ministry continued a long series of official visits to Russia.

The Middle East

Greek governments have traditionally pursued a policy of friendship with the Arab states. This relationship is based on both historical and contemporary factors. Greece shares with the Arabs a common history of subjugation by the Ottoman Turks, and a large proportion of Christian Arabs are of the Greek Orthodox faith. Many Arab states have had large and prosperous Greek communities within their boundaries. The largest such community was in Egypt. In the 1950s, however, the Egyptian government forced most resident foreign businessmen, including Greeks, to leave the country in an effort to foster growth in the Egyptian middle class by reducing foreign business competition.

After the 1967 Arab-Israeli War, as the politics of the Middle East grew more complex, Greece called for Israel's evacuation of all occupied Arab land and supported the Palestinian struggle for an independent homeland. At the same time, Greece supported Israel's right to exist within safe and internationally guaranteed borders; this position was consistent with Greece's de facto recognition since 1948 of Israel's right to statehood.

In the wake of the oil crisis and the Turkish invasion of Cyprus, both in the mid-1970s, Greece's Middle East policy appeared to slant strongly toward the Arabs. The change was dictated by two needs: Arab support for Greece's Cyprus policies and stable oil supplies from the Arab oil producers.

In the 1980s, PASOK administrations followed an actively pro-Arab policy, culminating in the granting of diplomatic status to the Palestine Liberation Organization (PLO), whose connection with terrorist acts had made it an outcast to most Western nations. Even while PASOK support of the PLO was unwavering and contacts increased with hard-line Arab states such as Algeria, Iraq, Syria, and Libya, the Greek socialist regime also pursued a parallel policy of greater accommodation with Israel.

The end of the 1980s brought a significant change in Greek policy in the Middle East, an event not unexpected in view of the negligible gains that the pro-Arab policy had made for the Greek cause in Cyprus. The end of the Cold War and the outcome of the 1991 Persian Gulf War pointed to a potentially different Mediterranean region free from the chilling prospect of superpower confrontations. Since its full de jure recognition of Israel in 1990, Greece has maintained cordial ties and strong economic bonds with all the states at the eastern end of the Mediterranean Sea.

In the 1980s and early 1990s, the Greek political system showed signs of stabilization after many decades of drastic shifts from civilian to military and liberal to conservative governance. In the 1980s, ND changed leaders without dissolving into factions, and PASOK was expected to do the same eventually upon the retirement of Andreas Papandreou. The year 1994 marked twenty years of domination by those two parties. Although political power has continued to shift frequently between conservative and liberal parties, both main party platforms have moderated in domestic and foreign policy. The largest remaining question for Greek democracy is how quickly the old clientalist relationships, which still prosper in many quarters, can be shed in favor of a more appropriately varied representation of public interests.

As it entered the mid-1990s, Greece found itself in a generally better-balanced geopolitical environment than it had enjoyed during most of the twentieth century. The heavy reliance on the United States and NATO for national security eased greatly when the bipolar nature of European military configuration ended and NATO began considering new international roles (and new members) for itself. The chronic and multifaceted disputes with Turkey remained an unresolved threat to national security, however, and multiple crises with the former communist nations to the north found Greece taking controversial positions that earned the disapproval of Western allies.

*   *   *

Among the most useful recent works on Greek politics are several collections of articles on social, political, and economic facets of socialist rule in the 1980s. They include two volumes edited by Richard Clogg, *Greece in the 1980s* and *Greece 1981–1989: The Populist Decade*; *Political Change in Greece Before and after the Colonels*, edited by Kevin Featherstone and D.K. Katsoudas; *The Greek Socialist Experiment*, edited by Theodore C. Kariotis; and *Greece, the New Europe, and the Changing International Order*, edited by Harry J. Psomiades and Stavros Thomadakis.

Nicos Mouzelis's *Politics in the Semi-Periphery: Early Parliamentarism and Late Industrialization in the Balkans and Latin America* provides insight into the current Greek political setting. English and Greek editions of the *Southeast European Yearbook* focus on additional aspects of foreign affairs and document official government positions, facts, and figures. In *Entangled Allies: U.S. Policy Toward Greece, Turkey, and Cyprus*, Monteagle Stearns covers a central problem in Greek foreign relations; an equally timely discussion of Greek attitudes toward the outside world is *Modern Greece: Nationalism and Nationality*, edited by Martin Blinkhorn and Thanos Veremis. (For further information and complete citations, see Bibliography.)

Chapter 5. National Security

Member of the Evzone (Presidential Honor Guard) on parade

THE EARLY TO MID-1990S have been a period of drastic change in the national security conditions of the member nations of the European Union (EU—see Glossary) and of the Balkan countries. For Greece, this change has been complicated by a domestic political metamorphosis that began in 1974 and has continued into the 1990s. Among the factors exerting influence on Greece's security situation during this period are political, economic, social, and leadership variables; Greece's regional setting in the Balkans and the eastern Mediterranean; and, in a broader global context, the replacement of Cold War bipolarity with the more transitional and fluid geopolitical order that emerged in the early 1990s.

In the post-Cold War world, the geopolitical environment of Greece includes a security network of stable nations—the North Atlantic Treaty Organization (NATO—see Glossary) and the EU—working toward common goals. A second element of that environment, however, is an increasingly active group of less stable nations characterized by conflicting territorial claims, violent ethnic disharmony, and the threat of conflict. The characteristics of the latter group are similar to those that prevailed in the region before World War I and during the interwar period. In the mid-1990s, Greece finds itself along the border between the two groups: a solidly entrenched member of Western military and economic alliances but strongly linked to the less stable communities by a combination of historical alliances (with Serbia, for example) and antagonistic territorial claims (against the Ottoman Empire, for example).

Greece is located at the junction of three continents: Europe, Asia, and Africa. It is an integral part of the Balkans, where it is the only country that is a member of the EU, the Western European Union (WEU—see Glossary), and NATO. Greece also is in close proximity to the oil-rich and politically sensitive Middle East. Most important, Greece's position in the Mediterranean region—a crucial area of contact between North and South—enhances its strategic importance.

This strategic position accounts for Greece's 1952 entry into NATO. During the Cold War, Greece provided an essential link in NATO's southeastern flank. The linkage was especially important considering Greece's proximity to Turkey, a fellow NATO member whose location has two unique aspects: it is the only NATO member nation bordering the former Soviet Union below the Arctic Circle, and it is the only member nation bordering potentially hostile countries of the Middle East. Greece thus constitutes the most direct connection between Turkey and Western Europe (although Greece itself has no land connection with a NATO nation except Turkey). In the opinion of many Greek decision makers, the country's strategic importance has been underestimated by the West and, at times, even neglected.

As early as the mid-1950s, NATO's southeastern flank was experiencing periodic cycles of international tension. The emergence of the Cyprus problem in the 1950s, the Greek-Turkish crises of the 1960s, the Greek junta-sponsored coup in Cyprus in 1974, and the resultant Turkish military intervention in Cyprus (beginning a standoff on the island that continues to the present day) were complicated by a series of Greek-Turkish frictions in the Aegean Sea (see Turkey, ch. 4).

In the 1970s and 1980s, the strategic importance of NATO's southeastern flank increased significantly with the continuing oil crises of 1973 and 1979 and the growing tensions and instability in the region of the Persian Gulf. Important elements of that instability were the Soviet invasion of Afghanistan in 1979; the fall of Western ally Mohammad Reza Shah Pahlavi, ruler of Iran, in 1979; the outbreak of all-out war between Iran and Iraq in 1980; and the increased involvement of the United States in protecting vital oil shipping lanes in the Persian Gulf.

Historical Background

The national security history of twentieth-century Greece can be divided into a pre-1974 period and a post-1974 period, when full civilian control of the military emerged, too late to forestall a disastrous misadventure in Cyprus but in time to end the continual internal political conflict that had made Greece vulnerable to outside domination and needing the support of powerful allies throughout the early twentieth century. The post-1974 period has brought enhanced internal stability and the desire for greater independence in national security matters.

National Security Before 1974

In the period 1912–74, Greece experienced considerable turbulence in its external and internal relations. Economically,

Greece was classified with the poor, agrarian, raw material-producing, trade-dependent, and externally indebted nations—in short, it was underdeveloped. The polarized political world of Greece featured political parties based on personality and patron-client relations and the largesse of a bloated state sector offered to supporters when the parties gained power. The years 1915–74 were marked by deep schisms between royalists and republicans, communists and nationalists, whose bitter struggles sapped the energy of reform (see The Venizelos Era, ch. 1). These conflicts resulted in frequent military interventions in politics, including military dictatorships in 1925–26, 1936–41, and 1967–74. In 1946–49, a bloody and destructive Civil War, following soon after the German occupation in World War II, deeply scarred all of Greek society (see The Terrible Decade: Occupation and Civil War, 1940–50, ch. 1).

Although modern Greece had enjoyed sustained and functional democratic institutions throughout the second half of the nineteenth century, the twentieth century brought with it nearly constant challenges to democratic institutions by competing models of monarchical authoritarianism and communist totalitarianism. For this reason, during most of the twentieth century, political scientists classified Greece in the "praetorian zone" on the fringe of Western democracy, together with states such as Spain, Portugal, and Turkey.

In the turbulent twentieth century, the external relations of Greece were shaped by two world wars, totalitarian ideologies, competing nationalisms, and the Holocaust, as well as by more specific international conflicts such as the Balkan Wars (1912–13) and the Greco-Turkish War of 1921–22. All these events, which were very much a reflection of general turbulence in Europe (and particularly in the Balkans), affected the setting of Greece's boundaries as they were formally defined in 1923 by the Treaty of Lausanne and in 1947 by the Treaty of Paris.

Given its strategic location, throughout the twentieth century Greece was subject to competing bids for Great Power penetration. Being nearly totally surrounded by the sea placed the nation under the direct influence of two Great Powers that exercised naval control in the Mediterranean—Britain throughout the nineteenth century and up to 1947, and the United States after that time. The collapse of the last Greek military dictatorship, which was triggered by that government's attempt to establish a compatible regime in Cyprus in the summer of 1974, began a new era. The preconditions for change had already been put in position: extremely high rates of economic growth in the 1950s and 1960s, the rapid postwar urbanization of the population, and the consequent creation of a sizable middle class.

The Postjunta Transition

In 1974, following the collapse of the military dictatorship, Konstantinos Karamanlis returned from political exile to preside over a remarkably smooth transition process leading to the establishment of democratic institutions that proved durable over the next twenty years. Under Karamanlis the deep divisions of the past were gradually bridged, and the effective reintegration of Greek society commenced. Karamanlis's pragmatic approach to the thorny issues of domestic communists, the fate of the monarchy (whose abolition was confirmed in a December 1974 referendum), the recent show of power by Turkey in Cyprus, and punishment for the junta ended decades of mutual recrimination in the Greek political arena while reducing clashes among outside powers competing for influence within Greece.

The Cyprus Situation

In 1960 the Republic of Cyprus was created from a former British colony off the southern coast of Turkey in the northeastern corner of the Mediterranean Sea. The international agreements that created the nation attempted to guarantee the rights of the Turkish Cypriot minority (about 20 percent of a population that was otherwise almost entirely Greek Cypriot) in a fair allocation of governmental power and social privileges. In the years immediately following independence, however, the relative welfare and the interaction of the two ethnic groups in Cyprus became the object of constant quarrels, in which the nearby nations of Greece and Turkey naturally took great interest. A series of crises and armed conflicts, capped by the intervention of United Nations (UN) peacekeeping forces in mid-1964, forced the Turkish Cypriot population into enclaves that were circumscribed by the increasingly active Greek Cypriot National Guard. By 1964 the government devised by the 1960 agreements included only Greek Cypriots. In the years that followed, confrontations alternated with international mediation efforts; twice in that period, in 1964 and in 1967, Turkey made military preparations to invade the island and protect the Turkish Cypriot minority. At the same time, underground partisan groups, which had emerged in the early 1960s, gained much wider support in both communities. Such circumstances doomed the efforts of Cypriot President Archbishop Makarios III to preserve the island's independence. By the early 1970s, Cyprus was in fact a partitioned country, Makarios had lost all authority in the Turkish sector, and the government continued to function without its prescribed Turkish Cypriot contingent.

Makarios's position was further complicated by the support of the Greek ruling junta for Greek Cypriot backers of enosis (union with Greece). Finally, in July 1974 the junta backed the guerrilla organization EOKA B in a coup against Makarios, whose policies had blocked enosis. From the Turkish viewpoint, the attempt to join Cyprus to Greece was an unacceptable threat to the already isolated position of the Turkish Cypriot minority on the island. Acting officially as one of the three guarantors of Cypriot independence under the 1960 treaties (the others were Britain and Greece), Turkey responded to the coup with a swift and effective military occupation of northeastern Cyprus, which reinforced the de facto partition of the island into Greek and Turkish sectors.

Karamanlis Establishes Policy

When Karamanlis came to office in Greece in 1974, he was faced with three options in the Cyprus situation. The first was to go to war with Turkey. But the Greek dictators, paradoxically, had kept Greece militarily exposed by leaving the Aegean Islands undefended against a possible Turkish military operation. The second option was to seek a truce so as to gain time and later begin a massive rearmament that would enable Greece to push the Turks out of Cyprus at an opportune moment. Had this option been chosen, Greece and Turkey likely would have initiated a chain reaction of revanchist wars similar to those that occurred between Israel and its Arab neighbors. The result of that decision would have been a climate of high tension that would have prevented Greece from securing membership in the EC. The third option was to arm Greece for purposes of adequate deterrence of future Turkish expansionism in Cyprus, the Aegean, and Thrace, while at the same time applying political, economic, and diplomatic pressures to promote a viable settlement in Cyprus and the Aegean.

Karamanlis took the third option, believing that at that point Greek national security required maximum integration into the European Community (EC—see Glossary), even though from the Greek viewpoint that course meant abandoning certain territorial and nationalistic goals. Although Greece subsequently withdrew from the military structures of NATO in protest against perceived Western failure to prevent the Cyprus "invasion," Karamanlis's decision set an important precedent for Greek national security policy for the ensuing twenty years.

Policy in the 1980s and 1990s

Spirited debate in the 1970s preceded Greece's entry into the EC. The Panhellenic Socialist Movement (Panhellinion Socialistiko Kinima—PASOK), which had gained a significant political following in opposition to Karamanlis's weakening New Democracy (Nea Demokratia—ND) party, strongly opposed Greek membership. Since Greece formally entered the EC in January 1981, however, membership in the EC and its successor organization, the EU, has become almost universally accepted by all political parties as the centerpiece of Greece's foreign policy and national security institutions. Especially after 1990, that association exerted influence on nearly every aspect of Greek life (see International Economic Policy in the 1990s, ch. 3).

Between 1981 and 1994, EC/EU membership provided Greece an important foreign policy tool in relations with Turkey (see Greece and the European Community, ch. 4). Because membership in the EU is an important goal of Turkish foreign policy, Greece has used its membership as a lever to try to prevent Turkish membership (and large-scale EU aid to Turkey) until Cyprus and other Aegean issues are resolved to Greece's satisfaction. While presiding over the EU in the first half of 1994, Greece also attempted to capitalize on its EU status in its dispute against the Former Yugoslav Republic of Macedonia (FYROM—the internationally accepted name of the Socialist Republic of Macedonia after it declared independence from Yugoslavia in 1991) in order to prevent the latter from assuming (or expropriating, in the Greek view) the historical name of ancient Greek Macedonia. (Other issues, such as FYROM's use of Alexander the Great's sunburst symbol on its new flag, became subordinate to the "name" issue as negotiations proceeded.)

At the same time, membership in a highly institutionalized structure has restrained Greek foreign policy. In issues concerning both Turkey and northern neighbors such as FYROM,

Greece has found that its membership in the EC/EU has prevented it from pursuing nationalist or irredentist goals. The stabilizing influence of the EC/EU prevented Greece from taking sides in the chronic hostilities that followed the collapse of Yugoslavia in 1991, and instead promoted participation in a constructive (if self-interested and futile) search for Balkan solutions (see The Balkans, ch. 4).

New Post-Cold War Concerns

During the four decades of the Cold War, the undisguised adversarial relations between NATO and the Warsaw Pact (see Glossary) provided a high degree of stability in the Northern Hemisphere, albeit under the threat of general nuclear war. The end of the Cold War left previously well-defined global structures in a state of flux and raised the potential for new kinds of conflict—based, for example, on long-standing ethnic animosities—to erupt in many areas of the formerly stable North. To promote its security interests most effectively in this context, Greece has sought to integrate its policies with those of its EU partners and its NATO allies. In particular, this attitude has meant wide acceptance of the notion that collective Atlantic-European policies will facilitate a stable, conflict-free transition to political democracy and a market economy in postcommunist societies in the Balkans, hence meeting Greece's national security goals.

Since late 1991, however, adherence to these general guidelines has been considerably impeded by Greece's high-profile involvement in an emotional dispute over the nomenclature to be used for newly independent Slavic Macedonia. In the mid-1990s, there was considerable political friction between Greece and fellow EU members as a result of Greece's unilateral embargo against FYROM. The action provoked sharp disapproval and threats of legal action by the EU (see Greece and the European Community, ch. 4). In addition, Greece's pro-Serbian sympathies and its refusal to back or in any way facilitate NATO air strikes on Serbian positions in Bosnia, as well as its refusal to contribute troops to peacekeeping forces in Bosnia, exacerbated Greek-EU tensions. Greece's efforts in the early 1990s to broaden and deepen ties with the EU, the WEU, and NATO were also complicated by disunity in the NATO alliance in the face of the strategic and ideological vacuum that remained after the collapse of the Soviet Union.

The External Elements of National Security

The three most important external elements of Greece's security profile are the EU, the WEU, and NATO. The nations of the EU, whose extensive commitment to regional governance has indirectly solidified and supplemented Greece's national defense position, would assumedly use diplomatic and military force to protect their investments in Greece against potential attack from outside.

The second element is the WEU, originally intended as the military arm of a united Europe, then resurrected after being abandoned in the 1970s and the 1980s. By the mid-1990s, the WEU was touted as the European pillar of NATO's defense forces. For Greece's security structure, however, the WEU offers uncertain benefits, mainly because the organization's eventual role remains unknown. The unanswered question is whether the WEU will evolve into the exclusive defense component of the EU, or whether other, non-EU European states might be brought into an inclusive European pillar of NATO. The WEU could assume quite substantial significance for Greece if the United States were to reduce dramatically its military presence in Central Europe and the Mediterranean. In any case, in the future Greece is likely to rely on the WEU for at least some part of the collective security of its region.

Finally, the most far-reaching element of national defense and security is the collective defense structure of NATO. Membership in the "Atlantic community" represented by NATO integrates Greece into the most powerful military alliance ever assembled. Although internal politics have made Greek relations with NATO problematic in past decades, reliance on the alliance's security mechanisms has become a firm foundation of national security policy in the 1990s—even though the alliance's automatic support would be doubtful in case of dispute or hostilities with Turkey.

Membership in other international institutions such as the Conference on Security and Cooperation in Europe (CSCE— see Glossary) and the Council of Europe (see Glossary) further enhances the likelihood that Greece can settle disputes through peaceful processes. Greece's participation in the CSCE process (which now has been applied in the Caucasus, beyond the southeastern border of Europe) ensures that Greek perspectives are heard in an international forum where human rights, minority issues, and confidence-building measures are discussed.

The Role of the United States

In 1953 the first defense cooperation agreement between Greece and the United States was signed, providing for the establishment and operation of American military installations on Greek territory. Major installations included the Hellinikon Air Base and Nea Makri Naval Communications Station (both near Athens), Heraklion Air Station, Gournes Communications Station, and Souda Bay Air Base and Port (all in Crete). In the mid-1990s, the only operating facility that remains is the base at Souda Bay, which provides direct operational support for the United States Sixth Fleet in the eastern Mediterranean. In the past, bases in Greece also provided the United States surveillance of Soviet naval activities in the eastern Mediterranean, ammunition and supply storage sites, and support for the United States Air Force Europe and Military Airlift Command (MAC). The installations were under joint Greek and United States command. In 1972 an agreement with the military dictatorship provided home-port access for the Sixth Fleet at the port of Eleusis near Athens. A controversial issue in Greece even under the dictatorship, the project was abandoned in 1975 after the fall of the military regime.

Bilateral defense relations between Greece and the United States have been regulated by Defense and Economic Cooperation Agreements (DECAs), as well as Defense and Industrial Cooperation Agreements (DICAs). Despite occasionally harsh rhetoric toward the United States in the early 1980s, the socialist government of Andreas Papandreou nevertheless signed a new DECA in September 1983. In 1990, after several years of negotiation, a Mutual Defense Cooperation Agreement (MDCA) on the establishment and operation of United States forces in Greece was signed. The 1990 agreement was facilitated by unilateral United States decisions to close some of its military installations in Greece (see The United States, ch. 4). The 1990 agreement is scheduled to expire in 1998.

Geopolitical Considerations of National Security

In the mid-1990s, Greece's most critical concerns were chronic disagreements with and a perceived security threat from fellow NATO member Turkey and instability in the Balkans. Greece's tense relationship with Turkey is its most intractable international problem and has colored postwar economic and defense planning. In the mid-1990s, the public and all

Greek political parties continued to regard Turkey as the principal threat to Greek security, and this perception was used to justify increased military spending (see Turkey, ch. 4). The effects of instability in three former communist countries (Albania, Bulgaria, and the disparate elements of the former Yugoslavia), where various degrees of internal friction could overflow into neighboring countries, are also of immediate concern to Greece. Protection of human rights for the Greek minority in Albania and the need to resolve the domestically delicate question of recognition of FYROM and the conflicts this question arouses between Greece and its allies in the EU and NATO are primary security worries as well (see The Balkans, ch. 4).

Assessing the Turkish Threat

Assessment of the potential military threat from Turkey has long been a key concern of public opinion and the topic of constant debate among Greek security planners. The issue's urgency is rooted in the 1974 Cyprus crisis, which can be regarded as a turning point in post-World War II Greek security orientations. The alarm caused in Greece by the Turkish military intervention was the stimulus for a general reevaluation of national security doctrine.

Since the invasion, periodic nationalist declarations by radical factions in Turkey, which usually make headlines in Greek newspapers, have intensified Greek fears. A second factor in Greece's fear of Turkey is the program of armed forces modernization that Turkey has undertaken since 1991. Greece's perception of Turkey as a threat to national security has long been used to justify increased military expenditures and weapons procurements by Greece. But a continued, major expansion of Greek arms procurement is something the Greek economy can ill afford.

Greek military planners envision that the Turkish threat might take one of several forms: a Turkish attempt to extend its Cyprus occupation zone; to take over Greece's easternmost islands in the Aegean Sea, control of whose continental shelf is a burning issue; and/or to "protect" the Muslim minority in Thrace.

In late 1994, the issue of territorial waters between Greece's Aegean Islands and the Turkish mainland assumed greater urgency, at least on a rhetorical level. From the Greek perspective, a major concern is the prospect of a Turkish seizure of

Military parade on National Day (Independence Day), March 25
Courtesy Press and Information Office,
Embassy of Greece, Washington

Greek islands in response to a de facto Greek extension of the territorial waters limit of its islands from six to twelve miles. Such a move would be in accordance with the UN Convention on the Law of the Sea, which went into effect for most of the world in November 1994. (Through the end of 1994, Greece had signed but not ratified the treaty.) Were Greece to ratify and activate the terms of the treaty, it would in effect control sea access to ports on Turkey's west coast and to the Black Sea to the north. Turkey has repeatedly warned that such an act would be considered a casus belli (see Turkey, ch. 4). The Greek position has been that Greece has the right to extend territorial waters at some time in the future, but that Greece has no immediate intention of doing so. When the treaty went into effect for signatories in November 1994, Greece and Turkey both were holding naval maneuvers in the Aegean, and the rhetoric of both countries escalated.

A related source of Greek-Turkish tension is the dispute over the airspace above the Aegean. The issue, which surfaced in 1931, when Turkey refused to recognize the ten-mile territorial air limit first claimed that year by Greece, gained intensity after 1974. In the early 1990s, mock dogfights occurred frequently between Greek and Turkish pilots, whose interpretation of appropriate use of airspace differed. The frequency of these incidents plus the speed of the aircraft and the compactness of the airspace markedly increase the probability of a real air engagement with potential for escalation. Moreover, resolution of the airspace issue is a key to gaining both Greek and Turkish support for funding of NATO airbases at Larisa in Greece and at Izmir in Turkey.

Greek policy makers also view the Muslim population of northeastern Greece (Greek Thrace), estimated at 120,000, as a potential threat to national security. The Muslim population is composed of 50 percent Turks, 34 percent Pomaks (Muslim Bulgarians), and 16 percent Roma (Gypsies). By mutual consent of Greece and Turkey, the status of this minority has been tied to the fortunes of the Greek population in Istanbul and on the offshore islands of Gokceada (Imroz) and Bozcaada (over 200,000 strong in 1923 but only about 3,000 in 1994). The gradual depletion of the Greek minority in Turkey has changed the balance of this understanding, however. The demographic strength of the Muslims, coupled with pro-Turkish activity in Greek Thrace, occasionally has created tense relations between Christian and Muslim citizens in Greece.

Occasional threats by Turkish nationalist extremists such as the Bati Trakya organization to intervene in Thrace "to liberate their oppressed kin" have not been echoed by responsible Turkish authorities, nor have they attracted significant attention outside the immediate region. Nevertheless, Greek planners take potential Turkish aspirations in Greek Thrace seriously. In addition, in the Greek view, Bulgaria's treatment of its own Turkish minority, which the communist regime of Todor Zhivkov attempted to Bulgarianize in the 1980s, could play a role in ethnic conditions in Thrace because of that region's close proximity to Bulgaria's Turkish communities.

Security in the Balkans

For reasons of geographical proximity and historical connections, Greece has a compelling interest in the Balkan region. In the late 1980s and the early 1990s, several factors have radically altered the basic premises of Greece's traditional Balkan policy. Those factors are Turkey's increasing Balkan activism, regional political and economic instability, the disintegration of Yugoslavia and the prospect of revisions in its southern border, and the strategic reorientation of Bulgaria.

Besides the other burdens on the Greek-Turkish relationship, Turkey's perceived desire to become a regional power in the Balkans is a security worry for Greece. In the Greek view, the existence of Muslim communities and minorities in Albania, Bosnia and Herzegovina, Kosovo, Bulgaria, and FYROM might tempt Ankara to develop a "Turkish network" in the Balkans that would isolate Greece and Bulgaria in this area.

Greece's fears of outside orchestration of events in the Balkan region have inflated the "Macedonia issue" into a far wider international concern than normally would be warranted by a small, land-locked entity such as FYROM. This distraction has been particularly worrisome because Greece's responses to the FYROM situation (as well as its divergent views on Bosnia and Serbia) have created animosity toward Greece within the EU (see Greece and the European Community; the Balkans, ch. 4).

Greece seeks stability in the Balkans, and, as the Balkan state that is comparatively the most affluent, stable, democratic, and Western-oriented, it is ideally situated to play the role of interlocutor in the region. But it is unclear whether such a role is now possible, given Greece's festering disputes with Turkey and its strained relations with the EU.

Greece's approach to its security interests in the Balkans has not been influenced by irredentist claims on its neighbors. Although the Megali Idea (Great Idea) of including all Greeks in the Greek state played an important role in foreign policy before World War II, the Greek government has renounced all territorial claims on southern Albania, still called Northern Epirus by Greek nationalists. An important national security consideration in this region, however, is the possibility that violent ethnic hostilities in FYROM could bring outside powers into the region or trigger a large-scale refugee movement into Greek territory. In a period of recession and high unemployment, large numbers of illegal workers place extra pressure on the struggling Greek economy (see Emigration and Immigration, ch. 2).

In the 1980s, Greece's security doctrine deemphasized the Warsaw Pact as a security threat, in spite of the shared border with Bulgaria, the Soviet Union's most loyal Warsaw Pact ally. Because of its defense relationship with the United States, complemented by participation in NATO, Athens could afford to devote relatively minor resources and energy toward security measures to its north. In an age of mutual nuclear vulnerability, it was correctly assumed, neither superpower would tolerate a regional interbloc conflict in the Balkans.

In the Cold War era, Greek-Bulgarian consultations on security matters were encouraged by the common threat felt by both countries from Turkish military power and political interests in the Balkans (Bulgarian-Turkish relations were particularly difficult as a result of Bulgaria's official efforts to Slavicize its large Turkish minority in the mid-1980s). In this context, commentators began to discuss an Athens-Sofia axis in the late 1980s. More recently Greece has become concerned about Bulgaria's potential role in encouraging integrative policies between Bulgaria and FYROM, especially considering that political relations between Sofia and Ankara have improved considerably since Bulgaria ended its status as a client-state of the Soviet Union. Nevertheless, the prospects for a true Turkish-Bulgarian rapprochement seemed remote in the mid-1990s, and Greek-Bulgarian relations began to improve again as Bulgaria adopted a more balanced approach in its relations with its two NATO neighbors. For example, in 1994 Greece and Bulgaria agreed on construction of an oil pipeline through Bulgaria and Greece, connecting the Black Sea to the Aegean and bypassing Turkey.

The deepening crisis in former Yugoslavia concerns Athens for economic and strategic reasons. First, there is the fear that Balkan instability, either limited to former Yugoslavia or more general, will inhibit the integration of Greece into the European mainstream. The economic dimensions of this problem are quite significant. Until the collapse of Yugoslavia in 1991, Greece had relied on road and rail communications through that country for some 40 percent of its trade with the European market. Prolonged disruption of this vital link has crippled that connection, as did the imposition of UN sanctions against the rump Yugoslav state (consisting of Montenegro and Serbia) in 1992. In 1994 Greek authorities estimated that sanctions have caused losses of up to US$10 million per day, although Greece is known to have violated the embargo.

Also of concern to Greece is the fear that ethnic violence between the 90 percent Albanian Muslim majority and the Montenegrin and Serbian minority in the Serbian province of Kosovo might spill over into adjacent territory. Were an outbreak of Albanian separatism to include the neighboring Albanian-populated Tetovo region of FYROM, Serbian efforts to subdue Albanian Kosovan separatism might also cross the frontier, bringing FYROM into the conflict. But even if hostilities were to be contained within Kosovo, the movement of thousands of refugees to Albania or farther south might cause ethnic Greeks living in southern Albania to flee to Greece. The increasing role of Albanians in secessionism within FYROM, where they now constitute about 30 percent of the population, could further destabilize the area. Great population movements southward could have serious consequences for Greece as well as for the whole region.

National Security Doctrine

The evolution of Greece's national security doctrine since World War II has been determined by the country's own relative strength and by changes in threat perception. The Cyprus events of 1974 dramatically changed the country's view of its primary threat. Attention since then has focused almost exclusively on Turkey.

Historical Development

During the late 1940s and early 1950s, the difference between Greek conservatives and liberals (the communist party having been banned after the Civil War) on security issues and participation in NATO was one of emphasis. Both groups basically believed that Greece's main security threat emanated from the Warsaw Pact military power across its northern borders. NATO was viewed, therefore, as indispensable for the defense of the country, and the United States was treated as Greece's natural ally and guarantor.

From the end of the Civil War in 1949, Greek governments, given the nation's dependence on the United States, yielded to that power on most issues concerning national defense and security arrangements. The Greek armed forces were equipped exclusively with American arms, and the hundreds of Greek officers who received advanced military training in the United States welcomed the continuity of their host country's influence on the Greek armed forces.

The orientation of Greece's national defense doctrine until the mid-1960s was based on the United States credo that the main security threat was internal rather than external. The Greek army was primarily supplied and organized to face a domestic communist threat. According to NATO planning, in case of global war between the superpowers, Greece was only expected to cause some delay to Soviet and satellite forces.

When international tension relaxed somewhat in the late 1960s, the perception of a domestic communist threat being supported by Greece's communist neighbors diminished considerably. Rather, after the 1964 and 1974 Cyprus crises, a main concern became a confrontation between the two Balkan

NATO allies. Greek security planning could no longer focus only on internal danger and NATO defense prescriptions.

The end of the Cold War, the overthrow of Soviet-supported communist regimes in Eastern Europe, and the collapse of the Soviet Union have led, rather paradoxically, to a darkening of Greece's security horizons and a rather complete reassessment of national security requirements. Until the 1974 Turkish invasion of Cyprus, the Hellenic Armed Forces had two primary missions: defending the country against an attack by the Soviet Union or its Balkan satellites and assisting in the maintenance of Western control over the eastern Mediterranean Sea in time of conflict. After the 1974 invasion, the security focus shifted.

Defense Posture after 1974

Since 1974, the Hellenic Armed Forces' primary mission has been maintaining a balance of power with Turkey, specifically deterring infringement of Greek national interests and sovereignty and preventing a Turkish attack on the Greek Cypriot portion of Cyprus. As a secondary mission, Greece's status as a member of NATO requires military contributions to that alliance's efforts to deter threats in Eastern Europe, the Balkans, and the Mediterranean originating outside the region.

Greece's military doctrine is defensive on the strategic level, in accordance with the overall doctrine of NATO. The objective is to deter any threat or actual attack against Greece and to protect Greek national interests. The doctrine of forward defense has been adopted by the Hellenic Armed Forces.

On the tactical level, the doctrine may have a defensive or a counteroffensive orientation, according to circumstances. The impressive performance of the United States Armed Forces in the Persian Gulf War prompted Greece to reorganize its land forces, putting greater emphasis on smaller units (moving primary focus from divisions and regiments to brigades and battalions), combining the increased mobility of armored personnel carriers and helicopters with enhanced firepower. The main task of the air and naval components of the armed forces in case of armed conflict with Turkey would be to deter Turkish attempts to occupy Greek islands in the Aegean Sea and, concurrently, to support the defense of Cyprus. More specifically, the Hellenic Navy is expected to maintain control of the seas, intercept and destroy enemy amphibious forces, protect lines of communication, and transport reinforcements to the islands. The Hellenic Air Force is expected to maintain air superiority, support land and naval operations, attack first- and second-echelon forces in Thrace (providing at the same time close air support for Greek land forces), neutralize amphibious forces in the Aegean, and strike at vital targets on the enemy's territory.

In 1994 Greece and Cyprus announced the creation of a Joint Defense Area. According to this doctrine, as long as Turkey maintained an occupation force of more than 30,000 troops in Cyprus, Greek and Cypriot forces would remain in the posture of joint defense. In this context, any attack against the Republic of Cyprus would constitute a casus belli for Greece. In 1994 some 950 regular Greek troops were in Cyprus, and 1,300 Greek noncommissioned officers (NCOs) and officers were detailed to the Greek Cypriot National Guard, the republic's active armed force. That force's senior officer corps is composed mainly of Greeks; the commanding officer is a general of the Hellenic Army selected by the Ministry of Defense of Greece in consultation with the Hellenic General Staff when the command becomes vacant.

Greece in NATO

The evolution of NATO's post-Cold War European strategies toward deterrence and crisis management has played an important role in the development of Greece's military doctrine. Greek policy is to adopt new doctrines and strategic options prescribed by NATO whenever such changes are compatible with its national security interests. Greece has expressed its intention to contribute troops in the near future to the Allied Mobile Force of NATO's Allied Command Europe (ACE). In 1994 Greece was contributing one division to the ACE Rapid Reaction Corps (ARRC), and it will participate in the Multinational Division in the Southern Region.

Greece participates in NATO's Standing Naval Force Mediterranean (STANAVFORMED), which consists of destroyers and escort ships, and the Strategic Allied Command Europe prescribes a pivotal role for the Hellenic Navy in the Multinational Maritime Force in instances of limited aggression in the Mediterranean. The E–3A aircraft of NATO's Airborne Early Warning Force are manned by integrated crews from eleven nations, including Greece. The main forward operating base of the E–3A component is maintained at Preveza on Greece's Ionian coast. A number of NATO air defense installations also are located in Greece. Greece has offered headquarters facilities for the Multinational Division in Thessaloniki.

Nevertheless, disagreements between Greece and Turkey have hindered some aspects of the two nations' participation in the NATO alliance and have complicated the strategic preparations of the alliance. At the end of 1994, NATO was attempting to finalize establishment at Larisa of the NATO headquarters responsible for land defense of Greece and Italy (LANDSOUTHCENT). Greece had reversed its 1993 blockage of the arrangement, but in 1994 Turkey refused its support until Greek and Turkish airspace over the Aegean Sea is firmly defined. The Joint Staff of NATO had set its manning plan for the LANDSOUTHCENT headquarters in early 1994, but subsequent Turkish and Greek disagreements defied NATO efforts to find a satisfactory compromise on the timing of commitments. Until a comprehensive settlement of their differences is reached, such bickering will prevent both Greece and Turkey from making full contributions to NATO activities in the strategically sensitive eastern Mediterranean.

The Greek armed forces made a significant contribution to the UN effort in the Persian Gulf War of 1991. The Hellenic Air Force carried out air and sea surveillance and reconnaissance, and it relocated aircraft and deployed radar stations in its southeast sector. Most Greek airfields were made available to United States and allied aircraft. During the war, bases on Crete and Rhodes received nearly 3,000 aircraft from United States aircraft carriers in the Mediterranean. Greece also contributed a frigate to the allied Maritime Interdiction Force and supported UN sanctions against Iraq.

The National Defense Establishment

The current national defense system is designed to guarantee civilian control of the armed forces, a vital constraint in view of the 1967 coup and the seven-year military dictatorship that followed. The 1975 constitution, ratified one year after the collapse of the junta, fixes the mechanism of command. After the restoration of democratic rule in 1974 and the limited purge in the Hellenic Armed Forces that followed in its wake, civilian control over the military has never been in question (see The Junta, ch. 1). The role of the military has been limited to defense matters, and all significant decisions concerning national security issues are made by the government.

The Command Structure

According to the Greek constitution, as amended in 1986, the president of the republic is the supreme commander of the armed forces, but his powers are largely symbolic. Military command decisions are made by the prime minister and the government. The Government Council for Foreign Policy and National Defense, which convenes once a year and in emergency conditions, appoints the chief of the Hellenic National Defense General Staff (English acronym HNDGS) and the chiefs of staff of the three military branches: the Hellenic Army, Hellenic Navy, and Hellenic Air Force. The Joint Chiefs of Staff Council is an advisory board to the chief of the HNDGS.

The chief of the HNDGS is the supreme military commander of the armed forces in times of crisis or war. In peacetime, the chiefs of staff of the three branches report directly to the minister of defense (see fig. 12). The post of chief of the HNDGS alternates every two years on an almost regular basis among officers of the three branches. The branch chiefs of staff serve two-year terms, although the term can be extended if deemed necessary.

The Officer Corps

Officers have enjoyed a unique status in Greek society, to the extent that in some respects they have formed a separate caste. During the twentieth century, the military has repeatedly intervened in Greek political life, establishing a military dictatorship on three occasions, in 1925, 1936, and 1967 (see The Military in Politics, ch. 4). Since the restoration of democracy and the trial and incarceration of the leaders of the 1967 coup, however, officers have consistently refrained from intervening in political life. The converse of that statement has not always been true, however, particularly given that general and flag officers serve at the pleasure of the prime minister. In addition, shortly after PASOK's 1993 election victory, a new law legalized the recall of retired officers to active duty. When four retired officers with political connections with PASOK were recalled and appointed chiefs of staff, thirty-five senior army, navy, and air force officers resigned in protest. Although changes in top staff positions had occurred after previous changes of government, this was the first time in the postjunta era that officers had resigned in protest of a government action.

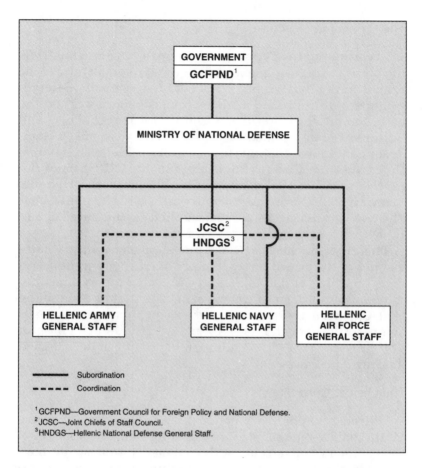

Source: Based on information from "Defence and Economics in Greece," *NATO's Sixteen Nations*, 37, No. 5, 1992, 45.

Figure 12. Organization of Defense Establishment, 1994

During the political schism between royalists and republicans that continued for most of the first half of the twentieth century, the armed forces were first strongly monarchist and then also strongly anticommunist. Then, the events of the Civil War (1946–49) pitted the World War II resistance forces, which were dominated by the republican Communist Party of Greece (Kommunistikon Komma Ellados—KKE), against a royalist Greek army that had largely spent the war in exile. This conflict further bolstered anticommunism in the officer corps. In the postwar period, however, time and the process of national reconciliation have largely altered the strong conservative attitude of the military—especially once the Karamanlis government reestablished democracy in 1974.

Military Personnel

The organization of the Hellenic Armed Forces of the 1990s is based mainly on United States standards. The number of individuals serving in the Greek military decreased by about 21 percent between 1985 and 1994; over the same period, defense expenditures as a percentage of gross national product (GNP—see Glossary) decreased by slightly less than 1 percent. National defense planning stresses training modernization in keeping with the selected goals of military doctrine.

Personnel Policy

According to the constitution, every male citizen capable of bearing arms has the obligation to serve in the Hellenic Armed Forces upon reaching his twentieth year. During the period of eligibility, exemptions may be granted for serious health problems and in some other cases, such as to fathers of more than four children and church officials. Deferments are granted for completion of university studies until the age of twenty-seven for undergraduate studies and until the age of thirty for graduate studies. It is estimated that 40 percent of each conscript "class" request and receive deferments for completion of their studies. Women are not subject to conscription, but they may enlist voluntarily in the armed forces.

The recruitment pool for the Greek armed forces has been shrinking gradually since about 1980 because the population is aging and each recruiting age-group is accordingly smaller (see Population Characteristics, ch. 2). In 1994 the prime recruiting group, ages eighteen to twenty-two, included 370,000 men. Because of the country's demographics, the Ministry of National Defense announced in 1994 that women may be required to participate in some military training in National Guard units.

In 1985 the armed forces had 201,500 persons. In 1994 the total number was 159,300, of whom 122,300 (77 percent) were conscripts and 5,900 were women. The Hellenic Army numbered 113,000, the air force 26,800, and the navy 19,500. Every year six "classes" of conscripts are inducted.

The youngest age at which a person may enlist voluntarily is seventeen. Each individual's case is reviewed by the local draft board, which evaluates all conscripts to determine the person's appropriate branch, specialization, and grade (officer, non-commissioned officer, or private). Classifications are computer-processed on the basis of qualifications. Those entrants selected to serve as officers spend four months at a reserve officers' school, after which they are designated "reserve officers." A few months before their release from active service, they are commissioned as second lieutenants.

In addition to active-duty personnel, the Greek military includes about 406,000 reservists. They are divided into three categories, according to age. Categories A, B, and C include personnel below age forty, between forty and fifty, and above age fifty, respectively. Reservists are subject to recall to participate in military exercises lasting one to two weeks per year.

Greece's conscription system operates effectively overall, and it is widely accepted by most Greeks. In the last few years, however, the issue of conscientious objectors has received increased publicity. Greece allows conscientious objectors who are religious ministers of "known religions" to serve in non-combatant assignments, but these are for twice as long as regular military service. In addition, the recruiting service of the armed forces has refused to recognize Jehovah's Witnesses as a known religion, and so has called them up for service, then prosecuted them for refusal. They may appeal for an exemption from service only after a conviction. As a consequence, these ministers have spent periods of a few months to over a year in jail while appealing their cases. Several human rights organizations have urged Greece to resolve this problem.

Induction and Training

The standard term of service for inductees is eighteen months in the air force, twenty months in the army, and twenty-one months in the navy, with maximum terms of nineteen, twenty-three, and twenty-one months, respectively. Male and female personnel may become career noncommissioned officers (NCOs) by serving an initial five-year term, after which they have the option to remain in the service as a career or return to civilian life. In 1994 some 24 percent of armed forces personnel were classified as professional soldiers (career NCOs or officers). Recent efforts to increase this percentage have been frustrated by the lack of funds to raise the pay scale and induce reenlistment.

Male and female volunteer NCOs undergo eight weeks of basic training at recruit training centers, after which they receive specialized NCO training, the duration of which depends on their specialization. The training cycle is completed with on-the-job training in the units to which the individuals are assigned.

Conscripts go through three training cycles. An eight-week orientation period provides physical training and knowledge of basic military skills. The twenty-six-week cycle that follows is conducted in special training centers that teach battlefield survival, fighting skills, and carrying out missions. The third cycle, which continues until the individual is demobilized into the reserves, aims to maintain the skills learned previously. All personnel participate in small-scale or large-scale army or interservice exercises at the conclusion of training. Reservists are called up periodically to refresh their skills or familiarize them with new equipment.

In 1994 about 16,700 officers served in the Hellenic Armed Forces. Officers receive training at one of four military schools. The Army Cadet Academy accepts 250 new students annually, the Air Force Cadet Academy adds 130 students annually, and the Navy Cadet Academy accepts seventy-five students annually. All three academies offer four-year programs. Entry to the service academies is very competitive; between 10 and 15 percent of applicants normally are selected. The Corps Officers' Military School offers a four- to six-year training program for medical and administrative officers, accepting 100 new officers annually. In addition, each service branch has several schools for NCOs, each offering a two-year course of study. The law provides that a fixed percentage of academy NCO graduates be commissioned every year.

In the course of their careers, selected officers are trained in higher military schools such as the Army War College, the Air Force War College, and the Navy War College, which accept captains and majors, and the National Defense Academy, which accepts lieutenant colonels and colonels. The course of study in all those schools is one year. A number of officers also study at military schools and academies in NATO-member countries and other allied nations.

The Hellenic Armed Forces

The structure and alignment of the Hellenic Armed Forces reflect the assessment that the most serious potential threat comes from the east. Accordingly, force deployment emphasizes Greek Thrace, the Aegean Islands, and Cyprus, and funding for modernization and expansion has been targeted to specific eventualities.

Modernization Plans

The Ministry of Defense's plans for modernizing its armed forces have concentrated on improving capabilities in eight areas: command, control, and information systems; electronic warfare; capability to conduct sustained operations; armor support firepower; air defense; achievement of air and sea control; logistics personnel; and survivability of forces. Modernization plans are funded by the state budget together with foreign and domestic loans. Planners place special emphasis on force-multiplier factors, such as electronic warfare and telecommunications, and on factors such as mobility that will enhance the position of Greek forces in the Aegean.

Also included in the modernization program in the planning period 1992–96 are improvements in training and living conditions and acquisition of more vessels for use in surveillance of the eastern Aegean. Where the purchase of new equipment is too expensive, refurbished equipment is acquired with German and United States assistance, as permitted by the Conventional Forces in Europe Treaty (CFE Treaty—see Glossary) signed in 1991 by NATO and the Warsaw Pact nations.

The Hellenic Army

The Hellenic Army, the Greek ground forces, includes 113,000 troops, of whom 100,000 are conscripts, and 2,200 of whom are women. The ground forces reserves include 350,000 troops, of whom 230,000 are trained for field army activity. The First Army, the only field army in the ground forces, is headquartered at Larisa in Central Greece and is divided into four corps, headquartered, respectively, at Kozani (First Corps, north-central Greece), Veroia (Second Corps, north-central Greece), Thessaloniki (Third Corps, on the north Aegean shore), and Xanthi (Fourth Corps, in Greek Thrace). The Higher Military Command of the Interior and the Islands (ASDEN HQ) is located in Athens.

The First Corps and Second Corps are responsible for protection of the country's northern borders. The Third Corps and Fourth Corps share responsibility for the Greek-Turkish border in Thrace and the islands. ASDEN, designated as a terri-

Hellenic Army armored and special forces troops participating in training exercises
Courtesy Embassy of Greece, Washington

torial defense force, is responsible for the rest of the country, as well as for the islands, acting in a complementary role to the field army.

The field army has a total strength of 82,000 troops. Besides the four corps headquarters, there are also one armored divisional headquarters and one mechanized divisional headquarters. The army includes nine infantry divisions, each of which has three infantry and one artillery regiment and one armored battalion. Of the divisions, two are category A (85 percent full combat readiness), three are category B (60 percent combat ready within twenty-four hours), and four are category C (20 percent combat ready in forty-eight hours). The army also includes five independent armored brigades, each of which has two armored battalions, one mechanized battalion, and one self-propelled artillery battalion, all of which are category A.

In addition, the army has one independent mechanized brigade, including two mechanized battalions and one armored and one self-propelled artillery battalion, all in category A. Those units are supported by two infantry brigades; one marine brigade, including three infantry battalions, one artillery battalion, and one armored squadron, all category A; one commando and one raider regiment; four reconnaissance battalions; ten field artillery battalions; six air defense artillery battalions; two surface-to-air missile battalions with upgraded Hawk missiles; two army aviation battalions; and one independent aviation company.

The ASDEN territorial defense forces are divided into four military command headquarters, one of which is in Athens. The forces include one infantry division, one paratroop regiment, eight field artillery battalions, four air-defense artillery battalions, and one army aviation battalion. A reserve force of 34,000 National Guard troops is responsible for internal security in wartime.

In the early 1990s, significant arms expenditures for the ground forces have included the purchase of new attack helicopters, modernization of tanks and transport helicopters, and modernization and enhancement of artillery firepower (see table 14, Appendix).

The Hellenic Air Force

The Hellenic Air Force lists several critical objectives in fulfilling its mission. Development of a modern command, control, and information system will aid in crisis management by

F–16 fighter jet of the Hellenic Air Force
Courtesy Press and Information Office, Embassy of Greece, Washington

linking the air force with other branches and commands in allied countries in a timely manner. An upgraded early warning system is considered another high-priority element of communications, to provide time for decision making. A second requirement is the capability for immediate reaction to unforeseen threats; to achieve that goal, the air force is emphasizing interoperability and compatibility of armaments and suppression of enemy air defenses.

A third goal is improving mobility, especially considering the requirement for Greece's assigned participation in the ACE Rapid Reaction Corps in the NATO force structure of the 1990s (see Greece in NATO, this ch.). An important element of this requirement is improved air transport capability. A fourth goal is improving support of ground-force operations by using air transport to preposition ammunition and supplies. Finally, the development of air defense is considered critical to maintaining control of the air in the cramped airspace of the eastern Mediterranean Sea. In its combat doctrine, the Hellenic Air Force aims not at permanently establishing air superiority (a prohibitively expensive goal) but at being able to control air space at specific times and places.

Greek military experts believe that between 1987 and 1994 the air force achieved satisfactory turn-around time for service and repair of aircraft, elements that are complex given the diversity of fighter types in the present NATO inventory. All major airfields in the country now can provide quick repair of battle damage. Most training in aircraft repair work is carried out abroad. Flight and ground safety were improved in 1992 by the reorganization of the Hellenic Air Force General Staff to include a Flight Safety Directorate.

The air force modernization program has aimed at reducing the number of aircraft in operation and increasing flexibility and tactical reconnaissance capability. Specifically, this policy has meant the procurement of F–4E and A–7E aircraft from the United States and NF–5A/B and RF–4E aircraft from the Netherlands and Germany, respectively, and phasing out outdated F/RF–104s and F–5A/B aircraft. Two squadrons of F–16 jets with modern weapon systems have been added to upgrade defensive capacity, and the addition of C–130 and medium transport aircraft improved deployment and support capability in the early 1990s (see table 15, Appendix).

The Hellenic Air Force includes 26,800 troops, of whom 14,400 are conscripts and 1,100 are women. The three commands are the Tactical Air Command, headquartered at Larisa, and the Air Support Command and the Air Training Command, both based in Athens. The Tactical Air Command includes eight combat wings and one transport wing. The combat wings have six fighter ground-attack squadrons. There are ten fighter squadrons, one regular reconnaissance squadron, and one marine reconnaissance squadron. Three transport squadrons and two helicopter squadrons form the organization of the air portion of the Tactical Air Command. The Air Training Command includes four training squadrons.

The eight major air force installations are located at Larisa, Nea Ankhialos southeast of Larisa, Eleusina west of Athens, Thessaloniki, Tanagra north of Athens, Souda Bay, Araxos in the northern Peloponnesus, and Andravida. Other airports supporting military operations are located on the Aegean Islands of Karpathos, Santorini (Thira), Rhodes, Skiros, and Lemnos, and at Kavala (Macedonia), Heraklion (Crete), and Tatoi/Dekelia, north of Athens.

The Hellenic Navy

Greece's location in the Mediterranean Sea and its long maritime tradition have led to emphasis on the role of the Hellenic Navy. The chief of the Hellenic Navy General Staff also is Commander Eastern Mediterranean (COMEDEAST) in the NATO command structure. Among the navy's missions is control of vital choke points in the Aegean and Ionian seas to ensure safe passage of NATO and domestic naval forces.

In the early 1990s, the navy was increasingly active in NATO exercises and in the STANAVFORMED, which was formed in

1992. Base facilities are provided to NATO ships at Souda Bay in Crete and at Salamis, near Athens. The navy is divided into three commands: the Fleet, the Naval Training Command, and the Naval Logistics Command. The most important operational part of the navy is the fleet. Greece's geographic position places special demands on the fleet because its possible area of operations ranges from the coastal areas and shallow waters of the Aegean to open waters in the Ionian Sea and the eastern Mediterranean Basin. All those areas are within range of land-based aircraft.

The demands of national security and NATO participation have inspired an expensive modernization program in the Hellenic Navy. Given fiscal restrictions, planners have concentrated on acquisition of modern naval platforms to replace outmoded Fletcher-class and Gearing FRAM I/II-class destroyers. The goals of the replacement program include manufacture of four MEKO–200H-class frigates—the first of which was delivered from Germany in 1993 and the other three of which are scheduled for later completion in the Hellenic Shipyards (see The Greek Defense Industry, this ch.).

Four Adams-class destroyers were leased from the United States Navy in 1992 and placed in the Greek Kimon class. The next year, three Knox-class frigates also were leased from the United States Navy and placed in the Makedonia class, and three Standard (Dutch Kortenaer)-class frigates were acquired from the Dutch Navy for use in the Greek Elli class. In all, the Hellenic Navy had fourteen major surface combatants in 1994. In 1993 Greek shipyards began construction of five tank landing ships (LSTs). The modernization program also includes acquisition of five Sikorsky antisubmarine warfare (ASW) helicopters from the United States to support the fleet's antisubmarine defenses. Four of Greece's eight Glavkos-type (GeT–209/1100) submarines have updated power plants and upgraded electronic equipment; Harpoon surface-to-surface missiles have been added to one. One of the submarines was modernized in Germany, the others at the Salamis Shipyard near Piraeus. The navy's command, control, and communications information systems are also in the process of modernization to improve information flow. A number of small combatants and support ships also have been built in the early 1990s.

Plans for the immediate future called for acquisition of eight P3 maritime patrol aircraft to replace the nine outmoded Albatross aircraft currently in use. The addition of new units also requires upgrading the naval facilities at Greece's two main bases, Salamis and Souda Bay, as well as the forward bases on the island of Skiros and on the Khalkidiki Peninsula, both in the Aegean Sea.

The Hellenic Navy includes 19,500 active-duty personnel, of whom 7,900 are conscripts and 2,700 are officers; 2,600 of the number are women. Greece is divided into three naval districts, covering the Ionian Sea, the Aegean Sea, and northern Greece. Besides fleet headquarters, which is the combat command component, the organization includes the Naval Logistics Command and the Naval Training Command. Other naval bases are located at Kavala and Patras in the Peloponnesus and at Thessaloniki. The navy's total equipment strength includes a wide range of vessels (see table 16, Appendix).

The Coast Guard is a paramilitary branch of the navy that comes under the purview of the Ministry of Merchant Marine in peacetime. The force has 158 patrol craft of various types and four light aircraft. The Coast Guard patrols all Greek harbors, coastlines, and territorial waters, monitoring antipollution measures and controlling merchant shipping. Officers train at the Navy Cadet Academy.

The Merchant Marine

In wartime, the Greek merchant marine, possessing one of the largest fleets of peacetime vessels in the world, would make an important contribution to NATO combat operations in the eastern Mediterranean. In 1990 NATO combat contingency plans called for 780 Greek merchant ships to be activated for military transport duty compared with 626 for the United States. This disparity is largely because Western shipping is increasingly configured for container transport, but most types of military equipment cannot be containerized. Thus Greece's large number of break-bulk ships and ferries would be very valuable in transporting military vehicles and helicopters. In 1992 the estimated capacity of the merchant marine was 85,000 passengers and 15,000 vehicles, and the fleet undergoes continuous modernization. The Ministry of Merchant Marine actively supported UN forces in the 1991 Persian Gulf War with immediate transport of fuel and equipment.

Overseas Basing

The only Greek armed forces overseas in 1994 were in Cyprus, where 2,250 troops are assigned, including two infantry battalions together with officers and NCOs assigned directly to the forces of the Joint Defense Area (see National Security Doctrine, this ch.). In addition, Greece has seven observers with United Nations Iraq-Kuwait Observer Mission (UNIKOM) peacekeeping forces along the Iraqi-Kuwaiti border and one observer with the UN's Mission for the Referendum in Western Sahara (MINURSO) peacekeeping effort in Western Sahara. The only foreign troops stationed in Greece are from the United States: sixty army and 200 navy troops at Souda Bay, and 500 air force troops located in two air base groups at Heraklion.

Ranks and Uniforms

The officer ranks of the three branches of the armed forces correspond precisely to those of the United States armed forces (see fig. 13). For enlisted personnel, the Hellenic Army promotes directly from sergeant first class (*archilochias*) to sergeant major (*anthypaspistis*), and the Hellenic Air Force promotes directly from master sergeant (*archisminias*) to chief master sergeant (*anthypaspistis*). The Hellenic Navy promotes enlisted personnel directly from seaman apprentice (*naftis*) to petty officer third class (*diopos*) and from chief petty officer (*archikelefstis*) to master chief petty officer (*anthypaspistis*) (see fig. 14).

Until the end of World War II, Greek military dress showed the strong influence of British uniform styles. After the war, however, Greek uniforms gradually came to resemble those of the United States, which also was the country that replaced Britain as Greece's strongest military ally.

Standard duty uniforms of army officers and senior NCOs are olive green. Army officers' dress uniforms are dark green, navy officers' are dark blue (a white dress uniform is used in the summer), and air force officers' dress uniforms are light blue. Trim and accessories for the dress uniforms may be changed to satisfy the requirements of various types of formal occasions.

Until 1994 battle dress consisted mainly of United States-style field uniforms. That year new camouflage uniforms were issued to replace the previous field uniform. Branches of the army can be distinguished by the color of the beret, which is worn with service dress, and in some cases with battle dress. The air corps of the ground forces is issued red berets; com-

GREEK RANK (ARMY)	ANTHY-POLOCHAGOS	YPOLOCHAGOS	LOCHAGOS	TAGMATARCHIS	ANTISYNTAG-MATARCHIS	SYNTAG-MATARCHIS	TAXIARCHOS	YPOSTRATIGOS	ANTISTRATIGOS	STRATIGOS
U.S. RANK TITLE (ARMY)	2ND LIEUTENANT	1ST LIEUTENANT	CAPTAIN	MAJOR	LIEUTENANT COLONEL	COLONEL	BRIGADIER GENERAL	MAJOR GENERAL	LIEUTENANT GENERAL	GENERAL
GREEK RANK (AIR FORCE)	ANTHY-POSMINAGOS	YPOSMINAGOS	SMINAGOS	EPISMINAGOS	ANTISMINARCHOS	SMINARCHOS	TAXIARCHOS	YPOPTERARCHOS	ANTIPTERARCHOS	PTERARCHOS
U.S. RANK TITLE (AIR FORCE)	2D LIEUTENANT	1ST LIEUTENANT	CAPTAIN	MAJOR	LIEUTENANT COLONEL	COLONEL	BRIGADIER GENERAL	MAJOR GENERAL	LIEUTENANT GENERAL	GENERAL
GREEK RANK (NAVY)	SIMAIOFOROS	ANTHY-POPLIARCHOS	YPOPLIARCHOS	PLOTARCHIS	ANTIPLIARCHOS	PLIARCHOS	ARCHIPLIARCHOS	YPONAVARCHOS	ANTINAVARCHOS	NAVARCHOS
U.S. RANK TITLE (NAVY)	ENSIGN	LIEUTENANT JUNIOR GRADE	LIEUTENANT	LIEUTENANT COMMANDER	COMANDER	CAPTAIN	REAR ADMIRAL LOWER HALF	REAR ADMIRAL UPPER HALF	VICE ADMIRAL	ADMIRAL

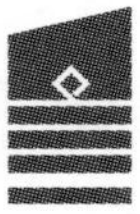

Figure 13. Officer Ranks and Insignia

302

GREEK RANK	STRATIOTIS	YPODECANEAS	DECANEAS	EFEDROS LOCHIAS	LOCHIAS	EPILOCHIAS	ARCHILOCHIAS		ANTHYPASPISTIS
ARMY	NO INSIGNIA							NO RANK	
U.S. RANK TITLE	BASIC PRIVATE	PRIVATE	PRIVATE 1ST CLASS	CORPORAL/SPECIALIST	SERGEANT	STAFF SERGEANT	SERGEANT 1ST CLASS	MASTER SERGEANT / FIRST SERGEANT	SERGEANT MAJOR / COMMAND SERGEANT MAJOR
GREEK RANK	SMINITIS	ANTHY-POSMINIAS	YPOSMINIAS	EFEDROS SMINIAS	SMINIAS	EPISMINIAS	ARCHI-SMINIAS		ANTHYPASPISTIS
AIR FORCE	NO INSIGNIA	NO INSIGNIA						NO RANK	
U.S. RANK TITLE	AIRMAN BASIC	AIRMAN	AIRMAN 1ST CLASS	SENIOR AIRMAN / SERGEANT	STAFF SERGEANT	TECHNICAL SERGEANT	MASTER SERGEANT	SENIOR MASTER SERGEANT	CHIEF MASTER SERGEANT
GREEK RANK	NAFTIS	NAFTIS	NO RANK	DIOPOS / DOKIMOS KELEFSTIS	KELEFSTIS	EPIKELEFSTIS	ARCHI-KELEFSTIS		ANTHYPASPISTIS
NAVY	NO INSIGNIA		NO RANK	  PETTY OFFICER 3D CLASS	 PETTY OFFICER 2D CLASS	 PETTY OFFICER 1ST CLASS	 CHIEF PETTY OFFICER	NO RANK	
U.S. RANK TITLE	SEAMAN RECRUIT	SEAMAN APPRENTICE	SEAMAN					SENIOR CHIEF PETTY OFFICER	MASTER CHIEF PETTY OFFICER

Figure 14. Enlisted Ranks and Insignia

mandos and airborne forces, green; armored troops, black; infantry and artillery, khaki.

When on parade or standing guard, the Evzone (Presidential Honor Guard) wear the colorful traditional costume of the mountain warriors who fought the Ottomans in the Greek War of Independence (1821–32). This dress uniform includes tasseled cap and shoes, white stockings and the *fustanella*, a shirtwaist with pleated skirt of white fustian.

The navy's winter service uniform coat is navy blue, and its summer equivalent is white. The eight-buttoned, double-breasted blouses, blue caps, and white shirts, worn by naval commissioned and petty officers in winter, are of British cut, as are the summer blouses, which are buttoned to the collar. Short-sleeved shirts, worn open collared without blouses, are standard daytime wear for naval officers and petty officers in warm weather. Uniforms for sailors are also patterned on British styles.

The air force has adopted uniforms and insignia modeled after those of the United States Air Force. For all ranks, the uniform, including cap, is light blue; it is worn with a gray-blue shirt and black tie.

Roles in International Security

Greece's membership in NATO and the EU brings with it active participation in Western defense organizations and activities connected with those organizations. In the 1990s, Greece took an increasingly active role, in proportion to its resources, in peacekeeping and arms control around the world.

United Nations Peacekeeping

Greece has been generally supportive of UN peacekeeping operations. In the Korean War, the first UN military action, Greece contributed one infantry battalion and one air transport squadron. More recently Greek military personnel have participated in the United Nations Operation in Somalia (UNOSOM) and other missions in Kuwait, Northern Iraq, Western Sahara, and the former Yugoslavia. Through the end of 1994, Greece chose not to contribute troops to the United Nations Protection Force (UNPROFOR) in Bosnia and Herzegovina, arguing that participation by any Balkan country or former colonial power would have a destabilizing effect. Greece has, however, contributed one major combat vessel to

Operation Sharp Guard, the UN's offshore observation force in the Adriatic Sea. In 1994 the Greek Ministry of National Defense declared the country's readiness to contribute troops to a new peacekeeping force in the Middle East if peace negotiations between Israel and Syria are successful and require international border monitors. Greece is also considering participation in UN peacekeeping forces maintaining ceasefires between Georgian and Abkhazian forces in Abkhazia and Armenian and Azerbaijani forces in Nagorno-Karabakh, as well as assisting in an eventual withdrawal of UN forces from Bosnia. Greece has also borne the second-largest share of the expenses of the UN's Force in Cyprus (UNFICYP), contributing about US$7.5 million of the estimated total expense of US$52.5 in 1994.

Arms Control

Greece has signed nearly all the multilateral arms control agreements concluded in the 1980s and the 1990s, as well as many older pacts still in force. Among those agreements are the 1925 Geneva Protocol, the Antarctic Treaty, the Partial Test Ban Treaty, the Outer Space Treaty, the Nuclear Nonproliferation Treaty (NPT) of 1968, the Seabed Treaty, the Biological Weapons Convention, the Enmod Convention, the "Inhumane Weapons" Convention, the CFE Treaty, and the Chemical Weapons Convention.

Greece's very limited nuclear activities have been for peaceful purposes. The only nuclear installations in the country are a five-megawatt pool-type research reactor at the Demokritos National Research Center, which uses 20 percent enriched uranium, and a subcritical installation at the National Polytechnic University of Athens. The Demokritos reactor is mainly used for the training of scientists and for the production of radioisotopes for medical uses. Both facilities operate under the safeguards of the International Atomic Energy Agency (IAEA) and the European Atomic Energy Program. Although Greece exports almost no nuclear materials, it has pledged to apply international safeguards on any shipments of nuclear technology through its territory. In preparation for the 1995 NPT Review and Extension Conference, Greece has expressed strong support for indefinite and unconditional extension of the treaty.

Greece is also a member of the Australia Group for the Control of Chemical Exports and of the Missile Technology Control Regime. It has also signed the Chemical Weapons Convention and is preparing to implement the treaty's provisions fully. Greece was a member of the Coordinating Committee for Multilateral Export Controls (CoCom), an international organization aimed at controlling international movement of strategically sensitive items. As an upgraded export control organization was being established to replace CoCom in 1994, Greece prepared for full participation in the new regime. Greece's official view, however, is that the most effective arms control measures are political solutions to conflicts causing security threats, rather than exclusive reliance on international policing.

Military Funding and Procurement

Defense Expenditures

Since 1974, when Turkey began its occupation of Cypriot territory, Greece has maintained the highest level of defense expenditures as a percentage of gross national product (GNP—see Glossary) among NATO countries. More specifically, high military expenditures and intensive training have been deemed by Greece to be necessary to compensate for Turkey's quantitative advantage in military equipment and manpower. Although there is consensus among major political parties and the Greek people that this expense is necessary for national security, military expenditures constitute a heavy burden for the Greek economy.

In the early 1990s, total defense expenditures remained relatively even. Between 1992 and 1994, the amount increased from US$4.4 billion to US$4.5 billion. As a percentage of GNP, expenditures in the same period remained at 5.5 percent, compared with an average of 6.3 percent in the last years of the Cold War (1985–88). As a standard of comparison, in 1992 Turkey spent an estimated 3.6 percent of its GNP on defense, Italy 1.7 percent, and the United States 4.9 percent.

The Greek Defense Industry

Efforts to develop a defense industry began in Greece in the mid-1970s, although several isolated industries existed long before that date. In the mid-1990s, the defense industry supplied a wide variety of equipment to the Hellenic Armed Forces, and it has had moderate success in exporting military equipment to other countries.

Development of the Industry

The objectives of the initial policy were to satisfy national military needs and to increase the participation of domestic manufacturers, reducing Greece's heavy dependency on foreign military suppliers. Beginning in the 1970s, Greece was able to establish the technological base for producing military vehicles, aircraft components, guns, and ships. By the early 1980s, a substantial base of regional sales outside Greece had developed. However, significant economic problems have arisen because of the small domestic market, which seriously affects the viability of production lines, and because of management mistakes. The latter difficulty has included delayed response to technological developments and the changing needs of the armed forces and the rather inefficient use of offset agreements (by which Greek plants supply components to foreign military manufacturers in return for aircraft and equipment). Military aid programs, Defense and Economic Cooperation Agreements (DECAs) with the United States, and memoranda of understanding with partners in Western Europe have not been used effectively.

As a result, some state-owned defense industries are in a precarious financial position that may necessitate privatization to ensure profitable operation. Furthermore, defense planners now generally agree that the only way for the Greek defense industry to survive is through the coproduction of equipment with defense enterprises of other countries. In 1994 the industry, which employed 22,000 persons, had an annual turnover of about US$250 million.

The Defense Industry Directorate (DID) is the advisory body of the Ministry of National Defense for formulating and implementing national policy toward enterprises engaged in defense manufacturing. The DID constitutes the connecting link between the armed forces and the defense industries; its general purpose is to foster an increase in the domestic production of military equipment. The responsibilities of the DID also include management of specific new projects in the defense industry and the modernization and expansion of already existing industries that are either wholly or partially state-owned, as well as the codification and standardization of the armed forces matériel.

Defense Enterprises

The defense sector of Greek industry is dominated by a few major companies. The Greek Vehicle Industry (Elliniki

Viomikhania Okhimaton—ELVO) manufactures a wide range of special-purpose vehicles for civilian and military use. ELVO obtained its technical expertise by license from Austria's Steyr Daimler Puch and the Mercedes Benz corporation of Germany. Among other items, ELVO produces or coproduces Leonidas I, Leonidas II, and Pandur APCs, and a 2.75-ton jeep. At the end of 1994, the firm had made about 400 vehicles for domestic use and export, with current contracts calling for delivery of about 100 more vehicles to the ground forces in 1995 and 1996. At the end of 1994, the Hellenic Army was considering purchase of a new mechanized infantry combat vehicle from Norway's NFT, the DAF Special Products Company of the Netherlands, or the Santa Barbara corporation of Spain. The new model would be built by ELVO under license, under the name Alex-andros.

After beginning in 1908 as a producer of commercial explo-sives for the domestic market, the Powder and Cartridge Com-pany (Piromakhika kai Kalikes—PIRKAL) has a workforce of 1,500 that now produces three types of hand grenades, five types of rifle grenades and smoke hand grenades, flares, and mining boosters. The firm also has manufactured many types of ammunition used in a wide range of military operations. PIRKAL cooperates with leading European and American industries in ammunition manufacture, and since 1985 it has participated in Europe's Stinger missile production program.

Established in 1975, the Greek Aerospace Industry (Elliniki Aeroporiki Viomikhania—EAV) now employs 3,250 workers. It has become one of the region's leading aeronautical compa-nies, supplying more than seventy customers. Among these cus-tomers are the Greek armed forces and buyers in more than twenty foreign countries, including the United States, Britain, France, Portugal, and various Arab states. EAV has the capabil-ity to maintain, overhaul, modify, and test almost all types of Western aircraft and helicopters, offering particular expertise in Mirage, F–1, and C–130 airplanes and Bell helicopters. EAV services more than twenty types of engines and related accesso-ries and components. It also manufactures and puts together subassemblies for large commercial aircraft such as the Boeing 757 and military aircraft such as the F–16, small and medium-size static subassemblies for military and commercial engines, and aircraft modification and upgrade kits for military and commercial markets. EAV's custom design of electronic and telecommunications products also sells to military and commercial markets. The firm provides training services in all phases of aircraft engine and electronics support, modification, and manufacturing, as well as management and logistics.

The Greek Arms Industry (Elliniki Viotekhnia Oplon— EVO) is a group of companies established in 1977. The industry has five plants with a total workforce of 1,450 employees, making it the largest private defense industrial group in Greece. In 1994 EVO purchased PIRKAL. EVO manufactures a wide variety of small arms, light and heavy machine guns, mortars, nitrocellulose, trinitrotoluene (TNT), aircraft bombs, complete rounds of artillery ammunition, drop fuel tanks, pylons, external stores, antiaircraft defense systems, medium-caliber guns, and components for howitzer retrofitting. In the 1980s, EVO's proposed sale of its sophisticated Artemis–30 antiaircraft system to Libya, as part of a larger economic agreement, caused an international controversy. The group's companies also have produced sophisticated electra-optics (night-vision systems) and communications equipment, precision mechanical equipment for the modernization of tanks and APCs, and metallic components for both military and civilian applications.

The Hellenic Shipyards and the Eleusis Shipyards, which employ 3,150 and 2,350 workers, respectively, were scheduled for privatization in the mid-1990s. The Hellenic Shipyards at Piraeus on the Gulf of Saronikos is the largest shipbuilding, ship-repairing, and rolling-stock operation in the eastern Mediterranean and one of the largest in Europe. In the thirty-five years of the firm's operation, its two dry docks and three floating docks have accommodated repairs for over 8,200 vessels of all types and sizes. Its two slipways have seen the construction of 110 commercial vessels and warships, including frigates, fast-patrol missile boats, replenishment tankers, and fast-attack boats, up to 40,000 deadweight tons. At the end of 1994, the Hellenic Shipyards were completing the first Greek-built MEKO–200H (Hydra-class) frigate. Two additional frigates were in earlier stages of construction for the Hellenic Navy, and Hellenic Shipyards had designed three offshore-patrol vessels for delivery to a foreign customer in 1996. The yards also build railroad freight and passenger cars and electrically powered trains.

Greece's second major shipbuilding firm, the Eleusis Shipyards (also located on the Gulf of Saronikos near Athens), has a wide range of activities, including shipbuilding, ship repairs and conversions, and industrial construction. In late 1994, the major military contract at Eleusis was for five large LST landing craft for the Hellenic Navy.

Military Procurement from Abroad

The beginning of the post-Cold War period stimulated diversification of Greece's foreign military contacts and agreements. Diversification has occurred in both arms supply contracts and broader military cooperation agreements.

The Hellenic Armed Forces were built up progressively after World War II with British and United States aid. Between World War II and 1985, Greece received more than US$3 billion in military aid from the United States. During that period, the United States furnished the majority of Greece's major weapon systems. Between 1980 and 1990, the average annual value of United States military sales to Greece was about US$400 million. For the period 1991–93, the United States sold Greece a total of US$410 million worth of arms; at that point, Germany was the top supplier (US$480 million), followed by the United States and France (US$360 million). The United States also has exerted considerable influence in all other areas of the military, including organization, doctrine, training, and even uniforms. After 1974, and in view of the perceived United States bias toward Turkey in the Greek-Turkish conflict, Greece tried to lessen this dependence, turning to France as a partial alternative (see Karamanlis and the Restoration of Democracy, ch. 1). Nevertheless, since 1974 the United States has remained the main source of defense equipment for the Hellenic Armed Forces.

In 1964 Greece received military aid for the first time from the Federal Republic of Germany (West Germany), within the framework of assistance programs to other NATO members. In the decades that followed, German arms sales to Greece have increased steadily. Between 1967 and 1976, they averaged US$16.1 million per year; then, between 1979 and 1983 they averaged US$60 million per year. Under the cascading process provided for by the CFE Treaty, since 1991 Greece has received a large number of main battle tanks, armored personnel carriers, artillery pieces, mortars, and other equipment from NATO allies reducing their armaments as required by the CFE Treaty to balance reductions in the countries of the former Warsaw Pact and Soviet Union. In the early 1990s, Greece signed new defense cooperation agreements with Britain, France, Ger-

*Presidential Honor Guard greets visiting United States President
George H.W. Bush, summer 1991.
Courtesy Press and Information Office,
Embassy of Greece, Washington*

many, Spain, and Norway. In 1994 Greece signed military
agreements with nations of the former Soviet sphere in the
framework of NATO's Partnership for Peace initiative.

In upgrading equipment to incorporate recent technological developments, the Hellenic Armed Forces have ordered a
number of major weapons systems since 1990. Special emphasis
has fallen on weapons platforms whose smart-weapon capability provides a force-multiplier effect.

In the foreseeable future, Greece will continue to import
most of its defense equipment, especially for its land and air
forces, mainly from the United States, with France as a secondary source. For naval equipment, Germany will remain a major
supplier. The possibility of equipment purchase agreements or
equipment coproduction with Russia and Israel has been considered, although no concrete measures had been taken at the
end of 1994.

Military Justice

The Greek system of military justice is based on Article 96 of the constitution. Each branch of the armed forces has first-degree courts, and a single second-degree (appeals) court serves all three branches. In accordance with Article 406 of the Military Code of Justice, the appeals court has the power to hear cases referred to it and to annul decisions from lower courts.

All enlisted personnel (including conscripts) accused of criminal acts are tried by military courts, with specific exceptions cited in articles 247 and 248 of the Military Code of Justice. Those exceptions, which are tried by civil rather than military courts, include robberies, drug-related crimes, and embezzlement of more than million drachmas (for the value of the drachma—see Glossary).

In 1994 the Military Code of Justice was amended. Changes include lighter sentences for a variety of crimes, abolition of the death penalty for any act during peacetime, and a more balanced composition of military courts (now to be divided almost equally between military and civilian judges).

Public Order

For many years after the end of the Civil War, Greek police forces were employed by national administrations to persecute communist and leftist activists and sympathizers. Thousands of persons were exiled to various "prison islands" in the Aegean. The military dictatorship of 1967–74 widened this practice to include subjecting all of its critics, regardless of their political or ideological orientation, to arrest and exile. The threat of communism, however, was most often the pretext for such procedures. The military regime rarely respected articles of the constitution prescribing civil and political liberties, although no steps were taken to suspend such articles. During that period, military courts tried many civilian crimes, and in many cases such trials deprived opponents of the regime of their citizenship.

Immediately after the fall of the junta, the Karamanlis government restored civil liberties, and the constitution ratified in 1975 fully guarantees equality before the law, due process of law, and the inviolability of individual rights. In the mid-1990s, police brutality is a rare occurrence, and police officers who exceed the limits of their authority during arrests or police interrogations are immediately suspended pending the results of an official inquiry on each case.

The crime rate in Greece is fairly low. A recent increase is attributed to the large influx of illegal immigrants. According to Greek police sources, among the refugees who left Albania in the early 1990s were a large number of convicted criminals who were encouraged to depart by the regime of Albania's President Ramiz Alia. For the indigenous population of Greece, however, ethnic and religious homogeneity has combined with close-knit family structures to instill a sense of social discipline and acceptance of authority (see The Social Order, ch. 2).

Nevertheless, the police still do not enjoy great popularity in Greece. After governments had used them repeatedly to oppress the people (most notably after the end of the Civil War and during the rule of the 1967–74 junta), the police were treated by the public with suspicion and even animosity. In the aftermath of the junta, a number of police officers were tried for human rights violations, and others were dismissed from service. In 1984 a series of reforms culminated in the merging of the City Police and the Gendarmerie, placing routine police activities under local rather than national control.

Organization of Public Security

Before the 1984 reform, the public security establishment was divided into the City Police, which had jurisdiction in the cities of Athens, Piraeus, and Patras and the island of Corfu, and the Gendarmerie, which had jurisdiction in the rest of the country. Today, there is a single national police force, the Hellenic Police (Elliniki Astinomia—EL.AS), which operates under the direct supervision and control of the Ministry of Public Order. The commandant of the EL.AS is an officer with the rank of lieutenant general.

The police force remains paramilitary in character, and officers carry sidearms and clubs while on duty. The police occasionally receive training with heavier weapons. Special riot units are equipped with UR–416 APCs, and six NH–300 helicopters are in service, mainly for traffic monitoring. In 1994 the strength of all branches of the EL.AS was approximately 26,500 men and women. In the past, women served only in an auxiliary capacity, but the number of women in the regular force is gradually increasing.

Other branches of the police include the Tourist Police, which operates in Athens and various other tourist areas to protect and assist tourists in any way possible; the Forest Police;

and the Customs Police, whose task is to combat smuggling and collect duties at various points of entry into the country. The departmental structure of the EL.AS is similar to that of most major Western police forces. The force includes contingents specializing in cases of homicide, counterfeiting and white-collar crimes, vice, narcotics, and traffic control, as well as special weapons and tactics (SWAT) teams.

The problem of illegal migrants has become so acute in the mid-1990s that the government is considering creation of a special body of border guards. The objective is to enable Greece to comply with the Schengen accords, which prescribe EU standards for border controls among member-states.

Special Security Forces

The Operations Division of the EL.AS has two types of special security units. The main objective of the special tasks and missions units is to maintain or restore order in case of riots, mass protests, and other types of civil disturbance. The Special Forces Squad, which receives military commando training, is deployed in airports and other sensitive points to deal with emergencies such as hijackings, terrorist activities, and attacks against public officials and foreign diplomats (see Terrorism, this ch.). The squad's tactics and equipment resemble those of the police SWAT teams.

Another specialized police force, the Counterterrorism Squad, is under the jurisdiction of the Security Department of the Ministry of Public Order. Equipped and trained to deal with the activities of terrorist groups, this unit emphasizes investigative work that is conducted in close cooperation with counterpart agencies in other countries. In October 1994, the Ministry of Public Order began negotiating changes in the verbal agreement by which United States Central Intelligence Agency (CIA) and Federal Bureau of Investigation (FBI) units assisted in terrorism investigations. (To avoid charges of United States interference in domestic security matters, no formal agreement has existed.)

In August 1994, the Papandreou government announced a new support program to reduce crime and terrorism. The program included restructuring of the antiterrorism forces, emphasizing specialized personnel; coordination with other police forces in antiterrorism activities; and the addition of 2,000 personnel to antiterrorism and general crime forces. The changes were not implemented in 1994, however.

Training and Conditions of Police Service

There are two police academies, one for officers and one for rank-and-file policemen. Candidates are required to be high-school graduates to qualify for the competitive enrollment. The program, which includes courses in law, criminology, sociology, psychology and other academic subjects, law enforcement methods, physical education, and paramilitary tactics, lasts seven months for policemen and three years for officers. A number of officers receive advanced training abroad. NCOs with good service records can be promoted to officer rank after passing an examination and studying further at the academy. All police recruits are required to meet certain physical standards. The ministries of public order and justice lifted some constraints on trade unionism in the police force in late 1994.

Crime

The crime rate in Greece has risen in the 1990s, but the incidence of most types of crime has remained relatively low. Narcotics-related crime, however, has accelerated markedly and has been identified as the most serious challenge to public security.

Conventional Crime

The crime rate in Greece is relatively low compared with other nations in the region. The majority of offenses are crimes against property (especially in the big cities), simple assaults, and infractions of commercial and motor vehicle regulations. An increased rate of armed robberies since 1990 has been attributed to the influx of illegal aliens and economic refugees from the Balkans and the Middle East. In 1994 the rates for major crimes were two rapes and two murders per 100,000 population and 475 thefts per 100,000 population.

Narcotics-related crime is an ever-increasing area of concern. Greece is an important transshipment point for illegal narcotics moving from Asia to markets in Western Europe and the United States. Drug-related crimes began to increase in Greece in the late 1980s, and control of domestic drug abuse and shipment has become a major emphasis of the legal authorities (see Narcotics Sales, this ch.)

Gun control is strictly enforced in Greece. Possession of firearms of any type, except those licensed for hunting, is forbidden. Any violation of gun-control regulations (possessing, importing, selling, or transporting weapons and ammunition of a military type) brings a multiyear prison sentence.

In traditional Greek society, acts of revenge against a person perceived as having assaulted a family's honor often went unpunished. In the 1980s and the 1990s, some incidents of "vigilante justice" still occurred in rural areas, but authorities have become far less lenient in cases of assault and property damage instigated by a revenge motive.

Narcotics Sales

Greece's location, on the route for illegal narcotics from production centers in the Middle East and Asia into Europe and North America, exacerbates two drug-related problems. Those problems are the control of drug transfers through Greek territory and the increase of drug use by Greek citizens.

One of the major routes for the transportation of heroin and opium from Turkey and the Middle East to Western Europe is through the Greek-Turkish border in Thrace and then through the Balkans. Greek authorities have, however, been quite successful in intercepting a high percentage of shipments along this route. Drugs also move on small boats from western Greece to Italy.

As the EU member country located farthest to the east, Greece requires increased cooperation both from its European partners and from other neighboring countries to gain multilateral control of the problem. The Greek government has been active in the EU's narcotics control groups and in the Dublin Group, which monitors international drug movements in strategic corridors such as the "Balkan route" from the Middle East into Europe. In 1992 Greece signed an agreement with Russia for cooperation and mutual assistance in narcotics cases. Greece has ratified the 1988 United Nations Convention on Drugs, although its drug legislation is not yet in full conformity with the terms of that agreement.

The Customs Police and the Hellenic Police are the primary agencies of drug law enforcement. A new state narcotics agency, the Okana, was established under the Ministry of Health, Welfare, and Social Security in 1993 to coordinate the reduction of narcotics demand. The Central Narcotics Council, activated in 1993, coordinates drug enforcement activities among the Hellenic Police, the Coast Guard, and the Customs Police. In 1992 several heroin dealers apprehended in Greece received life sentences in prison. Although several police officers were convicted of drug trafficking in 1992, narcotics-related corruption among government officials has been rare in Greece. Legislation passed in 1993 stiffened penalties for drug trafficking and use.

Narcotics Abuse

Although the number of drug users is proportionally lower than in most Western countries, in the early 1990s drug use of various kinds rose sharply, especially among unemployed urban youth. Deaths from drug overdoses increased steadily between the mid-1980s and the mid-1990s, and heroin use became a regular occurrence in urban schools and parks. Amphetamines and barbiturates are widely available. Marijuana is grown in many parts of Greece for local use, and a high quality of opium is also produced locally. The annual turnover for drugs has been estimated at over US$1.5 billion, and in the early 1990s evidence appeared that organized crime was becoming involved in domestic drug sales.

A sudden increase in the number of deaths from drug overdoses during 1994 (reportedly 290) has led to greater attention to the problem and to increased interagency cooperation in the government to curtail supply and to assist users through special counseling programs and clinics. Nevertheless, drug users are still treated predominantly as criminals, meaning that they often go to prison, where drugs are easily obtained, rather than receiving medical assistance. The issue of decriminalizing drug use has involved a continuing debate among ministries that have jurisdiction, political parties, youth organizations, medical associations, and interested social groups.

Terrorism

In the mid-1980s, Greece was affected by the wave of terrorism that originated in the Middle East and swept Western Europe. Terrorist incidents declined elsewhere in Western Europe in the early 1990s; however, the rate remained quite constant in Greece, bringing accusations that Greek governments had created a permissive atmosphere for such acts of violence.

In the 1990s, two domestic terrorist organizations have been active. The 17 November organization is a small Marxist group (membership estimated at below fifty) established in 1975 and named after the student uprising that protested against the military regime in November 1973, contributing to the regime's fall the next year. Within its general opposition to any foreign military and economic presence in Greece, the group's position is anti-United States, anti-Turkey, anti-NATO, and anti-business. It is committed to violent overthrow of the government and removal of all United States military bases. The 17 November group may have links with the Red Brigades terrorists in Italy and Middle Eastern terrorist groups. The main activities have been bombings and assassinations of politicians, business executives, newspaper publishers, and United States citizens living in Greece.

The second group, the Revolutionary People's Struggle (Ellinikos Laikos Agonas—ELA), is a small, left-wing, anticapitalist, anti-imperialist revolutionary group. Its primary mode of operation is bombing buildings after giving half-hour warnings, apparently to avoid endangering lives. Connections have been established between ELA and 17 November, although the precise relationship is not known. A total of sixteen smaller terrorist organizations have been identified in Athens and Thessaloniki; all mimic the tactics and the anarchistic posture of the larger groups.

The two most serious terrorist incidents of 1994 were assassinations in Athens. The 17 November organization claimed responsibility for (and apparently used the same gun in) the January killing of a former director of the Greek National Bank and the July killing of an undersecretary of the Turkish Embassy—in the name of Kurdish and Cypriot victims of Turkish "ethnic cleansing." The latter act was the third assassination of a Turkish official in the last five years. (In the fall of 1993, the newly elected PASOK government had repealed the law prohibiting media publication of terrorist statements of responsibility for assassinations, a move that brought substantial criticism when the January 1994 assassination occurred.)

United States personnel and facilities have been frequent targets of terrorist attacks. In June 1988, a United States military attaché was assassinated. In 1994 a series of rocket attacks struck United States business establishments. Among United States offices and property attacked in 1994 were the American Life Insurance and IBM offices in Athens. An unsuccessful rocket attack at Piraeus on the British aircraft carrier *Ark Royal* was discovered only later. There also were frequent bombings of diplomatic, business, and government cars and buildings, often with prior telephone warnings. Almost all such incidents were traced directly or indirectly to one of the two terrorist organizations; both 17 November and ELA took credit for one bus bombing in September. Experts noted that most targets were European, and the acts of 1994 were defined as statements on Europe's role in Bosnia or on the treatment of Kurds in Europe (especially Germany).

Meanwhile, Turkish authorities have accused Greece of supporting the Kurdish Workers' Party (Partiya Karkere Kürdistan—PKK), which has operated to destabilize Turkish society, and tourist trade in particular, in its terrorist campaign for separatism for the Kurdish minority in southeastern Turkey. The PKK mode of operation often has included the killing of Turkish security personnel and the planting of explosives in urban areas. Turkey has cited the existence of a Greek-Kurdish Solidarity Committee and visits to Greece in 1994 by a top PKK official as evidence of Greek complicity. In 1994 Turkey accused Greece of training PKK terrorists and then allowing them to cross the border into Turkey.

In the 1980s and the early 1990s, Greek antiterrorism measures received substantial international criticism because of the frequency of terrorist incidents after new enforcement campaigns had been announced. To combat terrorism, the EL.AS operates an Antiterrorist Service, which cooperates closely with its American counterparts, as well as with agencies in the other member-states of the EU and in Russia, Israel, Turkey, and Armenia. The terms of United States cooperation, which has focused on elimination of 17 November, caused controversy in Greece in 1994 when the level of involvement by the United States CIA and FBI was disclosed publicly for the first time. The four-year-old informal agreement was revised in the fall of 1994 as part of the reorganization of the Antiterrorist Service. The revision, like its predecessor a nonpaper agreement, calls for a more equal sharing of intelligence. The Greek service had complained that its American counterparts were not disclosing information and that information leaks were jeopardizing operations. The other steps of the reorganization added analytic staff and streamlined nonessential functions.

Criminal Justice

The Greek criminal justice system is based on West European models. The constitution and civil laws include strict protections for the rights of the accused. The judiciary is an independent branch of government within which jurisdiction in various types of criminal justice proceedings is clearly defined.

The Criminal Code

The criminal code is based on the Bavarian codes, which were transferred by King Otto, the first king of independent Greece (r. 1833–62) from his homeland in the 1830s, but considerable revision has occurred since that time. According to the constitution, the judiciary is independent and judicial powers are vested in the courts of law, while the creation of extraordinary courts is expressly prohibited. The court system is divided into administrative, civil, and criminal sections (see The Branches of Government, ch. 4).

The criminal code defines three grades of crime: petty offenses, misdemeanors, and felonies. Sentences at the lower court level can be appealed. Unusual punishment is prohibited by the constitution. Custodial sentences for petty offenses and misdemeanors range from ten days to five years, while those for felonies range from five to twenty years. Offenders sentenced to imprisonment for a term of less than eighteen months can have their sentences converted into fines. The option of capital punishment is maintained for some categories of serious crime (not including political crimes), but the death penalty has not been imposed since the late 1970s.

How the System Works

Greek law classifies any person between seven and seventeen years of age as a juvenile. The crime rate among juveniles in Greece is rather low compared with those in other Western countries. It is confined mainly to petty theft and property damage. Police officers may arrest persons caught in the act of committing a crime; citizen's arrests also may be considered valid. In no other case can a person be arrested without a judicial warrant. Suspects must be brought before an examining magistrate within twenty-four hours of arrest. Within three to five days of arraignment, magistrates are required either to release a suspect or to issue a warrant for imprisonment pending trial. The maximum detention permissible before trial is nine months, or, if cause is demonstrated by the prosecutor, eighteen months. Administrative measures to restrict the movement of citizens are prohibited unless they are backed by a court ruling.

Public prosecutors represent the state whenever a criminal case is brought before a court. Before a suspect is remanded by the police to court authorities, the public prosecutor conducts a preliminary investigation, the results of which are passed to the court for further investigation or establishment of a trial date. An injured party may initiate prosecution when the appropriate public prosecutor fails to act.

The constitution provides full protection of the rights of the accused. The public prosecutor must explain comprehensibly to the accused all aspects of the case, including his or her rights and options and all documents bearing on the case. Illegally obtained confessions may not be used against the accused. Bail may be posted except for the most serious crimes. Criminal and political offenses are tried by juries composed of judges and lay people in so-called mixed courts that combine the functions of judge and jury in common law courts. The accused is present during the trial and may compel the appearance in court of defense witnesses. The court must appoint legal counsel if the accused lacks a lawyer. Criminal trials are open to the adult public. Although the criminal code specifies rules for the presentation of evidence, judicial panels are given considerable latitude in arriving at their verdict. The burden of proof rests with the prosecution.

Legal limits restrict the length of sentence or amount of fine that a presiding judge may levy at each level of the judicial system, as well as the applicable penalty for each kind of offense. Magistrates in juvenile courts are permitted considerable discretion in sentencing youthful offenders. Punishment for juvenile delinquency may range from a reprimand to committal to a training school or correctional institution.

The Greek court system is overburdened, especially at the lower levels of magistrates' courts and courts of first instance. Because of the large number of trivial cases (mostly misdemeanors, traffic violations, and accidents) that are not resolved before reaching the stage of trial, many cases wait for trial for two or three years.

The Penal System

Greece has several types of penal facilities, including central penitentiaries (the basis of the penal system), correctional farms, open and minimum-security prisons, reformatories, and training schools for juvenile offenders. Additional facilities include prison hospitals and sanatoriums. Conditions inside the great majority of those facilities are generally regarded as satisfactory. Since the 1980s, a major building program has replaced outdated buildings with modern facilities. No distinction is made inside prisons on the basis of social class, race, or religion, but men and women and adults and juveniles are housed in separate facilities. Occasionally, people serving life sentences for execrable crimes are housed in separate prison wings, although they are free to mix with other prisoners in social and athletic activities. The death penalty is prescribed by law for heinous crimes, but it has not been put into effect since 1972, and in the 1990s there was considerable support for abolishing it. Visits by family members are allowed three times per week. Under a 1994 law, a prison director may grant permission to prisoners to leave the prison and stay with their families for periods of five to ten days.

The Greek penal system emphasizes the rehabilitation of prisoners through education, vocational training, and productive labor. Probation officers assist ex-convicts in securing employment upon release from prison. Particular emphasis is placed on rehabilitation of juvenile offenders. Special training schools and institutions provide academic and vocational education.

Trends and Problems in Domestic Security

Besides ordinary crime, the main problems in maintaining public order in the 1990s are narcotics control and the influx of illegal migrants from the Balkans and the Middle East. In order to meet those challenges, the Hellenic Police is trying to modernize its structure and methods along the lines of Western police forces. To assist in modernization, in 1994 Prime Minister Andreas Papandreou promised US$27 million to upgrade police equipment and acquire helicopters. Experts have also identified improved police training as a major requirement, both at the basic level and at the more advanced level of modern investigative methods. To expedite achievement of those goals, Greece has developed numerous programs for cooperation with Western countries, including the United States, as well as with Russia, Israel, and other countries that have well-developed security institutions.

*   *   *

For current information about Greece's national security position and policies, a number of publications of the Hellenic

Foundation for Defense and Foreign Policy are authoritative sources, but most of them are available only in Greek. Among the topics the foundation's publications cover are the Cyprus situation, Greece in relation to the Middle East, United States policy toward Greece and Turkey, and Greece's policy toward Yugoslavia. For current statistics and a complete description of the Greek armed forces, the best source is *Jane's Sentinel: The Balkans*, which is updated annually. *Southern European Security in the 1990s*, edited by Roberto Aliboni, describes the security concerns of nations in Greece's region of the Mediterranean. Tozun Bahcheli's *Greek-Turkish Relations since 1955* reviews the history of the relationship, with special emphasis on Cyprus. Theodore Couloumbis's *The United States, Greece, and Turkey: The Troubled Triangle* and Monteagle Stearns's *Entangled Allies: U.S. Policy Toward Greece, Turkey, and Cyprus* provide historical background on the United States role in the 1974 Cyprus crisis and its results over the following two decades. *Greece and EC Membership Evaluated*, edited by Panos Kazakos and Panayotis Ioakimidis, describes the impact of EC (now EU) membership on Greece's economic and national security situation. Greece's narcotics problems and policies are described in the *International Narcotics Strategy Report*, an annual publication of the United States Department of State's Bureau of International Narcotics Matters. Specific national security topics such as arms purchases and events in the eastern Mediterranean are reported in the Federal Broadcast Information Service's *Daily Report: West Europe*, a daily summary of press items. (For further information and complete citations, see Bibliography.)

Appendix

1 Metric Conversion Coefficients and Factors
2 Economic Activity in the Adult Population, 1989, 1990, 1991
3 Urbanization, Selected Years, 1941–71
4 Evolution of the Greek Language, ca. 2000 B.C. to 1976
5 Schools, Teachers, and Students at Various Education Levels, Selected Years, 1975–89
6 Financial Structure of the Public Sector, 1989–93
7 Price and Wage Movement, Selected Years, 1985–93
8 Structure of Economic Output, 1989–93
9 Export Trade by World Economic Group, 1989–93
10 Import Trade by World Economic Group, 1989–93
11 Exports by Commodity, 1990–93
12 Imports by Commodity, 1990–93
13 Circulation of Leading Newspapers, 1991
14 Major Army Equipment, 1994
15 Major Air Force Equipment, 1994
16 Major Navy Equipment, 1994

Table 1. Metric Conversion Coefficients and Factors

When you know	Multiply by	To find
Millimeters	0.04	inches
Centimeters.....................	0.39	inches
Meters..........................	3.3	feet
Kilometers	0.62	miles
Hectares	2.47	acres
Square kilometers	0.39	square miles
Cubic meters	35.3	cubic feet
Liters	0.26	gallons
Kilograms	2.2	pounds
Metric tons	0.98	long tons
....	1.1	short tons
....	2,204	pounds
Degrees Celsius (Centigrade)	1.8 and add 32	degrees Fahrenheit

Table 2. Economic Activity in the Adult Population, 1989, 1990, 1991
(in thousands of persons over fourteen years of age)

Activity	1989	1990	1991
Agriculture, forestry, and fishing	929.9	889.2	806.5
Mining and quarrying	21.4	22.6	19.3
Manufacturing	714.9	719.9	699.0
Utilities	36.0	36.6	36.6
Construction	238.9	252.4	245.7
Trade, restaurants, and hotels	624.2	653.9	660.4
Transportation and communications	240.9	249.4	252.4
Finance, insurance, real estate, and business services	169.2	184.1	192.7
Community and social services	694.8	709.5	719.8
Other	0.7	1.5	0.0
Total employed	3,670.9	3,719.0	3,632.4
Total unemployed	296.0	280.8	301.1
Total labor force	3,966.9	3,719.0	3,933.5
Males	2,500.1	2,516.4	2,527.5
Females	1,466.8	1,483.4	1,406.0

Source: Based on information from *The Europa World Year Book, 1994, 1*, London, 1994, 1305.

327

Table 3. Urbanization, Selected Years, 1941–71
(in percentages of total population)

Year	Athens	Thessaloniki	Other Urban	Rural
1941	15.3	3.7	13.0	68.0
1951	18.0	4.0	14.9	63.1
1961	22.1	4.5	16.1	57.3
1971	29.0	6.4	17.4	47.2

Source: Based on information from Lila Leontidou, *The Mediterranean City in Transition*, Cambridge, 1989, 104.

Table 4. Evolution of the Greek Language, ca. 2000 B.C. to 1976

Period	Description
First half of second millennium B.C.	Greek speakers arrive in southern Balkan peninsula.
Second half of second millennium B.C.	Greek first written, then syllabary lost after fall of Mycenaea around 1100 B.C.
Late eighth century B.C.	Phoenician alphabet adopted and modified.
Sixth century B.C.	Greek literary tradition established.
404 B.C.	End of dominance of Athens, which had made Attic Greek lingua franca and literary language.
Mid-fourth century B.C.	End of predominance of several mutually intelligible dialects of city-states and literary variants depending on genre.
323 B.C.	Death of Alexander the Great ends expansion of Macedonian Empire, which had spread with it Attic Greek.
Third century B.C. to fourth century A.D.	Common language (Koine) develops for international trade, politics, and administration.
A.D. 330	Christian church adopts educated form of Koine as its official language.
Sixth century A.D. to fifteenth century	Byzantine period; complex, undocumented evolution of spoken form from that used in written texts.
Seventh century	Demotic (modern spoken Greek) assumes modern morphological and syntactic form.
Seventh to ninth century	During struggles against Arabs, Attic literary model not used.
Ninth to fifteenth century	Revived use of Attic model.
1261–1453	"Declassicized" texts simplify literary form for the uneducated.
Early fourteenth century	Vernacular literature (poetry) approximates spoken form.
Late sixteenth to early seventeenth century	Cretan vernacular used in drama and poetry.
Late eighteenth century	Influence of Enlightenment politicizes language in Greek communities of Ottoman Empire and in Western Europe.

Table 4. Evolution of the Greek Language, ca. 2000 B.C. to 1976

Period	Description
1834–36	Katharevousa adopted as offical state language of Greece after being devised by Adamantios Korais (1748–1833).
1888	Ioannis Psicharis, champion of demotic, publishes My Journey, model for demotic literary movement.
1901	Riots in Athens to oppose demotic New Testament translation.
1917	Introduction of demotic in lower grades of elementary school.
1946–57	Prose writing career of Nikos Kazantzakis, influential writer in demotic movement.
1967–74	Military junta government attempts to reinstate Katharevousa in schools at all levels.
1970s–1980s	Regional dialects lost in many parts of Greece.
1976	Demotic of Athens becomes official language, called common or standard Greek (Neohelliniki).

Source: Based on information from Robert Browning, *Medieval and Modern Greek*, London, 1969.

Table 5. *Schools, Teachers, and Students at Various Education Levels,*
Selected Years, 1975–89

	1975	1980	1985	1989
Preschools				
Schools	3,279	4,576	5,203	5,474
Teachers	4,137	6,514	7,617	8,307
Percent female teachers	100	100	100	100
Pupils	108,357	145,924	160,079	141,756
Percent female pupils	48	49	49	49
Primary schools				
Schools	9,633	9,461	8,675	7,755
Teachers	30,953	37,315	37,994	42,485
Percent female teachers	47	48	49	41
Pupils	935,730	900,641	897,735	839,688
Percent female pupils	48	48	48	48
All secondary schools				
Teachers	n.a.[1]	39,571	50,388	57,975
Percent female teachers	n.a.	49	53	54
Students	661,796	740,085	813,534	843,732
Percent female students	43	46	48	48
Vocational (secondary) schools				
Teachers	n.a.	7,834	8,138	9,434
Percent female teachers	n.a.	24	34	35
Students	132,591	100,415	109,415	130,738
Percent female students	13	20	29	32
All postsecondary schools				
Teachers	n.a.	10,542	11,878	13,451
Percent female teachers	n.a.	32	30	32
Students	117,246	121,116	181,901	194,419
Percent female students	37	41	49	50
Universities				
Teachers	5,956	6,924	6,934	8,104
Percent female teachers	35	35	28	29
Students	95,385	85,718	110,917	117,260
Percent female students	37	42	48	53

[1] n.a.—not available.

Source: Based on information from United Nations, Department for Economic and
Social Information and Policy Analysis, Statistical Division, *Statistical Yearbook,*
1992, New York, 1994, 62, 74, 86, 99.

Table 6. Financial Structure of the Public Sector, 1989–93
(in percentages of GDP) [1]

	1989	1990	1991	1992	1993
Budgetary indicators					
Primary receipts[2]	28.8	31.4	32.0	32.7	33.0
Primary expenditures[2]	37.7	37.6	36.5	35.7	35.8
Primary budget balance	−8.9	−6.2	−4.5	−3.0	−2.8
Net interest	−5.6	−7.7	−8.5	−8.7	−10.7
General government budget balance	−14.5	−13.9	−13.0	−11.8	−13.5
Savings	−10.3	−10.2	−8.9	−7.8	−10.1
Expenditure and tax structure					
General current expenditures	40.3	43.1	42.3	42.3	44.7
Transfers....................	13.1	12.7	12.7	12.2	12.7
Subsidies....................	4.1	4.4	4.2	4.1	4.7
Tax receipts..................	28.8	31.4	32.0	32.7	33.0
Personal income tax	3.5	4.0	3.6	3.1	3.2
Corporate tax	1.2	1.6	2.0	2.3	2.3
Social security contributions	11.8	12.2	11.8	11.7	12.5
Consumption taxes	12.2	13.7	14.6	15.6	15.0
Value-added tax[3]	6.6	7.4	7.6	7.9	n.a.[4]

[1] GDP—gross domestic product (see Glossary).
[2] Excluding interest.
[3] Largest category of consumption taxes.
[4] n.a.—not available.

Source: Based on information from Organisation for Economic Co-operation and Development, *OECD Economic Surveys: Greece 1995*, Paris, 1994, 101.

Table 7. Price and Wage Movement, Selected Years, 1985–93

	1985	1990	1991	1992	1993
Consumer price index[1]					
Food	66.4	144.3	172.2	196.4	221.3
Alcoholic beverages and tobacco	54.0	146.7	176.8	218.2	258.2
Clothing and footwear	55.5	134.4	156.5	178.4	198.0
Housing	63.7	136.1	172.0	201.8	233.7
Durable goods and household supplies	59.1	127.5	149.5	167.9	182.7
Transportation and communications	65.5	134.9	161.1	193.8	230.3
Overall consumer prices	61.5	136.9	163.6	189.5	216.8
Wholesale price index[2]					
Domestic finished products consumed in Greece	245.3	474.3	563.2	631.2	706.9
Foreign-produced finished products	281.1	541.7	620.6	699.0	783.9
Exported domestic products	269.7	413.4	457.8	487.1	542.3
Overall wholesale prices	255.2	473.7	553.0	615.7	689.1
Hourly wages in manufacturing[3]	100.0	210.5	245.7	279.4	308.8

[1] 1988 = 100.0.
[2] 1980 = 100.0.
[3] In enterprises employing at least ten persons.

Source: Based on information from Organisation for Economic Co-operation and Development, *OECD Economic Surveys: Greece 1995*, Paris, 1994, 94.

Table 8. Structure of Economic Output, 1989–93
(in percentage of GDP) [1]

Economic Activity	1989	1990	1991	1992	1993
Agriculture, forestry, and fishing	12.8	11.0	12.5	12.1	11.9
Mining and quarrying	1.9	1.9	1.8	1.8	1.7
Total manufacturing	18.8	18.6	17.9	17.4	16.9
Food, drink, and tobacco	4.3	4.1	4.2	4.4	n.a.[2]
Textiles	3.1	3.1	2.7	2.5	n.a.
Chemical and related industries	3.2	3.1	2.9	2.8	n.a.
Stone, clay, and glass	1.5	1.6	1.3	1.3	n.a.
Metals, engineering, and electric goods	1.9	1.7	1.8	1.8	n.a.
Construction	5.4	5.8	5.4	5.2	5.0
Utilities	4.2	4.1	4.3	4.5	4.6
Trade services[3]	26.8	27.7	27.8	28.6	29.0
Nontrade services[4]	24.0	24.6	24.4	24.0	24.4
Other	6.1	6.4	6.0	6.4	6.6

[1] GDP—gross domestic product.
[2] n.a.—not available.
[3] Transportation, communications, wholesale and retail trade, banking, insurance, and real estate.
[4] Ownership of dwellings, public administration and defense, and health and education services.

Source: Based on information from Organisation for Economic Co-operation and Development, *OECD Economic Surveys: Greece 1995*, Paris, 1995, 100.

Table 9. *Export Trade by World Economic Group, 1989–93*
(in millions of United States dollars)

Group	1989	1990	1991	1992	1993
Total OECD[1]	6,088.6	6,425.5	6,759.1	7,347.9	5,850.0
European Community[2]	4,990.9	5,202.6	5,515.2	6,108.0	4,748.4
Britain	558.6	587.7	592.8	660.5	484.7
France	664.3	777.1	656.0	689.2	526.0
Germany[3]	1,623.5	1,792.5	2,073.0	2,197.8	2,012.8
Italy	1,535.5	1,384.0	1,441.4	1,718.2	1,127.1
Other OECD Europe[4]	484.7	570.0	580.7	646.7	547.9
North America	480.5	498.9	528.7	436.0	417.9
Central and East European countries[5]	348.4	342.6	431.4	608.5	886.5
OPEC[6]	284.2	318.0	321.5	323.8	312.1
Other	845.8	934.4	1,151.0	934.2	1,085.7
Total exports[7]	7,567.1	8,020.6	8,663.0	9,842.0	8,777.3

[1] Organisation for Economic Co-operation and Development, whose twenty-five members include all of Western Europe, all of North America, Australia, Japan, New Zealand, and Turkey.

[2] Until 1994, included Belgium, Britain, Denmark, France, Germany (West Germany through 1990), Greece, Ireland, Italy, Luxembourg, Netherlands, Portugal, and Spain.

[3] West Germany through 1990.

[4] Austria, Finland, Iceland, Norway, Sweden, and Switzerland.

[5] In 1993 included Albania, Belarus, Bulgaria, Croatia, Czech Republic, Hungary, Poland, Romania, Russia, Serbia, Slovakia, Slovenia, and Ukraine.

[6] Organization of the Petroleum Exporting Countries, whose members in 1993 included Algeria, Gabon, Indonesia, Iran, Iraq, Kuwait, Libya, Nigeria, Qatar, Saudi Arabia, United Arab Emirates, and Venezuela (Ecuador left in 1992).

[7] Figures may not add to totals because of rounding.

Source: Based on information from Organisation for Economic Co-operation and Development, *OECD Economic Surveys: Greece 1995*, Paris, 1994, 96.

Table 10. *Import Trade by World Economic Group, 1989–93*
(in millions of United States dollars)

Group	1989	1990	1991	1992	1993
Total OECD[1]	12,938.2	16,049.5	16,858.5	18,385.8	16,914.2
European Community[2] ..	10,052.4	12,697.6	12,955.7	14,514.6	13,190.7
Britain	935.7	1,040.3	1,149.8	1,277.4	1,337.9
France	1,106.1	1,595.9	1,668.0	1,814.5	1,739.7
Germany[3]	3,244.2	4,104.0	4,168.6	4,668.2	3,727.6
Italy	2,393.4	3,038.3	3,054.6	3,290.4	3,074.3
Other OECD Europe[4] ...	1,137.6	1,305.8	1,405.5	1,398.6	1,292.9
North America	623.3	792.2	985.3	902.0	880.7
Central and East European countries[5]	647.7	787.4	973.1	930.9	1,007.7
OPEC[6]	792.6	1,129.1	1,575.6	1,595.6	1,492.2
Other	1,700.9	1,735.4	2,243.0	2,494.4	3,345.6
Total imports[7]	16,079.5	19,701.4	21,650.1	23,406.8	22,759.8

[1] Organisation for Economic Co-operation and Development, whose twenty-five members include all of Western Europe, all of North America, Australia, Japan, New Zealand, and Turkey.

[2] Until 1994, included Belgium, Britain, Denmark, France, Germany (West Germany through 1990), Greece, Ireland, Italy, Luxembourg, Netherlands, Portugal, and Spain.

[3] West Germany through 1990.

[4] Austria, Finland, Iceland, Norway, Sweden, and Switzerland.

[5] In 1993 included Albania, Belarus, Bulgaria, Croatia, Czech Republic, Hungary, Poland, Romania, Russia, Serbia, Slovakia, Slovenia, and Ukraine.

[6] Organization of the Petroleum Exporting Countries, whose members in 1993 included Algeria, Gabon, Indonesia, Iran, Iraq, Kuwait, Libya, Nigeria, Qatar, Saudi Arabia, United Arab Emirates, and Venezuela (Ecuador left in 1992).

[7] Figures may not add to totals because of rounding.

Source: Based on information from Organisation for Economic Co-operation and Development, *OECD Economic Surveys: Greece 1995*, Paris, 1994, 96.

Table 11. Exports by Commodity, 1990–93
(in millions of United States dollars)

Commodity	1990	1991	1992	1993
Food and live animals	1,627.7	1,922.3	2,085.3	1,736.7
Beverages and tobacco	443.6	493.2	650.8	550.2
Inedible crude material except fuels	456.7	455.7	425.3	506.2
Mineral fuels and lubricants	588.0	773.4	518.9	688.5
Animal and vegetable oils and fats	302.5	222.2	550.7	314.2
Chemicals	314.9	338.0	372.7	409.7
Manufactured goods	3,754.1	3,888.0	4,527.8	3,878.9
Textiles	500.1	533.3	520.2	446.0
Iron and steel	415.0	412.4	471.1	251.2
Aluminum	279.3	287.2	311.9	269.5
Clothing	1,675.2	1,749.6	2,146.0	1,844.0
Machinery and transportation equipment	1,864.5	1,935.5	2,360.1	2,115.2
Other	532.1	197.9	238.2	143.0
TOTAL	8,020.6	8,663.0	9,842.0	8,777.3

Source: Based on information from Organisation for Economic Co-operation and Development, *OECD Economic Surveys: Greece 1995*, Paris, 1994, 95.

Table 12. Imports by Commodity, 1990–93
(in millions of United States dollars)

Commodity	1990	1991	1992	1993
Food and live animals	2,506.9	2,379.3	2,762.6	2,561.1
Beverages and tobacco	323.7	366.5	464.1	493.4
Inedible crude materials except fuels..	954.1	945.7	723.1	643.4
Mineral fuels and lubricants	1,530.5	2,097.3	2,301.3	2,430.7
Crude petroleum	997.2	1,368.9	1,718.3	1,733.0
Petroleum products	456.1	623.7	490.8	612.0
Chemicals	2,068.1	2,238.7	2,472.5	2,504.4
Manufactured goods	4,306.3	4,300.9	4,263.0	3,809.8
Machinery and transportation equipment	6,120.4	7,124.1	7,969.6	8.012.5
Road motor vehicles	1,981.0	2,417.0	3,112.0	2,437.3
Aircraft	109.9	324.5	165.7	266.8
Ships and boats	527.1	886.1	819.7	1,486.0
Other	1,891.4	2,197.6	2,450.6	2,304.7
TOTAL	19,701.4	21,650.1	23,406.8	22,759.8

Source: Based on information from Organisation for Economic Co-operation and Development, *OECD Economic Surveys: Greece 1995*, Paris, 1994, 95.

Table 13. Circulation of Leading Newspapers, 1991

Newspaper	Circulation	Orientation
Akropolis	50,800 M[1]	Center-right, independent
Apogevmatini	80,000 A[2]	-do-
Avgi	55,000 M	Organ of Greek Left Party
Avriani	51,000 A	Center-left
Eleftheros Typos	135,000 A	Right-wing, independent
Eleftherotypia	108,000 A	Center-left, independent
Ethnos	150,000 A	Left-wing, independent
Express	25,000	Business, independent
Kathimerini	935,000 M	Center-right
Makedonia	55,000 M	Independent
Rizopastis	40,000 M	Organ of Communist Party of Greece
Ta Nea	133,000 A	Center-left
To Vima	195,000 S[3]	-do-

[1] M—Daily, morning.
[2] A—Daily, afternoon.
[3] S—Sundays only.

Source: Based on information from Harry Drost, ed., *The World's News Media*, New York, 1991, 192–94.

Table 14. Major Army Equipment, 1994

Type	Model	Number
Main battle tank	M–26	250 (in storage)
	M–47	396 (in storage)
	AMX–30	156 (in storage)
	Leopard 1A4	170
	Leopard 1A3	109
	M–48A1	299
	M–48A3	212
	M–48A5	599
	M–60A1	359
	M–60A3	312
Light tank	M–24	67
Reconnaissance vehicle	M–8	48
	M–20	180 (reserve)
Armored infantry fighting vehicle . . .	BMP–1	500
	AMX–10P	96
Armored personnel carrier	Leonidas	130
	M–2	114
	M–3 half track	403

Table 14. Major Army Equipment, 1994

Type	Model	Number
	M-59	372
	M-113A1 and M-113A2	1,346
105mm howitzer	M-56	18
	M-101	469
140mm howitzer	5.5 inch	32
155mm howitzer	M-114	271
203mm howitzer	M-115	85
105mm self-propelled howitzer	M-52	76
155mm self-propelled howitzer	M-44A1	48
	M-109A1	51
	M-109A2	84
175mm self-propelled howitzer	M-107	12
203mm self-propelled howitzer	M-110A2	100
107mm mortar	M-30	773
81mm mortar		690
122mm multiple rocket launcher	RM-70	150
Antitank guided weapon (ATGW) . . .	Milan	394
64mm rocket launcher	RPG-18	
90mm recoilless launcher	EM-67	1,057
	M-40A1	763
20mm air defense gun	RH-202 twin	101
23mm air defense gun	ZU-23-2	300
40mm air defense gun	M-1	227
	M-42A twin self-propelled	95
Surface-to-air missile	Improved Hawk and Redeye	42
Aircraft	Aero Commander	2
	Super King Air	2
	U-17A	20
Helicopter	CH-47C1	9
	UH-1D/H/AB-205	85
	AH-1P	9
	AB-212	1
	AB-206	15
	Bell 47G	10
	Hughes 300C	30

Source: Based on information from *The Military Balance, 1994–1995*, London, 1994, 53.

Table 15. *Major Air Force Equipment, 1994*

Type	Model	Number
A–7 fighter aircraft	A–7H	38
	TA–7H	7
	A–7E	40
	A–7K	7
F–5 fighter aircraft	F–5A	64
	F–5B	8
	NF–5A	11
	NF–5B	1
	RF–5A	6
F–4 fighter aircraft	F–4E	52
	RF–4E	20
F–16 fighter aircraft	F–16C	32
	F–16D	6
Mirage fighter aircraft	F–1	25
Transport and training aircraft	HU–16B	2
	C–47	4
	C–130H	10
	C–130B	5
	CL–215	11
	Do–28	12
	Gulfstream I	1
	T–2	36
	T–33A	30
	T–37B/C	29
	T–41D	19
	Ys–11–200	6
Helicopter	AB–205A transport	14
	AB–212 transport	3
	Bell 47G liaison	5
	AH–64 attack	12
Surface-to-air missile	Nike Hercules	36
	Sparrow	40

Source: Based on information from *The Military Balance, 1994–1995*, London, 1994, 53.

Table 16. Major Navy Equipment, 1994

Type	Model/Class	Number
Submarine	Glavkos (GeT–209/1100)	8
Destroyer	Kimon (U.S. Adams)	4
	Themistocles (U.S. Gearing–FRAM I)	2
Frigate	Hydra (MEKO–200H)	1
	Elli (Kortenaer)	4
	Makedonia (U.S. Knox)	3
Corvette	Niki (Ge–Thetis)	5
Missile craft	Laskos (La Combattante II/III)	14
	I. Votis (La Combattante IIA)	2
	Stamou	2
Torpedo craft	Hesperos (Jaguar)	6
	"Nasty"	4
Coastal patrol craft	Armatolos (Osprey)	2
Inshore patrol craft	Tolmi/PCI	5
Minelayer	Aktion (LSM–1)	2
Mine countermeasure craft	Alkyon (MSC–294)	9
	Atalanti (Adjutant)	5
Amphibious craft	Samos tank-landing ship	1
	Nafkratourssa (Cabaldo) dock landing ship	1
	Inouse (County) tank-landing ship	2
	Ikaria (LST–510)	4
	Ipopliarhos Grigoropoulos (LSM–1)	2
	Medium landing ship	2
Antisubmarine helicopter ..		
Helicopter	AB–212	22
	SA–319	4
Antiship missile battery	Exocet MM40	2

Source: Based on information from *The Military Balance, 1994–1995*, London, 1994, 54.

Bibliography

Chapter 1

Alastos, Doros. *Venizelos*. Gulf Breeze, Florida: Academic International Press, 1978.

Alcock, Susan E. *Graecia Capta: The Landscapes of Roman Greece.* New York: Cambridge University Press, 1993.

Alexander, Alec P. *Greek Industrialists: An Economic and Social Analysis.* Athens: Center of Planning and Economic Research, 1964.

Alexander, George E. *The Prelude to the Truman Doctrine: British Policy on Greece, 1944–1947.* Oxford: Oxford University Press, 1982.

Alexander, John. *Brigandage and Public Order in the Morea, 1685–1806.* Athens: Paragoge, 1985.

Alexandris, Alexis. *The Greek Minority of Istanbul and Greek-Turkish Relations, 1918–1974.* Athens: Center for Asia Minor Studies, 1983.

Alivizatos, Nikos K. *Political Institutions in Crisis, 1922–74.* Athens: Themelio, 1985.

Amen, Michael Mark. *American Foreign Policy in Greece, 1944–49.* New York: Lang, 1978.

Amnesty International. *Torture in Greece: The First Torturers' Trial, 1975.* London: 1977.

Andreopoulos, George J. "Liberalism and the Formation of the Nation-State," *Journal of Modern Greek Studies* [Athens], No. 7, 1989, 193–225.

Andrews, Kevin. *Greece in the Dark, 1967–1974.* Amsterdam: Hakkert, 1980.

Angelopoulos, A., ed. *Essays on Greek Migration.* Athens: Greek Social Research Center, 1967.

Angold, Michael. *The Byzantine Empire, 1025–1204: A Political History.* London: Longman, 1984.

Augustinos, Gerasimos. *Consciousness and History: Nationalist Critics of Greek Society, 1897–1914.* New York: Columbia University Press, 1977.

Baerentzen, Lars, John O. Iatrides, and Ole Smith. *Studies in the History of the Greek Civil War, 1945–1949*. Copenhagen: Museum Tusculanum Press, 1987.

Bahcheli, Tozun. *Greek-Turkish Relations since 1955*. Boulder, Colorado: Westview Press, 1990.

Baynes, Norman H., and H.St.L.B. Moss, eds. *Byzantium: An Introduction to East Roman Civilization*. Oxford: Clarendon Press, 1948.

Bickford-Smith, R.A.H. *Greece under King George*. London: Bentley, 1893.

Bosworth, A.B. *Conquest and Empire: The Reign of Alexander the Great*. Cambridge: Cambridge University Press, 1988.

Bower, Leondard, and Gordon Bolitho. *Otho I King of Greece*. London: Selwyn and Blount, 1939.

Branigan, Keith. *The Foundations of Palatial Crete*. London: Routledge and Kegan Paul, 1970.

Browning, Robert, ed. *The Greeks, Classical, Byzantine, and Modern*. New York: Portland House, 1985.

Cameron, Averil. "Rome and the Greek East." Pages 203–14 in Robert Browning, ed., *The Greeks: Classical, Byzantine, and Modern*. New York, Portland House, 1985.

Clogg, Richard. *A Concise History of Greece*. Cambridge: Cambridge University Press, 1992.

Clogg, Richard. *A Short History of Modern Greece*. Cambridge: Cambridge University Press, 1986.

Clogg, Richard, ed. *Greece in the 1980s*. New York: St. Martin's Press, 1983.

Clogg, Richard, and George Yiannopoulos, eds. *Greece under Military Rule*. New York: Basic Books, 1972.

Collard, Anna. "The Experience of Civil War in the Mountain Villages of Central Greece." Pages 223–54 in Marion Sarafis and Martin Eve, eds., *Background to Contemporary Greece*. New York: Barnes and Noble, 1990.

Couloumbis, Theodore, John A. Petropoulos, and Harry J. Psomiades. *Foreign Interference in Greek Politics*. New York: Pella, 1976.

Crawshaw, Nancy. *The Cyprus Revolt: An Account of the Struggle for Union with Greece*. Boston: Allen and Unwin, 1978.

Dakin, Douglas. *The Greek Struggle for Independence, 1821–1833*. London: Batsford, 1973.

Dakin, Douglas. *The Greek Struggle in Macedonia, 1897–1913.* Thessaloniki: Institute for Balkan Studies, 1993.

Develin, Rita. *The Jews of Ioannina.* Philadelphia: Cadmus Press, 1990.

Diamandouros, P. Nikiforos. *The 1974 Transition from Authoritarian to Democratic Rule in Greece.* Bologna: Johns Hopkins University Bologna Center, 1981.

Dickinson, Oliver. *The Aegean Bronze Age.* Cambridge: Cambridge University Press, 1993.

Diehl, Charles. *Byzantium: Greatness and Decline.* Rutgers: Rutgers University Press, 1957.

Dontas, Domna N. *Greece and the Great Powers, 1863–1975.* Thessaloniki: Institute for Balkan Studies, 1966.

Eddy, Charles. *Greece and the Greek Refugees.* London: Allen and Unwin, 1931.

Esche, Matthias. *Die Kommunistische Partei Griechenlands, 1941–1949.* Munich: Wien, 1982.

Finlay, George. *History of the Greek Revolution and the Reign of King Otho.* London: Zeno, 1971.

Frazee, Charles. *The Orthodox Church and Independent Greece, 1821–1852.* Cambridge: Cambridge University Press, 1969.

Gallant, Thomas. "Greek Bandit Gangs: Lone Wolves or a Family Affair?" *Journal of Modern Greek Studies* [Athens], No. 3, 1988, 269–90.

Gallant, Thomas. *Risk and Survival in Ancient Greece.* Stanford: Stanford University Press, 1991.

Gruen, Erich S. *The Hellenistic World and the Coming of Rome.* Berkeley: University of California Press, 1984.

Haas, R.N. "Managing NATO's Weakest Flank: The United States, Greece, and Turkey," *Orbis*, 30, Fall 1986, 457–73.

Hart, Parker T. *Two NATO Allies at the Threshold of War: Cyprus, a First-Hand Account of Crisis Management, 1965–1968.* Durham: Duke University Press, 1990.

Hitchens, Christopher. *Cyprus.* London: Quartet Books, 1984.

Hondros, John Louis. *Occupation and Resistance: The Greek Agony, 1941–1944.* New York: Pella, 1978.

Hourmouzios, S.L. *Starvation in Greece.* London: Harrison, 1943.

Housepian, Marjorie. *The Smyrna Affair.* New York: Harcourt Brace Jovanovich, 1966.

Howarth, David. *The Greek Adventure: Lord Byron and Other Eccentrics in the War for Independence.* New York: Atheneum, 1976.

Iatrides, John O., ed. *Greece in the 1940s: A Nation in Crisis.* Hanover, New Hampshire: University Press of New England, 1981.

Inalcik, H. *The Ottoman Empire: Conquests, Organization, and Economy.* London: Variorum, 1978.

Jelavich, Barbara. *History of the Balkans.* Cambridge: Cambridge University Press, 1983.

Jelavich, Charles, and Barbara Jelavich. *The Balkans in Transition.* Berkeley: University of California Press, 1963.

Jennings, Ronald C. *Christians and Muslims in Ottoman Cyprus and the Mediterranean World, 1571–1640.* New York: New York University Press, 1992.

Kaldis, William Peter. *John Capodistrias and the Modern Greek State.* Madison, Wisconsin: State Historical Society, 1963.

Kalthas, Nicholas. *Introduction to the Constitutional History of Modern Greece.* New York: Columbia University Press, 1940.

Kofas, Jon V. *Authoritarianism in Greece: The Metaxas Regime.* New York: Columbia University Press, 1983.

Kofos, Evangelos. *Nationalism and Communism in Macedonia.* Thessaloniki: Institute for Balkan Studies, 1964.

Kokosalakis, N. "Religion and Modernization in 19th-Century Greece," *Social Compass,* 34, 1987, 223–41.

Koliopoulos, John S. "Brigandage and Irredentism in Nineteenth-Century Greece," *European History Quarterly,* 19, 1989, 193–28.

Kourvetaris, George A. "Political Elites and Party Organization in Greece: An Entrepreneurial Model," *Journal of Social, Political, and Economic Studies,* 14, No. 2, 1989, 189–205.

Kourvetaris, George A., and Betty A. Dobratz. *A Profile of Modern Greece in Search of Identity.* Oxford: Clarendon Press, 1987.

Kousoulas, D. George. "The Origins of the Greek Military Coup, April 1967," *Orbis,* 13, No. 1, March 1969, 332–58.

Kousoulas, D. George. *Revolution and Defeat: The Story of the Greek Communist Party.* London: Oxford University Press, 1965.

Ladas, Stephen P. *The Exchange of Minorities: Bulgaria, Greece, and Turkey.* New York: Macmillan, 1932.

Legg, Keith R. *Politics in Modern Greece.* Stanford: Stanford University Press, 1969.

Leon, George B. *Greece and the First World War: From Neutrality to Intervention, 1917–1918.* New York: Columbia University Press, 1990.

Leon, George B. *Greece and the Great Powers, 1914–1917.* Thessaloniki: Institute for Balkan Studies, 1974.

Loulis, John C. *The Greek Communist Party, 1940–1944.* London: Croom Helm, 1982.

Mavrogordatos, George. *The Stillborn Republic: Social Coalitions and Party Strategies in Greece, 1922–1936.* Berkeley: University of California Press, 1983.

Mazower, Mark. *Greece and the Inter-war Economic Crisis.* Oxford: Oxford University Press, 1991.

Mazower, Mark. *Inside Hitler's Greece: The Experience of Occupation.* New Haven: Yale University Press, 1993.

Miller, William. *The Ottoman Empire and Its Successors, 1801–1927.* Cambridge: Cambridge University Press, 1936.

Murray, Oswyn. *Early Greece.* Glasgow: Fontana, 1980.

Norwich, John Julius. *Byzantium: The Apogee.* New York: Knopf, 1992.

Obolenski, Dimitri. *The Byzantine Commonwealth, 500–1453.* London: Weidenfeld and Nicholson, 1971.

Papandreou, Andreas. *Democracy at Gunpoint: The Greek Front.* Harmondsworth, United Kingdom: Penguin Books, 1971.

Papayannakis, Michalis. *The Crisis in the Greek Left.* Washington: American Enterprise Institute, 1981.

Pentzopoulos, Dimitri. *The Balkan Exchange of Minorities and Its Impact upon Greece.* The Hague: Mouton, 1962.

Petrakis, P.E., and N. Panorios. "Economic Fluctuations in Greece, 1844–1913," *Journal of Economic History,* 21, No. 1, 1992, 31–47.

Renfrew, Colin. *The Emergence of Civilization: The Cyclades and the Aegean in the Third Millennium B.C.* London: Metheun, 1972.

Richter, Heinz. *Greece and Cyprus since 1920: Bibliography of Contemporary History.* Stuttgart: Nea Ellas Verlag, 1984.

Roubatis, Yannis. *Tangled Webs: The U.S. in Greece, 1947–1967.* New York: Pella, 1987.

Sarafis, Marian, and Martin Eve, eds. *Background to Contemporary Greece.* London: Merlin Press; Savage, Maryland: Barnes and Noble, 1990.

Saraphes, Stephanos G. *ELAS: Greek Resistance Army.* London: Merlin Press, 1980.

Shepherd, William Robert. *Historical Atlas.* New York: Barnes and Noble, 1962.

Smith, Ole L. "Marxism in Greece," *Journal of Modern Greek Studies* [Athens], 3, 1985, 45–64.

Snodgrass, Anthony. *The Dark Age of Greece.* Edinburgh: Edinburgh University Press, 1971.

Stavrianos, Leften S. *The Balkans since 1453.* New York: Holt, Rinehart, and Winston, 1965.

Stavrou, Nikolaos. *Allied Politics and Military Interventions: The Political Role of the Greek Military.* Athens: Papazissis, 1977.

Stearns, Monteagle. *Entangled Allies: U.S. Policy Toward Greece, Turkey, and Cyprus.* New York: Council on Foreign Relations, 1992.

Tsoukalis, Loukas. *The European Community and Its Mediterranean Enlargement.* Boston: Allen and Unwin, 1981.

Venizelos, Eleutherios. *The Vindication of Greek National Policy, 1912–1917.* London: Allen and Unwin, 1918.

Walbank, F.W. *The Hellenistic World.* Glasgow: Fontana, 1981.

Woodhouse, C.M. *Modern Greece: A Short History.* (5th ed.) London: Faber, 1991.

Zakinthos, D.A. *The Making of Modern Greece: From Byzantium to Independence.* Oxford: Blackwell, 1976.

Chapter 2

Allen, Peter S. "Positive Aspects of Greek Urbanization: The Case of Athens by 1980," *Ekistics,* 53, Nos. 318–19, May–August 1986, 187–94.

Baxevanis, John J. *Economic and Population Movements in the Peloponnesus of Greece.* Athens: Greek Social Research Center, 1972.

Baxevanis, John J. "Population, Internal Migration, and Urbanization in Greece," *Balkan Studies* [Thessaloniki], 6, No. 1, 1965, 83–98.

Browning, Robert. *Medieval and Modern Greek.* London: Hutchinson University Library, 1969.

Campbell, John K. *Honour, Family, and Patronage.* Oxford: Clarendon Press, 1964.

Campbell, John K., and Philip Sherrard. *Modern Greece.* New York: Praeger, 1968.

Cavounides, Jennifer. "Capitalist Development and Women's Work in Greece," *Journal of Modern Greek Studies* [Athens], No. 2, 1983, 321–38.

Clogg, Richard. "Elite and Popular Culture in Greece under Turkish Rule," *Indiana Social Studies Quarterly,* 32, No. 1, 1979, 69–88.

Clogg, Richard, ed. *Greece in the 1980s.* New York: St. Martin's Press, 1983.

Demertzis, Nicolas. "Greece: Greens at the Periphery." Pages 193–207 in Dick Richardson and Chris Rootes, eds., *The Green Challenge: The Development of Green Parties in Europe.* London: Routledge, 1995.

Dicks, T.R.B. *The Greeks: How They Live and Work.* New York: Praeger, 1971.

Du Boulay, Juliet. *Portrait of a Greek Mountain Village.* Oxford: Clarendon Press, 1974.

The Europa World Year Book, 1994. London: Europa, 1994.

European Economic Community. Hospital Committee. *European Health Services Handbook.* Leuven, Belgium: Acco, 1994.

Galani-Moutafi, Vasiliki. "From Agriculture to Tourism: Property, Labor, Gender, and Kinship in a Greek Island Village, Pt. 1," *Journal of Modern Greek Studies* [Athens], No. 2, 1993, 241–70.

Giannitsis, Tasos, I. Katsoulis, and P. Kazakos, eds. *Greece Facing the Year 2000.* Athens: Papazissis, 1988.

Guterschwager, Mary C. "Nea Aeolia: Persistence of Tradition in a Greek Urban Community." (Ph.D. dissertation.) Chapel Hill: University of North Carolina, 1971.

Hart, Janet. "Women in Greek Society." Pages 95–122 in Marian Sarafis and Martin Eve, eds., *Background to Contemporary Greece.* New York: Barnes and Noble, 1990.

Hart, Laurie Kain. *Time, Religion, and Social Experience in Rural Greece.* Lanham, Maryland: Rowman and Littlefield, 1992.

Herzfeld, Michael. "'Law' and 'Custom': Ethnography of and in Greek National Identity," *Journal of Modern Greek Studies* [Athens], No. 2, 1985, 167–86.

Husen, Torsten, and T. Neville Postlethwaite, eds. *International Encyclopedia of Education.* Oxford: Pergamon Press, 1985.

Kariotis, Theodore C., ed. *The Greek Socialist Experiment.* New York: Pella, 1992.

Katsoulis, Basil D., and John M. Tsangaris. "The State of the Greek Environment in Recent Years," *Ambio* [Stockholm], 23, Nos. 4–5, 1994, 274–79.

Kayser, Bernard, and Pierre-Yves Sivignon. *Exode rural et attraction urbaine en Grèce.* Athens: Greek Social Research Center, 1971.

Kenna, Margaret. "Institutional and Transformational Migration and the Politics of Community," *Archive of European Sociology,* 24, 1983, 263–87.

Kenny, Michael, and David I. Kertzer, eds. *Urban Life in Mediterranean Europe: Anthropological Perspectives.* Urbana: University of Illinois Press, 1983.

Kommantos, George, and Christine Stambelou. "Greece: 'Digesting' the New Family Law," *Journal of Family Law,* 28, No. 3, 1989, 517–25.

Kunz, Didier. "Greece Accused on Minorities' Rights," *Manchester Guardian Weekly* [Manchester, United Kingdom], 151, No. 26, 1994, 12.

Lambriri-Dimaki, Jane. *Social Strategy in Greece, 1962–1982.* Athens: Sakkoulas, 1983.

Leontidou, Lila. *The Mediterranean City in Transition: Social Change and Urban Development.* Cambridge: Cambridge University Press, 1989.

McNeill, William H. *The Metamorphosis of Greece since World War II.* Chicago: University of Chicago Press, 1978.

Massialas, Byron G. *The Educational System of Greece.* Washington: GPO, 1981.

Moustaka, Calliope. *The Internal Migrant.* Athens: Greek Social Research Center, 1964.

Organisation for Economic Co-operation and Development. *Trends in International Migration: Annual Report.* Paris: 1994.

Organisation for Economic Co-operation and Development. Directorate for Employment, Labour, and Social Affairs. *The Reform of Health Care Systems: A Review of Seventeen OECD Countries.* (Health Policy Studies, No. 5.) Paris: 1994.

Papas, George, and George Psacharopoulos. "The Transition from School to the University under Restricted Entry: The Greek Tracer Study," *Higher Education*, 16, 1987, 481–501.

People-to-People Health Foundation. *Request for Proposal to Provide the Ministry of Health, Welfare, and Social Security of the Hellenic Republic with Technical Assistance to Prepare a Comprehensive Health Plan.* Millwood, Virginia: Project HOPE, 1993.

Pesmazoglou, Stephanos. *Education and Development in Greece, 1948–1985.* Athens: Themelio, 1987.

Petras, James. "The Contradictions of Greek Socialism." Pages 97–126 in Theodore C. Kariotis, ed., *The Greek Socialist Experiment.* New York: Pella, 1992.

Pollis, Adamantia. "Gender and Social Change in Greece: The Role of Women." Pages 279–304 in Theodore C. Kariotis, ed., *The Greek Socialist Experiment.* New York: Pella, 1992.

Pollis, Adamantia. "Greek National Identity: Religious Minorities, Rights, and European Norms," *Journal of Modern Greek Studies* [Athens], 10, 1992, 171–96.

Psacharapoulos, George. "Education and the Professions in the Light of 1992," *European Journal of Education*, 25, No. 1, 1990, 61–74.

Psacharapoulos, George. "Greece: System of Education." Pages 2079–85 in Torsten Husen and T. Neville Postlethwaite, eds., *International Encyclopedia of Education.* Oxford: Pergamon Press, 1985.

Richardson, Dick, and Chris Rootes, eds. *The Green Challenge: The Development of Green Parties in Europe.* London: Routledge, 1995.

Sanders, Irwin. *Rainbow in the Rock: The People of Rural Greece.* Cambridge: Harvard University Press, 1962.

Sant Cassia, Paul, and Constantina Bada. *The Making of the Modern Greek Family: Marriage and Exchange in Nineteenth-Century Athens.* Cambridge: Cambridge University Press, 1992.

Skalkidis, Yannis. "Greece." Pages 81–84 in European Economic Community. Hospital Committee. *European Health Services Handbook.* Leuven, Belgium: Acco, 1994.

Stevis, Dimitris. "The Politics of Greek Environmental Policy." *Policy Studies Journal*, 20, Winter 1992, 695–709.

Tsoucalas, Constantine, and Roy Panagiotopoulou. "Education in Socialist Greece: Between Modernization and Democratization." Pages 305–33 in Theodore C. Kariotis, ed., *The Greek Socialist Experiment.* New York: Pella, 1992.

United Nations. Department for Economic and Social Information and Policy Analysis. Statistical Division. *Statistical Yearbook, 1992.* New York: 1994.

World Resources Institute. *The 1994 Information Please Environmental Almanac.* Boston: Houghton Mifflin, 1994.

Chapter 3

Agriantone, Christina. *The Beginning of Industrialisation in Nineteenth-Century Greece.* Athens: Commercial Bank of Greece, 1986.

Alogoskoufis, George, Lucas Papademos, and Richard Portes, eds. *External Constraints on Macroeconomic Policy: The European Experience.* Cambridge: Cambridge University Press, 1991.

Association of Hellenic Banks. *Report for the Reform and Modernization of the Greek Banking System.* Athens: 1987.

Athens Stock Exchange. *Annual Statistical Bulletin.* Athens: 1994.

Candilis, Wray O. *The Economy of Greece, 1944–66.* New York: Praeger, 1968.

Chalikias, Demetrios I. *Money and Credit in a Developing Economy: The Greek Case.* New York: New York University Press, 1978.

Clogg, Richard. *A Short History of Modern Greece.* Cambridge: Cambridge University Press, 1986.

Cononelos, Louis James. *In Search of Gold Paved Streets.* New York: AMS Press, 1989.

Constantelou, Natasha. "Liberalizing Telecommunications Markets: Political Externalities in the Greek Case," *Telecommunications Policy,* 17, August 1993, 431–45.

Drost, Harry, ed. *The World's News Media.* New York: Longman Current Affairs, 1991.

Droucopoulos, V., and Stavros Thomadakis. *Internationalisation of Economic Activity and the Development of SMEs: Greece.* Paris: Organisation for Economic Co-operation and Development, 1994.

Emerson, Michael, et al., eds. *One Market, One Money: An Evaluation of the Potential Benefits and Costs of Forming an Economic and Monetary Union.* Oxford: Oxford University Press, 1992.

Freris, Andrew F. *The Greek Economy in the Twentieth Century.* New York: St. Martin's Press, 1986.

Gianaris, Nicholas V. *Greece and Yugoslavia: An Economic Comparison.* New York: Praeger, 1984.

Giannitsis, A. "Globalisation, Technology Factors, and Industrial Restructuring in Southern Europe: The Greek Experience." Pages 162–72 in Marc Humbert, ed., *The Impact of Globalisation on Europe's Firms and Industries.* London: Pinter, 1993.

Gortsos, C.V. *The Greek Banking System.* Athens: Association of Hellenic Banks, 1992.

Hellenic Industrial Development Bank. *Investment Guide in Greece.* Athens: ETBA, 1993.

Humbert, Marc, ed. *The Impact of Globalisation on Europe's Firms and Industries.* London: Pinter, 1993.

Iatrides, John O. "Papandreou's Foreign Policy." Pages 127–60 in Theodore C. Kariotis, ed., *The Greek Socialist Experiment.* New York: Pella, 1992.

Iatrides, John O., ed. *Greece in the 1940s: A Nation in Crisis.* Hanover, New Hampshire: University Press of New England, 1981.

Jane's World Railways, 1994–95. Ed., James Abbott. Coulsdon, United Kingdom: Jane's Information Group, 1994.

Jouganatos, George A. *The Development of the Greek Economy, 1950–1991.* Westport, Connecticut: Greenwood Press, 1992.

Kariotis, Theodore C. *The Greek Socialist Experiment.* New York: Pella, 1992.

Katsenevas, Thodoros K. *Trade Unions in Greece.* Athens: Greek Social Research Center, 1984.

Kazakos, Panos. "Socialist Attitudes Toward European Integration in the Eighties." Pages 257–78 in Theodore C. Kariotis, ed., *The Greek Socialist Experiment.* New York: Pella, 1992.

Koniaris, Theodore B. *Labor Law and Industrial Relations in Greece.* Athens: Sakkoulas, 1990.

Lando, Steven D. "The European Community's Road to Telecommunications Deregulation," *Fordham Law Review,* 62, May 1994, 2159–98.

McNeill, William H. *Greece: American Aid in Action, 1947–56.* New York: Twentieth Century Fund, 1957.

Moraitinis, Pierre A. *La Grèce telle qu'elle est.* Paris: Firmin Didot, 1877.

Mouzelis, Nicos P. *Modern Greece: Facets of Underdevelopment.* London: Macmillan, 1978.

Nikolau, Kalliope. *Intersize Efficiency Differentials in Greek Manufacturing.* Athens: Center of Planning and Economic Research, 1978.

Noam, Eli. *Telecommunications in Europe.* New York and Oxford: Oxford University Press, 1992.

Organisation for Economic Co-operation and Development. *OECD Economic Surveys, 1992–1993: Greece.* Paris: 1993.

Organisation for Economic Co-operation and Development. *OECD Economic Surveys: Greece 1995.* Paris: 1994.

Organisation for Economic Co-operation and Development. *OECD in Figures: Statistics on the Member Countries.* Paris: 1994.

Petras, James. "The Contradictions of Greek Socialism." Pages 97–126 in Theodore C. Kariotis, ed., *The Greek Socialist Experiment.* New York: Pella, 1992.

Psomiades, Harry J., and Stavros Thomadakis, eds. *Greece, the New Europe, and the Changing International Order.* New York: Pella, 1993.

Saloutos, Theodore. *The Greeks in the United States.* Cambridge: Harvard University Press, 1964.

Svoronos, Nikos G. *Histoire de la Grèce moderne.* Paris: Que je sais, 1972.

Thomadakis, Stavros, and Dimitris Seremetis. "Fiscal Management, Social Agenda, and Structural Deficits." Pages 203–56 in Theodore C. Kariotis, ed., *The Greek Socialist Experiment.* New York: Pella, 1992.

Tsakalotos, Euclid. *Alternative Economic Strategies: The Case of Greece.* Aldershot, United Kingdom: Avebury, 1991.

Vergopoulos, Kostas. "The Political Economy of Greece in the Eighties." Pages 179–202 in Theodore C. Kariotis, ed., *The Greek Socialist Experiment.* New York: Pella, 1992.

(Various issues of the following publications were also used in the preparation of this chapter: Bank of Greece, *Monthly Statistical Bulletin* [Athens]; Economist Intelligence Unit, *Country Report: Greece* [London]; Foreign Broadcast Information Service, *Daily Report: West Europe*; *Financial Times* [London]; and

Greece National Statistical Service, *Monthly Statistical Bulletin* [Athens].)

Chapter 4

Alivizatos, Nicos C. "The Difficulties of 'Rationalization' in a Polarized Political System: The Greek Chamber of Deputies." Pages 131–53 in Ulrike Liebert and Maurizio Cotta, eds., *Parliament and Democratic Consolidation in Southern Europe*. London: Pinter, 1990.

Alivizatos, Nicos C. "The Presidency, Parliament, and the Courts in the 1980s." Pages 65–77 in Richard Clogg, ed., *Greece 1981–1989: The Populist Decade*. London: Macmillan, 1993.

Blinkhorn, Martin, and Thanos Veremis, eds. *Modern Greece: Nationalism and Nationality*. Athens: ELIAMEP, 1993.

Charalambis, Dimitris, and Nicolas Demertzis. "Politics and Citizenship in Greece: Cultural and Structural Facets." *Journal of Modern Greek Studies* [Athens], 11, 1993, 219–40.

Clogg, Richard. "Greece and the Balkans in the 1990s." Pages 421–35 in Harry J. Psomiades and Stavros Thomadakis, eds., *Greece, the New Europe, and the Changing International Order*. New York: Pella, 1993.

Clogg, Richard. "Troubled Alliance: Greece and Turkey." Pages 123–49 in Richard Clogg, ed., *Greece in the 1980s*. New York: St. Martin's Press, 1983.

Clogg, Richard, ed. *Greece in the 1980s*. New York: St. Martin's Press, 1983.

Clogg, Richard, ed. *Greece 1981–1989: The Populist Decade*. New York: St. Martin's Press, 1993.

Coufoudakis, Van. "The Cyprus Question after the Gulf War." Pages 135–43 in *The Southeast European Yearbook, 1991*. Athens: ELIAMEP, 1992.

Coufoudakis, Van. "Greece, Turkey, Cyprus, and the United States in the Changing International Order." Pages 379–90 in Harry J. Psomiades and Stavros Thomadakis, eds., *Greece, the New Europe, and the Changing International Order*. New York: Pella, 1993.

Coufoudakis, Van. "PASOK and Greek-Turkish Relations." Pages 167–80 in Richard Clogg, ed., *Greece 1981–1989: The Populist Decade*. New York: St. Martin's Press, 1993.

Coufoudakis, Van. "PASOK on Greco-Turkish Relations and Cyprus,1981–1989: Ideology, Pragmatism, Deadlock." Pages 161–78 in Theodore Kariotis, ed., *The Greek Socialist Experiment.* New York: Pella, 1992.

Couloumbis, Theodore. "Andreas Papandreou: The Style and Substance of Leadership." Pages 85–96 in Theodore C. Kariotis, ed., *The Greek Socialist Experiment.* New York: Pella, 1992.

Couloumbis, Theodore. "Greece and the European Challenge in the Balkans." Pages 75–88 in *Southeast European Yearbook, 1991.* Athens: ELIAMEP, 1992.

Couloumbis, Theodore. "Greek-U.S. Relations in the 1990s: Back into the Future." Pages 379–90 in Harry J. Psomiades and Stavros Thomadakis, eds., *Greece, the New Europe, and the Changing International Order.* New York: Pella, 1993.

Couloumbis, Theodore. "PASOK's Foreign Policies, 1981–9: Continuity or Change?" Pages 113–30 in Richard Clogg, ed., *Greece 1981–1989: The Populist Decade.* London: Macmillan, 1993.

Diamandouros, P. Nikiforos. "Politics and Culture in Greece 1974–1991: An Interpretation." Pages 1–25 in Richard Clogg, ed., *Greece 1981–1989: The Populist Decade.* London: Macmillan, 1993.

Diamandouros, P. Nikiforos. "Transition to, and Consolidation of, Democratic Politics in Greece, 1974–83: A Tentative Assessment," *West European Politics* [London], 7, No. 2, April 1984.

Doukas, George. "Party Elites and Democratization in Greece," *Parliamentary Affairs,* 46, No. 4, October 1993, 506–16.

Drost, Harry, ed. *The World's News Media.* New York: Longman Current Affairs, 1991.

Featherstone, Kevin. "The Party-State in Greece and the Fall of Papandreou," *West European Politics* [London], 12, No. 6, December 1989, 101–15.

Featherstone, Kevin. "Political Parties and Democratic Consolidation in Greece." Pages 179–202 in Geoffrey Pridham, ed., *Securing Democracy: Political Parties and Democratic Consolidation in Southern Europe.* London: Routledge, 1990.

Featherstone, Kevin, and Susannah Verney, "Greece." Pages 90–106 in Juliet Lodge, ed., *The 1989 Election of the European Parliament.* New York: St. Martin's Press, 1990.

Featherstone, Kevin, and Dimitrios Katsoudas, eds. *Political Change in Greece Before and after the Colonels.* London: Croom Helm, 1987.

Glenny, Misha. *The Fall of Yugoslavia: The Third Balkan War.* New York: Penguin Books, 1993.

Glenny, Misha. "Hope for Bosnia?" *The New York Review of Books,* 41, April 7, 1994, 6–8.

Iatrides, John O. "Beneath the Sound and Fury: U.S. Relations with the PASOK Government." Pages 154–66 in Richard Clogg, ed., *Greece 1981–1989: The Populist Decade.* London: Macmillan, 1993.

Iatrides, John O. "Greece in the Cold War and Beyond," *Journal of the Hellenic Diaspora,* 19, 1993, 11–30.

Iatrides, John O. "Papandreou's Foreign Policy." Pages 127–60 in Theodore Kariotis, ed., *The Greek Socialist Experiment.* New York: Pella, 1992.International Studies Association. *Greece: A Profile.* Athens: 1988.

Ioakimides, P.C. "Greece in the EC: Policies, Experiences, and Prospects." Pages 405–20 in Harry J. Psomiades and Stavros Thomadakis, eds., *Greece, the New Europe, and the Changing International Order.* New York: Pella, 1993.

Kapetanyassis, Vassilis. "The Communists." Pages 145–73 in Kevin Featherstone and Dimitrios Katsoudas, eds., *Political Change in Greece Before and after the Colonels.* London: Croom Helm, 1987.

Kapetanyassis, Vassilis. "The Left in the 1980s: Too Little, Too Late." Pages 78–93 in Richard Clogg, ed., *Greece 1981–1989: The Populist Decade.* London: Macmillan, 1993.

Kariotis, Theodore C., ed. *The Greek Socialist Experiment.* New York: Pella, 1992.

Katsoudas, Dimitrios. "The Conservative Movement and New Democracy: From Past to Present." Pages 85–111 in Kevin Featherstone and Dimitrios Katsoudas, eds., *Political Change in Greece Before and after the Colonels.* London: Croom Helm, 1987.

Kazakos, Panos. "Socialist Attitudes toward European Integration in the Eighties." Pages 257–78 in Theodore C. Kariotis, ed., *The Greek Socialist Experiment.* New York: Pella, 1992.

Kofos, Evangelos. "National Heritage and National Identity in Nineteenth- and Twentieth-Century Macedonia." Pages 103–

41 in Martin Blinkhorn and Thanos Veremis, eds., *Modern Greece: Nationalism and Nationality.* Athens: ELIAMEP, 1993.

Lagani, Irene. "Évolutions politiques à Skopje et leurs conséquences éventuelles dans la 'question macédonienne.'" Pages 189–207 in *Southeast European Yearbook, 1991.* Athens: ELIAMEP, 1992.

Lyrintzis, Christos. "PASOK in Power: From 'Change' to Disenchantment." Pages 26–46 in Richard Clogg, ed., *Greece 1981– 1989: The Populist Decade.* London, Macmillan, 1993.

Lyrintzis, Christos. "Political Parties in Post-junta Greece: A Case of Bureaucratic Clientelism?" *West European Politics* [London], 7, No. 2, April 1984, 99–118.

McDonald, Robert. "Prospects for the Greek Economy." Pages 89–106 in *Southeast European Yearbook, 1991.* Athens: ELIAMEP, 1992.

Mavrogordatos, George. "Civil Society under Populism." Pages 47–64 in Richard Clogg, ed., *Greece 1981–1989: The Populist Decade.* London: Macmillan, 1993.

Mouzelis, Nicos. "Continuities and Discontinuities in Greek Politics: From Eleftherios Venizelos to Andreas Papandreou." Pages 271–88 in Kevin Featherstone and Dimitrios Katsoudas, eds., *Political Change in Greece Before and after the Colonels.* London: Croom Helm, 1987.

Mouzelis, Nicos. *Politics in the Semi-Periphery: Early Parliamentarism and Late Industrialization in the Balkans and Latin America.* London: Macmillan, 1986.

Pesmazoglou, Stephanos. "The 1980s in the Looking-Glass: PASOK and the Media." Pages 94–112 in Richard Clogg, ed., *Greece 1981–1989: The Populist Decade.* London: Macmillan, 1993.

Petras, James. "The Contradictions of Greek Socialism." Pages 97–126 in Theodore C. Kariotis, ed., *The Greek Socialist Experiment.* New York: Pella, 1992.

Pollis, Adamantia. "The Impact of Traditional Cultural Patterns on Greek Politics," *Greek Review of Social Research* [Athens], No. 29, 1977, 2–14.

Pridham, Geoffrey, ed. *Securing Democracy: Political Parties and Democratic Consolidation in Southern Europe.* London: Routledge, 1990.

Pridham, Geoffrey, and Susannah Verney. "The Coalition of 1989–90 in Greece," *West European Politics* [London], 14, No. 5, October 1991, 42–69.

Psomiades, Harry J., and Stavros Thomadakis, eds. *Greece, the New Europe, and the Changing International Order.* New York: Pella, 1993.

Samatas, Minas. "Debureaucratization Failure in Post-Dictatorial Greece: A Sociopolitical Control Approach," *Journal of Modern Greek Studies* [Athens], No. 2, 1993, 187–217.

Samatas, Minas. "The Populist Phase of an Underdeveloped Surveillance Society," *Journal of the Hellenic Diaspora,* 19.1, 1993, 31–70.

Sotiropoulos, Dimitri. "Colossus with Feet of Clay: The State in Post-Authoritarian Greece." Pages 43–56 in Harry J. Psomiades and Stavros Thomadakis, eds., *Greece, the New Europe, and the Changing International Order.* New York: Pella, 1993.

Southeast European Yearbook, 1991. Athens: ELIAMEP, 1992.

Stavrianos, Levten S. *The Balkans since 1453.* New York: Holt, Rinehart, and Winston, 1965.

Stearns, Monteagle. *Entangled Allies: U.S. Policy Toward Greece, Turkey, and Cyprus.* New York: Council on Foreign Relations, 1992.

Thomadakis, Stavros. "European Economic Integration, the Greek State, and the Challenges of the 1990s." Pages 351–75 in Theodore C. Kariotis, ed., *The Greek Socialist Experiment.* New York: Pella, 1992.

Tsoucalas, Constantine. "Enlightened Concepts in the Dark: Power and Freedom, Politics and Society," *Journal of Modern Greek Studies* [Athens], No. 1, 1991, 1–23.

Veremis, Thanos. "Defence and Security Policies under PASOK." Pages 181–89 in Richard Clogg, ed., *Greece 1981–1989: The Populist Decade.* London: Macmillan, 1993.

Veremis, Thanos. *Greek Security Considerations: A Historical Perspective.* Athens: Papazissis, 1980.

Woodhouse, C.M. *Modern Greece: A Short History.* (5th ed.) London: Faber, 1991.

(Various issues of the following periodicals were also used in the preparation of this chapter: *Economist* [London]; Embassy of Greece, Press and Information Office, *News from Greece* [Athens]; Foreign Broadcast Information Service, *Daily Report: West*

Europe; *Kathimerini* [Athens]; *New York Times*; and *Ta Vima* [Athens].)

Chapter 5

Alford, Jonathon, ed. *Greece and Turkey: Adversity in Alliance.* London: Gower, 1984.

Aliboni, Roberto, ed. *Southern European Security in the 1990s.* London: Pinter, 1992.

Amen, Michael Mark. *American Foreign Policy in Greece, 1944–1949: Economic, Military, and Institutional Aspects.* New York, 1978.

Argyropoulos, Alexander. *Greece-Turkey: An Annotated Collection of Articles, 1986–1989.* Athens: Papazissis, 1990.

Attalides, Michael, ed. *Cyprus: Nationalism and International Politics.* Edinburgh: Q Press, 1979.

Attalides, Michael, ed. *Cyprus Reviewed.* Nicosia: Zavallis Press, 1977.

Axt, H.J. *Griechenlands Aussenpolitik und Europa: Verpasste Chancen und neue Herausforderungen.* Baden-Baden, Germany: Nomos, 1992.

Bahcheli, Tozun. *Greek-Turkish Relations since 1955.* Boulder, Colorado: Westview Press, 1990.

Barker, Elisabeth. *Macedonia: Its Place in Balkan Power Politics.* London: Royal Institute of International Affairs, 1950.

Barkman, Carl. *Ambassador in Athens.* London: Merlin Press, 1989.

Brown, James. *Delicately Poised Allies: Greece and Turkey.* London: Brassey's, 1991.

Chipman, John, ed. *NATO's Southern Allies: Internal and External Challenges.* London: Routledge, 1988.

Clogg, Richard, and George Yiannopoulos, eds. *Greece under Military Rule.* New York: Basic Books, 1972.

Constas, Dimitri, ed. *The Greek-Turkish Conflict in the 1990s.* London: Macmillan, 1991.

Coufoudakis, Van. "Greek Foreign Policy since 1974: The Quest for Independence," *Journal of Modern Greek Studies* [Athens], No. 6, 1988, 55–80.

Couloumbis, Theodore. *Greek Political Reaction to American and NATO Influence.* London: Yale University Press, 1966.

Couloumbis, Theodore. *The United States, Greece, and Turkey: The Troubled Triangle.* New York: Praeger, 1983.

Couloumbis, Theodore, John A. Petropoulos, and Harry J. Psomiades. *Foreign Interference in Greek Politics.* New York: Pella, 1976.

Couloumbis, Theodore, and John O. Iatrides, eds. *Greek-American Relations: A Critical Review.* New York: Pella, 1980.

Couloumbis, Theodore, and Sallie M. Hicks, eds. *U.S. Foreign Policy Toward Greece and Cyprus: The Clash of Principle and Pragmatism.* Washington: Center for Mediterranean Studies and American Hellenic Institute, 1975.

Couloumbis, Theodore, and Yannis Valinakis, eds. *The CFE Negotiations in Vienna and Their Impact on Southeastern Europe.* Athens: ELIAMEP, 1991.

Crawshaw, Nancy. *The Cyprus Revolt: An Account of the Struggle for Union with Greece.* Boston: Allen and Unwin, 1978.

Danopoulos, Constantine. *Warriors and Politicians in Modern Greece.* Chapel Hill, North Carolina: Documentary, 1984.

"Defense and Economics in Greece," *NATO's Sixteen Nations,* 37, No. 5, 1992, 4–67.

Dokos, Thanos. *Seeking Peace: Nuclear Proliferation and International Security.* Athens: Papazissis, 1992.

Eaton, Robert. *Soviet Relations with Greece and Turkey.* Athens: ELIAMEP, 1987.

Economides, Spyros. *The Balkan Agenda: Security and Regionalism in the New Europe.* London: Centre for Defence Studies, 1992.

Featherstone, Kevin, and Dimitrios Katsoudas, eds. *Political Change in Greece Before and after the Colonels.* London: Croom Helm, 1987.

Gianaris, Nicholas V. *Greece and Turkey: Economic and Geopolitical Perspectives.* New York: Praeger, 1988.

Helsinki Watch Committee. *Denying Human Rights and Ethnic Identity: The Greeks of Turkey.* New York: Human Rights Watch, 1992.

Hermes, Walter G. *Truce Tent and Fighting Front: United States Army in the Korean War.* Washington: Office of the Chief of Military History, United States Army, 1988.

Hitchens, Christopher. *Cyprus.* London: Quartet Books, 1984.

Iatrides, John O. *Revolt in Athens: The Greek Communist "Second Round," 1944–1945*. Princeton: Princeton University Press, 1972.

Iatrides, John O., ed. *Greece in the 1940s: A Nation in Crisis*. Hanover, New Hampshire: University Press of New England, 1981.

Ioannides, Christos. *In Turkey's Image: The Transformation of Occupied Cyprus into a Turkish Province*. New Rochelle, New York: Caratzas, 1991.

Jane's Sentinel: The Balkans. Ed., Paul Beaver. Coulsdon, United Kingdom: Jane's Information Group, 1993.

Kazakos, Panos, and Panayotis Ioakimides, eds. *Greece and EC Membership Evaluated*. London: Pinter, 1994.

Kitromilides, Paschalis, and Peter Worsley, eds. *Small States in a Modern World*. Nicosia: Zavallis Press, 1979.

Kofas, Jon V. *Intervention and Underdevelopment: Greece During the Civil War*. University Park: Pennsylvania State University Press, 1989.

Kofos, Evangelos. *Nationalism and Communism in Macedonia*. Thessaloniki: Institute for Balkan Studies, 1964.

Kofos, Evangelos. *The Impact of the Macedonian Question on Civil Conflict in Greece, 1943–1949*. Athens: ELIAMEP, 1989.

Kourvetaris, Yorgos A. "The Southern Flank of NATO: Political Dimensions of the Greco-Turkish Conflict since 1974," *East European Quarterly*, 21, January 1988, 431–46.

Kuniholm, Bruce. *The Origins of the Cold War in the Near East: Great Power Conflict and Diplomacy in Iran, Turkey, and Greece*. Princeton: Princeton University Press, 1980.

The Military Balance, 1993–1994. London: International Institute for Strategic Studies, 1993.

The Military Balance, 1994–1995. London: International Institute for Strategic Studies, 1994.

Munkman, C.A. *American Aid to Greece: A Report on the First Ten Years*. New York: Praeger, 1958.

North Atlantic Treaty Organization. *NATO Handbook*. Brussels: NATO Office of Information and Press, 1995.

Roubatis, Yannis. *Tangled Webs: The U.S. in Greece, 1947–67*. New York: Pella, 1987.

Salem, Norma, ed. *Cyprus: A Regional Conflict and Its Resolution*. London: St. Martin's Press, 1992.

Southeast European Yearbook, 1993. Athens: ELIAMEP, 1994.

Spyridakis, Emmanuel. *The "Macedonian Question": An Historical and Diplomatic Review.* Athens: ELIAMEP, 1991.

Stavrianos, Leften S. *Balkan Federation: A History of the Movement Toward Balkan Unity in Modern Times.* Northampton: Smith College Press, 1941.

Stavrianos, Leften S. *Greece: American Dilemma and Opportunity.* Chicago: Regnery, 1952.

Stavrou, Nikolaos. *Allied Politics and Military Interventions: The Political Role of the Greek Military.* Athens: Papazissis, 1977.

Stearns, Monteagle. *Entangled Allies: U.S. Policy Toward Greece, Turkey, and Cyprus.* New York: Council on Foreign Relations, 1992.

Stern, Laurence. *The Wrong Horse: The Politics of Intervention and the Failure of American Diplomacy.* New York: Times Books, 1977.

Stuart, Douglas, ed. *Politics and Security in the Southern Region of the Atlantic Alliance.* London: Macmillan, 1988.

Tsoukalis, Loukas. *The European Community and Its Mediterranean Enlargement.* Boston: Allen and Unwin, 1981.

Tsoukalis, Loukas, ed. *Greece and the European Community.* Farnborough, United Kingdom: Saxon House, 1979.

United States. Arms Control and Disarmament Agency. *World Military Expenditures and Arms Transfers, 1993–1994.* Washington: GPO, 1995.

United States. Department of State. Bureau of International Narcotics Matters. *International Narcotics Strategy Report.* April 1994. Washington: GPO, 1994.

Valinakis, Yannis. *Greece and the CFE Negotiations.* Ebenhausen: Stiftung Wissenschaft und Politik, 1991.

Valinakis, Yannis. *Greece's Balkan Policy and the "Macedonian Issue."* Ebenhausen: Stiftung Wissenschaft und Politik, 1992.

Valinakis, Yannis. *Greece's Security in the Post-Cold War Era.* Ebenhausen: Stiftung Wissenschaft und Politik, 1994.

Veremis, Thanos. *Greek Security: Issues and Politics.* London: International Institute for Strategic Studies, 1982.

Wilson, Andrew. *The Aegean Dispute.* London: International Institute for Strategic Studies, 1979.

Yannopoulos, George, ed. *Greece and the EEC Integration and Convergence.* London: Macmillan, 1986.

(Various issues of the following publications were also used in the preparation of this chapter: Foreign Broadcast Information Service, *Daily Report: West Europe* and *JPRS Report: Terrorism*).

Glossary

Conference on Security and Cooperation in Europe (CSCE)—Established as an international process in 1972, the group consisted of fifty-three nations in 1994, including all European countries, sponsoring joint sessions and consultations on political issues vital to European security. Charter of Paris (1990) changed CSCE from ad hoc forum to organization with permanent institutions. In 1992 new CSCE roles in conflict prevention and management were defined, potentially making CSCE the center of a Europe-based collective security system. In the early 1990s, however, applications of these instruments to conflicts in Yugoslavia and the Caucasus did not have a decisive impact. In January 1995, renamed Organization for Security and Cooperation in Europe (OSCE).

Conventional Forces in Europe Treaty (CFE Treaty)—An agreement signed in 1990 by the member nations of the Warsaw Pact (*q.v.*) and the North Atlantic Treaty Organization (*q.v.*) to establish parity in conventional weapons between the two organizations from the Atlantic to the Urals. The treaty included a strict system of inspection and information exchange and remained in force, although not strictly observed by all parties, in the mid-1990s.

Council of Europe—Founded in 1949, a thirty-three-member (1994) organization overseeing intergovernmental cooperation in designated areas such as environmental planning, finance, sport, crime, migration, and legal matters.

drachma—National currency unit of Greece, with an exchange rate of approximately Dr230 to US$1 in May 1995.

European Commission—A governing body of the European Union (*q.v.*) that oversees the organization's treaties, recommends actions under the treaties, and issues independent decisions on EU matters.

European Community (EC)—A grouping of three primarily economic organizations of West European countries, including the European Economic Community (EEC), the European Atomic Energy Community (Euratom or EAEC), and the European Coal and Steel Community (ECSC). Founded separately in 1952 and 1957, the three came to be known collectively as the EC. Executive power

363

rested with the European Commission (*q.v.*), which implemented and defended the community treaties in the interests of the EC as a whole. Greece gained full membership in January 1981. Members in 1993 were Belgium, Britain, Denmark, France, Germany, Greece, Ireland, Italy, Luxembourg, the Netherlands, Portugal, and Spain. Name changed to European Union (*q.v.*) in December 1993.

European currency unit (ECU)—Established in 1979 as a composite of monetary systems of European Community (*q.v.*) member nations, to function in the European Monetary System. Acts as the unit for exchange-rate establishment, credit and intervention operations, and settlements between monetary authorities of member nations.

European Union (EU)—Successor organization to the European Community (*q.v.*), officially established by ratification of the Maastricht Treaty, November 1993. Goal is closer economic unification of Western Europe leading to single monetary system and closer cooperation in matters of justice and foreign and security policy. To the members of the European Community (*q.v.*), the EU added Austria, Finland, and Sweden, effective January 1, 1995.

gross domestic product (GDP)—The total value of goods and services provided exclusively within a nation's domestic economy, in contrast to gross national product (*q.v.*), usually computed over a one-year period.

gross national product (GNP)—The total value of goods and services produced within a country's borders plus the income received from abroad by residents, minus payments remitted abroad by nonresidents. Normally computed over one year.

millet—In the Ottoman Empire's policy for governance of non-Muslim minorities, an autonomous community ruled by religious leaders responsible to the central government.

North Atlantic Treaty Organization (NATO)—An alliance founded in 1949 by the United States, Canada, and their postwar European allies to counter the Soviet military presence in Europe. Greece joined in 1952 but withdrew from military commitments 1975–80. Until the dissolution of the Warsaw Pact (*q.v.*) in 1991, NATO was the primary collective defense agreement of the Western powers. Its military and administrative structure remained intact after the threat of Soviet expansionism had subsided. The Partnership for Peace, originated in 1993, offered limited participation in NATO to East European countries and former Soviet republics with the possibility of eventual full membership by some or all of those nations.

Ottoman Empire—A Muslim empire, based in Istanbul (formerly Constantinople), that controlled southeastern Europe, the Middle East, and most of North Africa between the sixteenth and eighteenth centuries, and lesser territories between 1300 and 1913. Ottoman occupation was a major influence on all civilizations of southeastern Europe and caused ethnic animosities that remained long after the disintegration of the empire.

Sunni—The larger of the two fundamental divisions of Islam, opposed to the Shia (the other main division) on the issue of succession to Muslim leadership.

value-added tax (VAT)—A tax applied to the additional value created at a given stage of production and calculated as a percentage of the difference between the product value at that stage and the cost of all materials and services purchased as inputs. The VAT is the primary form of indirect taxation applied in the European Union (*q.v.*), and it is the basis of each country's contribution to the community budget.

Warsaw Pact—Informal name for Warsaw Treaty Organization, a mutual defense organization founded in 1955, including the Soviet Union, Albania (which withdrew in 1961), Bulgaria, Czechoslovakia, the German Democratic Republic (East Germany), Hungary, Poland, and Romania. The Warsaw Pact enabled the Soviet Union to station troops in the countries to its west to oppose the forces of the North Atlantic Treaty Organization (NATO, *q.v.*). The pact was the basis of the invasions of Hungary (1956) and of Czechoslovakia (1968); it was disbanded in July 1991.

Western European Union (WEU)—Based on the 1948 Treaty of Brussels and set up in 1955, the council is a forum for coordination of regional defense policy among its members, Belgium, Britain, France, Germany, Greece, Luxembourg, the Netherlands, Portugal, and Spain. Denmark and Ireland have observer status, and Iceland, Norway, and Turkey are associate members. After lying dormant for many years, the WEU was reactivated in 1984 to serve as the European pillar of NATO (*q.v.*) defenses and the defense component of the European Community (*q.v.*). In 1993 the WEU and NATO ran a joint arms embargo operation against Yugoslavia in the Adriatic. A Eurocorps of Belgian, French, and German troops was established at the end of 1993.

World Bank—Informal name for a group of four affiliated international institutions: the International Bank for Reconstruction and Development (IBRD); the International Development Association (IDA); the International Finance Corporation (IFC); and the Multilateral Investment Guarantee Agency (MIGA). The four institutions are owned by the governments of the countries that subscribe their capital for credit and investment in developing countries; each institution has a specialized agenda for aiding economic growth in target countries.

Index

abortion: legalization of, 118
ACE. *See* Allied Command Europe
ACE Rapid Reaction Corps (ARRC), 287, 297
Achaia, 19
acid rain, 105–6
acquired immune deficiency syndrome (AIDS), 136–37
Acropolis, 97; as tourist site, 190
Actium, Battle of, 18, 93
Adrianople, Treaty of (1829), 33
adult education, 136
adultery, decriminalization of, 79, 118
Aegean, University of the, 136
Aegean Islands, 44, 87–88, 286; climate of, 104; geography of, 101–3
Aegean Sea, 86; dispute over airspace above, 281; islands in, 44, 87–88, 101–3, 104, 286; issue over territorial waters in, 280; oil deposits in, 73, 254–55
Aeschylus, 12, 96
Afghanistan: Soviet invasion of, 272
AGET, 173, 226
Agnew, Spiro, 72
Agrapha, 26
Agricultural Bank of Greece, 178, 192; establishment of, 150
Agricultural Insurance Organization (Organismos Georgikon Asfaliseon—OGA), 143
agriculture, 175–79; contribution to export values, 40, 149, 177, 197; cooperatives in, 178–79; in Dark Age, 7; post Greek War of Independence, 34; in Macedonia, 23, 51; organizational aid to, 178; and use of fertilizer, 106; under Venizelos, 53
AIDS. *See* acquired immune deficiency syndrome
Aigispotamoi, 12
Air Force Cadet Academy, 293
Air Force War College, 293
air travel, 185–86
Akheloos River, 106

Albania (*see also* Northern Epirus), 86; fall of communism in, xli; foreign investments in, 148; Greek relations with, xlvii–xlviii, 250–51, 263–64; Greek territorial claims to, 283; and immigration policy, 114; and inter-Balkan conference, 260; as issue in Balkan Wars, 43–44; language of, 128; and refugee problem, xli, 250, 263–64.
Albert, Prince, 38–39
Alemanni, 20
Alexander I, 33, 47; death of, 48
Alexander the Great, xxxv, 3, 15–16, 128, 262
Alexandra (queen consort of Britain), 39
Alexandria: as commercial center, 19
Alexandroupolis, 168; airports at, 186; roads linking Igoumenitsa and, 183
Ali, Mahomet, 31–32
Alia, Ramiz, 312
Aliakmon River, 92
Allied Command Europe (ACE), 287
aluminum, 169
AMAG. *See* American Mission of Aid to Greece
Amalfi, 24
Amalia, Queen, 38
American Mission of Aid to Greece (AMAG), 65
Amsterdam: merchant colonies in, 28
Amvrakikos, Gulf of, 93, 95
ANA. *See* Athens News Agency
Anatolia, 4
Andravida, airport at, 186
Andrianopoulos, Andreas, 233–34; as opposition leader, xlvii
Andrianopoulos, Manos, 233–34
Andros, Roman Catholic Church in, 126
Ankara, Treaty of (1930), 53
Antarctic Treaty, 305
anticommunism, xxxvi, 63
Antioch: recapture of, by Macedonians, 23

Antwerp: merchant colonies in, 28
Apollo, Temple of, 190
Arab-Israeli War (1967), 265–66
Arab-Israeli War (1973), 153
Arafat, Yasir, 80
Arakhthos River, 93
Araxos: Hellenic Air Force at, 298
archaeological sites: tourism at, 190
Argos: growth of, in eighth century B.C., 7–8
Arianism, 21
Aristophanes, 12, 96
Aristotle, 15, 96
Aristotle University of Thessaloniki, 136
Armenia: recapture of, by Macedonians, 23
Armenian Rite church, 126
Armenians: immigration of, 114
arms control: role of Greece in, 305–6
Army Cadet Academy, 293
Army War College, 293
ARRC. *See* ACE Rapid Reaction Corps
Arsenis, Gerasimos, 231
Arta: Greek control of, 42
artisan associations, 39
asbestos, 169
ASDEN. *See* Higher Military Command of the Interior and the Islands
ASDEN territorial defense forces, 296
ASE. *See* Athens Stock Exchange
Asopos River, 96
Aspida group, 70, 72
Aspropyrgos Refinery, 166
assassinations, 318
Assembly, 209, 211; and choice of department ministers, 208–9; election of members of, 216–17; election of president by, 207–8
Association of Greek Industrialists (Sindesmos Ellinon Viomikhanon—SEV), xliii, 108, 242
Atatürk, Kemal, 49, 53
Athens: air pollution and smog in, 80, 104–5, 185; collapse of, 12; as commercial center, 19; construction of subway system in, 184–85; geography of, 96; Golden Age of, 10–12, 96; greater, as tenth region, 214; history of, 96–97; income level of residents of, 96; Jewish communities in, 58; local government of, 220; as major seaport, 180; migration to, 111; natural gas dis-

tribution in, 167; Ottoman Turk rule of, 97; and Peloponnesian War, 12; pollution in, 107–8, 174; population of, 111–12; population density of, 86; rise of, 9; and rule of Otto, 27, 34; sacked, in Persian Wars, 10; tent cities around, 51; in World War II, 97
Athens Academy, 135
Athens News Agency (Athenagence or ANA), 244
Athens Stock Exchange (ASE), xliii, 191, 193
Aurelius, Marcus, 19
Australia Group for the Control of Chemical Exports, 305–6
Automatic Indexation Scheme, 164
Averoff-Tositsas, Evangelos, 232
Ayios Evstratios, 103

Bactrians, 18
balance of payments, 194; need to improve, 40
Balkan Pact, 66
Balkan Peninsula: crisis in, xxxv, 243; and foreign policy, 259–60; nationalism in, 43–44; security in, 282–85; Slavic invasions of, 23
Balkan Wars (1912-13), 43–44, 273
banking and finance, 191–94, 221
Bank of Crete: and financial scandal, 221
Basil II, 23
Bati Trakya organization, 282
bauxite, 169; processing of, 169
Berisha, Sali, xlvii, 264
Berlin, Congress of, 42
Berlin Wall: collapse of, 248
beverage sector, 170
bilateral defense relations: with United States, 279
Biological Weapons Convention, 305
birth rate, 110
black market, 151–52
Black Sea, 101; Greek colonies on, xxxv
Boetia (Voiotia), 96
Bonaparte, Napoleon: defeat of, 29, 32
Bosnia and Herzegovina: 282; Serbian advances in, xlix, 261
Bosporus Strait, 101
Bozcaada, 282
Britain: and Balkan Wars, 43; and Crimean War, 38; and Cyprus issue,

Agreements (DECAs), 256–57, 259, 279, 307
Defense and Industrial Cooperation Agreements (DICAs), 279
defense enterprises, 307–10
defense establishment, 288; command structure, 289; officer corps, 289–91
defense expenditures, 306
defense industry, 306–10; development of, 307
Defense Industry Directorate (DID), 307
Delian League, 11
Deliyannis, Theodoros, 40
Delors Package Number Two, 148
Delos (Dilos), 102
Delphi: and tourism, 190
Democratic Army of Greece (DAG), 63, 66–67
Democratic Front, 236
Democratic Renewal Party, 239
demography, 110; emigration and immigration in, 112–14; ethnic minorities in, 114–15; population characteristics, 110–12
Demokritos National Research Center, 305
Demos, 12
Denktas, Rauf, 254
DID. *See* Defense Industry Directorate
Dinaric Alps, 87
Diocletian, 20
doctors: ratio of, to population, 141–42
Dodecanese (Dodekanisos) Islands, 25, 102, 115, 123; and coming of World War II, 56; families in, 116; Muslims in, 127; in Treaty of Lausanne, 50
domestic economic growth, 147
domestic security: trends and problems in, 322
drachma: devaluation of, 65, 66, 220; stabilization of, 65
drainage patterns, 87
drug use, 137; and crime, 137, 315, 316–17
Dublin Group, 315

EAM. *See* National Liberation Front
East European communist regimes: fall of, 252
EAU. *See* Greek Aerospace Industry
EC. *See* European Community

ECOFIN. *See* European Community Finance Organization
Economic and Monetary Union (EMU), 198
economy, 147–200; composition of national income in, 156–57; employment in, 158–59; energy sector in, 165–68; after Greek War of Independence, 34; growth of, in twentieth century, xxxv, xxxviii–xxxix; importance of tourism industry in, xliv–xlv; industry in, 165–74; international policies in 1990s, 198–200; under Karamanlis, 67; labor unions in, 159–60; and Marshall Plan, 64–65; in 1930s, 53–54; in nineteenth century, 149–50; from 1909 to World War II, 150–52; policy after 1974, 153–56; postwar recovery in, 152–53; privatization as key issue in, xliii; public sector and taxation, 161–63; role of foreign trade, 157–58; service sector in, 180,183–94; structure of, 156; underground, xxxix, 160; wages, prices, and inflation in, 163–65
Ecumenical Patriarchate of Constantinople, 124, 214
EDA. *See* United Democratic Left
Eden, Anthony, 68
EDES. *See* National Republican Greek League
Edict of Milan, 20–21
education, xxxviii, 130; administration of, 132; adult, 131, 136; advancement of women, 119; broad availability of, 85–86; historical background, 130–31; primary and secondary, 132–33; reforms in, 40, 131, 132–33; religious, 121, 130, 133; at university level, 86, 133–36; under Venizelos, 53
Egypt, 10; capture by Alexander the Great, 16; involvement in Greek War of Independence, 32–33
Egyptians, 6
Eisenhower, Dwight D., 68
EK. *See* Center Union
ELAS. *See* National People's Liberation Army
EL.AS. *See* Hellenic Police
elections: of 1946, 62–63; of 1950, 65; of 1951, 65–66; of 1952, 66; of 1961, 69; of 1967, 71; of 1981, 78; of 1985, 220; of 1989, 81; of 1993, 204, 218, 227–28

Contributors

Theodore A. Couloumbis is President of the Hellenic Foundation for European and Foreign Policy, Athens.

Glenn E. Curtis is Senior Research Specialist for Eastern Europe and Central Eurasia in the Federal Research Division, Library of Congress.

Thanos P. Dokos is a Research Fellow in the Hellenic Foundation for European and Foreign Policy, Athens.

Thomas Gallant is Associate Professor of History at the University of Florida.

Eleni Mahaira-Odoni is Chairman of the Greek Studies Group of the Center for European Studies, Harvard University.

Stavros B. Thomadakis is Professor of Economics at Baruch College.

Published Country Studies

(Area Handbook Series)

550–65	Afghanistan		550–36	Dominican Republic
550–98	Albania			and Haiti
550–44	Algeria		550–52	Ecuador
550–59	Angola		550–43	Egypt
550–73	Argentina		550–150	El Salvador
550–111	Armenia, Azerbaijan,		550–28	Ethiopia
	and Georgia		550–167	Finland
550–169	Australia		550–173	Germany, East
550–176	Austria		550–155	Germany, Fed. Rep. of
550–175	Bangladesh		550–153	Ghana
550–112	Belarus and Moldova		550–87	Greece
550–170	Belgium		550–78	Guatemala
550–66	Bolivia		550–174	Guinea
550–20	Brazil		550–82	Guyana and Belize
550–168	Bulgaria		550–151	Honduras
550–61	Burma		550–165	Hungary
550–50	Cambodia		550–21	India
550–166	Cameroon		550–154	Indian Ocean
550–159	Chad		550–39	Indonesia
550–77	Chile		550–68	Iran
550–60	China		550–31	Iraq
550–26	Colombia		550–25	Israel
550–33	Commonwealth Carib-		550–182	Italy
	bean, Islands of the		550–30	Japan
550–91	Congo		550–34	Jordan
550–90	Costa Rica		550–56	Kenya
550–69	Côte d'Ivoire (Ivory		550–81	Korea, North
	Coast)		550–41	Korea, South
550–152	Cuba		550–58	Laos
550–22	Cyprus		550–24	Lebanon
550–158	Czechoslovakia		550–38	Liberia

550–85	Libya	550–184	Singapore
550–172	Malawi	550–86	Somalia
550–45	Malaysia	550–93	South Africa
550–161	Mauritania	550–95	Soviet Union
550–79	Mexico	550–179	Spain
550–76	Mongolia	550–96	Sri Lanka
550–49	Morocco	550–27	Sudan
550–64	Mozambique	550–47	Syria
550–35	Nepal and Bhutan	550–62	Tanzania
550–88	Nicaragua	550–53	Thailand
550–157	Nigeria	550–89	Tunisia
550–94	Oceania	550–80	Turkey
550–48	Pakistan	550–74	Uganda
550–46	Panama	550–97	Uruguay
550–156	Paraguay	550–71	Venezuela
550–185	Persian Gulf States	550–32	Vietnam
550–42	Peru	550–183	Yemens, The
550–72	Philippines	550–99	Yugoslavia
550–162	Poland	550–67	Zaire
550–181	Portugal	550–75	Zambia
550–160	Romania	550–171	Zimbabwe
550–37	Rwanda and Burundi		
550–51	Saudi Arabia		
550–70	Senegal		
550–180	Sierra Leone